Legions of Death

The Nazi Enslavement of Eastern Europe

&

Cross of Iron

The Nazi Enslavement of Western Europe

Rupert Butler

PEN & SWORD MILITARY CLASSICS

Legions of Death first published in Great Britain in 1983
by The Hamlyn Publishing Group Ltd.
Cross of Iron first published in Great Britain in 1989
by Arrow Books Ltd.

Published in 2004, in this format, by
PEN & SWORD MILITARY CLASSICS
an imprint of
Pen & Sword Books Limited
47, Church Street
Barnsley
S. Yorkshire
S70 2AS

ISBN 1 84415 042 9

A CIP record for this book
is available from the British Library.

Printed in England by
CPI UK

Introduction by Rupert Butler

It is close on 60 years since the collapse of the Third Reich and the suicide of the man who had launched the juggernaut of death and devastation which was the Second World War. Any reappraisal of the events of those days has to take account, not just of the courage and fighting strength of those who opposed Hitler, but of the cruel consequences.

Thanks to a flood of books, television documentaries, war and video games, fresh generations are constantly made aware of most aspects of the conflict. These include the courage of resistants from all nations, placed alongside the prowess of armies in the field and, above all, the sufferings of the survivors.

Instances of resistance, both in the East and West theatres of the War, featured in two books which are being published in a single volume*. In the East, June 1942 provided a stirring example of Jewish courage in Poland. During that month the British Broadcasting Corporation transmitted from London a searing account of the fate of 700,000 Jews who had been murdered up till then. That information would never have reached London if it had not been for the determination of the Polish underground who, at terrible risk, smuggled the news to London out of Warsaw. A year earlier, Yugoslav resistants in the town of Kragujevac had lobbed bombs at German troops who had forced local people into an Orthodox Cathedral which they had then torched, burning the occupants or machine gunning frantic escapers. In revenge for the retaliation, the Germans rounded up the entire male population between the ages of 15 and 60. By dusk some 150 boys, dragged from a local school, were shot along with the other inhabitants.

In the west on 7 April 1944, the Germans launched a wide sweep against fighters of the French resistance, capturing some 20 agents who, a month earlier, had fashioned for the British, a highly detailed 55 foot map of the German defences of the Contentin peninsula, near where the cross-Channel invasion was planned. Once the invasion began, all were executed.

In both East and West, Jews from the occupied countries were earmarked for destruction. As far as Russia was concerned, Hitler had ordered that all those identified as political commissars or partisans 'should be taken aside and shot, reasoning that this was the only way whereby the people could be liberated from the oppression of a Jewish and criminal group'. The hatred which Hitler reserved for Russia – 'the cradle of Bolshevism' – had been expressed in the Commissar Order: 'The Commissars hold views directly opposed to those of National Socialism. Hence these Commissars must be eliminated. Any German soldier who breaks international law will be pardoned.'

Nor, of course, was the West to escape Hitler's obsession. By the end of September 1940, Jews in France's occupied zone were obliged to carry specially marked identity cards, while shopkeepers were forced to display yellow and black posters announcing 'Jewish business'. It was scarcely a day before writings by Jews were withdrawn. Jews were forced to register at police stations and to give family and professional details.

Furthermore, homes of Jews throughout Europe were broken into and pillaged shamelessly.

The mere mention of collaboration can still act as a raw nerve on the conscience of nations. However unpalatable, the blunt truth is that thousands of all ages from occupied or subjugated countries were prepared in some degree to serve the interests of their oppressors. A striking example was provided by the numbers of volunteers who served the Nazis in the various echelons of the Waffen-SS (Armed SS); numbers grew throughout the war and by the end of hostilities foreigners outnumbered native Germans. Just how committed many of them were was underlined by SS-Obergruppenführer (General) Felix Steiner, a prominent

Waffen-SS division commander, who wrote: 'They observed the good behaviour and discipline of the German troops and began to make comparisons that did not turn out to be unfavourable for the Germans.' At the post-war Nuremberg trials, a Herr Brill, a recruiting officer, testified: '...I read thousands upon thousands of applications for admission. I can say that the enthusiasm for the SS, for its decent and proper conduct was the main reason for volunteering'.

Collaborators, notably in France, paid conspicuously for their treachery. The purge known as 'l'epuration' stretched from September 1944 until the end of 1949. Trials resulted in 120,000 sentences, of which 4,785 were for death, of which an estimated 2,000 were carried out.

Accusations of collaboration post-war, rightly or wrongly, made few distinctions of degree. A Paris café owner, for example, could be pilloried for being obliged to serve German troops in order to remain in business. Although death sentences on women and minors were automatically commuted by General de Gaulle, President of the liberated Republic, French partisans settled old scores without bothering about legal niceties. Many thousands of collaborators, notably in the region of the Midi, a stronghold of the Resistance, were rounded up and executed. Minor offenders did not escape. Resistance workers enjoyed the humiliation of female compatriots known to have slept with Germans. As punishment, hair was shaved off, a visible sign of guilt which took months to grow back.

Many Russians who collaborated or had sympathy with their German occupiers had nursed bitter memories of the pre-war Stalinist purges and were happy to throw in their lot with the Nazis. Perhaps the most celebrated was peasant-born Lieutenant General Andrei Vlasov, who had led the Second Assault Army to relieve Leningrad in 1942. Totally surrounded in the Volkov marshes, he received what he regarded as an insane order from Stalin to hold out to the last man. This triggered a determination to rid his country of the Soviet's leader's regime of terror. When Vlasov was taken prisoner by the Germans, Josef Goebbels, the Propaganda Minster, eagerly seized on him as a useful instrument of propaganda, encouraging him to raise a patriotic 'Russian Army of Liberation' among his fellow prisoners. After the war, the Americans returned him to Moscow where he was hanged for treason in August 1946.

The old adage that revenge is a dish best eaten cold was not observed by many of Hitler's victims in the occupied countries, East or West. This applied particularly to the Jews who have never forgiven or forgot the guilty Nazis. Simon Wiesenthal, an Austrian Jew who had been a concentration camp prisoner, has devoted much of his life to hunting down 1,000 war criminals from his Jewish Documentation Centre, established in Vienna. It is surely significant that when the notorious Adolf Eichmann was arrested in Buenos Aires, the first question he asked his captors was: 'Are you Americans?', adding as the truth dawned: 'You must be Israelis. The others are not interested in me.'

As was inevitable with the passing of time, fever for denazification cooled as new problems, political and economic, crowded in on a shattered Europe. There are still many survivors, elderly and their numbers dwindling, who cannot forget, since they will literally carry the scars of war to their graves, whether in the form of physical disfigurement or mental anguish. In his masterly account of the War, the historian Sir Martin Gilbert wrote: 'The greatest unfinished business of the Second World War is human pain.'

* *Legions of Death: The Nazi Enslavement of Eastern Europe* (Hamlyn Paperbacks, 1983);
Cross of Iron: The Nazi Enslavement of Western Europe (Arrow Books Ltd, 1989), both by Rupert Butler.

'Once we have won the war, then for all I care, mincemeat can be made of Poles and Ukrainians and all the others who have run around here.'

Speech by Governor-General of Poland Hans Frank, 14 January 1944.

'Gentlemen: I am known as a brutal dog. Because of this reason I was appointed as a Reichskommissar of the Ukraine. Our task is to suck from the Ukraine all the goods we can get hold of, without consideration of the feeling or the property of the Ukrainians.

'Gentlemen: I am expecting from you the utmost severity towards the native population.'

Inauguration speech by Erich Koch, Rovno, September 1941.

1

The white flag fluttered in the wind from the mast of the central tower of Buchenwald.

Prisoners who had climbed joyfully to erect it glanced over the thickly wooded hills to the large oak forests of Ettersburg, some six miles from Weimar. To the north over a wide shallow plain lay lines of dull, monotonous hills. Beyond was the dark of the Harz mountains, while to the south-west stretched the high trees of Thueringer Wald and to the east the great plains of Saxony.

The region had once been a cradle of German culture, where Goethe and Schiller had come in search of peace among trees and flowers.

The Nazis had destroyed all that. On the sloping uneven ground they had constructed rough windowless huts of wood with floors of damp earth. There were two-storey brick blocks, and latrines which were nothing more than poles suspended over trenches.

Above the main gates of the camp was the inscription *Recht oder unrecht – mein Vaterland* (My country – right or wrong). Local people had their own sinister nickname for this place. They called it *Blutburg* (castle of blood). It had been the first of the main concentration camps of Nazi Germany to be overrun by American and British forces.

But now that nightmare was seemingly at an end. The prisoners who had climbed the tower noticed with satisfaction that the guards had fled their posts. Those below could now hear the sullen roar of the American heavy vehicles growing steadily louder. The vanguard of the US eightieth Division was approaching Buchenwald.

Liberation was at hand. Buchenwald, which had been a concentration camp since 1938, was soon to give up its terrible secrets to a shattered world.

Only a few days before, other vehicles had rumbled

through Weimar. They had contained a killer squad from the *Sicherheitsdienst* (SD, Security Police of the infamous SS) armed with flame-throwers and under orders to burn the camp to the ground.

But they had scuttled off hurriedly in the path of the rapid American advance.

And now the Americans were greeted by emaciated survivors – Jews, and Gentile Poles, Hungarians and Russians. In the hospital block they saw shelf cubicles without mattresses, where the excreta of dysentery patients dripped from tier to tier. Here each morning corpses had been collected and taken by cart to the crematorium or the pathological laboratories of the SS doctors.

Those who had survived were skin-and-bone scarecrows with ragged shirts or cotton jackets, beneath which protruded thighs no thicker than normal wrists.

Buchenwald's maximum capacity had been 120,000. By the end of April 1945, the total number of those who had died, been murdered or transferred to other camps was put at 51,570 – 17,000 of them in just three months.

But something rather more than cold statistics was needed to bring home the horrors of a camp whose atrocities, it was believed, were only surpassed by Auschwitz in Poland.

Newspapermen and radio reporters followed in the wake of the American army. One of the visitors to Buchenwald at the time of its liberation was the celebrated radio reporter Edward R. Murrow, who reported for CBS Radio:

> 'As I walked down to the end of the barracks, there was applause from the men too weak to get out of bed. It sounded like the handclapping of babies . . . They were so weak. As we walked out into the courtyard, a man fell dead.
>
> 'Two others, they must have been over 60, were crawling towards the latrine . . . In another part of the camp they showed me the children, hundreds of them. Some were only six. One rolled up his sleeves, showed me his number. It was tattooed on his arm. B-6030, it was. The others showed me their numbers. They will carry them until they die . . .'

Ed Murrow's despatch was by no means the first to reveal

the horrors of this particular camp. From the time that Hitler had come to power in January 1933, the *Manchester Guardian* had been running a series of articles on mounting Nazi atrocities.

A report on Buchenwald in August 1938 revealed:

'The prisoners have to parade at four o'clock in the morning. They work on the roads and in the quarries. Many are in a weak condition because of the bad food, the ill-treatment and overwork. Those who fail in the opinion of the guards, who are SS men, to do the required amount of work, are punished with twenty-five strokes of the lash, which is a heavy tapering thing of cowhide. These floggings occur daily, the victims being strapped to a trestle.'

It had always been intended that camps such as Buchenwald were to be murder factories, set up originally for the incarceration of German Jews. With the outbreak of war, they became repositories for the subjugated people of the east. These were the citizens of the vassal states which Hitler had vowed to overrun and ultimately to destroy.

Five weeks after the Germans had unleashed their mechanised might on Soviet Russia, lanky, blond, wasp-waisted SS Obergruppenfuehrer Reinhard Heydrich had every reason to be a happy man.

For a former naval officer who had been dismissed in disgrace from the service after refusing to marry a girl with whom he was involved, he had found life agreeably profitable under the Third Reich.

His mentor, SS boss Heinrich Himmler, had put him in charge of strengthening the country's intelligence service, which included the Gestapo and SD.

The Nazi spy machine had humble beginnings. As a newly promoted SS-Sturmbannfuehrer, Heydrich, his wife Lina and part-time SS help had begun with a few card indexes in a cramped fourth floor of a house at Turkenstrasse 23 in Munich. Then with infinite stealth and cunning, Himmler had managed to wrest power from the fat, self-indulgent Hermann Goering, who had built up the Gestapo in Prussia with immense energy during the early days of power.

Coldly and calculatingly, Heydrich had hitched his wagon

to Himmler's star. All the time, the startling blue ice-pick eyes were set firmly on the top job as head of the SD and effective leader of the Gestapo with its sinister headquarters at Prinz Albrechtstrasse 8 in Berlin.

A few years back, he had been a cashiered naval officer haunting the ports of Hamburg, Luebeck and Kiel, desperate for any sort of job. By the key month of July 1941, with the Nazis masters of not only western Europe but also of Austria, Czechoslovakia and a comfortable slice of Soviet Russia, Heydrich was given a fresh and altogether more decisive role.

For over two years, he had waited to activate the order which had been given to him by Goering, who had secured himself the title of Commissar of Jewish Affairs.

And now it had come. Onto his desk was dropped the official communiqué. It read:

> 'In order to complete the mission imposed on you, in the order of 24 January 1939, to solve the problem of the Jews by means of emigration or evacuation in the most suitable way in the circumstances leading to a possible solution; I hereby instruct you to make all the necessary organisational, practical and material preparation for a comprehensive solution of the Jewish question within the German area of influence in Europe.
>
> 'In so far as other central authorities are concerned they are to co-operate with you.
>
> 'I hereby instruct you further to submit to me as soon as possible a general plan with respect to organisational, practical and material means necessary – for the execution of the desired Final Solution (*Endloesung*) of the Jewish question.'

It was the green light for nothing less than mass murder.

For the task, Heydrich plainly needed help. He had long had in mind an able lieutenant – Adolf Eichmann, a former salesman who had edged his way into the SD as a filing clerk.

It was a job that most would have regarded as a mere stepping stone, but Eichmann devoted himself to bureaucracy with an almost mystical dedication. The key to success in anything, he reasoned, was organisation. The fact that the merchandise in question was going to be human lives made little difference.

Eichmann had a hatred of Jews nourished from childhood and was always self-conscious about his own swarthy complexion and Semitic appearance.

A motherless, introverted son of a failed garage owner, the child Eichmann had, as a pupil of the Wermingrode public school in Thuringia, captured the headlines of a local paper as the leader of a gang who had cruelly tormented a Jewish classmate, Ulrich Cohn.

The teenagers had beaten up the boy, torn his clothes and forced him to jump in the air while they danced around him. Eichmann's role in the affair was significant and gave a direct indication of what was to be his greatest value to the Nazi – as a tireless, meticulous bureaucrat.

He had kept a precise account of each child's turn to beat the Jewish victim. Needless to say, his own name had been at the top of the list.

Heydrich had combed Eichmann's SS dossier and was delighted with what it revealed.

As number 45326 in the SS and number 889895 in the Nazi Party, Eichmann had shown early promise in any number of ways. For example, on 22 April 1934, Eichmann, then aged twenty-eight, had visited a Munich tavern. Before long he had become involved in a fight. An SS officer who was also there filed a report:

'Tonight a fight occurred in a Munich tavern. Two men entered the tavern and insisted that the proprietor play Jewish records. The owner refused and the two became loudly insistent in their demands. Adolf Eichmann, SS Oberschuetze, was present. Eichmann interfered in the discussion, taking the owner's viewpoint, objecting to the playing of that kind of music. He attacked the two men. I, as an officer of the SS, restored order. At the same time, I checked the identity cards of those involved in the brawl, including Eichmann's. Eichmann said that he was on leave but I noted that according to his pass his leave had terminated a few days before and that therefore the pass had become invalid.'

No action was taken against Eichmann. Indeed, he had been promoted to SS Unterscharfuehrer a month later. His personal dossier also noted: *'Has great organisational abilities.'*

It was true, Eichmann was forced to admit, that in the 1920s he had worked in Austria for the Vacuum Oil Company of Vienna and had made a number of Jewish friends. Now he was suitably repentant, reconverted to a virulent anti-Semiticism both by the Austrian press and the effects of Hitler's speeches.

Eichmann confessed: 'After hearing the Fuehrer speak I felt a loathing of myself that I had mixed with those Jews who were the enemies of the German people and who defiled our blood . . .'

Heydrich had patently every reason to be satisfied with his choice.

The first consideration of the two men was those areas in the west which Hitler had occupied and where it had been ordained that a 'Jewish badge' should be worn on the left side of the breast. Jews were forbidden to leave their places of residence or use transport.

Then on 10 October 1941, a conference was held at the concentration camp at Theresienstadt to determine the future of Czech Jews. By November, Eichmann had placed before Heydrich a draft plan for carrying out the 'imminent' final solution. Heydrich declared that a meeting with members of all the Reich ministries must be held forthwith.

However, events in the wider theatre of war dictated otherwise. The Japanese unleashed their attack on Pearl Harbor, followed by the invasion of Allied territory in South-East Asia. Even the top Nazi leadership was caught on the hop. Heydrich's planned meeting was postponed until the following year.

It took place on 29 January 1942 in the pre-war headquarters of Interpol at Grossen Wannsee No 56-58 in a pleasant south-east suburb of Berlin.

Background preparations were in the hands of Adolf Eichmann and he set about his task with characteristic zest. But he was never allowed to forget that he was, at the end of the day, nothing more than his master's voice.

Eichmann, when he was tried as a war criminal in Israel many years later, denied vehemently that he had a major role in organising the conference, as had been alleged. Nevertheless, the pride of the born bureaucrat was still in evidence when he came to write his memoirs in Buenos Aires and to recall what he claimed was a humble role at Wannsee. He wrote:

'My orders from my superior, SS Gruppenfuehrer Mueller, were to ensure that the proceedings of the meeting were properly recorded and I spent most of the time sharpening the stenographer's pencils.'

Eichmann emphasised at his trial that one of the key reasons for holding the conference was to feed Heydrich's overweening vanity. Under cross-examination in the dock, Eichmann remarked: 'It was well known to us all that Heydrich was never satisfied with what he had and always wanted to increase the scope of his power.'

The eventual line-up for the Wannsee Conference included leading personalities from the Ministry for the Occupied Territories, masterminded by the party's prominent racial theorist, Alfred Rosenberg. Also present were officials from the departments of the Interior, Justice, Foreign Affairs and Economics. Numbers were further swollen by prominent Nazi Party members, Hitler's Chancellery and Himmler's Race and Settlement Office.

It was significant that there was also a sprinkling of talent from Heydrich's personally established department, the Directorate General of Security for the Reich (Reichssicherheitshauptamt or RSHA).

Heydrich, however, was not quite so consumed with vanity that he forgot his true objective: to emphasise to those present at Wannsee that he had become undisputed ruler of all Jews in those areas conquered by Germany.

Heydrich began by revealing briefly the two-pronged attack which had already been launched against the Jews. They had been forced out of individual sections of life (*Lebensgebitte*) of the German people and had been forced out of the living space (*Lebensraum*) which was rightfully the property of all Germans.

Up till then all was sweet reasonableness. Heydrich behaved for all the world like a managing director who felt his board needed a pat on the back before being urged to greater efforts. Much, he conceded, had been achieved. In what was now Reich territory there had been over a quarter of a million Jews in 1939. It was most agreeable now that there were only something like 131,800 left.

17

At this point Heydrich looked up from his statistics and his voice hardened. The time for bouquets was over.

Cold blue eyes raked the table. He said: 'In the Soviet Union, however, we are faced with five million – three million of them in the Ukraine. As for the Government General in Poland, it is cursed by two and a quarter million Jews.

'The Fuehrer has ordered the evacuation of the Jews to the east with the goal of arriving at the final solution. It is estimated that a total of eleven million Jews are involved.

'Gentlemen, you will doubtless wonder how this will be done.

'Under suitable management, the Jews will be moved, in the course of the Final Solution, to labour units in the east. Those capable of working will be transported in long labour columns, men and women separate, to build roads in that region; as a result of which, no doubt, a large part of them will fall out through natural losses.

'Those who ultimately remain, who will surely be those who have great powers of resistance, must be given special handling, because they will constitute a nucleus for the rebuilding of a new Jewry.

'For the practical execution of the Final Solution, Europe will be combed from west to east. In the occupied territories and the countries within our sphere of influence in Europe, the officer designated by the security police will operate in co-ordination with the appropriate representative of the Foreign Ministry.'

Heydrich had scarcely sat down before the flood of questioning began. Predictably, there were protestations from various ministries that the final solution process had already begun. After all, as more than one person present that day reasoned, it was important to make a favourable impression on Heydrich and Eichmann right from the start.

Dr Joseph Buehler, a representative of the Polish Government-General, stated that there might not be as many Jews available for work as Heydrich seemed to assume. Most of the two and a quarter million in his region came into that category.

Might it not, he suggested blandly, be a sound idea to put their future in the hands of the RSHA – a move which would, of course, be treated with the utmost co-operation from the Government-General?

Silkily Buehler added: 'I ask only that the matter be attended to as soon as possible.'

Otto Thierack (Reich Minister of Justice from September 1942) saw a good opportunity to make his mark. Certainly, in order to free the body of the German people of certain elements, including Jews, he was prepared to transfer the punitive authority over them to Heinrich Himmler in his capacity as Reichsfuehrer-SS.

In effect, it meant a transfer to Reinhard Heydrich, in *his* authority as head of the Reichssicherheitshauptamt.

The stenographer at the meeting dutifully took down Thierack's next remark.

> 'There is no sense in keeping them in prisons or in internment centres. By handing over those people to the police – who will be unfettered by the criminal law – better results will be achieved.'

In one sentence, the Jews had been sentenced to death.

Up till then, the meeting had been a rigidly formal affair. Heydrich, a master manipulator, reasoned that since he had got all he wanted and had suitably pliant colleagues, the time had come to relax the tension.

It was a remarkable transformation. The doors of the room were flung open. Waiters appeared, bearing trays of drinks. Alcohol, that notorious relaxer of tension, began its work. The conversation switched to the most effective means of execution. Suddenly, everybody was talking at once above the cognac fumes.

(At his trial, the prissy Eichmann, even after all the intervening years, was at pains to deny that anything so distressing had taken place at any meeting he attended.

Hastily, he assured the Jerusalem court:

> 'I do not want to say there was an alcoholic atmosphere. It was, of course, an official meeting but not a very formal one when everyone spoke in turn.')

Not surprisingly the stenographer was soon giving up. Heydrich ordered that such transcripts as there were should be delivered to him the next morning, by which time he had cleared his head.

The minutes of the second half of the Wannsee Conference did not survive.

Gerhardt Riegner, representative of the World Jewish Congress in Geneva, stared in stunned disbelief as the prominent German industrialist sitting opposite gave him a detailed account of the proceedings at Wannsee a few months before. He even specified one of the instruments of murder that had been discussed so casually over the cognac: prussic acid, the lethal ingredient of Zyklon B gas.

Riegner's agent was reliable. There was no question of that. He was the employer of more than thirty thousand war workers – and, most important, had direct access to Hitler. It was in the Fuehrer's circle, he said, that he had heard the order discussed.

Riegner sighed: 'Nobody is going to believe you. Nobody has dreamed of anything on this scale.'

Within hours, a cable sent to the State Department in Washington gave the essence of the Wannsee proceedings. It was followed swiftly by a memorandum from Howard Elting, American Vice-Consul in Geneva.

Elting wrote:

> 'When I mentioned that this report seemed fantastic to me, Riegner said that it had struck him the same way but that from the fact that mass deportations had been taking place since 16 July as confirmed by reports received by him from Paris, Holland, Berlin, Vienna and Prague, it was always conceivable that such a diabolical plan had actually been considered by Hitler.'

In addition, ever since the German invasion of the Soviet Union in June 1941, hundreds of thousands of Jews had been shot by the action groups (*Einsatzgruppen*) and special commandos (*Sonderkommando*). These were mobile killing units which followed in the wake of the Nazi armies and whose tasks were delicately designated as 'house cleaning'. Detailed reports of their operations had even found their way into the American press.

Riegner's doubts proved only too accurate. Eldridge Durbow, an official of the State Department's Division of European Affairs, declined to pass on the Wannsee intelligence to New York Jewish circles and the American and Allied governments. He wrote:

'It does not appear advisable in view of the fantastic nature of the allegations and the impossibility of our being of any assistance if such actions were taken . . .'

It seemed impossible to grasp that Hitler's programme of terror was now to begin in earnest, that it had been planned from the very start of the inexorable march east, right from the time, four years earlier, when the Fuehrer, as triumphant conqueror, had returned to his native Austria with delirious crowds laying flowers at the feet of his storm-troopers.

2

The thirteen open limousines and their occupants in jet-black SS uniforms with skull and crossbones on the caps moved slowly down the length of Vienna's Ringstrasse. Keen eyes sternly scanned the crowd for the least sign of danger.

Behind the cars and looking strangely insignificant in a vast armoured vehicle stood the brown-uniformed figure of Adolf Hitler, making an entry into the city which had rejected him in his vagabond youth and which he secretly hated.

Yet his eyes had always been fixed greedily on the land of his birth. Long ago, on the first page of his political manifesto, *Mein Kampf*, Hitler had insisted:

'German Austria must return to the great German motherland; not out of economic considerations of any kind. No. No. Even if this union made no difference from the economic point of view – even it it were positively detrimental – it must nevertheless take place. Peoples of one blood belong together in one Reich.'

The procession made its way rapidly past the Hofburg to the Hotel Imperial, whose guests had been evacuated for the conqueror.

On 9 April 1938, Hitler faced a crowd of twenty thousand at the disused Vienna North-West Station. He contemptuously dismissed the previous rulers of Austria as 'dwarfs'. Then he declared:

> 'Whether in a hundred years' time anyone will remember the names of my predecessors here, I do not know. But my name will stand as the name of the great son of this country.'

Then had come the regimented shouts of the obedient Nazi legions. From the throats of the besotted and the jubilantly fanatic there leapt the phrases:

Sieg Heil! Sieg Heil! Sieg Heil!
Ein Volk! Ein Reich! Ein Fuehrer!
Sieg Heil! Sieg Heil! Sieg Heil!
Heil Dem Fuehrer! Dank Dem Fuehrer!
Wir Danken Dir, Adolf Hitler!
Wir Danken Dir, Adolf Hitler!

But there were others, not daring to speak, who remembered another voice which had spoken to them over the radio just over a month ago.

> 'Austrian men and Austrian women: This day has placed us in a tragic and decisive situation. I have to give my Austrian fellow-countrymen the details of the events of the day.
>
> 'The German government today handed to President Miklas an ultimatum, with a time limit attached, ordering him to nominate as Chancellor a person to be designated by the German government and to appoint members of a Cabinet on the orders of the German government; otherwise German troops would invade Austria.
>
> 'I declare before the world that the reports put into circulation concerning disorders by the workers, the shedding of streams of blood and the allegation that the situation had got out of control of the government, are lies from A to Z.

'President Miklas asks me to tell the people of Austria that we have yielded to force, since we are not prepared even in this terrible situation to shed blood. We decided to order the troops to offer no serious' – here the speaker corrected himself – 'to offer no resistance.

'So I take leave of the Austrian people with the German words of farewell, uttered from the depths of my heart – 'God protect Austria' *(Gott schuetze Oesterreich).*'

The moving farewell from the Chancellor, Kurt von Schuschnigg, hounded out of office by the Nazis, was followed by Austria's national anthem. It was not to be heard again for a long time and it seemed to many listeners to be played with a new soft sadness.

The Anschluss (annexation of Austria) was decreed the day Hitler entered Vienna. The document began: *'Austria is a province of the German Reich.'* A once great empire was now Ostmark, a province, and Vienna, the former imperial centre, became nothing but a provincial seat of administration.

Without firing a shot and without the slightest interference from the other powers, Hitler at a stroke had added seven million subjects to the Reich and gained an invaluable strategic position. He had secured not only the gateway to south-east Europe but the certainty that neither France nor Great Britain would stop any future aggression.

On 11 March 1938, Heinrich Himmler, whose prim spectacles gave him a vaguely Mongolian appearance, was now martial and sinister in a brand-new field-grey SS uniform, as he left his Berlin headquarters in the Prinz Albrechtstrasse with a group of aides.

Himmler, who had never seen a shot fired in anger in his life, was almost childishly pleased with the two hand grenades dangling from his belt. He did not possess the force of personality to assert authority without question; the grenades were a useful symbol for what he found impossible to express.

But Himmler was not entirely brimming over with confidence. Even so besotted a Nazi had to admit that, until now, the role of National Socialists in Austrian affairs had been nothing short of disastrous.

Austria had been buffeted by politicians of the left and right ever since the demise of the Habsburg Empire in 1918. There had been an attempt to seize power in the summer of 1934, when Austrian Nazis had occupied the government building in the Ballhausplatz and murdered the diminutive Chancellor Engelbert Dollfuss.

But Hitler had regarded the timing of the death of Dollfuss as embarrassing and had disowned the killing because it would attract criticism from abroad.

The Fuehrer had been forced to be patient. It had looked for a time as if Schuschnigg, who succeeded Dollfuss, would restore stability to Austria. In the meantime, Germany was able to build her strength. The support of Austria by England, France and Italy grew progressively less reliable.

By February 1938, the Nazis had been able to turn the screws. Hitler had summoned Schuschnigg to Berchtesgaden and compelled him to include banned Nazis in the government. Then Schuschnigg was tumbled from office; the government passed into the hands of the Austrian Nazis.

But National Socialism was a tender plant in Austria. It had to be nurtured – and fast. Fortunately, Himmler realised, there was a strong tradition of anti-Semitism in the country which would help.

Himmler was clearly out of his depth, however, as an organiser of wholesale repression against dissident elements. That needed energy and a breadth of vision that went far beyond a talent for bureaucratic exactitude.

Heydrich and Eichmann, also speeding to Vienna, had work to do.

The hitherto banned Austrian Nazi Party was let loose on the streets in one vast brown tide. Stormtroopers, many of them barely out of their teens, sporting cartridge belts, carbines and swastika armbands swept toward the Jewish quarter of Leopoldstadt.

A British journalist, Eric Gedye, covering events for *The Times* recorded:

'The Seitenstaettengasse is a tiny, old world, cobbled street just off the busy Rotenturmstrasse. In the tall, shabby building is the principal synagogue of Vienna, together with the Jewish *Kultusgemeinde* – centre of the

24

religious, cultural and charitable work of the Jews of the capital. Since early morning the building had been occupied by SS guards. To it were accustomed to come the Jewish poorest of the poor, to the soup-kitchens provided by the Jewish community.

'The SS had closed the soup-kitchen and stolen all the food supplies. Then they had issued special passes to enter the building to poor Jews who came in search of relief . . .

'. . . Once inside the building they were taken into the synagogue, where the SS lolled about, smoking pipes and cigarettes. The Jews were forced to perform 'physical jerks', knee bending and stretching, holding a chair in each hand. The older and feebler ones who stumbled or collapsed were brutally kicked and beaten by the Nazis . . .

'They were forced to strap on the wrists the sacred *Tefillin* or praying bands with the ten commandments, and therewith to scrub the floors and clean out the bowls of the lavatories.'

War was declared on intellectuals and the professional middle classes. Almost overnight, one-sixth of the population of Vienna became outcasts. They were deprived of all civil rights, including the right to retain any property or to hold jobs or offer them. They were banned from restaurants, cafés, swimming baths and public parks.

Jews were arrested without charge and disappeared. Weeks later relatives would receive a small package and an accompanying letter which read: *'To pay, 150 Marks, for the cremation of your husband – ashes enclosed from Dachau.'* The usual intimation was simply a printed slip: *'The relatives of Herr X are informed herewith that he died today at Dachau Concentration Camp. (Signed) GESTAPO HEAD-QUARTERS.'*

It was necessary for the Nazis to tie up some distressing loose ends, the most pressing of which was the murder of Dollfuss.

Emil Fey, former Vice-Chancellor, had been at the Chancellery when the Nazis had seized the building and shot the Chancellor. A systematic campaign was launched against him and his family. There were insulting telephone calls and letters.

Fey had not the physical or moral strength to hold out for long. He summoned two of his closest friends and confided to them his fear of being arrested and made the subject of a show trial.

In vain, his friends tried to reassure him by saying there surely were enough witnesses to prove his innocence.

Fey shrugged: 'But do you think that would stop them finding hundreds of people, who in their enthusiasm for National Socialism, would be willing to swear they saw me shoot Dollfuss?'

Later, he summoned his son Herbert from the Military Academy in Wiener Neustadt. Friends who had offered to get Fey out of the country pleaded in vain. He declared that he had made up his mind to kill himself with his family. Letters of farewell were handed over.

The doctor's report noted that father and son had shot themselves. The death certificate for Fey's wife read: *'Two shots through the skull. Killed by another hand. Family suicide.'*

As soon as Kurt von Schuschnigg came to the end of that final emotional broadcast, the accumulated agonies of the last few weeks proved too much. He burst into tears and slumped forward. A number of his loyal ministers helped him to a chair, while Artur Seyss-Inquart, the man who was to succeed him as Chancellor and whom Schuschnigg had been forced to take into his cabinet after that bullying interview with Hitler at Berchtesgaden earlier in the year, resolutely ignored him.

It had been long obvious that Schuschnigg's days of liberty were numbered. Plans were laid by friends to spirit him out of the country but he had protested: 'I do not run away. My place is here in Austria.'

Directly after the broadcast he left for his home at the Belvedere Hotel, hotly pursued by Seyss-Inquart and a clutch of stormtroopers armed to the teeth with rifles and machine-guns.

At the Chancellery, six thousand stormtroopers and eight hundred SS swarmed up the ladders, leaping onto the balconies. They forced their way in, seizing President Miklas and his ministers.

Soon the main gates were being flung open; Seyss-Inquart

had simultaneously given orders for all public buildings to be seized.

For the civilised, cultivated Schuschnigg, lawyer and devout Roman Catholic, a deliberate, planned humiliation was in store.

Abruptly, one of the Gestapo snapped: 'Take the things you need and plenty of underwear and bedclothes.'

He was transferred to the temporary SS and SD headquarters at the Hotel Metropole. In his memoirs, *Austrian Requiem*, Schuschnigg later relived his experiences:

'At six a.m. the sentry shouts at me to get up. He closes the windows which, thank God, may be opened during the night.

'Then my day's work begins. First I wash. Then I clean the room. I dust the table and wardrobe, sweep the floor and walls, the radiator and the window frame as well as the opaque glass panels, all with my only towel. For sweeping the floor I was finally given an old broom. After my room has been cleaned, I am ordered to go next door to the room where the sentries sleep. I take my towel and my broom and begin the same procedure in their room, only here there is more work to do. Usually the guards have just finished washing, and I have to empty their washbasins and slop buckets. My towel is again used to wipe these utensils dry; then the floor and the walls. When I have finished, the guard in charge remarks: 'You'll get used to it. Dismissed!' I return with my sentry to my own room barely four paces away.'

Schuschnigg's guard ordered his prisoner to make his bed, then demanded that the blanket be folded from the right and the sheet tucked in another four inches. Schuschnigg obeyed meekly – then was ordered to do it eight more times.

After that, he was put to cleaning the toilet, but not until a selection of guards and prisoners had soiled it first. His food was carried from the kitchen on a tray and put down by the lavatory bowl so that he had to pick it up. The meal was meagre, because the SS charged the former Chancellor as if he were a hotel guest, and Schuschnigg had little money.

In a last desperate throw, he had planned a plebiscite in

which he asked voters whether they wanted a 'free, independent, social, Christian and united Austria.'

Hitler had riposted with a brutal ultimatum that unless the plebiscite was cancelled and a full Nazi cabinet under Seyss-Inquart appointed, the Nazis would invade forthwith.

Schuschnigg gave in. Jews, army officers, clergyman and nobility – all those who knew they were sure candidates for a Nazi death list – had dashed to the city's East Station. Cars weighed down with luggage clogged the roads.

Some of the trains, driven by Nazi sympathisers, had halted in open country. Stormtroopers of the SS, armed with dog whips, dragged off screaming passengers, including small children. Some refugees, allowed to continue their journey to Creclav on Czech soil, lost jewellery, watches and furs in an orgy of gleeful looting.

But the Nazis had their sympathisers among the Czechs, too. Many of those fleeing from Vienna got no further. They were ordered back – and soon were on a third journey to the concentration camps of the Reich.

Fearful of Hitler's wrath, few other countries were keen to absorb the steady stream from Vienna, claiming they had no facilities for stateless Austrians.

Reinhard Heydrich was more concerned with security directly inside the country. He affected a fastidious distaste for the sort of crude Jew-baiting which entailed making the wealthy middle-class scrub pavements or wash cars with the acid from batteries.

But, after all, what could you expect from a man like Ernst Kaltenbrunner, whom the Fuehrer had appointed chief of police for Austria? The fellow reminded Heydrich of a sweating ox. He had the sensitivity of an abattoir keeper and it was rumoured that he was sober for precisely four hours a day.

The staff of the SD, Heydrich made it clear, was the élite. His operatives were not in the business of making yesterday's politicians clean toilets. Their task was to work on the administrative integration of Austria into the Third Reich.

From Heydrich's office there poured out a positive torrent of laws and decrees. They amounted to the complete surrender of both the police and the security organisation of what had once been an independent country.

A mere two weeks after the Anschluss the SS propaganda newspaper, *Das Schwarze Korps*, which Heydrich himself had created, was able to announce the complete takeover of all political, criminal and administrative police in Austria.

Heydrich regaled his readers with an account of his new dominion in the east. He proclaimed:

'Austria is now an area where the will of the Fuehrer can be carried out as a result of the successful conclusion of the bitter fight against all political, spiritual and criminal elements who opposed the idea of a single German people.

'The former Austrian police were responsible for the death of a large number of good fanatical Germans. The honour of the force was rescued only by the National Socialist policemen who gave their lives and freedom for the dream of a greater Germany.'

Interference, of course, could not be tolerated. Heydrich arranged for a special train from Vienna to carry around two hundred leading opponents of the Nazis to the concentration camp at Dachau. Those who survived rotted there for seven years until relieved by the Allies.

The more fortunate were sentenced to short terms of imprisonment and then released. They were segregated from the very worst areas of the camp. The idea was that, on release, they would warn others of what foolhardy opposition to the Nazis could mean.

In 1933, the German Social Democratic Party had gone underground. But its members produced, in English and German, a clandestine magazine, *Germany Reports*.

Among its contributors were former Dachau prisoners from Austria. One wrote:

'We had an 18 hour night journey behind us, during which nobody had slept, and now we had to stand from 9 a.m. to 6 p.m. with no food at all. From the first day we were constantly beaten in Dachau. The Jewish prisoners worked in special detachments and received the hardest tasks. They were beaten at every opportunity – for instance, if the space between the barrows with which they had to walk or even run over loose flints were not correctly kept, they were overwhelmed with abusive epithets such as 'Sow Jew', 'Filth Jew' and 'Stink Jew'. During the working period the non-Jewish prisoners were issued with one piece of bread at breakfast – the Jews got nothing.

'On March 23rd all prisoners were formed up in a hollow square. The SS Kommandant Loritz announced that he was going to let us all see what happened to incorrigibles. Three prisoners were strapped down to a block, their heads muffled in blankets, and each given 25 lashes with four-foot cattle whips which had been left soaking in water for the purpose since the previous day. Three block leaders took it in turns to beat them. Further, twelve prisoners were given from one to two hours 'post hanging'. They were hung up on posts with their hands tied behind their backs so that with their toe-tips they could just touch the ground . . .'

Heydrich, however, was by no means to have everything his own way. Individual Nazis realised that Austria provided an excellent opportunity for them to make their own reputations – and enrich themselves most agreeably in the process. The Foreign Office of Joachim von Ribbentrop, which had a separate intelligence service, stuck its fingers in every conceivable pie.

Heydrich's own intelligence service, for all its speedy achievements in Austria, was hopelessly bureaucratic. It became increasingly obvious that what was needed was a single centralised authority to deal with Jewish affairs.

At first sight, Adolf Eichmann seemed scarcely fitted for the job he proposed for himself. He was, after all, only a junior SD officer. He had, however, one thing in common with his master: a prodigious sexual appetite.

In Berlin, Heydrich's main relaxation, apart from music, had been prowling the restaurants and nightclubs, picking up tarts and a lot of worthwhile information at the same time.

Eichmann had been brought up in Austria and was well acquainted with the more sleazy byways of Vienna. Heydrich began prowling around the local nightspots in much the same way as he had in Berlin; now he was invariably accompanied by Adolf Eichmann, who also had a taste for expensive restaurants and fleshy cabarets.

During one of these nocturnal adventures, Eichmann cautiously broached the subject of an office for Jewish emigration, to be set up in Austria but with its headquarters in Berlin.

What Eichmann proposed amounted to an extremely lucrative trade in human freedom. The office, suggested Eichmann, would become the sole Nazi agency authorised to issue permits to Jews seeking to leave the country. When all the Jews able to pay had quit Austria, there could be only one destiny for those who remained.

Eichmann was only too conscious that he had started his career in the SS as a filing clerk typing out data on freemasons in whom the Gestapo had been interested. If he put a step wrong with a man like Heydrich, a promising future would very rapidly dissolve. Heydrich must be persuaded that the original idea for an emigration office had been his own right from the start.

Eichmann was able to console himself with the thought that he was well in with the all-powerful Himmler, who had been almost touchingly grateful for Eichmann's intense interest in the Reichsfuehrer's Scientific Museum for Jewish Affairs. Eichmann had even gone to the trouble to learn some Hebrew and had made a brief trip to Palestine.

He had also made himself familiar with standard anti-Semitic literature and learned all he could about Jewish religious beliefs and customs and the various branches of the Zionist movement.

The emigration office was established eventually on 20 August 1938, but incidents of crude persecution continued. Day after day, large numbers of Jews could be seen scrubbing pro-Schuschnigg signs off the pavements and cleaning the gutters.

But deportation and plunder were now the main pre-occupations. Wealthy Austrians seeking to leave the country were issued with passports, but at the slightest whim these could be seized and held until a ransom was paid.

The passport of Baron Louis Rothschild was seized at the airport. It was torn up and flung in his face while Eichmann's agents opened negotiations with the Rothschild family.

The Baron was later able to buy his way out of Vienna by turning over his steel mills to the Hermann Goering Works in Linz.

Humiliation did not stop there. Eichmann summoned members of the German Jewish community in Vienna to Gestapo headquarters. The lowly bureaucrat, the eternal clerk who was in seventh heaven filing endless reports, was suddenly transformed into a brutal martinet.

Visitors were ordered to remain standing in his presence and then taken on compulsory tours to see how the Nazis were dealing with Austrian Jews.

A prominent Jew, Gerson Friedmann, who survived to testify at Eichmann's trial, told how he and others were forced to don Nazi helmets and swear their loyalty to the Gestapo on a bible.

But Eichmann's passion for bureaucracy never deserted him. Shoals of clerks were employed to stamp the applications of those Jews who were denied exit visas with a large D. It stood for Dachau.

The target of the Nazis was not simply Austrian Jews. War was declared on the very spirit of the country, on that mysterious *Gemuetlichkeit,* the abundant charm which the visitor invariably found so beguiling. Such nonsense, it was made clear, was to cease. Instead, the 'Eastern State' would become a new workhorse of the Reich.

The swaggering Hermann Goering, Hitler's heir apparent, who had helped mastermind the military incursion into Austria, was in bullying form at the opening of the Linz works named after him.

The scented Goering, with his liking for comic opera uniforms and gangster jewellery, told his audience harshly: 'Quick! Quick! You have to prove to the world that you are not easygoing.

'An eight-hour day is not enough. Work! Work!'

Life in the restaurants and pavement cafés gave way to the compulsory route march and physical training for young and old with the ever present threat of deportation.

Austria had once been a city of beautiful women, leisurely elegance and polished manners. But now, where there had been relaxation and good fellowship, there was fear and suspicion. Even a simple taxi ride was taken in silence. Strangers received terrified glances; news was passed on in hastily whispered asides.

At any time a hand could fall on monarchists, Catholics and Socialists as well as Jews. But Hitler's interest was already elsewhere. On 28 May 1938, he had spelled it out: 'It is my unshakeable will that Czechoslovakia shall be wiped off the map.'

The thoughts of Adolf Eichmann were soaring over the Austrian border too.

3

Out of the east that winter of 1939 came bitter winds bearing bullet-sized snowflakes to lash the lands of the Czechs and Slovaks. And, out of the west, eager and impatient for fresh conquest, burst Adolf Hitler.

The snow was carpeting thoroughfares of the busy Graben, all but blotting out from view the huge swastika flags unfurled on bank buildings. It turned to ice the tears of the Czechs who attempted in the milling crowds to raise their voice with the oddly pathetic words of the Czech national anthem: '*Where is my home? Where is my home?*'

Much louder were the ecstatic yells of '*Heil Hitler! Sieg Heil!*' The Germans of Prague were on the streets to greet the first soldiers of the 'liberating' Third Reich.

The German annexation of the Sudetenland area of Czechoslovakia with its German minority the previous October, turned out to be solely the prelude to the country's complete dismemberment. Now Hitler had threatened to destroy Prague unless the remaining areas in Bohemia and Moravia were surrendered. This was to be the price of the 'peace' with honour with which British Prime Minister Neville Chamberlain had returned from the notorious Munich conference in September 1938.

Nine hundred thousand inhabitants of Prague, most of whom had huddled the previous night before their wireless sets, heard at five a.m. the announcement:

'Citizens of Czechoslovakia! At six o'clock this morning the German army will begin the occupation of Bohemia and Moravia. In these grave hours more than ever we must show to the world our dignified orderliness and complete calm.

'Go, all of you, to work because in work lies our strength. In no circumstances must there be any incident. The railway, post and other services must work absolutely normally. Everyone is obliged to comply with the orders of the German military authorities.'

Then had followed the order from the elderly President, Dr Emil Hacha, who was also Commander in Chief of the Czech Army. All officers and men were ordered to stay quietly at their posts and not to offer resistance to the Germans. A communiqué by Foreign Minister Chvalkowsky told the Czechs of the previous night's conference between Hitler and Hacha in Berlin. The result had been that the Czech government had been obliged to occupy Bohemia and Moravia so that the nation could be saved from complete annihilation.

As soon as the first German armoured car had reached Melnik, thirty miles from Prague, a proclamation, bordered in red and bearing the German eagle and swastika which was to become familiar in every Czech town and village, had been posted on the hoardings.

Under this proclamation no one was allowed in the streets after eight p.m. without special German permission. The only exemptions permitted were for doctors and railway workers. All popular gatherings were forbidden and there was also an order for the surrender of weapons, munitions and wireless sets. Disobedience to these orders, the proclamation ended, would be severely punished under military law.

A casual visitor to Prague, up and about an hour after the wireless announcement, might not have found much amiss. The main square, Wenceslas-Platz, was alive as usual with the roar of trams. Motorists were driving with care to avoid skidding on the snow-wet pavements.

A closer look at the people hurrying to work might have revealed a rather tenser atmosphere than usual. Most looked as if they were on the way to a funeral; often a woman put a handkerchief to her eyes.

In the corner of the square a bank of loud-speakers had been rigged up. They suddenly cut into the early morning air with the oft-repeated warning: 'Citizens remain calm. There is nothing you can do. Don't resist German troops.'

The Nazi mechanised columns rumbled into Prague. There was a seemingly endless column of grey mudstained cars, the frozen snow clotting their windscreens. The robot-like figures who sat in them looked as if they had been turned to stone in the bitter cold. Indeed, it was almost impossible to see any faces at all, just rows and rows of goggles beneath intimidating steel helmets. On the knees of the men were light machine-guns, which pointed towards rooftops and windows and sideways into the crowd.

Within seconds, a German tank was surrounded. Everyone in the crowd had linked hands to sing 'Hroma Paklo', an age-old song of Slav defiance which dated back to the days of the Habsburgs. The refrain seemed to run like a lighted fuse through the rest of the crowd.

Motor-cycle escorts arrowed ahead, threatening to slice into any obstacle. Tanks, armoured cars and lorries with infantry made up the rest of the procession, brought to a sudden halt as, without warning, a section of the crowd burst through the police cordon.

But the loud-speakers were cutting in now, begging urgently: 'Citizens, remain calm; avoid bloodshed.'

It was a futile resistance in the face of armed might; all the crowd could do was pitch snowballs at the procession, which had now resumed.

And Adolf Hitler? By late afternoon he was installed in the ancient Hradcany Castle, a magnificent fortress set high above the River Moldau and which, as the former home of the kings of Bohemia, had guarded the destinies of Prague for eight hundred years.

The Fuehrer, a conquering Napoleon who intended the latest Czech adventure to be a mere stepping stone towards his declared objective of the gates of India, stared down thoughtfully on the twinkling lights of the capital of his latest vassal state.

If Hitler allowed himself a moment's reflection, his lieutenants back in Berlin wasted no time. Propaganda Minister Joseph Goebbels was soon at the microphone to issue a Fuehrer proclamation to the German people:

'A few months ago, Germany was compelled to protect against the unbearable regime of terrorism in Czechoslovakia those of our co-nationals living in areas inhabited chiefly by Germans. The same events have again occurred to an ever-increasing extent during the past week.

'In an area where so many nationalities are living side by side this must lead to an unbearable situation. As a reaction against these renewed attacks on their freedom, national groups have separated from Prague. Thereby Czechoslovakia ceased to exist.

'Since Sunday riots have occurred in many communities with many Germans as victims. Hourly they cried for help for the persecuted who steadily increased in number . . .

'In order definitely to eliminate this menace to peace and order and to create the prerequisites for the necessary new regulations in this area I have decided as from today to allow German troops to march into Bohemia and Moravia.'

For the Czechs, it meant that their country became downgraded to the status of a 'Reich Protectorate'. Except on festive occasions, they were allowed to fly only the Nazi flag and to carry German passports. Only German money and German postage stamps were issued.

As for Slovakia, to the east of the country, there was the dubious position of an 'independent state' – considered, nevertheless, part of Hitler's economic fiefdom in central Europe.

Adolf Eichmann had scarcely had time to perfect his Vienna operations as head of the Jewish emigration office before he was summoned by Heydrich.

The head of the SD came straight to the point, proclaiming: 'Since the setting up of the Central Office, we have managed to deport fifty thousand Jews from Austria.' With the suggestion of a sneer Heydrich added: 'This compares extremely favourably with the nineteen thousand Jews

36

deported from the rest of the Reich by the Ministry of the Interior.'

Heydrich's contempt for measures against the Jews taken by Interior Minister Wilhelm Frick was well known. Eichmann had no intention of being sucked into the Byzantine intrigues which riddled the Third Reich. Wisely, he kept quiet. Besides, Heydrich had changed the subject.

He leafed the pages of a beige file on his desk, murmuring: 'Your wife, I understand, is Czech, and you speak a little of the language. I see that you have a brother-in-law in the Prague police. How very useful!'

Eichmann felt a twinge of anxiety. What did this mean?

Back in January, things had looked very good. His organisation had been upgraded to Central Reich Bureau for Jewish Emigration and he himself had been promoted SS Hauptsturmfuehrer. But it never did to become complacent when dealing with Heydrich.

Keeping his voice as steady as he could, he stared Heydrich full in the face and replied blandly: 'Certainly, Herr Gruppenfuehrer. In addition, another of Frau Eichmann's sisters is married to a staff captain who lectures at the Czech Military Academy.'

Heydrich smiled slightly. Then he seemed to lose interest.

Instead he said: 'When we enter Prague, your instructions will be to get rid of as many Czech Jews as possible.

'To achieve this aim, you will at once set up in Prague a Central Office for the Jewish question in Bohemia and Moravia as a branch of our central department here in Berlin.'

Eichmann was granted an official interview with Monsignor Josef Tiso, the chubby, gluttonous pro-Nazi leader of the Slovak separatist government, who was every bit as anti-Semitic as Eichmann himself.

Tiso expressed himself delighted with the measures that Eichmann had taken against the Jews in Austria. The interview left Eichmann uneasy; a deep-seated middle-class inferiority in the company of those he regarded as his betters was largely to blame.

But there was another reason. Eichmann revelled in anonymity, in being the man in the shadows, a dutiful filing clerk with a prissy dislike for the limelight in any form.

Gratefully, he scuttled back to Prague. There, an enormous number of Jews began to fall into his hands. In the forced emigration that followed, some thirty-five thousand Jews left the Czech Protectorate.

Ironically, the Jews themselves helped to provide the machinery which made it possible.

For generations, the relief of Czech Jews throughout the entire country had been administered by the Prague Jewish Council, a body whose members were elected by the Jewish community.

The discovery was almost too good to be true; Eichmann set about exploiting it ruthlessly.

The Jewish Council was made the sole medium through which the Jews could approach Eichmann and his office. Here was a chance for bureaucracy to sprout and luxuriate: no less than thirty-two departments sprang into being. Eichmann gleefully moved his headquarters into the building of the Jewish Council itself.

Before the Jews were forcibly kicked out of the country, their property was confiscated. Then thousands were herded aboard German ships with bogus visas for Latin American countries or with British permits to enter Palestine.

The deported Jews, of course, had no money. Very well, the Jewish Council would pay the tax on each deportee – an admirable way of swelling the coffers of the Reich. Eichmann carried out almost daily 'negotiations' with Dr Klapka, an Aryan Czech who was the luckless head of the Prague City Council.

Then came the day when Klapka was driven to protest: 'It is quite impossible for me to raise any more money, Herr Haupsturmfuehrer. Your own people have blocked the Council's funds.'

Eichmann exploded in fury, shouting: 'If you don't get those damned Jews out of the country, I'll order the arrest of three hundred men per day. I'll send them to Dachau and Merkelgrun, where they'll be a damn sight more enthusiastic about emigration than you are!'

A shaking Klapka departed, but the threats and the bullying had their effect. Somehow, the money was forthcoming.

The policy of enforced emigration, however, soon began to

encounter snags. There were only a few countries, such as Argentina and Chile, which were prepared to be generous with immigration quotas. But the United States and Canada were decidedly niggardly. Practically no nation wanted penniless refugees and stipulated that an immigrant show either a certificate of land ownership or evidence of enough capital to support himself before getting a job.

Fearfully, Jews such as Dr Klapka realised that if immigration stopped altogether the certain fate of his people would be death and torture in concentration camps.

Secretly, the Jews began to set up an elaborate escape network which would make possible illegal immigration into Palestine. Organisation for this highly dangerous work was placed in the hands of Prague University student Naftali Palatin.

Possessed of an iron nerve, Palatin decided to put his head straight into the lion's mouth. He wrote to Eichmann direct, requesting an interview.

Eichmann had an office in a smart villa outside Prague. It was like a fortress, stiff with SS troops. A posse of them escorted Palatin to the third floor. He was ordered to stand at attention outside the office door until admitted.

Eichmann deliberately let a few minutes go by. Palatin heard a soft: 'Come in'.

It was a gentle, insinuating voice, which utterly disarmed the inexperienced visitor; a favourite technique adopted by Eichmann. He would suddenly induce a feeling of terror by switching without warning to a burst of hysterical ranting.

That morning, however, Eichmann seemed wholly sympathetic. Fatherly, almost. Gravely, he listened to Palatin's carefully prepared story that he had secured visas for three hundred and fifty Jews, that they were already to go and that negotiations were being made for a ship to take them to South America.

Eichmann was silent, possibly remembering the illuminating Gestapo report he had studied before Palatin's arrival. The Rhinelander's charm, if anything, became even more marked. The voice had a note almost of pity.

Eichmann sighed: 'Yes, I know who issued you with these visas to a South American country, but I will tell you that where you are really bound for is' – there was the merest pause – 'Palestine.

'You would have done far better to be frank with me. Now I want you to stop this nonsense and go downstairs and take all the necessary forms for the new emigration certificates – the real ones.'

Palatin felt encouraged. Clearly, Eichmann's main objective was to get rid of the Jews and he was not over-concerned where they went, even to the hated Palestine.

In his elation, Palatin increased his original list of three hundred and fifty passengers to five hundred and fifty. He hastened to get the certificates ready.

The Eichmann who greeted him on his next visit might almost have been a different person.

He snapped: 'So it is you again. When are you leaving?'

Slightly taken aback, Palatin stammered: 'We are just filling out the necessary documents.'

It was a match to a fuse. Eichmann advanced on the other man, bunching his fists and screaming: 'You're a liar. The documents are all ready.

'You have precisely fourteen days to get out. Otherwise, you won't get anywhere again alive. Do you understand?'

Palatin nodded in a mixture of misery and fear. Eichmann had been right. The documents were all completed, but the attempts by the Irgun Zvi Leumi headquarters in Palestine, in charge of illegal immigration, had been unable to find a ship.

Worse was to come. The orders from headquarters laid down that Palatin was to leave Czechoslovakia with his wife, but on no account could his six-year-old daughter Adina go with them. If the ship was attacked on the high seas, small children would present an obvious handicap.

The thought that he would have to face the unpredictable Eichmann again filled Palatin with dread, but he would have to seek permission for his wife to take Adina to her grandparents in Latvia and to return in time for the departure of the transport.

Outside Eichmann's office stood three SS carrying rifles and fixed bayonets.

One of them snapped: 'Are you the Jewish swine named Palatin?'

'Yes,' he answered.

'Come with us,' was the order.

40

Palatin realised with a sudden clutch of fear that he was being escorted downstairs and well away from Eichmann's office. Prodded with bayonets, Palatin was thrust in the direction of the cellars. This surely could only mean death. With Eichmann's lieutenants responsible for execution, there could be no guarantee that the end would be either swift or merciful.

The party stopped before a heavy wooden door. An order was snapped at Palatin: 'Knock!'

As soon as an old Czech woman appeared, one of the SS shouted: 'Ask her for the pruning shears!'

What form of refined sadism was Eichmann planning? Clutching the shears, Palatin was pushed and shoved up three flights of stairs to the familiar office.

Then the shears were snatched from him. Palatin saw a laughing Eichmann behind his desk looking genuinely puzzled.

Eichmann asked in mock innocence: 'What on earth did you think you were going to do with those shears? Kill me?'

This form of taunting sadism was all too common in Eichmann's treatment of the Jews. He liked a bit of cruel fun for its own sake, but there was a more serious purpose. He reasoned that an enemy who was cowed and demoralised would swiftly abandon any thoughts of rebellion. The shears had been a handy psychological tool.

Eichmann altered the mood yet again. Now he launched into a diatribe against the Jews.

He sneered: 'When we line you all up in the front of the ship and shoot you, we'll give you a choice as to where you stand in the queue. That way you'll be able to snatch a few more minutes of miserable life.'

Then all at once Eichmann appeared to tire of the game. Now his role was a harsh taskmaster willing to be merciful.

He sighed: 'All right, you can have an exit permit and a re-entry permit for your wife.'

Palatin could not remember leaving the villa. In a daze, he asked himself what possible sense could be made of Eichmann's techniques, save that they were meant to bewilder, to reduce life to one long nightmare from which there would never be the blessed balm of waking?

Palatin's wife was able to leave with the child for Latvia,

but for every mile of the journey there was the ever-present fear that Eichmann's cohorts might arrange a convenient accident, that the permits contained some deliberate error.

Amazingly, there were no difficulties; the journey was smooth. Palatin's wife took the baby to Latvia and returned. A week later, Palatin was again summoned by Eichmann.

The mask of the friendly uncle was firmly in place. All that remained now, he said smoothly, was to arrange the date of departure for the transport ship, a matter which should not present too many problems.

The first date suggested was the feast of Yom Kippur. Palatin had the temerity to shake his head firmly and say: 'You must know that such a day is completely out of the question.'

Eichmann sighed: 'Yes, I suppose it is. Very well, we will find an alternative. Now I'd like you to do me a favour.'

The last sentence was so extraordinary, coming from Eichmann, that Palatin could only stand and gape. His defences and powers of reasoning deserted him – which, of course, was precisely the effect Eichmann desired.

The mask of the uncle was torn off. The voice had become steel.

Eichmann said: 'What I would like you to do is to bring me the passports of your parents. They will certainly not be leaving with the transport.

'They remain as hostages. I give you fair warning that, should any of the Jews ever return to this country, your father and mother will be slaughtered like dogs. I will also kill them if, on your arrival in Palestine, you utter one word of criticism against the German Reich or even suggest that you have been ill-treated.'

The charade was over. Naftali Palatin and his wife left on the long journey for Palestine.

And then Adolf Eichmann acted. Palatin's father was hauled before a firing squad and his mother perished in the gas chambers. Killer gangs set out for Latvia; the small daughter and the grandparents were also murdered.

Eichmann this time had donned no mask, the true face had been shown at last.

The taste and fruits of power were indeed heady tastes for a

42

former filing clerk. But Eichmann also had to live with something far less agreeable; the stench of fear of the swift bullet from the forces of Czech resistance.

That fear could be kept somewhat at bay by travelling only in an official armoured limousine with machine-gun toting acolytes. In the pocket of his uniform there was always an egg-sized hand grenade with the fuse in his tobacco pouch.

Temporary oblivion could of course always be achieved through sex and alcohol, forms of release much favoured by his fellow merchant of terror, Reinhard Heydrich.

The head of the SD made frequent visits to Prague. The two men leched the nights away in a succession of bars and nightclubs whose owners had been wise enough to learn the virtues of unlimited tolerance.

It was common knowledge in Nazi circles that Eichmann's marriage to the former Veronika Liebel, a striking blonde Sudeten Czech, had long been on the rocks. Eichmann, it was said, had married only because single SS men were often overlooked in favour of those with families – likely in Himmler's view to be more stable and in the best position to breed magnificent new specimens for the racially pure Third Reich.

Eichmann, however, was devoted to his children – a quality which he incidentally shared with Heydrich and other Nazi leaders. Every weekend he made the journey from Prague to Berlin to see his two small boys.

Visits to the Czech-Austrian border were not always in the line of duty. An old girlfriend whom he had known before his marriage was now making a most agreeable mistress.

The daughter of a factory owner, with her own small estate, she was comfortably off. But Eichmann saw no reason why she should not better herself. A small prison camp was built in the grounds of the estate and it was only natural that the owner of the land should receive a handsome rent.

This blatant fiddle by Eichmann was too much for certain officers, even within the notoriously corrupt SS. The matter came to the ears of Himmler, a stickler for financial rectitude who himself accepted a comparatively meagre salary as the Reichsfuehrer-SS.

For a time it looked as if Eichmann would face courtmartial. In a panic, Eichmann pleaded with an SD crony in Vienna.

Incriminating papers were conveniently lost. A confidential report on Eichmann from the SD office in Vienna made no mention of irregular conduct.

Instead, the report blandly stated that Eichmann was an energetic and impulsive individual who in his special field had displayed great negotiating and administrative skill in dealing with difficult technical questions.

Eichmann himself doubtless reflected that it was of the highest advantage to have strong friends in the right places.

Gestapo and SS terror were in the meantime stepped up in the country. Already Hitler was looking with strong disfavour at what he regarded as the over-liberal attitude of Baron Konstantin von Neurath, the Reich Protector of Bohemia and Moravia. Neurath was a suave diplomat of the old school, just the type of statesman whom Hitler, the former Gefreiter of the trenches, loathed.

The Protector believed in trying to win over the Czech people through tactful persuasion, rather than outright terror, a policy which also found less than favour with Himmler and his cohorts.

Power began to slide away from Neurath. Only too willing to fill the gap as a man who, possibly even more than Heydrich, was to become the most hated of the Czech's oppressors, the brutal, swaggering sadist Karl Hermann Frank, once leader of the Sudeten Germany Party in the Czechoslovak Chamber and now Sudeten State Secretary in the puppet cabinet of President Hacha.

Foxy-faced Frank masterminded a group of informers among the Sudeten Germans whose activities were essential to the SS, most of whose operatives could not speak a word of Czech. These informers, infiltrated into hotels and cafés, were in addition given the job of censoring letters and tapping telephones.

Frank's agents were able to pave the way for the Gestapo's spectacular swoop at dawn throughout the Protectorate on Thursday, 31 August 1939.

By nine o'clock, thirty thousand had been arrested in Prague alone, including senior officers of the seven thousand strong Czech army, a picked organisation which had been formed by the Germans after the invasion. Jobs were swiftly allocated to the Wehrmacht.

Typical of events in Prague was the pinpointing by Sudeten Germans of the Café National as a centre of subversion.

Black Gestapo cars screeched to a halt in front of the terraces, where couples were sipping coffee and anxiously scanning the heavily censored newspapers.

Eight plain-clothes agents spilled out. Two waved revolvers menacingly, blocking the exits. Another, gun in hand, jumped on a chair shouting: 'Hands up! Gestapo raid. All stand up.'

An elderly man who moved too slowly was hauled up by the collar, his tormentor shouting: 'Can't you understand German by now?'

Café waitresses, many of them Nazi agents, were detailed to search the women under the eyes of the grinning Gestapo. Men were stripped; their clothes were deliberately stepped on and crumpled.

Then came the Gestapo vans, speeding with their new crop of victims to the Pankrac Prison, in the suburbs, where the SS had set up its own department. Up to three hundred suspects a day would be interrogated.

Sections of the SS were not content merely to humiliate their new vassal states; vicious attacks were made on proud national treasures such as the National Monument of Czech Liberation in Prague, which was broken up and its relics scattered. Pictures of Thomas Masaryk, founder of the republic, were slashed. Statues of other national heroes were bulldozed.

The Czech state was sealed off from the outside world. The inhabitants had to live in a land as forbidding and as inaccessible as Tibet, with fifty thousand Gestapo and SS troops as their absolute masters.

But the stubborn streak in the Czech character was such that the Germans by no means had everything their own way. The Czech had long experience of conquerors. Centuries of history had taught them to preserve national unity despite the harsh rule of foreign masters.

Students of history recalled that in 1620 the Czech nobility had been defeated catastrophically in the famous battle of the White Mountain. In the purge by the Habsburgs which followed, the Czechs were deprived of their leaders. It had been the ordinary people, peasants and workers, who had carried on the ideal of Czech nationhood under the hardship of oppression.

And now history was indeed repeating itself. The Germans found to their cost that there are few more obstinate creatures on the face of the earth than the average stolid Czech. When he was gabbled at in German, he merely turned a face of stone on his inquisitor – then went straight home to his clandestine radio set to tune into broadcasts, frequently in German, from London or Moscow.

A classic figure in Czech literature had walked out of the pages of fiction and become reality. In the 1920s, the writer Jaroslav Hasek created in *The Good Soldier Schweik* the sly, seemingly foolish Czech whose obduracy defeats the swagger of his Germanic masters. Now flesh and blood Schweiks proliferated, fuelled by the bitterness they felt at the cruelty of Nazi oppression.

Among all the new states that had been created by the peace treaties following World War I, Czechoslovakia had made a conspicuous start in democracy. Besides Schweik, the spirit of another hero stalked abroad – the fifteenth-century Bohemian religious leader Jan Hus, who had made the German crusaders of the Emperor Sigismund show a clean pair of heels. The Czech national spirit was showing every sign of surviving the centuries.

It soon became unwise for German soldiers in Prague to walk the streets alone at night. Members of the so-called 'Black Gang' leapt out of the shadows and either clubbed or garrotted their victims, a practice which became even easier with the blackout regulations later in the war. The Nazis retaliated with wholesale arrests, but the killings continued.

Typed Czech extracts from English and French newspapers and transcripts of speeches made in America by the exiled former President, Dr Eduard Beneš, formed the contents of an underground newspaper.

Each bulletin was accompanied by a footnote: *'If you are a loyal Czech you will make ten copies of this and pass them on to other Czechs, asking them to do the same.'* It was a chain-letter system which made it possible for eight million Czechs to keep themselves in touch with the news suppressed officially by their Nazi masters.

The biggest blow to the Nazi stranglehold of Czechoslovakia was dealt by the workers in the arms factories, regarded by the Germans as the richest part of their prize.

It was easy enough for a skilled engineer to make the smallest mistake in fashioning precision instruments, where a thousandth of an inch difference was every bit as good as a mile.

In the Waag valley of northern Slovakia the Germans had installed factories underground, safe from aerial bombardment. Czech resistance gleefully set about sabotaging them, in one case 'mislaying' blueprints for an automatic grenade-thrower.

Occasionally, harassing of the Nazi tormentors had a strong element of black comedy.

It was a particularly enraged SS officer, revolver in hand, who screamed a torrent of abuse at the mayor and council of Sternberg in east Moravia. The entire provisions of his company had unaccountably vanished overnight from the former police barracks. Mayor and council affected to understand not a single word the German was saying.

But, for the Protectorate, there was to be precious little to laugh at for six long years. A Czech student, before he perished in front of a Nazi firing-squad, shouted: 'It will be Hitler's turn next.'

Somehow that message of defiance reached the streets of Prague. The student's last words were adopted as a slogan and were soon chalked up on walls and intoned by one Czech to another by way of greeting.

The Gestapo was galvanised into fresh ferocity when, one dawn, houses throughout the Protectorate were raided, men hauled from their beds and a total of thirty thousand so-called 'subversive' Czechs hustled behind bars.

The date of the raid, Thursday 31 August 1939, was significant. Twenty-four hours later Hitler's columns were unleashed in Poland.

4

Adolf Hitler launched on Poland in September 1939 a vast army of a million and half, its fire-power complemented by the whine of diving Stukas annihilating the Polish Air Force even before its planes could leave the ground.

Focus for the assault was the port of Danzig and those other areas of Poland with predominantly German inhabitants. Thus was the Fuehrer provided with yet another pretext for his self-styled crusade of liberation.

But here was something new. Here Hitler was not marching to bloodless conquest as in Austria and Czechoslovakia. Here were the conditions of total war, of *blitzkrieg*, the lightning thrust and the ruthless knockout blow.

The attack began at four forty-five a.m. on 1 September 1939 with a massive assault by five German armies in the north and south. Whole tank divisions punched their way at the rate of thirty or forty miles a day. In a little over an hour of the start of hostilities, bombs were reigning down on defenceless Warsaw, screaming out of the sky on railways and roads, effectively quashing any attempt at mobilisation.

Pilots of the Luftwaffe had been given instructions that they were by no means to restrict their bombing to military targets.

During the siege of Warsaw, aircraft circled above the fields around the city, where women digging potatoes to take home were systematically machine-gunned. In the suburbs of Czerniakow, the blackened bodies of the dead lay in heaps for several weeks.

Similarly, corpses of those who had been fleeing eastward before the invasion of western Poland littered the Kutno-Warsaw road. Attacks were made on hospitals and Red Cross first aid stations, evacuation trains, and even on single cars carrying refugees.

About a third of the Polish land forces were trapped in a

pincer hold by the German Fourth and Third Armies.

Hero of the hour was *blitzkrieg* exponent General Heinz Guderian, whose Panzers had routed the proud brigade of cavalry. All those sporting the eagle of Poland on their field caps fought like tigers, but so many of them looked as if they had strayed out of the battle-fronts of wars centuries old. The long lance of the cavalry was pitched against the cannon of the tank.

Russia's hatred of Poland had proved every bit as keen as that of the Nazi dictator. History repeated itself and Poland's fate was to hark back to the days when Prussian kings and Russian emperors had agreed to partition the country.

Hitler had earlier secured an immediate agreement by the Soviet Union not to join Britain and France if they honoured their treaty obligation to come to the aid of a beleagured Poland. Stalin was given a free hand in the eastern Baltic.

On the day that the German pincer closed, news reached the armed forces that units of the Red Army had crossed into Poland over its eastern frontiers.

As for the Germans, their forces had wheeled south from Danzig, making for such towns as Bydgoszcz, where the puny Polish cavalry started a desperate corral of horses from the nearby forests, only to be swatted aside. On moved the inexorable wave of armour, orchestrated by the screaming hell that catapulted from the skies.

Buildings were seized and from their roofs German snipers emptied their weapons on anything that moved. A Red Cross station, prominently displaying its flag, was shelled without mercy, even as the stretcher-bearers struggled through the streets.

Hastily there came an order from Warsaw that citizens were to be armed. It was too little, too late. The mayor, sensing defeat, vowed to save all municipal documents and funds in a frantic drive to Warsaw. He had barely left before the Germans spread the news that he had deliberately absconded with the entire treasure from the church.

In the misguided hope of defending his honour, he rashly returned. The result was inevitable: the ponderous formality of a trial, then confirmation of a verdict of death by firing squad.

An English woman, Miss Baker Beall, who was stuck in

Bydgoszcz in the early stages of the Nazi occupation of the town, survived to produce her own account of those feverish days:

'Before the Germans had been a month in the town they forbade the use of Polish, both in the home and in the church . . . The *Volksdeutsche* are particularly brutal in enforcing this order. An elderly lady, who apparently did not know German, was speaking Polish very softly to her companion in the tram when a man got up, gave her a violent blow on the ear, and said: "Will that teach you not to speak your filthy language?"

'Men and women in the street were slashed across the face with dog whips if they spoke their mother tongue to one another, and one day a young lady told how, when a little girl about four years old and her brother, about seven or eight, were talking Polish together, she saw a *Volksdeutsche* policeman strike the baby in the face and beat the little boy unmercifully in the street.'

It was only the beginning.

On 22 August Hitler had told his senior commanders of his clear intention to send his SS units into the country 'to kill without pity or mercy all men, women and children of Polish race or language.'

Indeed, Hitler went even further, announcing that he would follow the annihilation of the Poles with an attack on Soviet Russia. Thus was revealed the real reason for the seizure of Danzig: Germany would have at its disposal the roads and railways which ribboned across the corridors.

To his appalled but helpless generals Hitler had proceeded to spell out his intentions towards Poland in even more detail. He ordered the political 'cleaning up' of the country, and nobody was deceived by the obscene delicacy of the phrase. Foreign Minister Joachim von Ribbentrop had weighed in with a pet scheme to fake an uprising of Ukrainian minorities against Poles, thus allowing all farms and houses in those regions to be burnt to the ground.

And the generals were put firmly in their place. Much of what would happen in Poland would 'not be to their taste' and they were warned that they 'should not interfere in such matters but restrict themselves to their military duties'.

In the same month, Hitler had conferred with General Eduard Wagner, his Quartermaster General, and proclaimed: 'We have no intention of rebuilding Poland. The Polish intelligentsia must be prevented from establishing itself as a governing class. A low standard of living must be conserved with cheap slaves. Total disorganisation must be created.'

At first sight, the man given the title of Governor-General of Poland seemed to possess irreproachable, civilised credentials.

The rise to prominence of Hans Frank had been eminently respectable – right from the days when he had graduated from law school in 1927. He had become Bavarian Minister of Justice and president of both the Academy of Law and the German Bar Association.

Well-read, devoted to music (as, incidentally, was Reinhard Heydrich) and with a seemingly liberal intelligence, Frank presented to the world a persona which was in refreshing contrast to most of the unabashed power-seekers surrounding the Fuehrer.

The impression was dangerously misleading. On the surface Frank was a genial family man. In reality, the Reich had as its servant a cold, calculating technician of dictatorship who, on hearing that Neurath had put up posters announcing the execution of seven Czech university students, commented to a Nazi journalist: 'If I wished to order that one should hang up posters about every seven Poles shot, there would not be enough forests in Poland with which to make the paper for these posters.'

The all-important job of liquidating the Jews in the Polish Government-General was given jointly to Himmler and Heydrich, who promptly appointed Frank their deputy.

It was made clear to him that he would be expected to squeeze food and supplies out of the country to help boost the economy of the Reich. The primitive and detested Poles

51

would in addition supply an admirable source of forced labour.

Brutal and subtle when it came to terror, but strangely coy and prim when actually designating responsibilities, the Nazi masters came up with a masterly code name for the Operation: 'Extraordinary Pacification Operation' (*Ausserordentliche Befriedigungsaktion*) or, as it came to be known, AB Action.

It took Frank a little time to move his intimidating new machine into operation, and it was not until the following late spring, when the German offensive in the west had switched the attention of the world from Poland, that he was able to achieve tangible results.

His own diary demonstrated that by 30 May 1940 he was boasting in a report to police aides that the removal of 'some thousands' of Polish intellectuals had been carried out.

On that occasion, Frank was begging earnestly:

> 'I pray you, gentlemen, to take the most rigorous measures possible to help us in this task.
>
> 'These are the Fuehrer's orders. The men capable of leadership in Poland must be liquidated. Those following them must be eliminated in their turn. There is no need to burden the Reich with this, no need to send these elements to Reich concentration camps. They will be put out of the way right in Poland itself.'

Frank also noted in his journal that the chief of the Security Police, in a progress report, had stated that about two thousand men and several hundred women had been apprehended 'at the beginning of the Extraordinary Pacification Action', most of whom had already been 'summarily sentenced'.

A second batch of intellectuals was now being rounded up 'for summary sentence'. This would mean that altogether 'about 3,500 persons', those reckoned to be the most dangerous of the Polish intelligentsia, would thus be taken care of.

Although malignly happy in the intoxication of his power, Hans Frank had only one complaint. The direct task of extermination was not in his hands but in that of the SS and Gestapo. Himmler and his lieutenants were pathologically jealous of even the barest suggestion that their territory was being poached upon.

On the third day of the Polish campaign, three special trains crossed the frontier in the area of Katowice, the first two containing Hitler and Goering and their staff. The third was Himmler's designated *Sonderzug* (special train) *Heinrich* – a name destined to figure prominently at the head of much SS and SD correspondence in the following six years.

The Reichsfuehrer was to relish to the full a resounding new title of High Commissioner of the Office for Germanisation of the East.

On 7 October, Hitler signed a decree, countersigned by Goering and Oberst-General Keitel, appointing Himmler as Commissioner and entrusting him with the 'Germanisation' of Poland.

The Reichsfuehrer's brief was to bring back to the Reich true Germans living abroad, 'to eliminate the sinister influence of foreign sections of the populace presenting a danger to the Reich and to the community of the German people, and to form new German colonies'. To bring that about Himmler was granted an entirely free hand.

He lost no time in adapting Hitler's general instructions to his own ideas.

He proclaimed:

'It is not our duty to Germanise the East in the old meaning of the term, that is to say to teach the people there the German language and law, but to see that only people of pure German blood live in the East. The cleansing of foreign races outside the incorporated territories is one of the essential aims to be accompanied in the German East.'

Poles, as members of a subhuman race, were not to be permitted the luxury of an intellectual élite. Land belonging to Polish farmers was to be 'freed' to Germans. Children were to be adopted, or if necessary stolen or kidnapped. Himmler went on: 'Where we can win good blood which we would use ourselves, we shall give it a place in the bosom of our people.

'Now perhaps you might find this cruel, but nature is cruel and we shall destroy all alien and inferior blood.'

By a decree of 12 December 1940, Himmler founded the 'racial register'. On it had to be recorded:

(1) Pure-blooded Germans who had exercised political activity in a Nazi organisation;

(2) Pure-blooded Germans who had taken no part in politics;

(3) Descendants of pure-blooded Germans or persons married to a pure-blooded German;

(4) The descendants of Germans absorbed by the Polish nation and thus regarded as renegades.

Poland, it was clear, was to become the testing ground for the refined methods of Nazi terror. Expropriations, evacuations and transport of those expelled to Germany and of the colonials in the 'liberated lands' would be carried out by Reinhard Heydrich as head of the RSHA.

But it was Frank who was to bring the rule of fear to every town and village in the western part of Poland that formed the Government-General.

Centuries of Polish culture were frozen in the halls and columns of the ancient royal Wawel Castle in Cracow which had been completed in the sixteenth-century. That the Nazis' prize intellectual thug should install himself there was bad enough; but the Germans also turned the two Gothic Halls into beer and wine bars and one of the finest of the turrets was made into a toilet area. Frank further expressed his contempt for Polish traditions; the name Wawel Castle was forbidden. A decree declared that only the expression 'Cracow Castle' (*Krakauer Burg*) could be used.

The cultural humiliation of Cracow was only just getting into top gear. It was to become a monstrous obsession with Frank.

The full blaze of his fury was next directed against the ancient university, founded in the fourteenth century by King Casimir the Great and widely acknowledged as one of the finest in central Europe.

A seemingly innocuous and apparently friendly invitation was despatched to the university and to the Polish Academy of Science and Letters. A lecture, stated the invitation, would be delivered by a German on the subject of 'The attitude of the National Socialist authorities to science and teaching'.

The German in fact turned out to be Dr Obersturmbann-fuehrer Bruno Mueller, chief of Cracow's Gestapo.

There was to be no lecture. Mueller contented himself with a single ranting declaration from the platform:

'In view of the fact that (1) the professors of the University were intending to begin lectures; (2) they had not interrupted their work in the scientific institutes and seminaries; and (3) the University of Cracow had been a bastion of polonism for more than 500 years, all the professors would be arrested.'

Mueller's men burst into the lecture hall, wielding clubs and batons. The professors were beaten, kicked and shoved into the waiting cars. The Gestapo kept one hundred and sixty of them for a few days' amusement at its Cracow headquarters. They were then sent to Breslau and ultimately to the concentration camp at Oranienburg-Sachsenhausen near Berlin.

The conditions there were appalling. In full knowledge that most of the academics were men in their sixties and seventies, the Germans kept their prisoners deliberately in unheated huts in the unbearable winter. Windows remained open all day. All warm clothing was forbidden; the sole prison garment was a shapeless affair of rough cotton. Food consisted only of ersatz bread and turnip soup.

And then there were the tortures. With seeming amiability, a highly apologetic member of the prison staff would assure the prisoner that the arrest had been a dreadful mistake and that he would soon be on his way home. In the meantime, a hot shower would obviously be welcome.

And then the mood would change. The prisoner would be hustled out of the shower into the open air. There came the order: 'Stand to attention'. Clad only in the pitiably in-adequate cotton garment the victim remained sometimes for as much as an hour. At the first sign of his knees caving in, a Gestapo whip would slash across his shoulders.

Jewish professors were humiliated most of all and were shut up with the criminal dregs of the camp. Desperation and bitter cold inevitably took their toll – seventeen of the professors died at Oranienburg-Sachsenhausen.

After three months, survivors, broken, emaciated and in some cases virtually unrecognisable, were returned to Cracow. What they badly needed was rest and medical attention. But Hans Frank was master there; inevitably the number of deaths increased.

A further thirty-nine professors and assistants, together with four students, were put to hard labour at Dachau. The fate of the rest went unrecorded.

Possessed of an energy to match his intellect, Frank and his staff raced to missions of terror throughout the territory of the Governor-General. Frank had taken over the Czech legation in Chopin Street in Warsaw; his presence there inevitably heralded more arrests.

Anyone refusing to display the German flag or the portrait of the Fuehrer was seized immediately. Orders were given that Poles were to bare their heads before German officers.

Frank's growing power and overbearing vanity led him to style himself 'the German king of Poland'. It was a title that in fact told only half the truth. Himmler could not be left out of the reckoning. The war against the Jews was the essential province of his SS.

Just what this came to mean to the Jews was recorded in a series of sneering reports in the Nazi-controlled Polish press. Thus on 2 December 1939, the *Krakauer Zeitung* was trumpeting under the headline 'JEW BEWARE!':

'As from 1 December, a decree came into force whereby Jews have to wear a white armlet bearing the Star of Zion. These "stars" could be seen yesterday for the first time twinkling in the streets of Cracow.

'All over the town, not only in the neighbourhood of the Jewish quarter, you met these white armlets with the blue Star of Zion, and you were surprised to realise how the Jew had spread himself out in Cracow under Polish protection. It is high time that he should be kept under observation. This is the main purpose of the white armlets. The Jews can no longer move about under camouflage. Wherever he goes you will notice him. Let the white armlet be a warning to him and to us.'

That this was no mere idle threat soon became only too apparent. This was shown by a sentence passed against a Jewess and published in the Nazi paper at Constance, the *Bodensee Rundschau,* on 21 August 1940.

The woman was sentenced in Cracow to eight months' imprisonment, because she was discovered in a café without an armlet. She stated that she had been ashamed to enter the café sporting it. The paper commented: 'Really, she only wanted to conceal her Jewish origin and make acquaintances among the Aryans.'

It came to seem to the Jews that they were waking up each morning to a fresh set of regulations constituting high treason.

Jews were soon forbidden to use the railways, a decree particularly relished by the *Krakauer Zeitung,* which revelled in the heading: 'GERM-CARRIERS BANNED FROM THE RAILWAYS.' When the ukase was extended to tramcars, the paper was on cue with the comment: 'The separation of the Germans from the Poles and particularly from the Jews, is not merely a question of principle, but, as far as Warsaw is concerned, a hygienic necessity.'

Wholesale massacres of Jews were carried out by the SS, whose *Einsatzgruppen* followed German forces into Poland as execution cadres.

Individual incidents of horror proliferated. Three Jews who had been herded into a concentration camp in Poznan were summarily sentenced to death for stealing bread and being in 'illegal possession of honey.'

On the day before the execution the trio were paraded around the city with sandwich boards proclaiming in German: 'Tomorrow I shall be hanged at eleven o'clock.'

Next morning, the other inmates of the camp were force-marched to Poznan's athletics stadium, where armed members of the Gestapo thrust them forward to the gallows. Prisoners were made to kick away stools from under the condemned men, who struggled and gasped in slow strangulation.

There was to be an extra touch of sadistic artistry.

Immediately after the executions, mobile food kitchens were wheeled on in full sight of the gallows. Survivors in the camp queued up, the corpses dangling in front of them.

In the town of Chelm, eighteen thousand Jews were forcibly assembled by machine-gun-toting SS.

One of the officers addressed the Jews. His message was terse: 'All Jewish men are to leave the town immediately. You are held responsible for the outbreak of war and are the greatest and most dangerous enemy of the Reich.'

The address was immediately followed by an order to surrender all money and valuables, as well as papers and documents. The Jews were then told to bid their families goodbye and leave; they chorused national songs on their way.

Nazi lorries and cars edged the group forward. The men were a mixture of the dark-suited middle class and bearded Orthodox Jews in their black robes. Their destination, they were told, was the town of Hrubieszow.

An order was given to speed up. The elderly, unable to move fast, were urged on by kicks and blows.

The procession had been on the road for an hour when the order came to stop. An officer stepped forward and announced: 'One of you Jews has attempted to escape. There will be appropriate punishment.'

Twenty-five men were hauled from the column to the side of the road. The machine-guns spoke, raking along the detached column. The officer smiled at the survivors and declared: 'Very well. Next time we will make it fifty, and the number will be doubled with each escape.'

Soon tiredness overcame the pathetic procession; the more elderly of the Jews stumbled and fell. Again, hostages were taken and the bodies left at the side of the road like broken dolls once the SS execution squads had done.

Those who survived were herded into a field not far from Hrubieszow. The bright light of a German searchlight bored into them throughout the night.

In the morning, the group of Jews was swollen by fresh numbers who had been rounded up in the town. Like cattle, they were driven towards the Soviet border. The frontier, however, was only three miles away, which to the SS seemed not far enough. The prisoners were taken along a different route and the journey stretched to ten miles, with executions continuing.

There were the individual tragedies. Towards the end of the second day, a young boy collapsed through sheer exhaustion. It was his death warrant, but in a desperate effort to save him, his older brother stepped forward and offered his life instead.

The officer sneered: 'So you want to die; nothing easier!' There was a swift nod and the machine-guns slaughtered them both.

Few men were left by the time they reached the Soviet border and were ordered to make the crossing by wading into the Bug river. Many of the elderly Jews could not swim; they were either drowned or cut down in waters which soon turned crimson.

For those who managed the crossing, there was no relief, however. Soviet sentries forced them back and the Germans pushed them into the water. At one time, both Russians and Germans were shooting at the same time.

News of this SS atrocity reached the outside world through a survivor, Israel Mayer, who with a party of some half a dozen boys who were good swimmers had allowed the current to carry them downstream. By a miracle, they found a spot where some willows kept them afloat.

They were able to crawl out unobserved in the morning. Soon they were behind the lines of Soviet sentries.

A fortnight later, Israel Mayer managed to cross the Carpathian mountains in Hungary and found himself in Budapest. He later stated that some two thousand Jews had been murdered during the trek and claimed that a single officer had boasted of despatching seventy-five single handed.

On his first day in Budapest, Mayer idly picked up a German newspaper. A headline caught his attention. 'GERMAN AUTHORITIES SUPPRESS JEWISH REVOLT IN CHELM' is what he read.

Hans Frank was never tired of boasting that he had but one single ambition in life, to make Poland *Judenrein* (pure of Jews). It was an aim shared, of course, by Himmler, but the Fuehrer, now supreme war lord as well as dictator of

Germany, was forced to recognise that he simply did not possess the resources to eliminate all of Poland's three million Jews. Priority had to be given to defeating the Allies; as for the Jews, they must be forced to emigrate.

The job was turned over to an Estonian shoemaker's son, Alfred Rosenberg, who had thrown in his lot with the Nazis as early as 1919 and had impressed Hitler with his all-consuming hatred of Bolsheviks and Jews. Rosenberg became accepted as the 'intellectual' of Nazi Germany, insinuating his way into the post of head of the Foreign Political Section of the National Socialist Party.

Rosenberg's aides evolved a plan to settle one million European Jews in the occupied Polish region of Lublin, a territory of about four hundred square miles close to the Russian border. The task of implementation was given to Reinhard Heydrich, who in turn informed Adolf Eichmann that now Danzig, western Prussia, Poznan, and Upper and Lower Silesia were to be cleared of Jews who would be moved to the Lublin reservation. Eichmann would be in charge of transporting the Jews.

It was the sort of assignment in which Eichmann revelled. One of his proudest achievements, he was to boast, was that in a brief four months he managed to send 87,883 Jews and 30,000 gypsies to Lublin.

On the face of it, the Lublin Plan seemed modest, and those gullible enough to be taken in by bland statements from the Third Reich might have supposed that the Nazis were setting up a Jewish state. But in fact the Jews who arrived at Lublin could not be economically self-sufficient; thousands were to die of disease.

In December 1939, an American, Oswald Garrisson Villard, wrote in the British weekly, *The Spectator:*

> 'What may prove to be the final act of the incredibly brutal and cruel tragedy which Adolf Hitler has inflicted on the Jews in his power is now going on, and without receiving the attention of the world as it should because of the pressure of war news. With practically no publication of the plan in the German newspapers, Adolf Hitler is going ahead with the creation of a so-called Jewish State, located in Poland, near Nisko, on the San, south-west of Lublin.

'A stretch of land, about 50 by 60 miles in area, has been set aside. It is enclosed by a barbed-wire fence, and only Jews will be allowed to live therein. Into this small territory are to be crammed no fewer than 1,945,000 Jews. What is to become of the Poles who have inhabited this region is not stated, but it is said in various quarters that the land is exceptionally poor.

'For these unfortunate people are forbidden to leave with more than 300 marks. They are permitted to take with them only such hand-bags as they can carry. All the rest of their belongings, the furniture in their apartments, the rest of their means, their jewels, everything is stolen from them.

'. . . No preparations are made for their reception; they are simply to be dumped in and left to shift for themselves. If they cannot find shelter in the deserted homes of the evacuated Polish peasantry, why, they can freeze to death, or build new homes, without means, without materials, without tools, without anything . . .'

The reservation at Nisko was one of ten set up by Odilo Globocnik, who already had an impressive track record in brutality. Under the old Austrian Republic he had been jailed for throwing stones at Jews, a job which Hitler considered made him admirably qualified to be Gauleiter of Vienna.

Now Globocnik received impressive promotion and lost no time in proving that he was worthy of it. His brief had a threefold aim: deportation of Jews (Eichmann's province); confiscation of Jewish property; exploitation of Jewish manpower and, eventually, annihilation.

At the same time, Globocnik had set up four extermination camps: Belzek, Majdanek, Sobibor and Treblinka.

Globocnik's devotion to the cause of National Socialism and the routing out of the detested Jews was not entirely without self-interest. He was anxious to head an industrial empire of his own; clearly there were rich pickings to be had with such an achievement.

Factories were set up in Lublin and fifty thousand Jews drafted in to work them. Casualties among them were heavy, but that scarcely mattered since there was always a generous pool of reserve manpower.

61

Globocnik, together with three partners, set up a corporation which was named Eastern Industries Limited. Of course, all property confiscated from the Jews and all profits flowing from the factories belonged to the Reich. Indeed, a special account for this purpose was in existence in Berlin.

In fact, the vast bulk of the profits of Eastern Industries was destined to stick firmly in the podgy fingers of the partners of Eastern Industries Limited.

Schemes like the Lublin Plan, however, had one serious drawback. They needed a vast amount of organisation if they were to succeed, and that took time.

Some infinitely more drastic plan was needed for the satisfactory resettlement of the detested Polish Jews.

5

Of all the Nazi old guard who had survived Adolf Hitler's bloody, brawling road to power, few at the outbreak of war were more fortunately placed than Paul Joseph Goebbels.

The sinister dwarfish club-footed Rhinelander had at one time flirted with the more avowedly socialist arm of the Nazi Party. But he had repented his error in time to avoid the fate of other dissidents whom the SS went on to eliminate in a succession of bloodbaths.

In purple prose, Goebbels had once proclaimed the extent of his infatuation for Hitler by writing in his diary:

'We bow to him with the manly, unbroken pride of the ancient Norsemen who stand upright before their Germanic feudal lord. We feel that he is greater than all of us, greater than you and I. He is the instrument of the Divine Will that shapes history with fresh, creative passion.'

The reward for such passion was, in the mid-1920s, the post of Gauleiter of Berlin – red Berlin, with its predominance of Socialists and Communists. In seven short years it was to be 'cleansed' of Bolshevism and, as the capital of the Reich, conquered for the new age of National Socialism.

Goebbels was just twenty-nine years old when he got the job. There was plenty of time for other infinitely more flamboyant successes – the most important of which was as architect and orchestrator of the Fuehrer myth itself.

In an early Nazi cabinet, Goebbels was made Minister of Propaganda. His brief was to manipulate the German people through the mass media; press, radio and films must be made to serve the purposes of the new regime exclusively.

And it was Goebbels who stage-managed the vast Nuremberg and Berlin party rallies, who helped to mesmerise the German people into following their Fuehrer with trance-like obedience.

The record of Goebbels ministry had been undeniably impressive. With the invasion of Poland in September 1939 Hitler had yet another job for the able young disciple.

Goebbels was summoned to the Reich Chancellery. Hitler told him: 'The present methods of resettling the Jews are proving far too slow. I want you to go to Poland and look around for new ways. Then you will have to explain them to the German people.'

Goebbels, who had received his Ph.D. from Heidelberg in 1921 at the age of twenty-four and had studied at a number of the more famous German universities, was more soundly educated than most of the other Nazi leaders.

As far as Poland was concerned, he did not look upon the country merely as a ragbag of sub-cultures ripe for extermination. The history of the Poles, he reasoned, could be studied with profit. Such lessons as were gained could be adapted cynically and ruthlessly for Nazi purposes.

His tour of Poland took in the cities of Warsaw and Lodz. He learned that for generations Jews in many parts of Poland had lived in different districts of the towns.

Why, he eventually suggested to Hitler, should they not continue to do so? But this time there would be a segregation backed by the law. There would be an end to the nonsense of Jews being able to move about quite freely. From now on, areas would be barred totally to them. The idea of the ghettos was born.

Goebbels was barely back in Berlin before he authorised a series of broadcasts to the German people and then to the occupied countries. The first bulletin was a bland announcement that the Nazis had decided to herd all Jews together in special walled-off parts of towns.

Then the tone became vituperative. Goebbels screamed:

'The Jews are ulcers which must be cut away from the body of the European nations. The inhabitants of these ghettos must be completely isolated. This is not merely a problem of forbidding marriage between them and members of other races, it is not a question of a single individual who commits a crime, but of a focus from which all crimes have their origin.

'These people must be completely isolated or the whole of Europe would be poisoned.'

Goebbels had set the wheels in motion; now it was up to the authorities of the Government-General in Poland to make the proposals concrete reality.

By no means all the Nazis were happy. Rosenberg viewed the prospect of the ghettos with considerable alarm. Not, it may be said, out of a feeling of compassion for the Jews. If the Lublin Plan collapsed, he reasoned, his own authority might well go down with it. He decided to play for time.

In Warsaw, leaders of the Jewish community were warned by the Germans what was afoot. The only way they could delay building a ghetto was to pay a massive fine to their conquerors.

The Jews paid up. But Rosenberg knew that any postponement could only be a matter of months.

Those entrusted with carrying out the recommendations of Dr Goebbels struck during the first April of the occupation. High walls appeared in the centre of the city, which the Germans dubbed 'the closed contaminated area.'

In one synagogue, the news that the Jews were to be confined in a ghetto arrived just as the cantor was about to start *Neilah,* the closing service of Yom Kippur, when Jews pray for salvation before the heavenly gates of mercy are closed. At once the cantor halted the service, saying that there was no further point in praying. The gates were already locked.

A string of orders was issued by the Governor of Warsaw, Fischer, and his deputy, Leist. Jews were to be given six months to move into the new section designated for them and all Aryans were to quit.

The result for Warsaw was administrative chaos. The time limit set by Fischer and Leist was impossible to enforce. Many of the homes within the ghetto confines had been destroyed in the bombing of the city and there was a chronic shortage of transport. The original deadline was put off until the end of October 1940.

As time ran out, there was an almost hysterical rush. Then the Germans discovered that many of the walls had not been put around the traditional Jewish quarters at all.

The limits of the ghetto were changed twice: on one occasion reduced and on another enlarged. Pathetic knots of Jews, forbidden to carry anything with them but essential hand luggage, wandered the streets in bewilderment.

The myth of German administrative efficiency had been severely punctured. A veritable shoal of conflicting orders continued to be issued until mid-November. Then without warning the ghetto areas were finally determined. The Jews were now confined behind an eight-foot-high wall. No further supplies of food were permitted. Groups of Poles who attempted to smuggle in supplies were shot on the spot.

Inside, the rule of the Gestapo was absolute, with sadism on the loose. Jews who did not raise their hats to Germans were severely beaten. Elderly men were ordered to exercise with bricks or concrete slabs on their hands. Many, as the playthings of their guards, were forced hour after hour to shin up and down telegraph posts.

The houses of rich Jews in fashionable districts now stood empty, their former inhabitants prisoners in the ghetto. The Germans could thus loot at leisure; furniture, money and even food were carried away in broad daylight.

Two years later, *The German New Order in Poland*, published in London by the Polish Ministry of Information, reported on what ghetto life had ultimately come to mean for the Jews. It stated:

'450,000 people now live in the Warsaw ghetto. They are crowded into a small area, the most neglected and the

65

dirtiest in the city. The Jewish cemetery is the only park, and there is only one square. The number of people per room (even before the war the ghetto was the thickly populated part of Warsaw) has risen to six, and in some cases to ten.'

The problem of food supplies, not only in Warsaw but in ghettos throughout the Government-General, soon became chronic. Prices inevitably soared; the result was malnutrition and, with the overcrowding, there was an inevitable increase in infectious diseases.

German newspapers were sometimes allowed to publish statistics. There was no reason to doubt the *Hamburger Fremdenblatt* of 29 October 1940, which reported that ninety-eight per cent of the cases of typhoid and spotted fever in Warsaw were in the ghetto. But the readers were not told the real cause.

By May 1941, it was reckoned that five thousand had died in the Warsaw ghetto. The Germans strenuously denied the figure and produced statistics to show that in fact numbers of those living were up, and life was proceeding more or less normally. The explanation was simple. As Jews died off, their numbers were replaced by the continual influx of Jews deported forcibly from provincial towns where the machinery did not exist to set up separate Jewish quarters.

The energy of Hans Frank continued unabated. Among his flood of decrees, the most crucial for the Jews was the 'Judenrat'. It provided that every Jewish community should elect a council of elders, who in their turn would elect a chairman and vice chairman.

Lest this be considered too liberal, Frank's law hastily went on to stress that the German District Governor had to confirm the appointments. If he did not like those who had been elected, then nothing could be simpler: he would simply appoint his own nominees.

To prevent any possible misunderstanding, Frank further stressed the mastery of the Nazis by declaring:

'The Judenrat is obliged, through its president or its deputy, to accept the commands of the German authorities. It is responsible for the conscientious carrying ot of these commands. The orders which it issues for the

66

carrying out of those German commands must be obeyed by all Jews and Jewesses.'

The setting up of the Judenrat was often a convenient way of making sure that collective fines could not only be levied on the Jews but that the money would be collected by members and handed over.

In Bedzin, the Germans levied a contribution of five kilograms of gold and twenty kilograms of silver. Just to make sure that there was no unseemly delay, one hundred and twenty hostages were taken as surety. A systematic programme of tortures and beating was instituted until the tribute was forthcoming. When, in Lwow, the chairman of the Judenrat had the temerity to refuse to hand over several thousand Jews for hard labour, he was beaten up and subsequently murdered.

Nazi intimidation of its puppet councils was naked and vicious. When Vilna was taken, the Germans summarily demanded five million roubles – one million to be paid within twenty-four hours, otherwise Judenrat members would be shot.

The news spread swiftly through the terrified town; the Jews forthwith instituted a compulsory levy on as many of their citizens as could be found in time.

There was a rush to surrender watches and jewellery, together with nearly seven hundred thousand roubles. But the figure was well short of what the Germans had demanded: the executions went ahead.

When the full amount had still not been paid, the Gestapo swept down on the Judenrat offices, and Vilna became a cowed and frightened city; orgies of seizures, arrests and killings continued unabated. Only six of the original Judenrat members survived. They were reconstituted into a new body, their dead comrades replaced by SS nominees.

The council of elders was made responsible for moving Jews into the ghettos and selecting those suitable for compulsory labour. Members were also held responsible for the upkeep of schools and Jewish hospitals, and for provisioning the ghetto with the meagre supply of food available. When it came to this last responsibility, resources were pitiful – just sixty-three communal feeding centres.

Reichsstatthalter (Governor) Artur Greiser was responsible for the *Reichsgau Wartheland* (abbreviated to *Warthegau*) which comprised Poznan province and adjacent districts. He was able to report:

'The 220,000 Jews in the district are isolated and have their own administration and police. At the head of the police there are officers who formerly belonged to the army. The Jews also have their own doctors and hospitals under Jewish administration. Most of the Jews work as tailors, shoemakers and carpenters. The uniforms of the German pilots and soldiers are made by the Jews in the *Warthegau* and so are the army boots.'

Frank's decree had brought into being a pool of labour for the occupying Germans, the suppliers of which could be slowly starved to death when they had served their purpose. And no one outside would be entirely sure of the fate of their fellow citizens behind the big high walls.

All over Poland, endless processions of weary men and women, babies in their arms and children at their sides, with bags, sacks and bedrolls on backs and around necks, made pitiable shambling progress to the ghettos. On 13 November 1940, the Jewish academic and writer Chaim Kaplan, who was eventually to be deported from Poland and to vanish, wrote: 'We are segregated and separated from the world and the fullness thereof, driven out of the society of the human race.'

Often the ghettos were sighted in the oldest, most run-down parts of the towns, sometimes in outlying areas lacking the most basic facilities. The dwellings were woefully dilapidated, victims of bombing, shelling and looting. The air hung fetid over those ant-heap cities, their streets choked with filth. A doctor in Vilna recorded:

'About 25,000 persons live in our ghetto, in 72 buildings on five street sections. That comes to one and a half to 2 metres per person, narrow as the grave.'

People crowded together could no longer observe even the basic conventions of decency and privacy. Despite themselves, many Jews began to lose their characteristic dignity.

But it is neither the smell not the squalor that survivors from ghettos still remember. What congestion produces, above all, is noise, a veritable clamour of suffering which in the Polish ghettos was perhaps the most unbearable torture of all.

A young girl in the Warsaw ghetto wrote:

'My ears are filled with the deafening clamour of crowded streets and cries of people dying on the side-walks. Even the quiet hours of the night are filled with the snoring and coughing of those who share the same apart-ment or, only too often, with the shots and screams coming from the streets!'

One of the main casualties of overcrowding was sanitation, inevitable when three and four families lived in space adequate for one. Toilets, running water, all plumbing and sewage were soon taxed beyond capacity, and the exhalations of latrines added to the already poisonous air. And in long, bitter Polish winters such water as there was froze solid in the pipes.

The cold was at least a seasonal thing; hunger and ultimately starvation had scant respect for the seasons. On 4 November 1941, the Germans issued special instructions for feeding the civilian population of the Occupied Eastern Territories, prescribing that Jews were to receive half the permitted maximum in grams because 'they are a population who do no work and are not worth mentioning.'

Quality meat products were forbidden absolutely. Average daily food ration provided about 1,100 calories per person – and that was only available if supplies had not been spoiled, stolen or made available on the black market.

Food and the lack of it became an obsessive topic at work, on breadlines and in the soup kitchens. Groups huddled to exchange recipes for concoctions that could be prepared from the available rations and which somehow would reduce the monotony of horsemeat or stinking fish that occasionally rolled in on wagons from the city outside. As another ghetto eye-witness put it: 'All became chemists mixing this with that – just to turn out something.'

Dumplings were made from sliced or mashed turnips mixed with potatoes and flour and seasoning. Ground horsemeat mixed with potatoes and rye flakes became meat patties, which were fried in a drop of oil.

Inevitably, rivalries and resentments built up within those cruelly confined communities. Polish Jews no longer had hate to give for the Germans. Now it was vented on Jews from Germany, Austria and Czechoslovakia deported to the Polish ghettos. Many arrived well dressed and bulging with property, able to pay the black market price for bread.

Soon the newcomers had cornered the market. But their sense of superiority was short-lived. Most of them had to be housed in buildings which had been intended as sleeping quarters. Lack of hygiene and inability to cope with the cold sent the death rate soaring. Many died huddling in their bunks, begging for mercy from Polish Jews whose own sufferings had bereft them of all pity.

Many, their money and goods long gone, begged in the streets and died ignored in the freezing cold. The tricycle-propelled hearses of the undertakers could not keep pace with the accumulation of corpses, and many bodies, covered with scraps of paper, lay untended for days.

Jewish police, drafted by the Germans to patrol many of the ghettos, proved a mixed blessing. Those who were not cowed by the calculated terror tactics of Hans Frank's minions were lenient in checking the identity papers and permits of those entering and leaving the ghetto. For those with no love for the Nazis, searches for contraband were apt to be perfunctory, but any form of backsliding discovered by the Germans was punished ruthlessly.

An elderly Jewess who brought a sack of potatoes into the Warsaw ghetto had it promptly confiscated by a German. A policeman intervened and begged for its return.

The result was swift and brutal. The policeman was promptly knocked down, bayoneted and hauled to the nearest wall. A burst of gunfire put paid effectively to any further argument.

A perilous new career was soon opening up for those Jews who found themselves in jail at the time of the arrival of the Germans. It was put to them that the tiresome apparatus of the Judenrat need not cause them undue concern. They would be co-opted into the Jewish police straightaway and without fuss. The Germans reasoned that the loyalty of such riff-raff could probably be taken for granted: even the dullest intelligence realised the likely fate of disobedience.

Such groups of shadow police were set up in Lodz, Kovno, Lublin and, in far greater numbers than anywhere else, Warsaw.

These roughneck policemen were given a dubiously responsible status. They were made members of an organisation given the imposing title of 'Control Office to Combat Black-Marketing and Profiteering in the Jewish Residential District'.

In charge was a Polish Jew named Abraham Ganzweich, who had lived in Vienna before the war and had been so ill-advised as to tangle with the Gestapo. He had no wish to repeat the experience. It was infinitely more sensible to consent to be put in charge of a group which became known as 'The Thirteenth', operating from 13 Leszno Street in Warsaw.

The Thirteenth, which had its own smart uniform and numbered some three hundred men, acted chiefly as an intelligence agency for the Gestapo; spies whose regulation weapons were the bludgeon and the rubber hose.

Weeded out mercilessly were the dodgers of forced labour and the smugglers whose pathetic currency was a few illicit potatoes or onions. Those police who had protected the ghetto inhabitants were removed. Only the naturally brutal and those who were corroded with the sole instinct of self-preservation were allowed to remain.

Yet the light of hope was very far from being snuffed out in the ghettos. Life, it was reasoned, need not be sustained simply by bread and potatoes. Ancient traditions of Jewish culture flourished with brave defiance. Committees were formed in the ghetto tenements to organise a variety of entertainments, often financed from the proceeds of card games, always a popular Jewish pastime.

In the Warsaw ghetto, professional and amateur singers and dancers performed in café and restaurants. Queues at soup kitchens were frequently entertained by comics and by variety acts. The horrors of ghetto life were made a mite more bearable by lampoons and comedy sketches.

In the large ghettos, music provided brief oblivion before the hour of enforced curfew. Ghettos in Warsaw, Lodz, Vilna

71

and Kovno boasted their own orchestras. At one concert, Lodz was able to muster twenty-five professional musicians and ten amateurs.

Jews were forbidden to play German music; a deprivation which many of the audiences found they could bear with equanimity. Many a Jew found, often for the first time, a hitherto latent taste for traditional Yiddish and Hebrew folk songs.

In Warsaw, the Germans shut down the public libraries and bookshops, which promptly went underground. Voluntary librarians were soon hard at work, running up and down the steps of tenement apartment blocks with heavy suitcases.

Education committees were formed in a desperate determination to keep some sort of schools in being. Inevitably the Nazis tried to control what was taught and the Jews became adept at hoodwinking them.

Lucy S. Dawidowicz, in her book *The War Against The Jews 1933-1945*, relates how one school in Lublin was set up in a basement shoemaker's shop behind a makeshift partition:

> 'When a warning was given that Germans were about, the classroom disappeared. Books and papers were hidden, the partition removed, the children dispersed, and the teacher, one shoe off, became the shoemaker's customer.'

Chaim Kaplan, who organised one school in his own home, describes in his diary on 15 February 1941, just what so perilous an undertaking meant:

> 'Jewish children learn in secret. In back rooms, on long benches near a table, little schoolchildren sit and learn . . . In time of danger the children learn to hide their books. Jewish children are clever – when they set off to acquire forbidden learning, they hide their books and notebooks between their trousers and their stomachs, then button their jackets and coats.'

For a few brief hours each day, the ghetto Jews managed to cling to their traditional culture and loyalties, triumphing over the unrelenting efforts of their tormentors to extinguish their civilisation. Outside the ghettos, the Nazi terror raged.

And soon it was to spread anew and roar like a tornado towards Soviet Russia's vast and still unviolated lands.

6

For burly Erich Koch, an unemployed railway clerk and Berlin street brawler, the advent of Adolf Hitler had begun as a decidedly mixed blessing.

It was true that many individuals who had been dubious misfits in the days of the Weimar Republic had managed to carve out agreeable careers for themselves after 1933, but Koch's relations with the Nazis had not been altogether happy and he was aware that the coming to power of the brown battalions frequently meant ruthless settling of old scores.

For, like Joseph Goebbels, Koch had allied himself with the extreme radical wing of the Nazi Party. Indeed, he had once been bold enough to proclaim: 'If it wasn't for Hitler, I would be a Communist today.' It was a dangerous statement and must have caused more than a twinge of anxiety when Hitler invaded the Soviet Union in 1941. But Koch had been wily enough to cover his tracks. Although he was disliked and distrusted by Himmler, he had managed over the years to curry favour with Goering, who eventually secured for him the useful position of Gauleiter of East Prussia.

As if by a miracle, the hitherto pro-Communist ideas of the man once nicknamed 'Erich the Red' disappeared literally overnight. From then on the Communists were utterly beyond the pale and to be rooted out. As if to atone for past misdeeds, Koch threw his considerable organisational abilities behind his new office. As satrap of East Prussia his activities were not entirely for the benefit of the Reich; unkind souls suggested that the specially set up Erich Koch Institute benefited its proprietor rather more than the economy of Nazi Germany.

Although an industrious toper, Koch was careful enough

to keep a clear head in his dealings not only with his mentor Goering, but also with the sinister Martin Bormann, party secretary and confidant of the Fuehrer. Koch's chief was nominally the pliable Rosenberg, but the Gauleiter did not allow that to inconvenience him. He frequently went over Rosenberg's head straight to the Fuehrer.

All of which must have been most agreeable for the small, bull-necked son of an Elberfeld coffee roaster whose total dedication to his Fuehrer extended even to sporting a Charlie Chaplin moustache.

On 16 July 1941, Hitler, at a top level conference, had drawn a blueprint for the occupation of the Ukraine, whose vast natural resources were vitally needed to feed Axis Europe.

The Fuehrer had exuded confidence. The Soviet Union, he was certain, could be brought to her knees in eight weeks. 'As for the Ukraine', he explained, 'it is to become the bread basket of the Reich.'

And Goering was on hand to argue that the man who could exploit that economic potential was Erich Koch. The indignant mutterings of Rosenberg were swept aside.

Here was awesome power indeed. Koch swiftly made up his mind that his new responsibilities could easily be combined with the East Prussian post. A few parts of Poland were tossed to him as well by Goering. Koch soon became fond of boasting that he ruled an area stretching from the Baltic to the Black Sea. The Polish kings of old had nurtured such a dream; by a strange quirk of history it had been fulfilled by a braggadocio ex-clerk with a weakness for the bottle.

Goering had described the likely future of the Russian people under Nazism with a resigned world weariness, telling Italian Foreign Minister Galeazzo Ciano: 'This year between 20 and 30 million persons will die in Russia of hunger. Perhaps it is well that it should be so, for certain nations must be decimated. But even if it were not, nothing can be done about it.' Koch's language was decidedly cruder. He lost no time in spelling out his job during his inauguration speech at Rovno:

'Gentlemen: I am known as a brutal dog. Because of this reason I was appointed as a Reichskommissar of the

Ukraine. Our task is to suck from the Ukraine all the goods we can get hold of, without consideration of the feeling or the property of the Ukrainians.

'Gentlemen: I am expecting from you the utmost severity towards the native population.'

To an obsequious well-wisher, the new Reichskommissar snapped: 'The Ukrainians will be handled with cheap tobacco stalks, vodka and the whip.'

His intentions were clear enough: the Ukrainians, a veritable reservoir of artisans and the professions, were to be worked to maximum capacity.

It was a brutal enough policy, but it had one fatal drawback. It left Himmler and his cohorts out of the reckoning. They had other plans in store for the Ukrainians.

On the morning of 22 June 1941, the sullen roar and the thud of tanks had jerked awake the Russian border guards. The most terrifying onslaught of mechanised warfare so far in the twentieth-century had been unleashed on the Soviet Union.

Hitler's Operation Barbarossa consisted of seven armies and four Panzer groups: three million men, 600,000 vehicles, 750,000 horses, 3,500 armoured combat vehicles, 7,184 artillery pieces and 2,100 aircraft.

Towards the vital Soviet artery of the Ukraine romped Army Group South under Generalfeldmarschall Rudolf Gerd von Rundstedt. With them, as sinister shadows, went divisions of the Waffen-SS contingents, the Leibstandarte and Viking. And within their ranks – with the blessing of Heydrich's central intelligence apparatus, the RSHA and the OKW (Oberkommando der Wehrmacht, High Command of the German Forces) – went the Einsatzgruppen.

Hitler had been well aware of the useful work in spreading terror that had been carried out by Heydrich's killer squads in Czechoslovakia and Poland. But that had been a mere dress rehearsal. In Russia the Einsatzgruppen would be given *carte blanche* for more serious tasks. Heydrich was to be granted authority for nothing less than mass murder.

To reinforce Heydrich's new powers, which, of course, came to him only with the blessing of Reichsfuehrer Himmler, Keitel proclaimed in mid-March 1941:

'By order of the Fuehrer, the Reichsfuehrer-SS has been given the special task arising from the conclusive and decisive struggles to be waged between the two opposing political systems (National Socialism and Communism). Within the limits of the set tasks *the Reichsfuehrer-SS will act independently upon his own responsibility.*'

The italics were not in the original. And for Heydrich, acting as Himmler's lieutenant in the implementation of Keitel's order, there was no need of them . . .

Heydrich was well aware that the Wehrmacht regarded the SS and its Einsatzgruppen with fear and loathing. This was not a situation that even he could ignore. After all, for the killer squads to work efficiently, it was obviously necessary for them to be placed on the same level as the army when it came to the provision of fuel, food, transport and, so that there could be a sensible chain of command, the army signals organisation.

Therefore, Heydrich recognised, the SS must be prepared to submit to military discipline; there could be no question, for instance, of freelance murderers roaming the combat areas. Heydrich conceded that the Einsatzgruppen must consider themselves 'tactical auxiliaries'. The army, on the other hand, must be made to understand that in no way could Heydrich tolerate interference in the operations of the Einsatzgruppen.

Quartiermeister-General Eduard Wagner was prepared to be co-operative. Up to a point, that is. Then he had the temerity to haggle with Heydrich over matters of detail.

With elaborate courtesy, the head of the RSHA summoned Wagner for an informal meeting. Heydrich spent most of the time talking of routine matters, but casually let fall at one point that he was in possession of Wagner's Gestapo dossier.

Heydrich left the meeting in considerable good humour. Wagner, on the other hand, was to be seen sweating and distressed.

Heydrich got precisely what he wanted. There was to be dual status for his Einsatzgruppen. In the front line and immediately behind it, his units were to place themselves entirely under army command.

In the rear areas already handed over to military government they became virtually autonomous. Keitel issued his order.

With the tiresome but necessary business of deciding who was boss at last sorted out, Heydrich was able to get down to fundamentals. He called a conference of senior RSHA subordinates.

During it he stated: 'It is my job to see that the newly occupied territories are secure and peaceful. I wish to make it clear that the end will justify the means. I need good men to carry out their tasks. It is my earnest hope that you, as my departmental chiefs, will be prepared to operate without restraint.'

Nobody went so far as to spell out Hitler's manifest intention of exterminating the Jews. There was the obvious need for security in the early stages of planning. But by the following year, 1942, Eichmann, as head of the appropriate department, received the written order for the Final Solution, outlined at the Wannsee Conference.

A seasoned SS talent was obviously needed for training the Einsatzgruppen and for making it perfectly clear just what was required of its members.

Excellent work, Eichmann considered, had already been carried out by SS-Brigadefuehrer Bruno Streckenbach, Heydrich's deputy and head of the RSHA Staff Office. Streckenbach had been chosen back in 1933 to run the Hamburg political police after it had been swallowed by the Gestapo. He had been concerned with the arrest of the professors at Cracow University and had been one of the architects of the effective implementation of the Extraordinary Pacification Action.

Streckenbach's work in Poland was now over and he had been ordered to return to Berlin for administrative duties. This, he considered, was a poor reward for years of conscientious service to the Nazi movement which had gone back years. But there were consolations.

After all, Governor Frank had actually staged a touching little farewell ceremony for him and had been most effusive in his praise.

Frank had enthused: 'What you, Brigadefuehrer Streckenbach, have accomplished in the Government-General must not be forgotten; you have no need to feel ashamed of it.'

Now, without warning, he had received a top secret order

to proceed immediately to the police barracks at Pretzsch on the Elbe. Awaiting him as the result of an equally peremptory summons were one hundred and twenty seasoned SS veterans who had already served Heydrich with distinction.

The fact that they were patently thugs was only to be expected, but soon Streckenbach found himself being joined by lawyers, university professors and intellectuals who at first sight might have been thought out of place in such crude company. In fact, they were members of the SD, the Gestapo and the police who were known to possess outstanding organisational and executive abilities.

During the weeks before the onset of the Russian campaign these men were trained and indoctrinated by Streckenbach and his cohorts. Veterans of many a Polish atrocity became members of one of four newly constituted Einsatzgruppen destined for Soviet Russia. They were built up to around battalion strength of between seven hundred and nine hundred men.

Streckenbach lost no time in spelling out their missions. They were to seize and destroy all political and radical enemy groups – Bolsheviks, gypsies, Russian secret police and Jews. Sabotage would be greeted with arrest and annihilation. 'Criminal and social elements' would be rooted out. In addition, the Einsatzgruppen were to report and evaluate material gained in every field of Russian operations and would collect titbits from agents and spies among the local Russian population.

The time for pussyfooting had passed. Streckenbach ordered that all enemies of the Third Reich were to be deported to concentration camps and execution. All hostages would be seized and shot, with the Jews receiving 'special treatment', which meant either destruction or confinement in ghettos.

The final pep talk before the invasion of Russia was delivered not by Eichmann, but by Reinhard Heydrich on the eve of the Russian campaign.

Heydrich told them: 'No mercy or human feeling must be shown to the enemies of the Third Reich. Women and children will be exterminated on the same basis as anyone else, particularly in anti-Jewish operations.

'These people must be exterminated because they are

potential avengers. The goal of all Einsatzgruppen operations will be to achieve permanent security of the newly occupied territories of the east and this can only be obtained if the children are killed.'

Whether Heydrich possessed the gift of prophecy is not known, although Eichmann, if he read the words of his chief, might well have wondered years later. Heydrich concluded: 'If these children are not killed, they will grow up and constitute no less a danger than did their fathers.'

If certain members of the Wehrmacht had held up pious hands in horror at the activities of the Einsatzgruppen in Poland, they showed no such sentimental scruples when it came to dealing with the Soviet Union.

On 10 October 1941, Generalfeldmarschall Walther von Reichenau, Commander-in-Chief of the Sixth Army, issued a directive which Hitler had previously dubbed 'excellent'.

'. . . In the eastern region, the soldier is not merely a fighter according to the rules of the art of war, but also the bearer of an inexorable national ideal and the avenger of all bestialities inflicted upon the German people and its racial kin.

'Therefore the soldier must have *full* understanding for the necessity of a severe but just atonement on Jewish sub-humanity. An additional aim in this is to nip in the bud any revolts in the rear of the army, which, as experience proves, have always been instituted by Jews.'

The SS and the army had sealed a compact in terror.

With an awesome competence the Einsatzgruppen performed their dreadful tasks. In they went with the Wehrmacht, shadowing the line of attack which extended with mechanised menace from the Baltic to the Black Sea.

In those early euphoric days, the pickings seemed rich indeed, even though the iron grim Russian winter loomed ahead like a malign spectre.

The campaign was but three weeks old when the Army Group Centre of Generalfeldmarschall Fedor von Bock, with thirty infantry divisions and fifteen panzer or motorised divisions, had punched 450 miles from Bialystok to Smolensk. Ahead, a mere 200 miles away, lay Moscow.

In the north, the army group of Generalfeldmarschall Ritter Wilhelm von Leeb knived through the Baltic states towards Leningrad, a glittering prize which Hitler regarded as the cradle of Bolshevism. Twenty-five infantry, four motorised, four mountain and five panzer divisions in the south romped towards the Dnieper river and Kiev – capital of the fertile Ukraine, coveted above all else by the German war lord.

On 8 October Orel, south of Moscow, fell. Marshal Semen Timoshenko, defending the capital, was trapped in two German pockets of steel. The southern armies of Marshall Semen Budenny had been wiped off the face of the earth.

And Leningrad? Some seventy divisions under Marshal Kliment Voroshilov, were surrounded.

In fact, such advantages were to be short lived. But Heydrich's murder band took full advantage of them. Einsatzgruppen C and D, operating in designated areas of the Ukraine, were among the very first to scent blood. Young Otto Ohlendorf was another of the displaced intellectuals who had been drawn to the SS on the eve of Hitler's bid for power. He had university degrees both in law and in economics and had been a professor at the Institute of Applied Economic Science. Indeed, he spent the war secure behind a desk in Berlin except for just one year. And during that time he was chief of Einsatzgruppen D.

At the Nuremberg trials – following which Ohlendorf and three other Einsatzgruppen members were hanged – he described how each Einsatzgruppe was divided into smaller units, Commandos, led by a member of the SD, the Gestapo or KRIPO (Criminal Police). The unit assigned to killing the Jews at a given place 'would enter a village or city and order the prominent Jewish citizens to call together all Jews for the purpose of resettlement. They were requested to hand over their valuables to the leader of the unit, and shortly before the execution to surrender their outer clothing. The men, women and children were led to a place of execution which in most cases was located next to a deeply excavated anti-tank ditch. Then they were shot, kneeling or standing, and the corpses thrown into the ditch.'

80

Accounts of the round-up of Jews and their executions abound. But there was one in particular which when it was recounted at Nuremberg produced a particular sense of horror, even among so case-hardened a gathering.

By Einsatzgruppen standards, the mass execution carried out at Dubno in the Ukraine was a fairly minor affair.

The court heard a sworn affidavit from Herman Graebe, manager and engineer of a branch office in the Ukraine of a German constructions firm. The object of the operation, which took place on a former flying ground, had been to liquidate the town's five thousand Jews:

'My foreman and I went directly to the pits. I heard rifle shots in quick succession from behind one of the earth mounds. The people who had got off the trucks – men, women and children of all ages – had to undress upon the order of an SS man, who carried a riding or dog whip. They had to put their clothes in fixed places, sorted out according to shoes, top clothing and under-clothing. I saw a heap of shoes of about 800 to 1000 pairs, great piles of under-linen and clothing.

'Without screaming or weeping these people undressed, stood around in family groups, kissed each other, said farewells and waited for a sign from another SS man, who stood near the pit, also with a whip in his hand. During the 15 minutes that I stood near the pit I heard no complaint or plea for mercy . . .

'An old woman with snow-white hair was holding a one-year-old child in her arms and singing to it and tickling it. The child was cooing with delight. The parents were looking on with tears in their eyes. The father was holding the hand of a boy about ten years old and speaking to him softly; the boy was fighting his tears. The father pointed to the sky, stroked his head and seemed to explain something to him.

'At that moment the SS man at the pit shouted something to his comrade. The latter counted off about 20 persons and instructed them to go behind the earth mound . . . I well remember a girl, slim with black hair, who, as she passed close to me, pointed to herself and said: "23 years old."

'I walked around the mound and found myself confronted by a tremendous grave. People were closely wedged together and lying on top of each other so that only the heads were visible. Nearly all had blood running over their shoulders from their heads. Some of the people were still moving. Some were lifting their arms and turning their heads to show that they were still alive. The pit was already two-thirds full. I estimated that it contained about a thousand people. I looked for the man who did the shooting. He was an SS man, who sat at the edge of the narrow end of the pit, his feet dangling into the pit. He had a tommy gun on his knees and was smoking a cigarette.

'The people, completely naked, went down some steps and clambered over the heads of the people lying there to the place to which the SS man directed them. They lay down in front of the dead or wounded people; some caressed those who were still alive and spoke to them in a low voice. Then I heard a series of shots. I looked into the pit and saw that the bodies were twitching or the heads lying already motionless on top of the bodies that lay beneath them. Blood was running from their necks.

'The next batch was approaching slowly. They went down into the pit, lined themselves up against the previous victims and were shot.'

In July 1941, Graebe had been visiting his sites at Rovno, where five thousand inhabitants of the ghetto in the town were to be exterminated. About a hundred of them had belonged to Graebe's firm and in a desperate bid to save them, he had run from one Einsatzgruppe leader to another, pleading that he was desperately short of labour.

All night the wave of appalling murders had continued. At ten in the evening, the SS had surrounded the Rovno ghetto, its powerful searchlights throwing the area into sharp relief.

The Einsatzgruppe had split into small detachments, breaking its way into houses by smashing the doors with rifle butts or flinging grenades inside. The Germans were armed with dog whips, belabouring the inhabitants to come out.

They emerged half clothed, while their children cowered behind in terror, screaming for their parents. Prisoners were lashed all the way to the waiting goods train, every carriage of which was soon completely filled. The air was rent with the continual screaming of women and children, the crackling of rifle fire, shouts and the hiss of whips.

The action continued throughout the long night. Individual scenes of horror witnessed by Graebe included children dragging their parents as far as the train by arms and legs. The houses they left behind them had ripped-off doors, smashed windows and everywhere clothes, shoes, stockings, jackets, hats and overcoats scattered all over the floor. Graebe added:

'I saw a small child less than a year old with its skull smashed lying in the corner of a house. Blood and brains were spattered on the wall of the house and on the ground around the child, who was wearing only a simple shirt.

'The Commandant, SS-Sturmbannfuehrer Putz, strode up and down, keeping watch on the column of 80 to 100 Jews squatting on the ground. He carried a heavy dog whip.'

Sara Sakola, a public library clerk in the town of Kharkov, was only thirty-eight years old when the Germans came. Yet, two years later, her Russian rescuers found a small, frail, prematurely aged cripple with both legs amputated after frostbite.

At first, Sara had lived undisturbed among Jewish families in the Pushkin Street apartment house. The arrests began sporadically in December 1941. The SS arrived with lists of names typed efficiently on clipboards.

Then came the day when she realised that she was the only Jew left. They took her to join a group of fifteen thousand others for a seven-mile walk to an abandoned tractor plant.

'So with a bundle of clothes and bedding and a small bag of food I set out,' she later recalled. 'Some people had hired carts to bear their possessions; some dragged them on sledges. But most were, like me, bowed down with bundles.

'Old people, little children and sick people lay dying beside the road. And we who walked were corpses, too. The guards told us nothing or amused themselves by spreading false hopes among us.'

The survivors on the long march were packed into windowless huts in which the doors were kept open.

Then came the order: 'There is to be complete silence at all times.' There were other petty rules; wardens and sentries took the opportunity to impose as many as they could and to fleece their victims in the process. Sara explained: 'Fines were imposed on mothers whose babies cried during the night. If the mothers protested that they had no money, the Germans informed them that the infants would be shot. What could the mothers do? The children were hungry and there was no milk.'

Residents of Kharkov besieged the huts with bandages and supplies. Money changed hands; friends were briefly united. Food kept the unspeakable cold at bay for just a few hours. Still more money delayed the final exodus from Sara's hut.

But respite could only be temporary. For the inhabitants of each hut, the pattern was the same. The prisoners were told that they were being sent elsewhere to work. One set of trucks was for baggage and possessions, the other for the Jews themselves. Men, women and children were soon on the move; the other lorries remained behind.

Those who awaited their turn were not slow to learn what was in store for them. News of Einsatzgruppen massacres a few miles away filtered back to the terrified Jews. Gradually, all the huts were emptied.

Sara Sakola told her rescuers: 'One day, towards the end, I went to the next hut. That morning the Germans had taken the last survivor away. It was a horrible sight. Fouled bedding and stale food lay in a horrible mess. On a trestle in one corner was a dead man, in another a baby was still alive, sucking a finger of its dead mother.

'That night we were ordered to get ready to leave the next day. And that night a woman in birth pangs was brought into our hut. She knew that the child she was bringing into the world was already condemned to death and in her agony she prayed that it might be born dead. That child's birth decided me to risk everything to escape.'

By moving from one hut to another, and eventually throwing in her lot with Ukrainian resistance, Sara was able to survive until the eventual rout of the Wehrmacht by the Russians in their sweep to the Dnieper river.

Kerch is a comparatively small town nestling on the edge of the Crimea's eastern strait. It and its people would have been more than happy to remain obscure from the rest of the world.

The Germans prevented that. And what happened there was to be recalled in all its horror six years later at Nuremberg as Exhibit USSR 63, subject of an Extraordinary State Commission for the Investigation of German Atrocities.

It was in November 1941 that Generalfeldmarschall von Manstein's Eleventh Army, supported by a Rumanian Army Corps, broke into the Crimea, where the Russian forces retreated in chaos to Sevastopol.

On the seizure of Kerch, an immediate order was issued: 'All family food stocks must be delivered to the German Kommando. Owners of undelivered supplies will be shot.'

The Town Council was ordered to register all livestock immediately. Poultry owners were strictly forbidden to use fowl and cattle for their own needs without the permission of the German Commandant. No sooner was the order issued than the Germans launched a wholesale dragnet of houses and apartments. The Gestapo dealt in kilograms: for each kilo of beans or flour discovered, the head of a family was promptly shot. Over the succeeding few days, the repression was stepped up with exquisite brutality.

The Commission reported at Nuremberg:

'According to instructions issued by the German Commandant, all the school children were ordered to appear at the school at a given time. On arrival the 245 children, school books in hand, were sent to a factory school outside the town, allegedly for exercise. There the cold and hungry infants were offered poisoned coffee and pies. Since there was not enough coffee to go round, those who did not get any were sent to the infirmary where a German orderly smeared their lips with a quick acting poison.

'In a few minutes all the children were dead. School children of the higher grades were carried off in trucks and shot down by machine-gun fire eight kilometres outside the town. The bodies of the first batch were brought to the same spot – a very large, very long anti-tank trench.'

Yet another Gestapo directive urged the inhabitants who

had previously registered with the Germans to present themselves within twenty-four hours at Sennaya Square. They were to bring with them enough food for three days. Anyone who failed to appear, regardless of age or health, would be publicly executed.

The group of young and old, including the pregnant, were herded into the Gestapo prison. There they were ordered to hand over the keys of their homes; all valuables were removed. Then the prisoners were stripped naked and the cohorts of Einsatzgruppe C moved in.

They were not content merely to slaughter. When, on 30 December, the Russians launched a bitter counter-attack and threw the Germans out they came across in the prison yard a formless mass of bodies of young girls, naked, mutilated and virtually unrecognisable.

In the nearby village of Baguerovo, motor coaches for three days ceaselessly ferried entire families to the anti-tank ditch which had been selected for their slaughter.

It was not until the following January that the Red Army stumbled across the Baguerovo ditch. The Soviet prosecutor at Nuremberg told the courtroom what was found:

'It was discovered that this ditch – one kilometre in length, four metres in width and two metres in depth – was filled to overflowing with bodies of women, children, old men, and boys and girls in their teens.

'Near the ditch were frozen pools of blood. Children's caps, toys, ribbons, torn-off buttons, gloves, milk bottles and rubber comforters, small shoes, galoshes together with torn-off hands, feet and other parts of human bodies were lying nearby. Everything was splattered with blood and brains.

'The Fascist savages shot down the defenceless population with dum-dum bullets. Near the edge of the ditch lay the mutilated body of a young woman. In her arms was a baby carefully wrapped up in a white lace cover. Next to this woman lay an eight-year-old-girl and a boy of five, killed with dum-dum bullets. Their small hands still gripped the mother's dress.'

Few of the Nazi conquerors attempted to disguise their exaltation at the success of the early military victories and the speedy despatch of hundreds of Jews by the Einsatzgruppen. True, Rosenberg and others favoured some form of autonomy for the Ukrainians, arguing that by dangling the carrot of self-government, sympathy and even support might be won for the Nazis. If Hitler played his cards right, so the argument went, the Bolshevik regime itself might collapse; history might repeat itself with the Russian armies disintegrating as in 1917.

Erich Koch was vocal in sweeping away such dangerous nonsense. In an address to Nazi Gauleiters he proclaimed flatly: 'There is no need to turn the land over to the Ukrainians. It will be reserved for the Germans.'

To underline that point Koch drafted a message for German troops on their way to the Soviet Union from East Prussia.

It read:

> 'As the Reichskommissar I have received the Ukraine with its rich soil and plant life, which at the will of the Fuehrer will be used for the needs of Europe . . . The confidence of the Fuehrer makes it possible for me to provide for everyone of you, so that there my comrades can be my loyal assistants in carrying out the tremendous task. I have already once given you my word that in the eastern regions conquered by you the first to receive establishments and a place of work will be you . . . You and your children will fill with German life the land that has been steeped in German blood.'

To make sure that the point really sank in, Koch went on the radio, announcing that 'the Ukraine will be settled by twenty-five million Germans and peoples kin to them, who need not fear difficulties since Ukrainians will be used for hard and skilled labour.'

If any of the 'sub-humans' were to be preserved at all, Himmler believed that it could only be because they would be of service back home in the Reich.

To bring such deportations about with peaceful persuasion was, on occasions, thought preferable.

There had been the instance of the little village of Batanog. To its inhabitants, the German conquerors had at first seemed pleasant enough. They had come, not as arrogant victors, but evidently as troops bored with the war and wanting only to tarry, swopping cigarettes and talking wistfully of the pleasant green land they had left behind.

Some time during the conversation, a question would be dropped with studied casualness: 'We need workers in the Reich. Badly. Are you interested?'

There was apathy, not out of distrust at this point, but because of reluctance to become uprooted from the homes of generations.

The Germans tried several times. On the last occasion, the tone of one of the officers had a distinct edge: 'Think again. We shall soon come for you.'

One night in July 1942, sleepy Batanog awoke to the rumble of armoured cars. The village was encircled with machine-guns. Troops, weapons at the ready, scattered among the cottages.

Householders were ordered to assemble at a single spot. The bulk of them stood their ground. Sixty-year-old Grigori Lukin, who had emerged as their spokesman, proclaimed stoutly: 'God preserve us, we want to stay at home. It will be far easier for you to kill us.'

There was a chorus of assent. Somebody said: 'None of us want to go. We were born here and we shall die here.'

One of the officers snarled, then snatched the revolver from the holster and shot the speaker at point-blank range.

He was yelling: 'Who will go to Germany now?'

Pavel Lavomyaga, another villager, kept his voice level: 'There is no need to shout. None of us is going.'

Seven hostages, along with Lavomyaga, were dragged away. Soon the sound of machine-guns was heard stuttering on the edge of the village.

The Germans took their time before they herded the women into the trucks. They were stripped to the waist and prodded with revolver butts.

The convoy roared away in a cloud of dust, drowning the frightened screams of the children left behind as the sole inhabitants of Batanog.

But the Germans had not finished. They returned a little later. They plundered everything they could lay their hands on, threw the children into the street and burned the village.

Yet Koch was uneasy. Elimination of Jews and deportation of Russians were all very well, but as he pointed out in a plaintive memo direct to Hitler:

'I have lost 500,000 Jews. I had to eliminate them because the Jews are a harmful element. But in this territory they were the only artisans . . . I have not a sufficient number of shoe-makers to repair shoes for our employees. I cannot get them. There are no artisans left.'

With supreme contempt by the conquerors, the cities of the Ukraine had been tossed starvation rations. There were no refinements such as milk and fat; bread was a rarity. Any attempts to secure extra food were forbidden and transgressions mercilessly punished. The youngest and healthiest citizens were herded into camps and deliberately allowed to starve or die of rampant plagues. It was a policy that satisfied racial theory, no doubt. In practical terms it proved disastrous.

An Economic Commission officer from the Ukraine commented in a report:

'If we shoot the Jews, liquidate the war prisoners, starve the major part of the big cities' population, and in the coming year reduce also a part of the peasants through famine there will rise a question: Who is going to produce the economic goods?'

The Einsatzgruppen were not in business to provide the answer. They merely went on killing. At Minsk in October 1942, sixteen thousand Jews, all that remained from the ghetto there, were executed in a single day.

It was an appalling statistic, of course. But Minsk was already historic for another reason. In the summer of the previous year, 1941, Heinrich Himmler had witnessed an event there which heralded another grim phase in Russian subjugation.

7

As Einsatzgruppen actions went, the mopping-up operation witnessed by Heinrich Himmler at Minsk in the summer of 1941 had been a relatively minor affair. It had certainly been very far from turning the stomachs of those efficient killing machines so ably trained by Brigadefuehrer Streckenbach.

Himmler, though, to his intense self-disgust and shame, had besmirched the name of the SS by swooning like a girl at the sight of blood.

The execution in question had been carried out in the normal manner of an Einsatzgruppe. The keynote had been, as always, speed. This was not for any humanitarian reason; it was simply that there were always a lot of executions to be performed. Even wounded who were alive were bundled into the graves alongside the dead.

At Minsk, Himmler had seen women groaning and struggling as the earth was scooped on them; later he regretted not having saved a young Jew who was fair-haired and looked Aryan.

Even so, to have shouted hysterically and then collapsed, was beyond the pale. In tears, the Reichsfuhrer had later confessed: 'I behaved like an intellectual.'

Himmler was by no means the only member of the SS present that day who was shaken visibly by what he had seen. Obergruppenfuehrer Erich von dem Bach-Zelewski, who was eventually to be called to the Nuremberg trials as a prosecution witness and who throughout his career had seen far more killings than Himmler, had rounded on his chief and cried: 'Look at the eyes of the men, how deeply shaken they are. These men are finished for the rest of their lives. What kind of followers are we training here? Either neurotics or savages!'

Himmler, by all accounts, had been incapable of speech.

He had clamped a handkerchief in front of his face and allowed himself to be led away.

Despite the fears of von dem Bach-Zelewski, remarkably few members of the killer squads ended up as nervous wrecks – and certainly not a man like Alfred Metzner, who, when being held in Augsburg prison in October 1946, confessed the extent of his involvement.

At the end of World War I, he had lived a rolling-stone existence in the unstable Germany of the Weimar Republic. At one time he had been a sailor, then a taxi driver in Berlin and had even been married to a half-Jewess.

The advent of Hitler came as a salvation; with the outbreak of war there was at last something useful for him to do. He was posted to Rosenberg's ministry as an interpreter and labour overseer. On the invasion of the Soviet Union he was sent to Slomin in White Russia, where there were some twenty thousand Jews.

One of Metzner's first duties was to drive a lorry-load of Jews to execution. Members of the Einsatzgruppe had been drunk. Jews were stripped and searched for valuables. Pregnant women were then shot in the stomach, many buried alive. The next day, Metzner felt able to drive a consignment of Jews who had spotted the blood-bespattered bodies of the previous day and made a vain attempt to escape.

By the following year, Metzner had been promoted and found himself a full-fledged member of a killing squad. He recounted:

'In my first action, 1,200 Jews of the community of Shirowitz were to be 'resettled' and a practice shoot was held a few days in advance to test whether the fusillade could be heard in the ghetto.

'The actual action lasted three or four hours and I paused only to load my carbine. I could not count the victims but 400 or 500 Jews were buried in a single pit in six layers. During the time, we drank a lot of schnapps to keep our spirits up. In the lower layers, the half-killed Jews were suffocated by the weight of the bodies and drenched in their blood. No one could survive that way.'

Nevertheless after his degrading experience Himmler did fall to pondering what ultimately must be the effect on the members of a killing group, many of them decent family men, who were expected to fire on women and children. Plainly, there was a danger that they would end up simply as brutalised morons worse than useless to the Reich. There could of course be no question of discontinuing the executions. It was merely the method; with a little thought an acceptable alternative could surely be found.

Back in Berlin, Himmler put the problem gravely to his star SS engineer, SS-Untersturmfuehrer Dr Becker. From his fertile brain sprang the notorious S trucks.

Otto Ohlendorf stated at Nuremberg that:

'The true nature of these vans could not be seen from the outside. They were like ordinary closed wagons and were built so that when the engine was started the exhaust gas was led inside the car, bringing death to the occupants within ten to 15 minutes . . . The victims were loaded into the trucks, which were driven to the place of burial, the place used for mass executions. The time of the journey was enough to ensure the death of all the occupants.'

The inventive Dr Becker was extremely solicitous of his vans; it was essential that they were used properly. He stated blandly: 'With the correct position of the valve, death comes quickly and the condemned then fall asleep peacefully.'

Soon a succession of S trucks, each crammed with twenty-five men, women and children, dying slowly of asphyxiation, were bumping over the Ukrainian roads. It was the final journey for those aboard; the end would be a trench already half-filled with its quota of convulsive corpses.

And not only in the Ukraine. Soon the S trucks were fanning out in convoys across Czechoslovakia and Poland. The very existence of these trucks was classified Top Secret within the SS. But the strain proved too much for many of the drivers, who had the horrific job of opening the trucks and prising out the contents.

Inevitably, there was no way in which this new method of mass-killing could remain an indefinite secret. At Minsk, a driver who got drunk and talked about his work was hauled before the SS tribunal. The firing squad followed swiftly. Bureaucracy, however, proved the ultimate betrayer. The minutely documented proceedings of the case survived to be produced at Nuremberg.

The weedy Reichsfuehrer, the unquestioning believer in the pseudo-mystic trappings of the SS creed, had flinched at the first sign of violence. Adolf Eichmann, away from his filing cabinets and his dutiful army of clerks, fared little better on coming face to face with the results of his own scrupulous organisation.

He also went to see an Einsatzgruppe at work. Near Minsk in 1942 he too saw the young killers shooting into a pit already full of writhing bodies. At his trial interrogation, he said: 'I can still see a woman with a child. She was shot and then the baby in her arms. His brains spattered all around, over my leather overcoat.'

Eichmann claimed that the experience had brought him to his knees. If that were true, it was not a posture he suffered for very long. He was soon on the move again, turning up with his Einsatzgruppen wherever the Wehrmacht found the pickings easiest.

Then came a specific instruction from Himmler; a meeting of the highest importance had been arranged for Eichmann with SS Hauptsturmfuehrer Rudolf Franz Ferdinand Hoess, currently operating in the Polish area of Oswiecim.

The world has come to know the place rather better as Auschwitz.

Of all the servants of the Third Reich qualified not only to be the commandant of a concentration camp but a mass killer as well, few were as ideal as Rudolf Hoess.

This son of a devout Catholic Baden-Baden shopkeeper who had once been destined for the priesthood had, within a year of joining the Nazis in 1922, been implicated in the murder of a schoolteacher named Walter Kadow.

Kadow, whose loyalty to the fledgling Nazis was questionable, was suspected of being a Communist. He was plied with drinks, then bundled into a cart. At a convenient spot, Hoess and his companions went to work on their victim, pummelling him with fists, sticks and rubber truncheons.

The infidel was next hauled into a field. Hoess broke off a sapling maple and brought it down with full force on Kadow's skull. His throat was then slit with a pocket knife and two bullets pumped into his brain. The blood-smeared car was washed down and the dead man's effects burnt. The next day, Kadow's body was buried in a grave of pine seedlings.

Hoess was jailed for ten years as an accomplice, but released in a general amnesty in 1928. By 1934, he was a member of the Totenkopf group of the Schutzstaffel, one of whose tasks, significantly, was guarding the camps.

The wisdom of specialisation is often advocated as a formula for professional success. Hoess adopted it. And wisely so. There were to be plenty of outlets in Nazi Germany for his particular talents.

Indeed, once war had broken out, his rise was spectacular. On 1 May 1940, he was transferred to Auschwitz, which was situated some 160 miles south-west of Warsaw. His previous post had been at Sachsenhausen, north-east of Berlin, where he had been adjutant to the commandant since 1935. In his new job, he was supremo not only of Auschwitz, but also of its neighbouring extermination centre, Birkenau.

For Himmler, Jews could never be exterminated fast enough. Quite apart from the distressing effect on the executioners, shooting by the Einsatzgruppen was messy and inefficient, and altogether too public. Admittedly, the SS themselves were scarcely discreet. No self-respecting SS man ever travelled without his Leica, whose cold lenses recorded a multitude of killings.

The SS trucks had proved satisfactory, but the speed of extermination had to be maintained. The camps must be made to play their part. Himmler summoned Rudolf Hoess to Berlin.

Hoess, who lived with his wife, children and dogs in considerable comfort not far from Auschwitz, was in many ways a simple soul. His job, as he saw it, was simply to obey orders. It was a song to be warbled constantly by self-justifying Nazis at the end of the war, but Hoess, who seemed to inhabit a complete moral twilight, believed in his duties implicitly and never made the slightest attempt to deny that he authorised the atrocities.

His meeting with Himmler was to the point. The Reichsfueh-rer used the chilling phrase *die Lœsung der Judenfrage* which loosely translated meant 'the solution of the Jewish problem'.

Himmler went on: 'Auschwitz would seem to be ideal for the purpose we have in mind. It is isolated and camouflaged easily enough.

'You will learn further details from Sturmbannfuehrer Eichmann of the RSHA, who will be calling on you before long. Plans for certain installations will be required from you. Please let me have them as soon as possible.'

Eichmann immediately set out on his mission to Auschwitz. Himmler, the health food fadist and puritan, would doubtless have discussed the gassings of millions of Jews over tea brewed from herbs that he encouraged to be grown in the garden of the camps. This was not Eichmann's way. The likely future of Auschwitz was outlined by two professionals sinking copious draughts of cognac.

However, Eichmann and Hoess remained sufficiently sober to design the construction of gas chambers on the spot and the final blueprint was drawn up. Indeed, Hoess stated: 'Eichmann had the entire plan of the camp figured in his head. As a matter of fact, he had planned it previously.'

Eichmann himself explained: 'We shall be expecting a great number of people. Technically it would prove very hard to shoot them. The shouts of the women and children would disturb the SS and cause great inconvenience.'

So it was that an entirely new enterprise was launched – the constructions of the *Vernichtungslager*, the annihilation camp. Two civilians from Hamburg were despatched to Auschwitz. Their job was to school the staff in the use of Zyklon B, originally commercially manufactured as a strong disinfectant but now to be put to a sinister new use.

Matters progressed at a speed which must have pleased even the insatiable Himmler. By September 1941 in the notorious Block II, the first gassings were carried out on 250 patients from the hospital. Next were 650 Russian prisoners of war who had been snatched away by the Einsatzgruppen. Construction forged ahead at Birkenau, which was to become Auschwitz's killing centre.

The pattern was repeated at various other centres throughout the eastern occupied territories. The first death camp completed was at Chelmo, thirty-five miles from Lodz, which was intended to house local Jews. The technicians of death went on to build the camps of Sobibor, Majdanek and Treblinka.

However, Hoess and his fellow camp commandants were not permitted to carry out their grisly appointed tasks with complete freedom. Eichmann, whose devotion, administration and executive efficiency was almost mystical, maintained an iron control.

Killings by gas would only be carried out with his express permission. The SS officer in charge of each convoy turned up with a mountain of official documentation, including notification whether or not a train was to be directed to a camp of extermination. There were precise instructions as to what the fate of the victims would be. Letters A or M on a file would indicate either Auschwitz or Majdanek. These dossiers were a passport to the gas chambers.

It was a system that worked well. In the years that Germany rode the high tide of conquest there were few administration tangles. Eichmann could be forgiven self-congratulation.

Disguise of the camps and elaborate security were further achievements of which Eichmann could be proud. One of his most able lieutenants, Christian Wirth, former Commissioner of the Kripo (Criminal Police) in Stuttgart, was put in charge of extermination camps in the forests and marshes of east Poland which had been laid out according to Eichmann's precise specifications.

In order that the charade could be acted out with maximum conviction, Wirth was instructed to weed out from among the Jewish population a number of criminals who would not be adverse to sacrificing their own people if there was prospect of a profit.

The importance of the particular layout of the camps soon became obvious. An eyewitness recorded:

'They were built in false perspective . . . That is to say, the arrivals had the impression of coming to a large town or a large nexus of dwellings. The train entered a false station, and after the escort and the train had left, the tracks were opened and the Jews got out.

'They were immediately surrounded by the renegade Jewish detachments and Commissioner Wirth or one of his deputies made a speech.

'He said to them: "Jews, you have been brought here to

be transplanted, but before organising this new Jewish state it is obvious that you must learn a new profession. Here you will learn that everyone has to do his duty.

"'As a first step everyone must undress, which is the regulation, so that your clothes may be disinfected, that you may be given a bath, for you must not bring any vermin into the camps.'"

To the new arrivals, it all seemed remarkably relaxed and reasonable. After all, it was smiling Jews, not Germans, who separated the men and the women and who courteously took their hats, jackets, shirts and finally shoes and socks.

The whole operation was carried out with such speed that the prisoners barely glanced at the watch towers with their machine-guns behind which the SS crouched. Guards with their slavering Alsatians remained well hidden behind the perimeter wire.

Then came the last halt. The group entered what had been described to them as the bath-house. The doors were then shut; the gassings began. The bodies were discreetly removed by a back door and incinerated. It was soon time for the next batch.

Wirth did not find the necessary organisation at all complicated. He had learned his trade in a good school – as part of the extermination programme of incurables, embodied by Hitler in a special euthanasia decree. The results of this had been thoroughly approved by Eichmann; hence his new 'confidential mission'.

Chimneys of the charnel houses of Auschwitz made the air stink even above the fetid marshes; the air was often dipped in flame red. But in the cities of Hitler's eastern vassal states, some form of pretence could be preserved, providing the stage management was shrewd enough.

So that the Jews of Slovakia should go meekly to the death camps, Eichmann unearthed a suitably pliant Czech journalist, Fritz Fialla, to write articles describing the wonderful conditions of Auschwitz.

Orders were also given to force Jews in the camps to send their relatives tasteful postcards marked 'Waldsee' with a printed inscription saying: 'We are doing very well here. We have work and are well treated. We await your arrival.'

Often the cards were sent long after the writers were dead.

Not all arrivals at Auschwitz were orderly. Gertrud Mosonyi was a young Jewess who had spent her early childhood in the fiercely anti-Semitic Hungarian town of Szombathely. She had been arrested with her parents following the total occupation of Hungary by the Nazis in 1944.

Gertrud, the daughter of a distinguished gynaecologist, today works in London as an archivist and librarian in Jewish studies. She remembers:

'In our particular camp the Germans separated the medical people and the lawyers and their families – the group to which I belonged.

'We were herded into the smallest cattle wagon and told we would be subjected to "special treatment" for intellectuals.

'At first when we were locked in we took it calmly. We built a row of seats with our luggage and then sat back to back, so as to enable everyone to have the same amount of space. Next to the door a bucket had been placed. The only ventilation came from two very small barred windows.

'When the train started with a tremendous jolt we all fell on top of each other but eventually settled down. This is how we travelled for the first two days, during which the heat and the stench became unbearable with everyone suffering from thirst. The bucket overflowed and we had no means of emptying it. People started to fight, abandoning all self-control.

'On the third day we thought that we would have a merciful break. Then we were told to get out of the train. But after a little while the journey continued. Again there was the terrible jolt and again we all fell on top of each other.

'There was mass hysteria with people beating each other, screaming and fighting. One old man died and we had his body for the rest of the journey. By that time my mother and others had been driven insane.

'Three times more the grim farce of stopping and decanting and starting again was repeated. Our last stop was Cracow. Then a few hours later, the doors opened. We were told to leave our luggage and were pushed out of the wagons.

'We had arrived in Auschwitz-Birkenau.

'The men were separated straightaway from the women. That was the last time I saw my father and mother. She could hardly stand and by this time was scarcely aware of what was going on. Although my poor mother at 48 was scarcely young, she had become like an old woman of 80 and was quite senile. I hope that she did not suffer much and that the assertion that going to the gas chamber was rather like taking a shower was true.

'Then those of us who were left behind were told to form up in rows of five and were made to march and drag ourselves along as best we could before a file of SS.

'Inevitably we were separated into different groups and that was the moment when I lost my parents.'

Gertrud was herded with a large party of other women into an ice-cold hall and ordered to strip. Then every hair on the body was shaven by the SS and each prisoner was smeared with a painful disinfectant. It was not the only indignity.

'While we were standing naked, the lights went out and some of the SS pinched, hit or pushed us in the dark and when the screaming started they began to shoot.

'The survivors were herded out of the hall and led to a barracks. These consisted of a number of enormously long buildings which stood on yellow mud and were separated by a ditch and surrounded with barbed wire.

'On the corner of these fences there were watch towers and guards with machine-guns and trained Alsatian dogs. There was not a tree, not a blade of grass anywhere.'

As if re-running for the thousandth time a clip of film, Gertrud can recall in all its vividness and horror one particular day in Auschwitz – 19 July 1944:

'I'm shivering and I'm hungry. And I'm terribly dirty and thirsty. It is dark, only the guard-towers are lit. There are 1,200 of us and we are shoved into one barrack of Birkenau B Lager.

'Another dreadful night is facing us. I think it's round

99

about 9.00 p.m. It is dark and cold. For the last three days I have had dysentery and am trying to be one of the last to go in so that I am near the latrines. But I don't succeed and am pushed further into the barracks. There is no going back.

'We try to form rows back to back, knee to knee so that at least we can sit down.

'It is freezing cold in spite of our being huddled up against each other. The windows are all wide open and in this desert of barracks where there is not a blade of grass, only dirty sand and sharp stones, the contrasts are terrible. It must be below zero. My one piece of clothing – a dress and no panties – is not enough in this cold. But as it is black it is far too hot in the daytime.

'I am tired yet I cannot sleep. I am alone here among all these shaven-head human beings . . .'

It was a morning of intense cold in August after the routine *Zaehl-Appell* (roll call) that the women of Birkenau were ordered to strip naked and stand in rows.

'We were told there would be a "medical inspection" for possible typhus germs. But it meant 15 hours standing naked and without food before Rudolf Hoess and a group of SS actually carried out their inspection.

'This excuse for sadism was played out as a gruesome charade. Hoess and the party even went through a show of examining our throats and the palms of our hands.

'A few days later, our group began to receive innoculations against typhus and diphtheria, but the programme was never completed.'

A journey to the showers of Auschwitz meant an eight-kilometre march along a sharp flinted road. Once when the pain of the stones made Gertrud stumble and step out of the line of prisoners, she was hit by a guard with such force that she staggered and fell.

Gertrud Mosonyi spent one month in Auschwitz, escaping the inevitable tattooing only because of an air raid.

'The lights had been turned off and we were left standing naked and freezing for some four hours.

'After the raid, we were told that there was no time for

further tattooing. Instead we were handed grey-flannel under-clothes, one dress and shoes which had wooden soles. On the soles it was stamped that the shoes had been made from the skins of Jews.'

Gertrud survived Auschwitz, herded in the path of the Allied advance into Germany. She ultimately found her way to France, where she was liberated.

Himmler may have seen the camps purely as powerhouses of slaughter for recalcitrant Jews and foreigners who were largely from the eastern territories, but back in Berlin were bureaucrats with more mundane preoccupations. They were determined that, above all, the camps must be made to pay for themselves; to be profligate with human lives did not allow for waste elsewhere.

At Majdanek, near Lublin, the Jews had been forced to build camps which would eventually engineer their own deaths.

Majdanek was laid out neatly for killing: a spacious network of roads winding between high watchtowers. The guards, as in so many camps, were keen gardeners and flowers luxuriated outside the house of the commandant and in front of the camp offices.

In the centre, serving as a fountain, was a ten-foot-high replica of a medieval castle. The Jews had built that too, and there was more than a dash of calculated sadism in the way their captors had ordered Jewish gravestones to be dug up for the purpose. Prisoners had endured this blasphemy as well as the lash of the whips of the Gestapo overseers who supervised the building.

When the gas chambers had disposed of between 150 and 200 people every five minutes in a succession of shifts over twelve hours, it was time to get down to the business of making the dead literally pay for it all.

The obsession with profit could be found right beside the ovens of the camps where piles of tin urns lay. The contents were sold to families misguided enough to believe they were actually buying the remains of their loved ones who had regrettably perished of cardiac disorder and been cremated. It was to prove a profitable trade; it was not uncommon for urns piled with the ash of the crematoria to be sold by the Nazis for high prices.

Waste was abhorred above all by the camp commandant. There was a shortage of clothing back in Germany and the new settlers in the east also needed to be clothed. At Majdanek there was clothing in profusion.

Allied newsmen, touring Majdanek on the heels of the victorious Red Army in 1944, were shown a building, some 50 feet wide by 100 feet long. It was devoted solely to the storage of hundreds and thousands of pairs of shoes destined for a deserving Reich. They ranged from the footwear of babies to gold evening shoes and the high-laced boots of the elderly.

In Lublin, the witnesses were shown a warehouse of four floors filled with the worn but fumigated personal possessions of thousands long dead. The inventories were impeccable; every item of women's underclothing was detailed, along with combs, vanity cases, nail files and scissors. An entire shelf ran round the walls of one floor; it was stuffed with children's books and tiles still smudged with the prints of small hands.

Winters are cold in Lublin; but they were always warm for one of the guards, Moosveld, the 'crematorium fuehrer'. Moosveld had been careful to site the bedroom of his house not ten feet away from the incineration ovens behind a wall. And his bath was heated by the same fires that consumed the remains of his victims.

During his trial as a war criminal, Hoess said with ill-concealed pride that he obeyed the instructions of both Himmler and Eichmann to speed up the extermination at Auschwitz. So successful was he that, he claimed, he had set up new records by gassing six thousand prisoners a day.

Hoess added: 'We had two SS doctors on duty at Auschwitz to examine the incoming transport of prisoners. These would be marched by one of the doctors, who made spot decisions as they walked by. Those who were fit to work were sent into the camp. Others were sent immediately to the extermination plants. Children of tender years were invariably exterminated since by reason of their youth they were unable to work.'

Here Nazi racial theory had been a normal part of medical

training; physicians had been subject to an indoctrination in the same way as any participant in Nazism.

The purely sadistic role of these doctors in the camps was outlined during the trial of SS Sturmbannfuehrer Dr Fritz Klein, who had been the chief SS doctor for the women's camp at Auschwitz.

At his trial, he elaborated on the evidence of Hoess and stated that when a transport of prisoners arrived he had orders

'. . . to divide it into two parts, those who, because of their age, could not work, who were too weak, whose health was not very good, and also children up to the age of 15. This selection was done exclusively by doctors. One look at the person and, if she looked ill, asked a few questions, but if the person was healthy then it was decided immediately . . .'

What was decided could vary in its horror. Prisoners could be placed in pressure chambers and subjected to high-altitude tests until they ceased breathing. There could be injections with lethal doses of typhus and jaundice; there were 'freezing' experiments in icy water and even dissection of the dead.

A prisoner at Auschwitz, Dr Miklos Nyiszli, No. 8450, who was forced to work with the camp medical personnel, gave in his memoirs, *Auschwitz: A Doctor's Eyewitness Account* a description of the bodies on the dissection table with which he was forced to deal:

'I noticed a thick black line across his neck. Either he had hanged himself, or been hanged.

'Taking a close look at the second body, I saw that death had here been caused by electrocution. That much could be deduced from the small superficial skin burns and the yellowish-red colouration round them. I wondered whether he had thrown himself against the high tension wires, or whether he had been pushed. Both were common . . .

'The formalities were the same, whether it was a case of suicide or murder. In the evening, at roll call, the names of the deceased would be scratched from the muster list, and their bodies loaded into "hearses" for transportation to the

103

camp morgue. There another truck would pick them up, at the rate of 40 to 50 per day, and bear them to the crematorium.'

After the dissection, Dr Nyiszli was forced to make a report to a group of resident SS doctors, who listened as impersonally as any pathology class in a medical school. The notes were filed away in SS archives.

Some of these doctors did not concern themselves overmuch with Himmler's racial theories. They were straightforward killers: represented in all their malignity at Auschwitz by SS Obersturmfuehrer Dr Endreid and his staff, who between them were accused of no less than twenty-five thousand murders by injection of phenol.

Retribution came to some of them. At the so-called Doctors' Trial at Nuremberg in 1948, Colonel Telford Taylor, the prosecutor, said:

'The 20 physicians in the dock range from leaders of German scientific medicine, with excellent international reputations, down to the dregs of the German medical· profession.

'All of them have in common a casual lack of consideration and human regard for, and an unprincipled willingness to use their power over the poor, defenceless creatures who have been deprived of their rights by a ruthless and criminal government.'

It has been estimated that there were fewer than two hundred men who besmirched the good name of German medical science. When it ultimately became clear that the war was lost and that the Allies would overrun the camps, Himmler ordered the execution of a number of these awkward medical witnesses.

Some did, however, survive to stand trial. Seven of them were condemned to death and hanged. To the end they defended their lethal experiments as patriotic acts which had served the fatherland.

Only a few were contrite. At a trial of medical underlings, Dr Edwin Katzenellenhogen, a former member of the faculty of the Harvard Medical School, begged the court for the death sentence. He cried:

'You have placed the mark of Cain on my forehead. Any physician who commited the crimes with which I am charged deserves to be killed.'

The court was not prepared to be so accommodating: he was given life imprisonment.

Fate intervened in the strangest ways to save the lives of the tattered humanity who staggered eventually out of Himmler's death camps.

Time and again survival had been a matter of accident or of luck. One prisoner, Josef Kret, who had seen the hell of Auschwitz and lived to talk about it, provided a vivid example:

'. . . In the yard we recognised the voices of Grabner, head of the Political Section, of the camp leader Aumeier and of SS Haupsturmfuehrer Schwartz, head of the Employment Office.

'One voice we did not recognise. The four of them were talking in low voices, while they stood near the opening of the rectangular ventilation shaft of our cell. After a while we heard the steps of several persons in the yard and the block leader's loud announcement:

'"You are sentenced to death for murdering the Chief of the German Aviation in Cracow."

'Four small arms shots followed the announcement. It was repeated again and we heard again four shots. The conversation near our ventilation shaft had stopped. We were listening intently and felt more and more frightened – a massacre was going on! Could it be a cleaning out of the cells? The block leader's hoarse voice kept repeating its announcement in intervals of a minute, each time shots would follow and then the dull thud of falling bodies was heard. Once, before we heard the shot, a voice cried out: "Long live Poland!"

'"What did the cur say?" asked Aumeier. The block leader translated and Aumeier began to hurl abuse at the Poles who gave him so much trouble, who would not be mastered . . .

'The shooting did not cease. We had counted more than 160 shots. Suddenly, the conversation of the SS men at the

105

aperture of our ventilation shaft stopped. Grabner stooped down, put his head near the aperture and shouted in German: "Is anybody there? Is there anybody or not?" I noticed that my companion was already opening his mouth to answer. I gave him a rapid sign to be quiet.

'It was clear that Grabner, head of the Political Section, that is the head of the camp Gestapo, had belatedly realised his words might be overheard in the cell below. He wanted to make sure if anyone had been in the cell. If we had answered we would probably have been shot, too, together with the others.

'The shots were finally no longer heard and the four dignitaries departed. Lorries began to arrive and the corpses were thrown into them with heavy thudding. We began to breathe more freely . . .'

Survivors from other camps owed their lives to decidedly more gruesome strokes of fortune. Dr Leon Wells, a Jewish scientist in optothermics, was hauled out of his camp at Lvov in the Ukraine on a macabre mission. The Nazis had been keen to incinerate the contents of one particular grave containing 182 bodies of prisoners executed a year earlier.

But the Germans were not merely content with matches and paraffin. The grave had to be opened and the bodies checked against the Nazis' exact records of its location and the number of people in it.

Dr Wells suddenly realised that the grave was located precisely where he had originally been captured; his comrades had perished and his name was high on the list of the victims.

At Eichmann's trial, in which he appeared as a witness, Dr Wells said: 'Of course, when we opened up the grave it contained 181 bodies. Mine, it was discovered, was missing. We dug for three days in search of my own body, before we were ordered to give up and move on.'

Wells realised only too well that if the Nazis had discovered his identity, he would have been shot instantly.

Adolf Eichmann had always been keen on tidy records.

8

The arrogant crunch of German high boots on cobbled streets sliced rudely into the sleep of the inhabitants of Kragujevac.

It was a sound that was to become depressingly familiar all over Yugoslavia to the victims of Hitler's ruthless excursion into the Balkans – an adventure that had come originally as a swift curtain-raiser to the rape of the Soviet Union.

But the footfalls of the conquerors in Kragujevac were not destined to die away into silence that night. No one was ever able to determine precisely from where the bombs had been thrown, but they were tossed directly into the centre of the marching columns. The carefully planned ambush on that October night in 1941 was chillingly successful. Within minutes ten Germans lay dead and twenty-six seriously wounded.

The Yugoslav resistance had carried out an act of calculated revenge. Those same German troops who now lay dead and shattered in the Kragujevac street had previously carried out a sweep against bands of alleged 'Communist partisans' at nearby Gornji Milanovac.

The town had shuddered under an artillery bombardment of enthusiastic thoroughness. Before the Germans put a torch to it, they had locked up several hundred people in the Orthodox Cathedral. When the heat had become unbearable, the frantic captives broke down the doors and rushed into the streets – only to be mown down by machine-guns. A bare handful reached safety.

Now Kragujevac had answered back; but as an act of revenge it was to prove terrifyingly futile.

Barely had the bodies of the Germans been removed before the town's military commander, Oberst Hankelmann, acted.

An immediate round-up was ordered of the entire male population between the ages of fifteen and sixty. On the morning of 21 October, a cordon was flung round Kragujevac. No one was allowed to leave or enter. Peasants from the surrounding villages bringing their produce to town were turned back. Kragujevac was now in an iron clamp and Hankelmann could carry out his counter-reprisals at leisure.

A Catholic priest who had arrived in Kragujevac with numerous Croat and Slovene refugees and who was to survive the terror, left an account of the day's business:

'It was exactly four months after the Germans invaded Russia. In my memory I shall always be able to see those events as vividly as if they were taking place before my eyes. The Germans cordoned off every block in the town. Then they went from house to house, dragging out all the male inhabitants. They collected them together and sent them out of the town, heavily escorted by armed guards.

'They collected the newspaper boys from the streets, the waiters from the restaurants, the cab-drivers from their cabs. They even invaded the district court, abruptly ordered the proceedings to terminate, and marched out judges, prisoners, prosecutors and witnesses, all in one batch. They entered the high school, interrupted the classes, and took out all the pupils of the fifth, sixth, seventh and eighth grades together with their teachers and their headmaster, Pantelic, who despite his 64 years refused to leave his pupils. The Germans also collected some six to seven hundred labourers who had been working on the banks of a nearby river.

'How many men in all they collected I do not know. But I do know that not one of them had any inkling of the terrible fate that was in store for them. Most of them thought that the Germans intended them for work on some project or other, or else for the factories or farms of German Europe. This applied particularly to those work-men who had until recently been employed by the local arsenal, and who had lost their jobs when the arsenal closed down, presumably because of sabotage. I saw one Slovene refugee quarrel with his wife because she had used her knowledge of German to get him away from the guards. "Everyone but me will get some sort of job," he complained, "and all because of your foolishness." The other prisoners chatted easily among themselves, confident in the belief that no harm awaited them. "We have done no harm to anyone," they reasoned. "Therefore no one can do harm to us."

'The prisoners were herded into the Topovske Supe military barracks, and there they were left overnight. Though they felt some anxiety, spirits were generally high. They quickly organised an exchange of matches, food, cigarettes and other sundries; many of them even sang.

'The following morning, they were awakened at five o'clock, divided into units of 40, and marched out of town in various directions. Shortly afterwards the sound of machine-gun fire was heard in the town. Horror fell like a pall upon the people. So that was what it all meant! Hour after hour, all day long the machine-guns continued . . . Soon from the houses, and then from whole streets, there came the wailing of women and children . . . The streets emptied, the shops closed. Not a soul was anywhere to be seen. Kragujevac was a place of the dead.'

Oberst Hankelmann let it be known that the official rate of reprisal was one hundred Yugoslav lives for each German killed and five hundred for every soldier wounded. The full quota would have been 2,300. When he was informed that the quota had been reached, Hankelmann shrugged: 'We might well have to do the same thing tomorrow morning. Why not save ourselves the trouble of having to do it twice?' Instructions were given for the quota to be ignored.

The schoolboys, some 150 of them, were mown down by firing squads, together with their teacher. The headmaster, Pantelic, according to one account, knelt before the Germans and begged them to kill him along with the pupils.

Just before the volley, Hankelmann smilingly replied: 'Bitteschön!' ('You're welcome.')

By dusk, the outskirts of the town were littered with six thousand bullet-ridden corpses. Sixty per cent of the male population had been slaughtered. Two thousand who were spared were ordered to bury the bodies. When the uniformed executioners had finished, a detachment of heavy tanks drove over the mounds of freshly dug earth, levelling the field of the dead and crushing the weight.

The massacre at Kragujevac was to have its parallel in countless towns and villages in those territories of the east overrun by the Nazis, but in the Balkans there was one essential difference. Resistance to tyranny was already stirring. And in Yugoslavia, Hitler's will was questioned directly on the eve of his projected invasion of the Soviet Union.

On 4 March 1941, Yugoslav's Regent, Prince Paul, was summoned in secret to an audience with Hitler in Berchtesgaden. The Regent was treated to the standard threats; Hitler needed to be rid of Yugoslavia in order to pave the way for his invasion of Greece. But in Vienna Foreign Minister von Ribbentrop informed the Yugoslav leaders of Germany's 'determination' to respect 'the sovereignty and territorial integrity of Yugoslavia at all times'.

No sooner had the Yugoslav returned to Belgrade after signing the Axis pact, than the entire Government and the Prince Regent were overthrown by a popular uprising led by a number of prominent Air Force officers with the support of most of the army.

The new regime swiftly offered to sign a non-aggressive pact with Germany. But by then Hitler was beyond all reason. He had wanted a puppet state in Yugoslavia and had been thwarted.

A tide of anti-German feeling swept through Belgrade. The rage of the Fuehrer surpassed anything that his immediate entourage could remember. Military chiefs were summoned hastily to the Chancellery. Hitler screamed for blood. He was determined, he stormed, 'without waiting for possible declarations of loyalty of the new government, to destroy Yugoslavia militarily and as a nation. No diplomatic enquiries will be made and no ultimata presented'.

Goering was ordered 'to destroy Belgrade in attacks by waves', sending in bombers from Hungarian air bases. Directive 95 was forthwith ordered – even if it meant the postponement of Barbarossa by a month. And so at dawn on 6 April, the Wehrmacht fell upon the small Balkan country with total ferocity. Armies crashed across the frontiers of

Bulgaria, Hungary and Germany itself. The army bulldozed rapidly against poorly armed defenders dazed by the advance bombing of the Luftwaffe.

Hitler's punishment of the Balkans had begun.

The Baltic nations of Latvia, Lithuania and Estonia had suffered their own indignities before Barbarossa. While Hitler had been busy in 1940 with his stupefyingly successful campaigns in the west, Stalin had moved armies of occupation swiftly into the Baltic States.

Thus when Hitler unleashed Barbarossa against Soviet Russia on 22 June 1941, the prospect did not seem unduly alarming to the little Baltic states. Indeed, they were gripped with a new-found fever of patriotism. Liberation from the Soviet yoke seemed a real prospect; freedom, it was felt, was advancing at high speed.

As early as 1 July, Russian troops had been driven by the Germans out of Riga; in a burst of nationalist pride, flags were unfurled throughout the city. Soviet emblems were incinerated in a multitude of small fires kindled in the streets. The Red Terror was lifted; the German liberators had arrived to be welcomed with flowers. Something of the same fever even spread to the hard-pressed Russian armies and there were wholesale surrenders and desertions.

In Lithuania, the crash of German bombs was hailed as a signal of revolution. It was as if an earnest prayer for war had been answered. More than one thousand Lithuanians turned on their hated Soviet oppressors. A Red Army in full retreat had abandoned the main cities of Kaunas and Vilna. A coalition provisional government was hastily scrambled together; it was prepared to greet the Germans as allies.

But Stalin had not done with Lithuania yet; the NKVD was given Kaunas as a plaything. Anyone suspected of as much as heaving a sigh of relief at the sorry state of the Red Army was sought out and punished. Stalin ordered that no political prisoners were to be allowed to fall into the hands of the Germans. If they were permitted to survive, they might well, it was reasoned, form the nucleus of resistance.

At Lukiskes, the largest prison in Vilna, the inhabitants were hustled into trucks by the Russians and machine-gunned in the Cherven Forest of White Ruthenia. At

Kretinga, near the German border, Lithuanians who at the time of the Nazi invasion were caught attempting to flee, were confined to a special camp hastily built by the NKVD. A favourite method of execution was to place victims inside a giant wooden hoop and set fire to it.

Estonia, too, was to have no reason to love the Russians. On the day of the German invasion, the strained, hoarse voice of Foreign Minister Vyacheslav Molotov had come on the radio to announce the attack. In restaurants and cafés, the news was greeted with cheers that were not directed at the Red Army. Stalin acted with characteristic spite; the NKVD went in to scatter the dissidents and deal with nationalist partisan groups which had suddenly sprung up.

But such squabbles within the Soviet family were of necessity short-lived. The magnificent machine which was the German armed forces rolled on relentlessly and Riga fell. A gigantic gate had been smashed from its hinges. Through the space and across northern Latvia coursed the Wehrmacht. In the town of Tartu, in Estonia, the distant rumble of artillery vibrating through the close hot summer air was the advance warning of the Nazi juggernaut.

Estonian military detachments were forced into Red Army uniforms. In the streets, Soviet propaganda harangued the masses into resistance they were conspicuously reluctant to show.

Leading Communists in Lithuania, with somewhat less romantic views of the Nazis, deserted in droves for what they regarded as a safe haven in the Soviet Union itself.

Estonians allowed themselves to wallow in national fervour, to parade once again their blue, black and white colours, which the Russians had forbidden.

The Red Army, now hopelessly cut off, could do nothing to prevent the arrival of German troops into Tartu. Members of the *Feldkommandantur* installed themselves in the best quarters of the university building. Artillery and tanks poured in. German aircraft circled the town and an observation balloon looked out for the severely depleted Soviet batteries.

The way in which isolated pockets of Soviet resistance were dealt with by the Germans in Tartu gave the first hint of what Nazi occupation would really mean for Estonia.

The Gestapo located a secret radio station on the top floor of an apartment block. It was swiftly ignited. Those who managed to flee were lined up in the street and shot.

The search for Jews was put into action even before the battle for Tartu was over. Objectives of the Gestapo were air-raid shelters situated beneath the university and the cathedral. Any person with non-Aryan features was dragged away.

The destination of those arrested was significant. They were dragged off to a house in Pepleri Street. The choice of the Gestapo made sense: after all the building had previously been occupied by the NKVD.

In northern Estonia, some forty thousand deportees were assembled at the extreme north in Tallinn. From there they were shipped to Leningrad and an eventual destination that could only be guessed at. Political detainees never left the country alive. Details of tortures eventually reached the outside world: the gouging out of eyes before the shot in the back of the neck; the impaling on stakes and enforced sewing up of eyelids.

Such refined tortures were not, however, the work of the Nazis but of Stalin's battalions of destruction. The scorched-earth policy was as often as not carried out literally. Whole villages and settlements were systematically burnt; whole districts were laid waste.

No planned programme for the evacuation of inhabitants existed. To scuttle across the border into the Soviet Union was to court oblivion, either from the NKVD or the advancing Wehrmacht.

In Tartu, the bleak, depressing and monotonous days of Nazi occupation stretched into months. The new lightened mood which had brought a brief sparkle of optimism to the Estonians had long since ebbed away. Cynics who had seen governments come and go pointed out that in one sense people were lucky: things were no worse than before and everyone seemed to have survived.

After all, ran the argument, what had really changed? There had previously been a hated flag hanging from the university flagpole. There still was, even if the red was a bit

113

brighter and the crooked cross had taken the place of the hammer and sickle. If you looked in the shop windows you still saw, not enticing consumer goods, but pictures of politicians. Now it was Hitler and Goering who glared out at passers-by. Were they really any worse than Stalin or Beria?

True, it was only safe to talk about the family and the weather in restaurants, because one's next-door neighbour was probably from the secret police. But what was new about that? In one sense there was an advantage: a German rat was easier to detect than a Russian one.

But there were changes. The Town-Hall Square was now renamed Hitler Square. German troops marched along the streets in an endless column of greenish grey. Homes were cold and overcrowded; main buildings had long since been seized by the invaders. In the university library, a large staff of earnest young disciples of Alfred Rosenberg were deep in lists of the cultural treasures which would be transferred to Germany as soon as Leningrad, Russia's northern capital, was starved out of existence.

Ants Cras, who was head of the library of his faculty at the university, wrote of darkness being the greatest friend of the inhabitants of little Estonia:

'On those dark evenings, the Gestapo, seldom shy of publicity, but averse to discomfort, scarcely carried out any arrests.

'Nevertheless, any ringing of the doorbell downstairs – unless it was two short sharp rings and a long one, the agreed signal for a few of our most intimate friends – made our hearts give a nervous jump, for it *might* mean an official visit from the house in Pepleri Street – a raid for foodstuffs or something even more ominous than that.

'Keeping as close to the ill-heated stove as we could, with all available coverings on us, we used to sit in our armchairs, often avidly listening to broadcasts for some unadulterated news from the outside world and always welcoming the ringing strokes of Big Ben – except when the vagaries of our dilapidated wireless set made them ring out with such a frantic clamour that we feared some passer-by in the street might hear it: after all there were German officers living not very far away.'

114

Hitler's avowed aim was to bleed the Baltic states dry. Imports – beyond German books and a few trifles – were forbidden. In Estonia, the textile and shoe industries worked solely for the Germans; at home their products became virtually unobtainable. Even the tobacco factories had to work almost exclusively for the Reich; the Nazis seized the more expensive cigarettes, and inferior brands were doled out to male Estonians at one hundred a month. Women received none.

Food rationing became so severe that a lack of talent for black-market bargaining inevitably meant eventual death from malnutrition. Eggs, butter and sugar became distant memories. Meat, fish and vegetables either filled German stomachs locally or rolled back to the Reich in a seemingly endless flow of freight trucks.

The Nazis had declared themselves 'heirs to the Soviet inheritance'. An official communiqué of 19 October 1941 proclaimed:

'At the start of the German-Soviet war, private property did not exist in the countries under Soviet rule, so nobody can claim to be a legal proprietor. By sacrificing the blood of German soldiers, all these countries have been liberated. The German Reich, therefore, became the legal heir to the Soviet inheritance.'

Hot on this imprimatur for tyranny came the Central Colonisation Office. Favoured terms for immigrants had previously been advertised throughout Germany. The settlers, it was made clear, would be privileged beings who would be positively encouraged to milk their new-found countries. German farmers were not expected to meet the stringent grain quotas for at least five years, neither would they pay any taxes.

The process of colonisation was spelt out in the following circular presented to the Lithuanian authorities and amounting virtually to a licence for confiscation:

'A German settler . . . is appointed to take over the farm which up till now you have managed. From this day on he takes over the management of the farm. You will remain with your family on the farm and will help the

German settler to run it until such time as you are transferred to a new farm. You will be properly compensated and you will receive proper provision according to former conditions. Wilful desertion of the farm will be treated as sabotage and punished accordingly. In a similar manner any insubordination will be punished. These penalties will be of such a nature that anybody who does not obey the new owner of the farm will forfeit his right to compensation for the farm. All judicial cases will be dealt with individually and with due regard to common interests.

'Therefore everybody must remain on the farm to live peacefully, must not raise any disturbances and must help with his family in war work. Only in this manner can transfer of the farm be effected without loss to the former owner of the farm. For the same reason all former owners are enjoined to show German settlers all their friendship and support in this enterprise.

(Sgd) Commissioner-General of
the Kaunas Colonisation
Headquarters.'

In practice, the former owner was reduced to the status of labourer or ejected altogether with the clothes he stood up in and with a few sticks of furniture. Needless to say, there was no compensation either. Native farmers and their workers were no longer in a position to fulfil the grain quotas. They were arrested just the same. The local commissar for the Vilna district of Lithuania, an SS officer Wolf had a weakness for dramatics. He carried out mass public shootings of delinquent farmers on market day and left their bodies to rot as a warning.

In the early stages, the progress of the war in Russia and the swift overrunning of the Balkan states was a matter of considerable satisfaction to Hitler. One man, however, was far from being happy: the business of rounding up Jews in the Balkans was going far too slowly for the liking of Adolf Eichmann.

In Lithuania, for example, there were known to be 150,000 Jews, but they were slipping through the Nazi net at an alarming rate. The Jewish councils seemed to be suspiciously short of records, and no amount of torture and threats produced the names which Eichmann was positively itching to enter on his new stack of filing cards.

So far, Himmler had shown more interest in German and Russian Jews, but at any moment he might turn his attention to the Baltic states and start asking distressing questions. It was plainly necessary to do something drastic: if the Jews persisted in going into hiding, then wheedling them out by trickery was indicated. Eichmann took the first opportunity to visit Latvia and, specifically, Riga.

His first move startled his SS subordinates. He told them: 'All arrests and shootings of Jews are to cease immediately in the Riga area. From now on, Jews are to be given every consideration. You can leave the rest to me.'

Eichmann possessed a good figure and the ability to wear the smart SS-Sturmbannfuehrer uniform with plenty of style. It galled him to lay it aside and don civilian clothes, but it was essential for the next step in his plan.

With a few soldiers also in mufti on hand in case of trouble, Eichmann did a few rounds of Jewish clubs and houses. He spoke the language well and was possessed of sharp, almost Semitic features, so there was no reason why he should excite suspicion in those who did not know him. A little bit of friendly flattery and some discreet questions soon produced some useful names and addresses of Jewish families.

Eichmann set out on a series of social calls. To the terrified families who opened their doors, Eichmann was bland and reassuring. He continued to pose as a Jew but did not attempt to conceal he was also a German. He pointed out that, since he was not in uniform, his visit was unofficial.

Then came the confession: 'The fact is that I am out of my depth and badly need your help.'

Eichmann went on to say smoothly that, due to misunderstanding and administrative muddle, a number of arrests and shootings of Jews in Latvia had taken place. Liaison between the Germans and the Jewish Council was bad; the sole object of his call was to straighten things out.

It seemed plausible. Executions of Jews had indeed declined markedly in recent weeks. The Jewish councils had perhaps erred overmuch on the side of suspicion. The fact that a *Jew* had actually been sent by the Germans to invite

117

co-operation settled the issue in the minds of the unsuspecting families waiting for Eichmann's baited trap.

In front parlours throughout Riga, Eichmann talked sentimentally of the old days in the Jewish quarter of Vienna. His listeners dared themselves the luxury of hope. After all, this Jew knew other Jewish leaders by name and could discourse with great knowledge of Jewish customs and festivities. Precious hoarded titbits were fetched out of store cupboards and Eichmann was given a meal. Confidence was complete.

These occasions always ended in the same way. Eichmann would again become apologetic. He would say: 'I'm afraid there is very little time. I'll have to report back to the authorities. Otherwise they will think that I have betrayed them.'

The next bit needed careful handling. Eichmann's tone was deliberately casual. He suggested: 'I think it would help if you could see your way to introduce me to one or two of your leaders so that I can get their help.'

It took a few more visits to entirely allay suspicion, but eventually Eichmann achieved his object. He was accepted by the Jews as one of themselves.

A prominent member of the community, Anatol Fried, was detailed to work out negotiations.

Eichmann told him: 'I don't know how long the Germans can be persuaded to hold off making fresh arrests. They must have evidence of friendly intentions from the councils. A list of names and addresses of known prominent Jews and others would certainly prevent any fresh persecution.'

Not for one moment did Fried or the other Jews know the real identity of the charming Jewish Viennese. The names and addresses were handed over.

The Jews had sealed their own fate; the next day Latvia's holocaust began.

There was no need to conceal that uniform now – the smart full-dress affair with the gleaming buttons and the shining death's head skull on the peak cap. Eichmann drove into the centre of Riga like a conqueror, flanked by outriders, and with SS trucks and armoured cars as cohorts.

The SS and some Latvian auxiliaries stalked the city; their instructions were to arrest every man, woman or child on the lists. All were rounded up and taken to the woods outside the town. There, Eichmann and senior SS officers directed the shooting and the carnage. Out of the total of 150,000 Latvian Jews, only 15,000 survived.

The cruel efficiency of Jewish persecution, masterminded with immaculate exactitude by Adolf Eichmann, spread throughout the Baltic states.

The pattern was the same as in the rest of eastern Europe: the setting up of ghettos, the public humiliation of the Jews by forcing the rabbis to shave their beards and break the Talmudic rules by slaughtering pigs. But the harshness went even further. The Nazis drew up a set of rules which forbade Jewesses to bear children. Those who neglected to arrange abortions were shot.

All the time, mounting hatred for the Germans fuelled the forces of the resistance.

Men like Albert Kalme were waiting in the wings.

9

Albert Kalme was a Latvian patriot quite prepared to take on either the NKVD or the Gestapo. Both instruments of terror gave him the chance.

He had been arrested the first time by the Russians during their period of occupation. They flung him into Riga's central prison, made sure that powerful spotlights shone into his cell throughout the night and fed him on a diet of cold water and uncooked peas.

True, he was not beaten, but such crude methods were unnecessary: the sound of beatings and screams from the other cells was quite enough to induce terror. The Russians were evidently prepared to bide their time. A steady improvement in diet and a measure of consideration by hitherto taciturn Russian guards led him to suspect something was in the offing.

Then came a summons by a senior NKVD officer.

He glanced at Albert and asked with a grin: 'How are you getting on?'

Despite himself, Albert laughed and pulled ruefully at his seven-day growth of beard and waited for further questions.

They did not come. Instead the Russians handed him a sheaf of paper with the curt direction: 'Read these and sign them. Then you are free to go.'

The first document was an affidavit in which the prisoner was to give an undertaking that he would say nothing about his arrest or treatment. Albert reasoned it would be worth signing to get out of the place.

But the next form was something altogether different. It was an NKVD form enrolling him as a police spy. His jailer explained patiently: 'It's really very simple. All you have to do is report to us any underground activities and any other signs of rebellion against the administration.

'Your rations will be generous and we will pay for each tip you give us. It will really pay you to be sensible. We know that you are in the Latvian underground and as such you can be of the greatest use. I assure you that you can expect a very promising career. We need good Latvians.'

Albert reasoned that if he did not sign, then he would never leave the central prison alive. Once outside, however, he could make it his business to rejoin the underground as soon as possible.

Mentally crossing his fingers, he scrawled his signature. The police chief smiled and shook his hand, reaching into his desk for the prisoner's wallet and passport.

Albert was conducted to the door with grave courtesy. In mock affection, the Russian patted his shoulder and kept his voice deliberately matter-of-fact: 'It would not pay you to double-cross us and we shall know if you do not keep your promises.'

Albert returned to his one-room apartment in the centre of Riga and was scarcely surprised to note that it had been turned over most efficiently by the NKVD. He reflected that the whole thing was much like a movie melodrama – even down to the NKVD man whom he had no difficulty in spotting from the upstairs window.

Albert realised that his first plan of reporting straight to the underground commander would have to be abandoned. He walked out into the hall and made for the downstairs apartment of his elderly landlady, who was able to confirm that the Russians had carried out their search immediately on his arrest.

Swiftly, Albert explained about the NKVD spy. Then he hastily scribbled a note to his commander, explaining what had happened. He told him that he would leave Riga for his uncle's farm. From there he would join the Latvian partisans in the woods near Valka. The landlady, who had no love for the Russians either, delivered the letter successfully.

Albert returned to his room, took one last glance at the man across the street and went to bed. Then next morning he donned an overcoat, crammed a few scraps of food into his pockets and strode out casually into the sunlight.

Really, the whole thing was getting progressively more Hollywood. The Russian, short, unshaven and with watery eyes, was actually propped against a wall pretending to read a newspaper.

A block further on, Albert dodged into a doorway opposite a bus stop. Both men leapt aboard the same time and Albert turned to the NKVD shadow as if he were an old friend. 'I am going to my old school to see if I can get a teaching job,' he said conversationally. The man merely grunted.

Albert walked into the school and made his way slowly towards the classrooms. Behind him, the shadow was staring at a noticeboard and puffing a cigarette. Albert kept the same pace, only starting to run when he reached the rear entrance leading to the school yard.

To take a taxi now would be madness; he knew there was at least a ten-mile walk ahead of him.

He had a quick lunch in a village inn and began to feel a little safer. He sat with a cup of coffee waiting for one of the farm wagons which would surely be passing at the end of the day.

He eventually hailed one and clambered aboard. The driver showed no surprise when his passenger crawled into the back and hid under the grain sacks.

Albert received an effusive greeting at his uncle's farm. He had previously steeled himself for the bad news that was inevitable -- such as the deportation of his parents during the time he was in jail. His brothers had fled to the woods.

Misfortune of that kind had to be accepted. What was important was the future of the anti-Soviet partisans, many of whom were hiding out in a barn.

Soon Albert was holding a rifle in his hands again and dreaming of killing Russians for the future of Latvia.

But by June 1941, the country had a new and brutal foe: the Nazis were in control.

All the nationalists were agreed that the Germans would need watching. The nationalists were grouped under a single command and the order went out: 'Take things easy. Wait and see what the Nazis do.' Albert was ordered to return to the University of Riga, ostensibly as a student but in reality to keep an eye on the Germans.

For months, he busied himself with engineering studies, but in fact was mostly busy with distributing copies of Latvian underground newspapers and broadsheets. Nights were spent stuffing them into mailbags and under doors.

In November 1942, the enemy struck. There came an order for Albert to report to the local employment officer.

The Nazi director was abrupt: 'Your studies are to be discontinued. From now on you will do some real work in Germany. Either that, or join the army.'

A move to Germany! Albert had imagined all sorts of unappealing fates that the Nazis might have in store for him. But service in the Reich, however brief, was not something he had bargained for.

The German was saying: 'We need writers in the Latvian section of the propaganda ministry in Berlin.' He held up his hands. 'It's no use arguing. Either you take the job or go to the Russian front.'

Albert begged for a day's grace; to his surprise it was granted.

His chief heard the news with delight. He gasped: 'A man inside the propaganda ministry! That's just what we need. Find out what they're doing there and contact us as soon as you can.'

The Berlin in which Albert Kalme eventually arrived was still a happy, prosperous-looking city. The people appeared well fed, confident of victory.

At the propaganda ministry Albert was put in the charge of

an impressive Balt named Zimmerman, who promptly gave him a stiff test to see how well he could translate German into Latvian. He passed impressively enough and was put to work.

There were still plenty of victories to report from the Russian front. But soon Albert, with scarcely concealed satisfaction, noted that the tide seemed gradually to be turning. Lame excuses were propounded for the defeat of Rommel's forces in Egypt and for the invasion of North Africa under Eisenhower.

Albert's off-duty hours were spent in clandestine contacts with Latvian nationals or sympathisers. There was a Latvian woman who had married a high Nazi official simply so that she could spy on him. And there were others who received whispered messages in restaurants or on park benches.

He never allowed himself to forget who his real masters were. Fresh instructions could reach him from Latvia without warning; indeed, the vital one arrived just before his first Christmas.

It said: *'We now know enough about German propaganda messages. You can be of more use here. Get back quickly.'*

Albert put through a request for leave in Riga. His bosses were furious. He had only been in the Reich for a month and here he was wanting to go home. Why couldn't he wait until the summer like everyone else?

Eventually, he settled for a few days. Then came a chilling order: 'Report to the Gestapo.'

At the notorious Prinz Albrechtstrasse 8, Albert was made to kick his heels for ten hours while various officials questioned him and telephoned for confirmation to Latvia. Permission to travel was granted on the strict understanding that he was to be back in Berlin on 27 December.

The efficient machinery of the Latvian underground hummed into action as soon as Albert reached Riga. He was whisked into hiding for debriefing, then told: 'We will find work for you here. There is no question of you returning to Berlin.'

A letter was hastily sent to Gestapo headquarters in which Albert pleaded that he was far too ill to travel and had a fever which must be allowed to run its course.

A Gestapo official was despatched to the farm of Albert's worried uncle. The Latvian doctor so obligingly on hand confirmed that indeed that there could be no question of Herr Kalme travelling to Berlin or anywhere else.

Early in January, Albert was ordered to join up with the partisans. Overjoyed, he raced to his apartment in Riga and began feverishly to pack. He stuffed a few clothes into a single suitcase and made for the door.

How long the three Gestapo officials had been the other side he never knew.

One of them smiled like a razor. With elaborate courtesy, he said: 'We're so glad you're ready.'

Albert tried to keep the fear out of his voice. 'Ready? Ready for what?'

'We have a warrant for your arrest. You are accused of subversive activities.'

The trio frogmarched him along the cold wet winter streets to Gestapo headquarters. Albert recalled ironically that he had taken precisely the same route when his captors had been the Russians. Then, too, there had been three men. Did they, he wondered, always travel in threes?

The former NKVD quarters had been turned into a tourists' gallery. Cynically, visitors were shown with glee just what the Communist barbarians had been guilty of. The real business of the building, however, was not a tourist attraction.

The Germans itched to get at Albert. Barely two minutes after he reached the building in Reimers Street they were on him with their beating and kicking. Ordered to strip, he was struck on the back of the head and kicked in the shins. He fell over and his head hit the stone wall. Before he could get up, the three were on him, raining down curses and kicks.

Then they used their Lugers to knock him unconscious.

A pail of cold water was poured over him and he was drenched and shivering. They got hold of him by the hands and feet, dragging him across the floor to the cells below.

They flung him against the cement floor and slammed the door shut. Albert felt the appalling cold and the throbbing chest pains. All at once he had a desperate yearning to be allowed to live. He sank to his knees and prayed.

At midnight they brought him food, and the diet was

almost identical to that which had been given him by the NKVD in the central prison.

Then he was yanked upstairs to the fourth floor and there was another Gestapo official, also wavering a Luger, who yelled: 'Out with the truth or else I'll shoot you on the spot.'

Two smaller men came in and set about him with blackjacks. Later, Albert was to recall that in their dreadful way they had been artists: varying the blows rhythmically between the head and the kidneys.

Idiotically, he begged for water. But they ignored him and repeated constantly: 'What were you doing in Berlin?'

'I was working there.'

'Yes, you pig! But not for Germany. You were spying for the Allies.'

The Luger crashed down on his head and he tumbled into a pit of darkness.

And so it went on for three days. In a delirium, Albert seemed to see Russian torturers as well as Germans. Perhaps, he thought, they had joined up for the sole purpose of finishing him off. Perhaps he had never been in the hands of the Germans at all and the whole time in Berlin had been the stuff of dreams.

The guards called for him again. At the sight of the tall German interrogator Albert's knees gave way beneath him and he shrank into a chair. A cup of scalding coffee was thrust into his hands, but before he could as much as smell it, it had been kicked away and the beatings began again.

Came the question: 'Are you ready to confess?'

He shouted in rage and fury: 'You are all alike! Confess! Confess! That's all I hear. I heard it from the Russians and now I hear it from you. I won't confess! I have nothing to confess! Do what you want!'

He might almost have saved his breath. The interrogator was speaking now. 'You are privileged, you stupid Latvian. The head of the Gestapo here wants to meet you.'

But there was a period of respite. Albert was left totally alone in his cell except for rations of watery soup and black bread three times a day.

It was ten in the morning when the summons came. The local Gestapo chief was a man who plainly took his job seriously. He had even modelled himself on Himmler, right down to the rimless glasses.

He said: 'You are to be shot for espionage and active participation in the underground movement directed against the German forces of occupation in Latvia.' He paused and pushed a few sheets of paper towards the prisoner.

Albert caught a glimpse of the confession that would send him to his death. He refused his signature.

The Gestapo chief did not seem unduly put out. He merely shrugged and rang a bell. Albert was taken to the courtyard and pushed into a closed van. Twenty minutes later he found himself at the gates of central prison.

He was back where he had been the previous year. But now he was a rather special prisoner. Every seam and hem of his clothing was examined scrupulously. The buttons were cut from his coat and trousers, the soles ripped from his shoes. Then his hair was clipped and he was marched to the condemned cell of Section II.

Albert was given a brew of hot water every other day and bread was thrown through a tiny window. Once the warden entered with a list of names, and when his own was called he knew that his time had come.

But, strangely, nothing happened. The days stretched into weeks, and when the order came he was marched not to the firing squad, but again to the office of the head of the Gestapo.

To his amazement, the man was almost civil. His first question was so ludicrous that Albert almost burst out laughing.

'How do you feel?'

He said: 'Terrible.'

The chief nodded and looked almost sad. He said: 'We have decided to let you free. Naturally, there are conditions. To be precise, two.'

What lunacy was this? The same thing had happened two years ago in the very same place. What were the new conditions to be?

'The first is that, soon after your release, you will present yourself before the Military Service Commission. After you have recovered your strength, you will be sent to the front. Germany needs soldiers in the fight against Bolshevism.

'The second is that you sign this statement promising to tell nothing of what has happened to you. If you so much as open your mouth, you will die. You may go.'

Albert staggered away, two guards hustling him quickly to the main gates in positive eagerness to be rid of him.

It was dark by the time he had reached his apartment, ripped off the stinking prison garb and run his bath.

Then the doorbell rang. Again and again it sounded through the tiny apartment, but it was an age before Albert could steel himself to open it.

Before him stood his elder brother. There was no time for anything beyond the barest greeting. Albert's brother snapped: 'Get dressed quickly. We're leaving.'

The couple stepped into a street carpeted with a fresh fall of snow. All at once the air-raid sirens began wailing throughout Riga. And then there was the drumming of aircraft overhead, the crunch of bombs and the sullen roar of the German anti-aircraft batteries.

Albert's brother said ironically: 'The war is coming home to them at last. They've got more to think about now than just torturing partisans in cellars.'

Albert could only repeat: 'But I still can't figure out why they released me.'

The other man replied: 'We bribed them. It took us three weeks to reach the right man.' He laughed. 'My God, you're expensive – 10,000 Reichsmarks, 50 pounds of bacon, 20 pounds of butter and a whole case of brandy. Mind you, they're getting more amenable. There's the fear in the back of their nasty minds that perhaps they aren't going to win after all.'

What had happened by the birth of 1943 was Stalingrad – a crushing, appalling and decisive defeat for the German Sixth Army under Generalfeldmarschall Friedrich Paulus. The reading over the Reich radio of the German defeat had been preceded by the roll of muffled drums and the playing of the second movement of Beethoven's Fifth Symphony.

Germany went into mourning. All theatres, cinemas and variety halls were closed. The blunt truth was that the high tide of Nazi conquest, which had rolled over most of Europe to the frontiers of Asia on the Volga and in Africa almost to the Nile, had begun to ebb. It would never flow again.

In the occupied lands of eastern Europe, new heart was put into the simmering resistance groups. In Latvia, Albert, obeying instructions, left Riga for Kurzeme; and there, in a log building deep in the forest, he met up with four men, all of whom began by digging their rifles suspiciously into his ribs.

In a few moments, though, they were feeding him hot tea laced with vodka, and then they were putting back into his hands the well-oiled rifle and the belts of ammunition.

Albert Kalme was a partisan once again.

10

Optimism and arrogance had fuelled the mighty forces of the Wehrmacht pouring into Soviet Russia on that proud June morning in 1941.

The simple German soldier could scarcely be blamed for his euphoria. After all, had not the Fuehrer triumphed already? Had not his troops cut through to the Channel ports in the west during the previous year with almost ridiculous ease? Surely failure was out of the question for three million fighting Germans buttressed for a magnificent new adventure with the finest technology the world had ever known?

But the Soviet Union was not just another country neighbouring the Reich. Here was a vast land mass made up of every conceivable form of terrain; the advance of the armies was from the pine-forested emptiness of northern Finland through the wide expanses of Russia's border zone.

And what of the land itself? To more than one fresh-faced novice of the barrack square it appeared nothing less than hell on earth. Above all, there were the foetid and inpenetrable swamps, the greatest of which extended a distance of over three hundred miles. To the south were the wide and monotonous steppes of the Ukraine and, below them, at the extreme southern part of the battle front, Georgia and the Caucasus and their sub-tropical climate. There were vast, dense forests, mountains, deserts and jungles.

And what of the enemy? Of that the German soldier knew next to nothing. How could he, since the knowledge of his superiors was in many respects scarcely better? The Fuehrer himself had screamed: 'The Russian is a clay colossus without a head.'

True, there was a Russian army, but everyone knew that it had lost most of its best talent in Stalin's succession of purges in the 1930s. Most of the commanders, it was proclaimed, lacked battle experience and were in charge of a rabble which could easily be routed by the military war machine.

There were fatal flaws in all the optimism. The German High Command was unaware that the Russians were equipped with many weapons, particularly tanks, which were qualitatively and numerically superior to its own. Ignorance of the extent of the Russian armed might soon became all too obvious.

But miscalculation was not simply military. Hitler made a grave mistake in so contemptuously dismissing the workers and peasants – groups incidentally which were to be the most foully treated by the Nazis. For these groups, many of them out-of-uniform Party comrades, added a new dimension to Hitler's war. They were prepared to fight like tigers until the Nazi yoke was lifted for ever from the east.

But little of that was apparent during that first July. By then the Germans had captured Minsk, capital of Belorussia, together with a large part of the Balkans and the western Ukraine.

In the Kremlin, fear stalked like a physical presence. Stalin spoke to the Russian people on 3 July 1941:

'In areas occupied by the enemy, diversionist groups must be organised to combat the enemy troops, to ferment guerrilla warfare everywhere, to blow up bridges and roads, damage telephone and telegraph lines, set fire to forests, stores, transports. In the occupied regions, conditions must be made unbearable for the enemy and all his accomplices. They must be hounded and annihilated at every step and all their measures frustrated.'

It was a crucial speech: nothing less than a match to the power-keg of Soviet resistance.

Units of guerrillas were, in fact, formed from nothing. The early weeks and months of the German invasion threw the Soviet Union into chaos. Russia's rulers had their work cut out holding on to territory and defending Moscow without contemplating the organisation of undercover forces.

Besides, the whole conception of a partisan or resistance movement was utterly alien to Soviet totalitarian rule. Stalin knew that there was always the fear that clandestine movements might form the basis of a counter-revolution.

But now there had to be quick rethinking.

Marshal Budenny, the Soviet Commander-in-Chief on the southern front, and Nikita Khruschev, secretary of the Ukraine Communist Party, made a spirited appeal to the population of German-occupied Soviet territory:

> 'We speak to those who are able to handle arms. Join guerrilla detachments; create new lines; annihilate the hateful German troops; exterminate Fascists like mad dogs.
>
> 'Derail their trains, interrupt communications, blow up dumps, so that no single ounce of grain is left to the enemy. Gather as much as you need for the near future, and destroy the rest. Destroy plantations of industrial crops – beetroot and flax.
>
> 'The hour of our victory is at hand. Make every effort to fight the enemy and exterminate him.'

Soon the Moscow printing presses were rushing out copies of a 400-page *Partisans' Guide* which set out the chief 'tactical rules of partisan warfare', the use of firearms captured from the enemy, how to destroy tanks and aircraft and the best ways of wrecking troop trains and motor transport. Here was set out in precise detail just how to kill an enemy motor-cyclist by stretching a wire across the road. Here were tips on more mundane subjects such as camping and camouflage.

Certainly there was an undeniably schoolboy element about a handbook which carried a glossary of useful German phrases, including *Halt! Waffen hinlegen!* (Halt! Lay down your arms!) or *Wo sind Minen gelegt?* (Where are the mines laid?).

But some fifty thousand copies were delivered not just to feed schoolboy fantasies. The hunt for partisans was on in deadly earnest. Orders were despatched to the army of bureaucrats who controlled all the vast resources of the Soviet Union, not only in the factories and towns, but also in villages with scattered homesteads and collective farms.

Cadres of partisans did not in fact exist in August 1941, but that did not stop the directive of the People's Commissars of White Russia implying that they did. In this way the morale of the people received the required boost.

Under the heading 'Organisation of the Partisans', section one read:

> 'Partisan units are formed at every plant, transport facility, at every government or collective unit. They consist of men, women and also adolescents, who are able to fulfil the tasks of the People's Defence (Partisans). The members of the partisan units are volunteers, patriots of our socialist homeland . . .
>
> 'The units are led by unit leaders who are selected by the competent councils from the officers' reserve of the Red Army, or from comrades having military training, as well as from political leaders and from political organisations who have proved themselves brave and well informed, wholly devoted to the Socialist cause.'

Stalin's dream of a ruthless, fanatical peasantry prepared to exterminate their conquerors with consummate ruthlessness was slow to get off the ground. For a time, those who greeted the German invaders could not think in terms of sniper fire and Molotov cocktails. Instead, Panzer commanders received floral bouquets from cheering civilians who greeted the Teutonic host as 'liberators'.

In fact, Ukrainian nationalists in eastern Galicia even went as far as rising against their Soviet masters – and were slaughtered for their pains by the retreating Red Army and the inevitable sinister shadows of the NKVD.

At first, the sheer speed of the German advance played havoc with any organisation of resistance bands. But the wholesale slaughter policy of the SD bred hardness and resource. The forcible requisitioning from the civilian population of horses, vehicles, foodstuffs and fodder bred the sort of resentment which drove young peasants and workers to throw in their lot with the partisans.

By the summer of 1942, Stalin was able to gauge that hatred of the enemy was running at an agreeably high level.

In an order of 1 May he proclaimed:

'Under the incomparable banner of the great Lenin, men and women guerrillas are to intensify partisan warfare in the rear of the invaders, to destroy the enemy's communications and transport facilities, to annihilate the staffs and war material of the enemy . . .'

Response was ecstatic. By now guerrilla groups were springing up in a spirit of competition.

According to a report of the German Eleventh Army dated 2 May 1942, the following competition form fell into its hands:

'We, the men and women guerrillas of the detachment Yalta are full of enthusiasm for the appeal of the Highest Soviet . . . We have unanimously decided to join the socialist competition. Our aim is to carry out all orders in the best possible manner, to succeed in all actions against the enemy, and to exterminate the invaders to the maximum possible extent.

'Therefore the detachment Yalta calls on all partisans to take part in this competition using the following methods of scoring:

'(1) Each partisan must exterminate at least five fascists or similar traitors.

'(2) He must take part in at least three actions a month.

'(3) Should a fighting comrade or Communist be killed or wounded in action, he must be carried from the battlefield.'

Partisan groups no longer consisted merely of scattered bands of cut-throats who were more anxious to forage for scarce food than kill the enemy.

The Nazis brought terror with them. Soon the partisans were in a position to return it with interest.

The Herr Gebietskommissar (German regional commissar) for a certain small town in the Ukraine was a supremely happy man in the second year of the war. Fate had been remarkably kind to him; there was hellish fighting going on further east, but by great good fortune he had managed to avoid it in his comfortable backwater.

Here, a comfortable one thousand miles from the front, there was little to do but requisition all corn, cereals, butter and other agreeably nourishing produce. Some of it, of course, had to be shipped back to the Reich, but there was ample opportunity for seeing that both he and his staff were properly looked after.

He had not found it necessary to work unduly hard. Civilians, after the initial occupation and the hanging in the market square of some dozen dissidents, were giving little trouble. Besides, only the elderly now remained. Young and able-bodied men had already been shipped to the labour camps in the Reich.

On this particular evening, the Herr Gebietskommissar was in benevolent mood, relaxing in bedroom slippers in his comfortable apartment.

It was a picture of cosy domesticity destined to be rudely interrupted. The German had a cup of coffee half way to his lips when he heard the sound of scuffles and shots. He darted to the door, shouting for his adjutant.

The look of fear on the other man's face was enough to make the Gebietskommissar grab his service pistol. The senior officer darted into the passage, his jibbering subordinate following reluctantly.

Neither got very far. Their way was barred by an extraordinary collection of individuals which seemed to consist most improbably of Wehrmacht rankers, SS officers, immaculately suited businessmen and others wearing their distinctive Ukrainian blouses.

And then the two terrified Germans were hustled unceremoniously to the same town square where they had previously strung up tiresomely unco-operative Russians. The partisans in their looted costumes went about their work swiftly and efficiently.

The next day, a Wehrmacht motorised detachment visiting the town found the whole place virtually deserted. It is doubtful, though, whether that was what the Germans noticed. Their attention was rooted on the bodies of the Gebietskommissar and his adjutant swinging from poplar trees.

The rest of the garrison had either fled or been abducted, along with a few elderly inhabitants of the town.

Then the apprehensive Germans noticed something else. There was a note scribbled on a scrap of paper lying on the dead Kommissar's desk. It read: *'To a speedy meeting, Bogdan.'*

Bogdan? The motorised detachment had just missed one of the greatest living legends of Ukrainian resistance, the man who became known and feared as 'Bogdan the Elusive.'

It was Bogdan who always left a visiting card, frequently tethered to a goat. Above all, it was Bogdan who, when it came to escaping, had powers which could be regarded as superhuman.

On another occasion, the Germans sent an entire division, reinforced with Panzers, to track down Bogdan and his band. It seemed an easy enough prospect: the partisans were caught between the junction of two rivers.

They were surrounded. But for two unbelievable days the guerrillas kept up an aggressive resistance. Meanwhile, others had cut down trees and built a bridge. Eventually Bogdan and his column escaped at night. Even then, so the story went, he left behind him the usual goat, complete with note: *'See you again shortly.'*

Bogdan had been a thorn in the flesh of the Wehrmacht for two years in central and west Ukraine. The secret of his success was speed. His band had romped through enemy occupied Kiev. An entire village and a garrison had been exterminated. The next exploit had been one hundred miles away – the mining of railway lines and blowing up of a munitions train. Bewildered Russians and terrified Germans spoke of bands of men in German, Italian and Slovak uniforms.

Such a trademark was not mere bravado but illustrated a common partisan technique: the sight of German uniforms had the habit of paralysing the enemy in the vital first minutes of an operation. Professionalism was a quality the partisans were learning fast.

SS Obergruppenfuehrer Erich von dem Bach-Zelewski positively relished the job Hitler had given him as a specialist in anti-partisan activities. The Fuehrer had been almost embarrassing in his fulsome praise of the man who would go on to command the SS forces which in 1944 put down the Warsaw uprising. Indeed, Hitler had enthused: 'Von dem Bach is so clever that he can do anything, get around anything.'

What that meant of course was that the good Erich was a ruthless thug without many principles, and as such sure of the pickings of good jobs going in the Third Reich. Hitler's words, in fact, were to prove more prophetic than he would ever know. Von dem Bach actually survived the war with his neck unbroken, was fortunate enough to stand in the dock at Nuremberg as a prosecution witness and die in his bed in 1971.

But in the summer of 1941, von dem Bach's sole thoughts were concentrated in Belorussia, around Mogilev.

Partisan resistance at that stage was feeble and ill-organised. Von dem Bach could perhaps be forgiven a little self-congratulation. The time had surely come to look around for a few pickings of victory.

Soon interesting news reached him from the Polyakovo state farm; rumour had it that a quantity of gold was hidden there.

Swift instructions were issued. A detachment was detailed to tear the collective farm apart and seize the gold. The terrified head of the settlement begged: 'Leave us alone for twenty-four hours and we will produce the gold. If you destroy our village entirely we shall be homeless for the winter.'

Normally, such an appeal would have been contemptuously ignored. But the prospect of gold proved altogether too strong. The Germans withdrew at dusk, warning that if the gold was not forthcoming by the next morning then the farm would be burnt and all the inhabitants placed under arrest.

Four men from the detachment, Fischer, Hahn, Neudeck and Grose, were detailed to remain behind to supervise and return to the unit with the booty.

By mid-morning, von dem Bach had heard nothing. Shortwave radios were scarce; it was decided to make a quick return to the farm in six armoured cars.

Von dem Bach led the procession of SS back to the Polyakovo. It was the smell of burning which first alerted them, and soon they were in sight of the blackened shell which had been the collective farm.

All attention, however, was elsewhere. One building, the office of the head of the settlement, had been untouched.

Von dem Bach fanned out his men and slowly they edged forward, kicking in the door. The building had been completely stripped of all furnishing, but in the centre of the floor in the office was a heavy leather box, the word *Geld* scrawled across it in white paint.

A booby trap with a partisan bomb that would blow them all to eternity? There was only one way to find out. A heavy boot crashed into the lid.

There were four objects inside. Von dem Bach and his men stared mesmerised at the heads of Fischer, Hahn, Neudeck and Grose.

Partisan operations of any sophistication, however, were slow to develop. Hunger and sickness plagued many of the units whose members were not weather-hardened and battle-conditioned troops.

Guerrillas suffered badly from rheumatism, scurvy, boils, toothache, stomach and intestinal disorders. Few units boasted doctors; understandably, valuable medicines were diverted to the battlefronts.

Achievements that recalled lurid comic strip adventures undoubtedly happened. But one unnamed guerrilla, who was eventually to die in a partisan engagement, came closer to the truth when he wrote in 1942:

'We are crossing the Lebyashka swamp. The villages round about are in flames. In the distance the thunder of cannon can be heard. Every five to six hundred yards we have to rest. We sit right down in the water and after ten minutes move on. Everyone is weak. The swamp sucks us down. We sink in often, sometimes up to the hips. There is no end . . . Finally the order is given to rest until dawn . . . Camp fires are forbidden; the swampland is flat and the Germans are all around.'

The true partisan, however, was also a technician with pride in his work. He learnt, for example, how to build dug-outs in groups of three facing each other, so that each could be covered by small-arms fire from the other two.

A German report in 1942 revealed:

'Each dug-out had space for 15 to 30 men. The average size was 18 by 20 feet, with small passages leading off from the sides for protection against shell fragments in case of attack. The depth at the entrance was about four feet, and the floor slanted towards the rear to a depth of nine feet. The doorway was slightly more than a yard high. Beside the door there was a glassed-in window which offered observation into the forest and could serve as a fire port. The dug-outs were blended into the forest cover.

'Trees of various sizes were planted on the roofs of the dug-outs, and the excess earth from the excavations had been hauled away. A yard-wide passage ran down the centre of each dug-out. Wooden platforms built on either side of the passage served as bunks. The walls were faced with small logs, partly covered with boards. A stove for heating and cooking was built in one corner. Most of the cooking, however, was done in a separately constructed kitchen dug-out. The chimneys ran up through the roofs, usually into a tall tree, so that the smoke would be dispersed among the leaves and branches. Each dug-out also had a table and benches.

'At the time the work on the dug-outs was begun, large stocks of food – salt, pork, beef, flour, and so forth – were brought into the forest and buried in sealed containers. The food caches were scattered over an extensive area and carefully concealed. Ammunition and explosives were stored in well-built underground storerooms, likewise well camouflaged.'

Many a civilian partisan started his own personal resistance to the Germans in a spirit of youthful idealism, with a heady sense of adventure. As the war in Russia ground on, even the youngest became mere killing machines, prepared to loot from their own people in order to keep alive – or, just as often, to deny supplies to the Germans. Collective farms, like the one near Mogilev, were burnt down without compunction, along with their inhabitants.

With the gaining of experience and confidence, the

partisans became chillingly effective with selective terrorism: killing key German officials and Russian collaborators.

The careful selection of targets was to pay off dramatically in Belorussia, cradle of partisan activity, during September 1943.

Target for liquidation was the area's Generalkommissar, Wilhelm Kube. He was an old Nazi war-horse, a veteran of those far-off days when Hitler's followers had consisted largely of rabble-rousers whose political sophistication extended little beyond bashing the heads of Communists in street battles.

Kube had been Minister-President for Brandenburg, much addicted to delivering pompous speeches on every conceivable occasion. Hitler's loyalty to old cronies was notorious; in the case of Kube, affection was tinged with exasperation. The Fuehrer once commented that there was never any need to give Kube a loudspeaker since he had lungs like a rhinoceros.

And seemingly a skin to match. Denouncing Jews was all very fine, but Kube had gone so far as to suggest that the racial ancestry of certain top Nazis was questionable. This was too much, even for Adolf Hitler. Kube had been stripped of appointments and sent to cool his heels in a concentration camp. However, he had made amends by insisting on joining the SS at the age of fifty-three.

Hitler forgave his old comrade. White Russia was to a certain extent a backwater. The area's supply lines had to be kept open for the Wehrmacht, but Hitler was far more interested in subduing Moscow or the Ukraine. Here was a handy place in which to lose the bellicose old bore who had at least had the virtue of repenting his former ways.

If the posting was a disgrace, Kube did not see it in that light. Indeed, his main interest in Belorussia was that it was agreeably plentiful in what he described as 'blondies and blue-eyed Aryans'. The former he pursued on every conceivable occasion, but performance was undoubtedly vitiated by the vodka bottle.

The Gestapo kept an eye on him throughout his rule, but Himmler's secret police were not concerned with morals. Distinctly more worrying were signs that Kube possessed a certain tipsy humanity; he appeared genuinely to abhor the bestiality of his comrades and was not afraid to say so.

Even so his scruples were not allowed to interfere with his leading the good life in Belorussia. He made a point of employing as many beguiling 'blondies' as he could, most of them attached to his domestic staff.

They were not the only commodities to share his bed. One of the girls, insinuated into his lavishly equipped Kommissariat, dutifully obeyed the instructions of her partisan superiors and slipped an anti-personnel mine between the sheets.

On 22 September 1943, it blew Wilhelm Kube to pieces.

11

The year of Kube's death saw some dramatic and ultimately decisive changes in the fortunes of Nazi Germany.

How, in 1942, could defeat even be envisaged for Adolf Hitler? The Mediterranean had been to all intents and purposes an Axis lake, with Germany and Italy holding most of the northern shore from Spain to Turkey, and the southern shore from Tunisia to within sixty miles of the Nile. This was the time when Hitler's troops had stood guard from the Norwegian North Cape on the Arctic Ocean to Egypt, from the Atlantic to the borders of central Asia.

But things had began to go wrong, perhaps from the time when Wehrmacht troops of the Sixth Army reached the Volga just north of Stalingrad on 23 August.

Within just two months all cause for congratulation vanished. A tough Russian armoured force broke clean through the Rumanian Third Army just north-west of Stalingrad. The Russians drove in awesome strength from the north and south of the city to cut it and to force the Sixth Army of Generalfeldmarschall von Paulus either to retreat or be surrounded.

On the morning of 10 January 1943, the Russians had opened the last phase of the battle of Stalingrad with an artillery bombardment from three thousand guns. By the thirtieth, von Paulus was radioing Hitler: 'Final collapse cannot be delayed more than two hours.'

By 2 February, 91,000 German soldiers and twenty-four generals, half-starved, frostbitten, many of them wounded, hobbled towards the dreary prisoner-of-war cages of Siberia.

Other disasters followed thick and fast. At the battle of the Kursk bulge, involving Army Groups Centre and South, the greatest tank battle in history to date ended with a bloody nose for the Germans.

But what put new heart into the Russian people and particularly the partisans was that by the start of 1943, the Red Army had been able to go on the offensive – prising open a land corridor into Leningrad, a city under siege since early September 1941, when German forces had closed on the southern approaches.

Leningrad! The former St Petersburg which throughout its history had been a cradle of Russian culture.

Peter the Great, the first of the Emperors, had sunk massive piles into the morass of the Neva estuary at the cost of tens of thousands of lives, to build first the fortress of Peter and Paul, then the Kronstadt naval base on one of the hundreds of the islands of the Neva delta, and finally palaces, boulevards, grandiose squares. There emerged a city of slender bridges, lowering skies and the endless cold and snow of winter. Here Mussorgsky had written dark, tempestuous musical whirlpools, Pavlova had danced and the Imperial Ballet had spawned Diaghilev, Fokine and Nijinsky.

Adolf Hitler hated Leningrad.

On 18 September 1941, the Fuehrer had issued strict orders:

> 'A capitulation of Leningrad . . . is not to be accepted or even offered.'

And on 29 September:

> 'The Fuehrer has decided to have St Petersburg (Leningrad) wiped off the face of the earth. The further existence of this large city is of no interest once Soviet Russia is overthrown . . .
>
> 'The intention is to close in on the city and raze it to the ground by artillery and continuous air attack . . .

'Requests that the city be taken over will be turned down, for the problem of the survival of the population and of supplying it with food is one which cannot, should not be solved by us. In this war for existence we have no interest in keeping even part of this great city's population.'

It had appeared during September that the Germans would eventually inundate the defences of Leningrad. Then General Georgi Zhukov, Deputy Supreme Commander of the Red Army since the previous August, had been ordered to take command.

A new spirit swept through the Soviet forces. But for the people of Leningrad there remained twin agonies. There was little respite from the almost incessant bombing and shelling of the Germans. Since the area was becoming increasingly isolated with no more than a trickle of essential supplies getting through, a grim and merciless spectre was soon hovering over the unhappy city.

It was not the prospect of mere hunger: the tightening of stomach muscles in protest at a meal postponed. It was the near certainty of nothing less than sheer starvation for thousands. All too soon it was to be realised.

On 6 September 1941, Peter Popkov, the Mayor of Leningrad, sent a cypher telegram to the State Defence Committee in Moscow, reporting that his city was on the verge of exhausting her food reserves. Food trains must be expedited or the city would starve.

Translated into cold statistics, Leningrad had enough flour for 14 days; cereal for 23 days; meat and meat products for 18 days; fats for 20 days; sugar and confectionary for 47 days. Stocks dwindled with alarming speed.

Action by the authorities was swift and ruthless. Supplies were severely rationed. To buy on the black market, to steal or hoard became a criminal offence. But already the city's communal cupboard was emptying.

Leningrad housewife Yelena Skryabina was, by 6 November, recording in her diary that her son Dima was reduced to chewing coffee grounds 'or those abominable oil cakes which were once fed to cattle'.

And she went on to write:

'All of Leningrad eats oil cake now. They pay whatever is asked for it: shoes, stockings, pieces of material. You take any valuable article to the market-place and you get this substance in exchange. It is so coarse that you can't bite into it. You can't even cut it up with an axe. You have to shave it like a piece of wood to get something like sawdust. And from this you bake pancakes. They are extremely unappetising. And after you eat them – heartburn. The bread, too, is barely edible. There is a minimal per cent of flour in it. Mostly it consists of oil cake, celluloid, and some other unknown substance. As a result of these ingredients the bread is dry and heavy. Nevertheless people are ready to cut each other's throats for it. In the morning on the way home from the bakery, you must hide it carefully. There have been many instances in which the bread has been stolen right on the street.'

Around half a dozen bowls of yeast soup per head were available in a specially set up mess hall. It consisted of yeast and water and its nourishment was nil.

But what people would remember was starvation's horrific effects. In contrast to mere hunger, it does not make the human frame emaciated. It makes the body swell obscenely. Apathy takes over. Yelena saw her son turning old, standing for hours by the single stove in his winter jacket, pale with deep blue circles beneath the eyes, indifferent to life or death.

It became only too obvious in the Leningrad of those years that civilisation is a very thin veneer, as hitherto devoted families clawed at one another for a mere twist of bread.

Yelitzaveta Sharypina, a school teacher, witnessed in a store in Borodinsky Street a woman beside herself with fury, reigning blows on a child, who was sitting on the floor and cramming his mouth with thick black bread. A circle of spectators stood around silently.

Indignantly, Yelizaveta grabbed the woman in a desperate bid to stop her battering the child, only to receive the indignant protest: 'But he's a thief.'

The woman's ration for that day had lain briefly on the counter. It was the worst mistake anyone could make in Leningrad. Not surprisingly, the child, no more than ten years old, had snatched the loaf and devoured it, deaf to shouts or blows or indeed anything that went on around him.

It was a situation that only the stoutest and most independent spirits could endure. Few came as tough as poet and writer Vera Inber, who had fled from Moscow to join her doctor husband in Leningrad.

Yet there was a note of desperation even from her when she wrote:

> 'It seems to me that if in the course of ten days the blockade is not lifted the city will not hold out. Leningrad has taken the full brunt of the war. What is needed is that the Germans on the Leningrad front receive their due . . . If only someone knew how Leningrad is suffering. The winter is still long. The cold is ferocious.'

The anniversary of the Bolshevik Revolution came on 7 November. In any other year, it would have been a time for joyful, even riotous celebration. There would have been wine, vodka, fat turkeys, suckling pigs, roasted hams, sausages. But in 1941 there was barely an extra cup full of sour cream to spare for the children. As for the grown-ups, five picked tomatoes and an extra litre of wine was all that could be managed.

Outside a store, a German shell sliced into a crowd of housewives waiting eagerly for the wine. The corpses lay battered and bleeding; those who survived merely stepped over the wreckage and were thankful that the queue was shorter.

The deaths had begun that first November. It was not only the hunger that killed. The elderly slipped away from a variety of diseases, of course. But age was no barrier to consumption, dystrophy and diarrhoea.

In such circumstances, an ulcer was a death warrant. Poisons worked with relish on under-nourished constitutions. Wallpaper was torn down and the paste eaten because it was believed to be made with potato flour. Some ate the paper itself, reasoning that since it was made from wood it must have some nourishment.

Before November ended, eighteen per cent of hospital cases in Leningrad were starvation-related. On 20 November, a single factory issued twenty-eight reports of dystrophy.

The next day the total had risen to fifty. The Vyberg region registry bureau was unable to keep up with the demands for death certificates. Harrison E. Salisbury in his book *The Siege of Leningrad* revealed that by the end of November at least 11,085 Leningraders had died of starvation.

As Yelena Skryabina expressed it:

'Today it is so simple to die. You just begin to lose interest, you lie on the bed and you never get up again . . .

'Death reigns in the city. People die and die. Today, as I made my way along the street, a man was walking ahead of me. He could barely put one foot in front of the other. Passing him, I reluctantly turned my attention to his blue, cadaverous face. I thought to myself that he would surely die soon. Here one could say that death had placed his stamp on the face of this man.

'After several steps I turned around and stopped to watch him. He sat down on a hydrant, his eyes rolled back, and then he slowly slipped to the ground. When I finally reached him, he was already dead.

'People are so weak from hunger that they are completely indifferent to death. They die as if they are falling asleep. Those half-dead people who are still around do not even pay any attention to them. Death has become a phenomenon observable at every turn. People are used to it. They are apathetic, knowing that such a fate awaits everyone, if not today, then tomorrow. When you leave the house in the morning, you come across corpses lying in the streets. The corpses lie around for a long time since there is no one to take them away.'

It became impossible for each corpse to be buried separately, since there were nothing like enough coffins. If relatives wanted to arrange a proper funeral, they had to wait until a coffin was ready. The preceding corpse was driven to the grave, taken out of its coffin and buried, and the coffin was handed down to those next in line.

A visit to a Leningrad apartment was reported by one woman:

'Frost on the walls. On a chair the corpse of a 14-year-old boy. In a cradle the corpse of a tiny child. On the bed the dead mistress of the flat. At the doorway, a neighbour looking without comprehension upon the scene.'

While the Germans pursued their barrage of the city, the NKVD did not hesitate to terrorise the Leningraders.

The Soviet secret police apparatus clamped its own ruthless discipline on the entire population, the more able-bodied of whom were put to work as a guerrilla army. The smallest violation of orders meant either the firing squad or death in another form through service in the labour battalions.

As in other countries either threatened by Nazi invasion or already suffering it, one of the greatest morale boosters remained the wireless. In Leningrad, families, even when cold and starving, continued to be faithful listeners to Radio Leningrad. It remained on the air in the most appalling conditions.

Broadcasts were of poetry, symphonies and operas. A regular contributor was a poet, Lev Uspensky, who on one occasion was puzzled to find in the cold studio a strange wooden device, a sort of rake without teeth and shaped like the letter T.

The director, Yasha Babushkin, explained: 'Many people are struggling here so weak that they can scarcely stand at the microphone. This helps to support them.'

It sounded melodramatic, but in fact another poet, Vladimir Volzhenin, had indeed collapsed in the studio from sheer hunger and had died a few days later. Another man, who had sung a role in Rimsky-Korsakov's *Snow Maiden*, had been so frail that he had supported himself with a cane. By nightfall he too was dead.

But somehow Radio Leningrad had kept going. One particular room was a fantastic sight. There were always twenty or thirty people crammed into the studio among cots, couches, office desks, files, newspapers and wooden packing cases.

Often there could be no question of broadcasters making for the studios. They were too weak to move. Microphones were slung across the room so that they could speak where they were resting.

Olga Berggolts, a poet, recalled: 'Not a theatre, not a cinema was open. Most Leningraders did not even have the strength to read at home. I think that never before nor ever in the future will people listen to poetry, as did Leningrad in that winter – hungry, swollen and hardly living.'

On 8 January 1942, the unthinkable happened. The radio fell silent. There was no more power available for transmission. Crowds centred on the building demanding to know when the studio would be back on the air. Engineers worked overtime in a desperate bid to restore the power. Eventually there was success; the voice of hope remained for the rest of the Leningrad blockade.

Starvation was by no means the only horror which stalked the streets of Leningrad throughout the long nightmare of that cruel siege.

Whenever hunger invades a city, crime can never be very far away. Soon murder became commonplace. Not murder for gain, but quite simply, for food. Inevitably, the victims were the old. Even in the long food queues they were far from being safe.

In broad daylight, gangs would attack – a vicious blow from behind, a quick tug at the handbag for purse and ration card. No one in their senses left a bakery unaccompanied. Youths quickly became experts with knives. They made no noise, and with practice a stabbing could be carried out quickly and the victim throttled before the alarm could be raised.

The Leningrad police, which after all were part of Stalin's apparatus of discipline, could not exactly be called incompetent. But soon they were powerless. There was no point in investigations following the pattern of more normal times. Hardened criminals were on file and the system was such that there was never any shortage of stool-pigeons. But records and narks were useless now. These new crimes were carried out by a cross-section of the population that it was virtually impossible to pin down. There were deserters from the front, ex-Red Army men; even Germans who slipped in from the suburbs and under-cover agents added enthusiastically to the general chaos.

Housebreakings were another terror. Gangs swept down on occupants of apartment blocks and rifled valuables. Prudent tenants soon learned to keep quiet; at the first sign of protest, gangs invariably let loose with petrol bombs.

146

The police turned over the few that they caught to the staff of Leningrad Party Secretary Aleksei Kuznetsov who later declared: 'Bread looters were put straight up against the wall.'

The military tribunals worked overtime. A sudden dragnet on shops revealed proprietors profiteering on the black market. There was a sideline in stolen flour and motor vehicles to add to the charge sheet. Those found guilty were promptly shot. The mildest sentence recorded was twenty-five years with hard labour.

The biggest racket of all which sprang up in Leningrad involved ration cards. Regional rationing bureaux replaced cards that had been lost or mislaid. When a total of twenty-four thousand extra cards had been issued, the authorities, already highly suspicious, pounced. From then on, obtaining a new ration card became a deliberate process of nightmarish bureaucracy that took months to complete.

In practice, to lose your ration card in Leningrad meant nothing less than death by starvation, anyway.

Weakness through starvation or not, armed resistance still had to be mobilised.

A Leningrad City Council of Defence was set up. Its task was to organise block-by-block resistance. Under the council were all-powerful troikas – three-member directorates – in each region of the city. A troika consisted of the party secretary, the local city executive chairman and the local NKVD commandant.

The tasks to be carried out through a chain of command were swiftly outlined and those involved were told to implement them within twelve hours.

Men, women and teenager citizens of Leningrad were allotted their defensive tasks. By the time that the deadline had run out, the citizens had 150 battalions – armed with shotguns, pistols, submachine-guns, Molotov cocktails, sabres, daggers and pikes.

In the various suburbs, there sprang up street barricades, fire points, machine-gun nests and anti-tank traps.

A further five days were set aside for machine-gun posts to be built in parks and open fields; the weapons were to be turned without mercy on German parachutists.

Much more was needed. Andrei Zhdanov, the virtual dictator of Leningrad, proclaimed:

'We have to teach people in the shortest possible time the main and most important methods of combat: shooting, throwing grenades, street fighting, digging trenches, crawling.

'The enemy is at the gates. It is a question of life and death. Either the working class of Leningrad will be enslaved and its finest flower destroyed, or we must gather all the strength we have, hit back twice as hard and dig Fascism a grave in front of Leningrad.'

No one was exempt from what amounted to the conscription of a city. The NKVD ruthlessly combed Leningrad for 'volunteers'. Back-sliders were punished for 'desertion' and were 'expelled'. No excuses were tolerated.

The Russian talent for circumlocution matched that of Himmler and his cohorts; expulsion of course meant death.

But how was Leningrad to be fed?

The best chance of survival for the city lay with the 125-mile length of Lake Ladoga. If it would freeze, food supplies that had been marooned on the far side could be brought across the ice.

It was not quite such a perilous undertaking as might have been thought. Ice formation around Leningrad seldom began until mid-November and sometimes as late as January. Once it had formed, it was like an iron floor. A plan was evolved to build a road twenty to thirty miles long across the lake as soon as the ice could support the horses and sleighs.

There were numerous reconnaissances. Then the first convoy, stretching five miles and consisting of 350 drivers in horse-drawn sleighs, was on its way.

It was a macabre procession. The horses were so weak from lack of fodder that they could scarcely stagger. All they could manage to pull was two hundred pounds per sleigh. But the food that would reach Leningrad might make the difference between subsistence level and total starvation.

The operation did not just involve loading up supplies of food. It was necessary to provide service facilities on the ice: first-aid stations, traffic control points, snow-clearing detachments, bridge-layers. It was a miniature army on the move.

Neither were the Russians left alone to get on with the job. The Luftwaffe shelled and strafed. Even worse, the ice at certain points was not as thick as had been thought; drivers of the trucks suddenly saw cracks looming up ahead. When the operation was completed, the entire exercise was seen to be pitiably inadequate. Between 23 and 30 November 1941, only 800 tons of flour had been brought to Leningrad. The city needed 510 tons for the needs of a single day.

One Leningrader commented wryly: 'This way we will continue to starve – only a little more slowly.'

The end of the year came with somewhat brighter news from the military front. On 11 November, Zhdanov learnt in Moscow that a new offensive was in prospect. There was to be a fresh push towards Mga to the east which was held by the enemy and was a key point on the railway leading to the city.

The people of Leningrad dared to hope: Army Group North would be annihilated and food would then flow in abundance across the river.

It all looked marvellous on the map. Statistics of the strength of both sides looked favourable. But statistics took no account of the fact that troops cannot fight on empty bellies. If food could not get through, neither could arms. Mga remained in German hands.

As for the ice road, it proved at first to be a sad delusion as a possible salvation. The city needed a minimum of 1,000 tons of food supplies a day. The road could carry only about 360.

A report on 1 January 1942 was simple and blunt: the city was starving.

The authors of the city's official history wrote:

'Never had Leningrad lived through such tragic days. Rarely did smoke show in the factory chimneys. The trams had halted and thousands of people made their way on foot through the deep drifts of the squares and boulevards. In the dark apartments those who were not working warmed themselves for an hour or so before their makeshift iron stoves and slept in their coats and scarves, covered with their warmest things.

'In the evening, the city sank into impenetrable darkness. Only the occasional flicker of fires and the red flash of exploding artillery shells lighted the gloom of the vast factories and apartment blocks. The great organism of the city was almost without life, and hunger more and more strongly made itself known.'

What made the ice road come into its own eventually was not successful organisation nor even the failure of the Luftwaffe to keep up its heavy bombing of the columns. The greatest ally of those who ran the road across Lake Ladoga was the mounting death rate in Leningrad.

Quite simply, the level of mortality was modifying the needs of the city. In November 1942, 11,085 people died of hunger. In December, the figure had climbed to 52,881. By the following January, when the siege was lifted, deaths were found to be rising to between 3,500 and 4,000 a day.

Eventually, it was relentless Russian harassment of German forces which gave the city a series of reprieves. Generalfeldmarshall Manstein was rushed to Leningrad to take command of Army Group North but found himself grappling with the Russians at Volkhov in the east; the heat was briefly off Leningrad.

The forces of resistance inside the city were matched with partisan strength in the surrounding districts. The 1943 Soviet offensive threw some of the German commanders into near-panic. The search was on for desperately needed supplies of arms, known to be in partisan hands.

In the thickly forested area of Pskov, the German Commandant hung notices ordering the handover of weapons, while the partisans moved with silent expertise from one village to another, often covering up to twenty miles on a single march. The Luftwaffe strafed their columns.

A group near Pskov, struggling under the weight of their wounded, carried on a running battle with Wehrmacht whose numbers were swollen by various garrison reinforcements. But the partisans knew the country better; they melted into the forests, eventually doubling back to their old base, weaving their way through the ambush positions of bushes and ditches.

Soon, however, the pursuing Germans had picked up the trail anew.

Fresh partisan legends were born that day as Ivan Tssivunin, group commander, and Alexei Klimov, a mortar-gunner, found themselves isolated with a small force.

The barrage of fire into the German columns continued relentlessly. Then Tssivunin's legs buckled in agony. He continued firing from the ground until there was only one bullet left. Klimov just had time to see his superior turn the weapon on himself. Then he prised the pin off one grenade and flung it into the advancing knot of Germans.

The final grenade he kept for himself.

Partisan warfare in the Soviet Union inevitably lacked the sophistication of the armoured clout of the Red Army. But it spread its own highly effective form of terror: the knowledge that the enemy was not confined to the battlefield but might be encountered anywhere.

Partisans even managed to tap the German telephone system. Officers demanding to speak, for example, to Generalfeldmarschall Manstein, were brave men indeed if they were not frozen in horror on hearing a reply in bad German: 'Manstein? Manstein kaputt. Germans kaputt. Soon you kaputt.'

While fighting on the eastern front was at its most bitter, Soviet propaganda gave partisans a patina of movie star glamour.

In fact, most of them, often poorly equipped, badly fed and living in hideous conditions, were loved by few and hated by many. And not just by the Germans. They extorted supplies from the villagers and were especially feared by those who only wanted to carry on living, even under Nazi occupation.

And their rewards? Soviet partisans received few. Once the war was over, all the credit was lavished on the victorious Red Army, who alone, it was said, had annihilated the fascist beast. Few former partisans allowed themselves to feel resentful once the war was over. At least, not publicly. The NKVD did not disappear with liberation.

At the time it did not matter. By 27 January 1944, the Germans had been driven more than fifty miles from Leningrad.

And the partisans? Their exploits had the added advantage of proving highly infectious. Elsewhere in the subjugated east, resistance was on the loose.

12

Sturmbannfuehrer Hermann Hoefle delivered his devastating news to the Judenrat in Warsaw on the morning of 22 July 1942.

Blandly, he told the assembled elders: 'All Jews living in Warsaw, regardless of age or sex are to hold themselves in readiness for resettlement in the east.'

What followed was one of the most appalling acts of the holocaust. Jews were despatched to the extermination camp at Treblinka at a rate which has been put at 5,000 to 6,000 per day; altogether not less than 450,000, it has been estimated, perished in Treblinka.

It was a model deportation exercise and Hoefle had every reason for self-congratulation. Unfortunately, however, Heinrich Himmler did not regard the exercise as a success. The Reichsfuehrer, in any case, was not the sort of man to hand out congratulations to an underling. He merely studied his beloved files and pointed out icily that, six months after the deportations had begun, some sixty thousand Jews were still alive.

Himmler reasoned that this was a matter in which he must exercise his interest personally. Early in January, a visit to the Warsaw ghetto demonstrated that matters were still not progressing fast enough. Plainly something more drastic was called for: the Jews must be rooted out of the ghetto by force.

Himmler's most senior subordinate in Warsaw was SS-Oberfuehrer Ferdinand von Sammern-Frankenegg. The Reichsfuehrer drafted in as Sammern-Frankenegg's assistant a police veteran serving in Greece, SS-Brigadefuehrer Juergen Stroop.

Himmler told both men bluntly: 'The Fuehrer's birthday is on 20 April. I want to give him a present - a *Judenrein* Warsaw.'

To make Warsaw 'clean of Jews', the Germans could muster a force of 2,842, plus an additional 7,000 members of the SS and auxiliary police who were brought to the non-Jewish sectors of the city.

As for the Jews, they fully recognised that resistance was unlikely to be successful against forces equipped with the most modern weapons and led by trained military personnel.

Emmanuel Ringelblum, one of the prominent Jews in Warsaw that day, spoke for them all when he declared: 'We realised that this was a struggle between a fly and an elephant. But their natural dignity dictated that the Jews must offer resistance and not allow themselves to be led to the wanton slaughter.'

On Sunday, 18 April 1943, the SS representatives and the chiefs of police held a conference. The plan for the ghetto attack was outlined. It was to be unleashed at dawn. By 2 p.m., mobilisation orders had been given out.

The Polish Blue police were told that by early evening they were to throw a cordon of steel around the entire ghetto. The key resistance unit, ZOB (Zydowska Organizacja Bojowa, the Jewish combat organisation) called a swift meeting to review tactics.

Doors of houses and entrances to streets were barricaded with furniture. Sandbags and pillows were placed on window sills for support and protection of snipers. It so happened that it was Passover night and more Jews living on the Aryan side were pouring in for Seder, the first night ritual.

By 2 a.m., the Polish Blue police presence around the ghetto had been buttressed by German police units and SS auxiliary formations consisting of Letts and Ukrainians. Every twenty-five feet stood a guard armed with a heavy machine-gun. Soon the various groups were marching in single file directly into the ghetto.

It must have seemed a puzzling place, a veritable city of the dead. For not a single Jew was abroad that night. But as the henchmen of Sammern-Frankenegg and Juergen Stroop penetrated even deeper into the ghetto they could be in no doubt that preparations were well ahead for resistance. At certain conspicuous places, banners had been hung out, including at least one with a proud five-pointed star. And on the walls of houses bordering the Aryan side were slogans calling on the Polish population to pitch in with their support.

Sammern-Frankenegg was anxious to attack the central ghetto first, reasoning that when other Jews saw how it was being put out of action, they would meekly surrender. On Monday, 19 April, the central ghetto was attacked.

The Lett-Ukrainians were sent in first, immediately followed by the Ordnungsdienst, the Jewish ghetto police.

It was not cowardice that made the Germans hang back. Sammern-Frankenegg had always been doubtful that when it came to the point Jew could absolutely be depended upon to shoot Jew. It was an instinct that proved correct: conscience-stricken police attempted to turn back at the very mouth of the ghetto. The SS mowed them down where they stood.

Over the prone bodies went the motor-cycles, the heavy trucks, panzer vehicles, infantry, heavy machine-guns, ambulances, field kitchen and field telephones. Behind all this ironmongery, the German and Ukrainian columns moved forward.

Their progress did not long go unchecked. The fighters of the ghetto were hidden behind windows, balconies and attics. Beside them were stores of Molotov cocktails, hand grenades, several pistols and one light machine-gun.

The Poles let the columns go a comfortable way into the ghetto. Then the Jews let loose with everything they had. The sudden onslaught caught the Germans entirely by surprise. Mounting panic turned into a riot as the armoury of the ghetto crashed into the invaders. All at once, the forces of Sammern-Frankenegg turned and ran, stumbling over the astonishingly large number of bodies littering the streets and sidewalks.

The effect on the hidden warriors of the ghetto was electric. Now they were leaping out of their homes, yelling in triumph and pursuing the fleeing Germans, their pistols spitting defiance all the way.

Something like incredulity gripped Sammern-Frankenegg as the news reached him at his headquarters. This emotion was followed by fear; the consequences of Himmler hearing of so disgraceful an episode would not bear thinking about.

Sammern-Frankenegg realised that he must act quickly. In

went reinforcements, but no one was going to make the mistake of trying a slow progress into the ghetto for a second time. There must be an all-out commando attack: troops would have to go in at lightning speed and shoot from the hip. Furthermore, all weapons would have to be emptied directly into the houses.

But the Jews were relishing the taste of blood. They held their ground; the Germans tumbled away to cover. Soon the victors were in the streets, wishing one another *mazeltov* (good luck) and hastily stripping off the uniforms from the German corpses and helping themselves in the process to helmets and weapons.

To Juergen Stroop fell the task of writing in a highly embarrassing report:

> 'At our penetration into the ghetto, the Jews and the Polish bandits succeeded, with arms in hand, in repulsing our attacking forces, including the tanks and panzers.'

News of the Jewish triumph spread to other parts of the ghetto. When the Germans were foolish enough to launch similar attacks there, the response was precisely the same. There was ignominious retreat under a hail of grenades and bullets and Molotov cocktails.

The Jews and the Poles were not the only threats to the Nazis. Letts and Ukrainians now regarded the Jews with something approaching sheer terror. And in their funk they turned upon the German contingents in a screaming but vain attempt to claw their way out of the ghetto.

The result was inevitable. The SS, whips in hand, drove the mutineers back to their positions to man the guns.

Tense, nervous and bewildered, officers began to re-group their scattered formations. The Jews did not, however, allow them the luxury of completing the task and there was a further retreat.

Sammern-Frankenegg reasoned that, since troops were not able to subdue the impudent 'bandits', then tanks must be sent in to do the job. They fared little better. At the very appearance of a tank, it was immobilised by several well-aimed Molotov cocktails and set on fire.

From ZOB came the report:

'The well-aimed bottles hit the tank. The flames spread quickly. The blast of the explosion is heard. The machine stands motionless. The crew is burnt alive. The other two tanks turn around and withdraw. The Germans who took cover behind them withdraw in panic. We take leave of them with a few well-aimed shots and grenades.'

And an eyewitness described the confusion in the German ranks:

'There runs a German soldier shrieking like a madman, his helmet on fire. Another one shouts madly, *"Juden . . . Waffen . . . Juden . . . Waffen!"*'

German losses of twelve men were, in the circumstances, small. But the Jews had fared even better: just one man had been killed.

Sammern-Frankenegg was reduced to stuttering imbecility. To Stroop he stammered that the only possible course left was to fly in waves of bombers from Cracow.

Stroop realised that if such action was followed, it would put paid to his own life as well as that of his frankly incompetent commander. If those attacking the ghetto had to rely on the Luftwaffe to subdue a few Jews, then the only course would be a swift pistol to the head. The forces given the job of wiping out the Jews would become a laughing stock.

Stroop decided to act on his own. Coldly, he told Sammern-Frankenegg: 'You have plainly lost your grip. I shall take command myself. You are dismissed forthwith.'

Sammern-Frankenegg had made the mistake of not returning to individual scenes of resistance, but of abandoning one section of the ghetto when the opposition proved too hot. Stroop was determined to punch holes at one section of resistance at a time and not to go into the next until the first objective had been achieved.

From now on those broaching the ghetto were to fan out and hug the buildings as they moved forward, under cover of artillery fire as if they were all on a battlefield.

When the forces went in under their new commander, the pattern of retaliation was the same. But light weapons were no match for an artillery bombardment. In any case, supplies within the ghetto were running out.

Static positions, maintained up till now, became impossible. The Jewish fighters changed positions by crossing through the attics from one house to another, hurling their grenades as they went.

Stroop introduced air attack; the Jews were soon forced to vacate bombed buildings. The only way that the combat organisation could match this move was to order the destruction of warehouses in the ghetto which had been taken over by the Germans.

Soon a whole succession of burnings coursed through the ghetto area. A Polish underground newspaper reported: 'The remaining Jews are dying with weapons in hand, first destroying the warehouses full of valuables and burning down the factories.'

Stroop's revenge was appalling. The ghetto hospital was bombarded and set on fire. Into the burning wards poured the German troops, dragging defenceless patients from their beds and tossing them into the flames. The heads of infants were smashed against walls; pregnant women were attacked with bayonets. Most of the hospital staff perished in the flames.

An ultimatum from the Germans proclaimed that unless the fighters laid down their arms by the next day, the ghetto would be razed to the ground. It was contemptuously rejected.

The firing of buildings was stepped up. The fighting groups clambered on blazing and charred roofs, running from corner to corner and from roof to roof until the machine-guns compelled them to melt back into the shadows.

Stroop had put all the responsibility for the failure of the ghetto incursion on the shoulders of the wretched Sammern-Frankenegg, but so far he was only too conscious that he had failed to do much better. What was it Himmler had said? 'The ghetto is partisan territory. Comb it out with ruthless tenacity.' The Reichsfuehrer-SS would want results. And soon.

In one particular, Himmler had been nothing less than correct. The ghetto *was* partisan territory.

Mordechai Anielewicz, commander of the resistance forces

within the ghetto, smuggled out a letter of 23 April to Yitzchok Zukerman, his representative on the Aryan side:

'Beginning with tonight, we are adopting the tactic of partisan warfare. Tonight three fighting units will go out into the combat area. They will have two tasks: armed reconnaissance and the capture of weapons. Bear in mind that small arms have absolutely no value to us today. We rarely use them. What we are terribly in need of are grenades, rifles, machine-guns and explosives.'

On the very day of Anielewicz's letter, Stroop had reported to his superiors: 'The action will be completed this very day.'

He was wrong. The defiance of ZOB blazed as furiously as ever. On 23 April, there appeared on the Aryan side of Warsaw a rallying poster for the entire population:

'For Our and Your Freedom!
'Poles, Citizens, Soldiers of Liberty!'

'Amidst the booming guns with which the Germans bombarded our houses, the homes of our mothers, women and children; amidst the rattle of machine-guns which we have captured from the gendarmes and SS men; amidst the smoke and fire and blood of the Warsaw ghetto we appeal to you, we, the prisoners of the ghetto, and we send you our brotherly greetings. We know that you are following with anguish and tears, with admiration and anxiety the outcome of the struggle we have been waging for the past several days with the invader.

'You have seen and will see that every doorstep in the ghetto is and will continue to be a fortress. We may all perish in the struggle but we shall not surrender. Like you, we are seething with the passionate desire to avenge all the crimes committed by our common enemy.

'It is a struggle for our and your freedom.

'For our and your human, social and national honour.

'We shall avenge Auschwitz, Treblinka, Belzek and Majdanek.

'Long live the brotherhood of weapons and blood of fighting Poland!

'Long live freedom!

'Death to the murderous and criminal occupants!

'Long live the life and death struggle against the German occupant!
THE JEWISH COMBAT ORGANISATION.'

For the new partisan offensive, Jewish fighters were sent out at night in groups of ten. Most of them wore captured German uniforms and helmets. Rags were tied around feet to muffle sound. The object was to reconnoitre for weapons and food, to ambush the enemy and attack patrols from behind.

On 25 April came a shambles. A reconnaissance group had penetrated to the Aryan side, where it was hoped extra reinforcements might be found. But the group ran straight into a German patrol. Fighting was brief and bloody; all but one of the Jews were killed. A seriously wounded survivor managed to make his way back to bunker headquarters and report the disaster.

The switch to partisan warfare meant inevitably that more conventional forms of defence had to be neglected. The Germans pressed their advantage; the area of the ghetto still in Jewish hands grew progressively smaller.

Another attempt was made to reach the Aryan side on 29 April, this time through the sewers. It ended in tragedy. The Germans had learned of a previous group that had surfaced successfully. All manholes were surrounded. The exhausted fighters who emerged found themselves face-to-face with the waiting Germans. The Jews had no stomach for the fight that followed.

The Germans were not the only enemy to threaten the fighters of the ghetto. In his book *The Warsaw Ghetto Uprising*, Professor Ber Mark wrote:

'. . . The role of the Polish police was generally a shameful one. It was particularly so during the uprising. Polish police hunted down Jews who were hiding on the Aryan side, blackmailed them, squeezed large sums of money from their victims and then handed them over to the Gestapo. They robbed and tortured Jewish food smugglers at the ghetto gates . . .

'Side by side with the Polish police, bands of civilian blackmailers, the so-called *szmalcovniki*, exploited the Jewish tragedy. They lay in wait at the ghetto gates and pounced on the despairing escapees from the conflagration and the German bullets. They pursued them, robbed them, and drove them back into the burning ghetto . . .

'Squeezing money out of Jews, putting fear into their hearts, giving them no rest, driving them out of their hiding places, collaborating with the Nazis in their hatred of the Jews, all this became a new source of income, a kind of sport for the "golden" youth, hypocritical fanatics, a part of the middle class who was eager to take over the commercial establishments left by the annihilated Jews, and even members of the professions. But at the head of them all was the Polish police with its arrogance and greed.'

The main benefit of partisan tactics was the ability to surprise, to swoop down in German uniforms in some dark alley. But there came a body blow to threaten the future of any further form of resistance.

The headquarters of ZOB was a gigantic bunker which served as a hiding place for three hundred civilian non-combatants and eighty members of the Jewish resistance. Here Mordechai Anielewicz laid plans and organised his contacts with the world outside. The bunker, the very nerve centre of resistance, was betrayed to the SS by informers.

The civilian population surrendered meekly enough, just before grenades were tossed in, and then came the hissing pipes of gas. Some choked to death, others turned their pistols on themselves. German reports spoke later of hearing Jewish songs before the last men were dead. Anielewicz fell with the rest.

By a miracle, a small group of ghetto fighters had managed to slip out of the bunker in the initial confusion. Since the Jews were badly crippled by the gas and totally incapable of resistance, their comrades decided to ferry them quickly out of the ghetto area. It meant a nightmare expedition through the filthy stinking water of the Warsaw sewers. Those who had been gassed were incapable of carrying weapons and had them tied around their necks by their comrades. Resistance fighters heaved the injured on to their backs; the march through the hell of the sewers lasted thirty hours. Through the yellow, cloying reek, after hours which they could not begin to calculate, the party heard an echoing explosion.

160

Its cause was not in doubt; manhole covers were being blown open. But by Jews or Germans?

Only when they had been led groping to the waiting trucks and the filth had been washed out of their eyes, did survivors from the Warsaw bunker recognise their rescuers as their own comrades. The Lomianka forest outside Warsaw was to provide a brief refuge.

But by no means for all. The trucks could not accommodate more than thirty of the survivors. Two journeys were necessary; those who were left behind in the sewers settled down to wait. This period seemed even more agonising than the previous thirty hours. The lack of air in the sewers made lungs feel as if they had been stuffed with explosives. Why was the truck taking so long to return?

The remaining Jews bore it for as long as they could. When their patience was exhausted, they clambered out of the sewers. The SS and their Ukrainian auxiliaries had waited willingly enough in the clean air above. They opened fire. There were no survivors among the Jews.

By the 25th day of the uprising, Stroop had given the order for the ghetto in Warsaw to be razed to the ground.

But the Germans were not getting things their own way. Word had reached the Soviet Union about the destruction of the ghetto: Russian bombers swooped in now to attack German positions, guided by the numerous fires.

The air attack lasted from midnight to 2 a.m. Several Jewish fighting groups regarded the intervention as a godsend. In the confusion they attempted to quit the ghetto, but the effects of the breakout were negligible.

By now the ghetto was a great grey ghost of charred ash. Stroop was able to report: 'The Warsaw Ghetto is no more.'

Yet as late as 31 May, Hans Frank had to admit that he 'was informed by the security police at Warsaw that the Jews were continuing their attacks and assassinations'. It was also declared that Hitler was taking a close interest in the fate of the ghetto and had personally ordered that bombardment was to continue until final capitulation.

It took a long time. Up until the following September, there were still reports that Jewish fighters, weapons in their hands, managed to slip past German guards to the Aryan side, leaving behind them a desert wrapped in total silence.

But not quite. Occasionally that silence would be broken by shots ringing out when some pitiable skeletal figure emerged from the rubble in search of food. Sometimes the shots were from his own weapon. More often than not, the weakened figure fell victim to the bullets of Stroop's men. The ghetto rebellion, the first major civilian revolt against the German forces in all of occupied Europe, was over.

Individual Jews hiding in ghetto caves somehow managed to survive until the whole of Warsaw, Jew and Gentile, rose up in two months of bloody insurrection from August 1944.

Jurgen Stroop, who in September 1951 was brought back to Warsaw and hanged for the murders in the Warsaw ghetto, put the number of Jews who perished at 56,065.

There is no reason to doubt so precise a figure. Stroop's report to his superiors, carrying the inscription: 'The Warsaw Ghetto No Longer Exists', was a document of scrupulous accuracy, complete with photographs and bound in the finest leather. It was a day-by-day account of the mass slaughter, and it survived to be produced at the Nuremberg trials.

A heroic failure? A futile act of resistance that could have had only one outcome? Whatever views there were on the ghetto uprising, one effect at least was positive.

Zydowska Organizacja Bojowa lit a fuse that ignited far beyond Warsaw. Uprisings erupted in Vilna, Cracow, Lodz and other Polish cities.

Indeed, as the military situation deteriorated steadily on more German fronts, there were indications that resistance to Nazism was becoming positively contagious.

13

The hand-picked contingent of sappers racing towards Sobibor in eastern Poland carried specific and urgent instructions from Reichsfuehrer-SS Heinrich Himmler.

The entire camp complex was to be razed to the ground, all buildings and watchtowers dynamited, and the diesel motors that propelled the gas for extermination were to be ground to powder, along with the remains of the camp victims.

It was an order which must have galled Himmler. Only just over a year before, on 8 May 1942, he himself had personally picked out the very small, obscure railway station situated between Wlodawa and Chelm as a suitable site for a death factory.

Sobibor had barely been allowed to operate at full efficiency. There had been a time when transports had arrived daily, carrying between 1,500 and 2,000 Jews from Poland, Czechoslovakia and the countries of western Europe. But now, due largely to a highly organised revolt by the inmates, it had been necessary to abandon the camp totally.

In happier days, it would have been possible to contain such an uprising, but now things were far from happy for Hitler's Reich.

It was October 1943. The seemingly invincible German army had suffered terrible defeats. And now those incarcerated in the centres of extermination had caught the mood and risen against their oppressors.

At Sobibor, insurrection was masterminded by a Red Army junior officer, Alexander Pechersky, who had originally been taken prisoner and sent to a punishment battalion in Borisov and from thence to Minsk, which turned out to be merely a half-way house to the horrors of Sobibor.

Pechersky later recalled:

'I had contracted typhus which in normal circumstances would have meant instant death at the hands of the Germans. But I managed to conceal the disease successfully. From that moment on, I had faith in my own survival.'

A daring escape plan evolved from Pechersky's carefully nurtured friendship with a fellow inmate of Sobibor, a jovial tailor named Baruch. A common interest in chess did not excite the suspicion of the guards; the two men talked freely whenever they were able to snatch a game.

Pechersky, of course, recognised the risk. The tailor, for all his joviality, could be a stool-pigeon for the Gestapo. Recently, however, a traitor had been discovered in the camp and the other inmates had beaten him into a pulp before stringing him up in the exercise yard, so there was probably less enthusiasm for siding with the Germans.

The soldier kept his voice deliberately casual: 'Do you know of any *useful*' – the word was gently stressed – 'shoemakers, furniture-makers and tailors?'

Baruch's reply had been prompt: 'Of course, I'll supply you anything you want.'

Pechersky decided to say no more for the moment; he merely contented himself with checkmating Baruch.

The cabinet-makers' shop in the camp became eventually the centre of resistance. A knot of camp craftsmen seemed sufficiently trustworthy to carry out what was sure to be thoroughly dangerous work.

At least one inmate present at a key meeting became an immediate object of hostility. A certain Brzecki was a privileged prisoner who was given to strutting around the camp as if he owned it, a whip forever in his hand. Among the women, he was detested and feared; he was always badgering the younger girls until they yielded to him.

None of this concerned Pechersky over-much. What mattered was that Brzecki had never been known to inform on anyone to the Germans.

Nevertheless Pechersky tested the man and asked him unexpectedly: 'Tell me, would you kill a German?'

Brzecki turned pale and bit his lip. Then he answered: 'If necessary, yes.'

'And supposing it was not vital. Supposing you were asked to kill them wantonly, just as they killed thousands of our brothers and sisters. Could you do it then?'

Brzecki had been thunderstruck, mumbling: 'Don't know. It's hard to tell. I have never given it much thought.'

The other man had considered the conversation encouraging. He reasoned that if the man had been a traitor he would have agreed to anything. In any case, co-operation with a privileged prisoner – a kapo – was vital to his plan.

Now Brzecki stood before a gathering of conspirators, conscious of hostile eyes. Pechersky looked at him coldly: 'We have decided to invite you to our meeting. The mere fact that you have come here at all has compromised you.

'Even so, if you betray us, we shall kill you. Is that understood?'

Brzecki understood only too well. All night he had pondered the problem. It was true that the camp commandant had assured the kapos that they would be spared, once the camp was liquidated after the war was won. Brzecki was not over-gifted with imagination but he had solid common sense: all the signs were that things were going badly for Germany. He had no doubt that his ultimate fate would be the same as all the others.

Now he contented himself with replying to the resistance cell: 'I understand. You needn't worry.'

Pechersky began to speak. He declared: 'My plan is to kill the officer group which administers this camp. Unless we do this quickly and ruthlessly and without a sound, we haven't a hope of getting out. I shall pick the killers myself.'

He turned to Brzecki. 'At 3.30 in the afternoon you will, on some pretext, take some men I shall indicate to Camp Two. These men will kill the Germans they find there. Baruch will see that the officers come individually into the room, where it will be possible to carry out the executions. Baruch must also see that from the moment that the executions begin no one must be allowed to leave the camp. If anyone tries to create trouble they must be silenced or killed. The operation must be completed by four o'clock.'

He then went on to outline plans to sever the telephone wires connecting Camp Two with the guard reserves. The wires would be cut at both ends and hidden so that repair would be delayed.

Unemotionally, Pechersky continued: 'The killing of the officers will then start. They will be invited individually to the workshops. Two people will carry out the executions. Within half an hour it will be all over.'

By then Brzecki and another kapo, Janek, would be lining up the inmates as though they were going out to work normally.

In the front row would be the members of the resistance with the job of attacking the weapons arsenal. The rest would seize the weapons, despatch the guards at the gate and turn their attention to the watchtower.

Pechersky added: 'If they open up we'll fire back and kill as many as possible.'

After the meeting broke up, Pechersky went up to the attic

of the cabinet-makers' shop, where he had a good view of the area on the other side of the fence. He noted that to the left of the camp gates was the railway and behind it the station and then the woods. To the right, some five hundred yards away, were more woods. Wooden blocks were scattered on the road; Poles were transporting them. To the right seemed to be the most sensible point of escape.

The following day, 14 October, was scheduled for the breakout.

That night, knives and small hatchets made to order by the camp blacksmith were distributed to Pechersky's men, together with warm clothing.

The plan was that the wire perimeter fence of the camp would be hacked through, near the officers' house. The escapees would hurl stones, which would cause some of the signal mines placed there to explode and allow a free passage.

Soon all was ready for the first victim.

Unterscharfuehrer Ernst Berg was looking forward particularly to the smart new uniform he had ordered, and he was always demanding to know when Juzef, the tailor, would want to carry out the first fitting. Now the message had come. Eagerly, Berg rode over to the tailor's shop, dismounted from his horse and went in with all the eagerness of a schoolboy receiving his first blazer.

Juzef came forward to receive him. To the intense relief of the other two men in the room, the German's first act was to remove his belt, together with his holster and pistol and lay them on the table. Then he started to take off his jacket. No one dared look down at the base of the table leg, where the hatchet, wrapped in a shirt, was resting.

Juzef was deferential. 'If the Unterscharfuehrer would have the goodness to turn round so that the light falls on his back. It will make the fitting easier . . .'

One of the plotters, Shubayev, moved behind the unsuspecting Berg. He brought the hatchet up above his head and slammed it down into the German's skull.

Berg let out a sharp scream. For a moment, the killers were unnerved as the horse started whinnying. One more blow was necessary. Then the body was quickly hauled under the bed in the corner and covered up. Swiftly, the spreading blood-stains were removed.

Oberscharfuehrer Erbert Helm was the next to enter the tailor's shop. The killing was swift and clean.

The chief of Camp Three, Oberscharfuehrer Goettinger was in a thoroughly sunny mood when he came to collect his shoes. He did not so much as glance at the man intent on repairing a stool in the corner. He was only concerned with the shoemaker, Jakub.

'Are my boots ready?' he queried.

Blandly, the shoemaker handed him the pair and invited: 'Try them on.'

Goettinger was rasping all their nerves with his flow of talk. 'Five days from now, Jakub,' he babbled, 'I shall be back in Germany. I shall expect you to have made a pair of slippers for my wife.'

Jakub murmured smoothly: 'I hope your wife will be satisfied.'

By then the stool-mender had crept up behind Goettinger. Soon the body was being dragged into a corner and covered with rags. Sand was scattered over the spreading pool of blood.

Oberscharfuehrer Greischutz was the next at the shop, for the uniform he had ordered . . .

More of Pechersky's band were now scurrying around the dead men's quarters looking for cartridges for the pistols they had taken from the bodies. It had been necessary to kill two more of the camp guards, notably one who had obviously become suspicious and entered a garage with his automatic drawn. One of the conspirators who had been working there had killed him with a single blow.

Time was getting on. Brzecki and Janek were due to march out the working party, fronted by some seventy Russians hand-picked by Pechersky.

Then all at once they were there, streaming out towards the exit. It had been neither possible nor desirable to involve all the inmates in the escape bid, but somehow everyone had a feeling of expectancy. The party moved forward swiftly.

Then came an unlooked-for interruption. The watchtower commander was inquisitive. He shouted: 'Hey, you sons-of-bitches, stop jostling. Get into line.'

Pechersky did not need to say anything. Several hatchets were simultaneously uncovered from undercoats. The butchery was messy; its effect looked like being disastrous to the escapers.

A shrill scream went up from women prisoners who witnessed the German being cut to ribbons. There was a sudden feeling of panic.

Pechersky shouted: 'Comrades, foward!'

The shout was taken up. As Pechersky later stated: 'Six hundred pain-wracked, tormented people, surged forward with a wild "hurrah" to life and freedom.'

In fact, it was not quite as simple as that. The attack on the weapons arsenal was a total failure. Guards let loose a burst of automatic fire, but the crowd kept on moving. Forward they surged, snatching weapons from the guards and trampling them underfoot. Stones and sand were hurled as the once seemingly disciplined working party poured through the central exit and made for the woods.

There were inevitable tragedies. Some men veered off to the left and straight into the minefield.

Pechersky and others hared towards the officers' house, forcing a passageway through the wire fence. The field behind was not mined, but the guards were there too, raking bullets into the fleeing prisoners. For those who escaped, there was the welcome shadow of the woods beyond.

Pechersky had given orders that there was to be no stopping in the woods and Soviet Jews would make their way as far to the east as they could reach.

For some time, the cacophony of rifle and automatic fire continued. But there was little that could be done by the remaining Germans in Sobibor. Robbed of their camp leaders, they were for a while bewildered as to just what had happened – which of course had been Alexander Pechersky's object. Telephone connections had been cut and it was impossible to order reinforcements. Then gradually the shooting died away.

Discipline among those escaping became rigid. Instructions had been given that there was to be no smoking, talking, lagging behind or running ahead of the party. Pechersky alone strode out in front, telling the rest that if he dropped to the ground, they were to do the same.

The group now numbered fifty-seven of the original seventy. Ahead of the party was a broad open stretch of land, sparsely covered with shrubs. It was soon the edge of dawn and it was clear that there was still to be no rest.

To remain in a single knot would invite detection, particularly from the air. A decision was made to fan out. The presence of a railway line was scarcely reassuring, and with the final advent of day came a light drizzle. Camouflaged lookouts were placed among the escapees and changed every few hours. Aircraft roamed overhead, and those near the railway line could hear the voices of workers.

Pechersky's plan was to attempt a crossing of the river Bug. At nightfall, the lookouts spotted two figures. They were moving cautiously as if to avoid detection, suggesting they were not Germans.

The two men had somehow become detached from the escaping party. There was a moment of joyful reunion, but the mood was short-lived. The couple had made their way to a small village not far from the river, but they soon found out that the area was stiff with Germans. All crossings were guarded heavily.

Pechersky took the decision. There must be a breaking up into even smaller groups, each of which would have to try its luck individually. Pechersky took nine men and they moved forward. In the scattered villages they were among friends. Food was gladly given and, even more vital, intelligence on enemy movement. The Germans, it was learnt, had launched a massive dragnet.

In some villages, the escapers met only fear; there was the ever-present spectre of reprisals from the enemy should any help be offered.

The young son of one family from a hamlet a mere mile and a half from the river offered to guide the party to a likely bank.

On the night of 19-20 October 1943, Pechersky and his companions were once again on Soviet soil. Pechersky later wrote: 'Although these parts were still occupied by the Germans, the air it seemed to us, was different here; it was fresher. And the roads, the trees, the sky were more familiar, more friendly.'

Three days later, the survivors met up with the partisan unit Voroshilov. For Alexander Pechersky, a new phase of the war was about to begin.

The Sobibor revolt secured an honoured place in the history of resistance by concentration camp inmates in the east. All six hundred had made the break for freedom during Pechersky's revolt and following it. About four hundred managed to break out, but half were destroyed by land mines, pursuing aircraft and the murder squads of SS and troops.

As a direct result of the Sobibor breakout, Himmler ordered the complete destruction of the camp. A death factory which had already claimed the lives of more than 600,000 Jews ceased to exist.

The rebels had killed ten of the SS. Thirty-eight Ukrainian guards working for the Germans were also despatched. Those that survived fled in a desperate bid to escape the vengeance of the NKVD.

Sobibor, as it turned out, was by no means the only centre of resistance in concentration camps with which Himmler had to contend.

14

The name of Treblinka does not excite quite the same thrill of horror as does the very mention of Dachau, Auschwitz and Belsen, yet what had been a small particularly unknown railway station near the town of Sokolow, about fifty miles north-east of Warsaw, has its firm place in the grisly history of Nazi extermination. Treblinka, too, as it happened, became a centre of heroic resistance by its inmates, who had been despatched there in sealed transports from Austria, Greece, Yugoslavia, Czechoslovakia, Poland and various parts of occupied Soviet territory.

Treblinka, a one-mile-square wooded clearing, was the second largest extermination camp after Auschwitz; 800,000 Jews perished there. And few members of the organised resistance within the camp survived.

When he first arrived, Samuel Rajzman felt a surge of

resentment that somehow he had been chosen to live when so many of his Polish companions had gone straight to the gas chambers.

The pattern was familiar. The party of prisoners were led out of the train to a nearby square enclosed by a high fence made of pine and fir branches. It was impossible to see what was behind the fence.

Women were directed to the barracks on the left, while the men had been marshalled to the right. Everyone was ordered to undress and to deposit all their valuables and money which, they were assured, would be returned to them after the bath.

Rajzman recognised a friend from Warsaw, an engineer named Galewski. In cold anger, he saw Galewski plead with a knot of SS that recruits were badly needed for the workers' brigades. Rajzman was told to get dressed and then was ordered into a group busy carrying bundles of clothes to the storehouses.

He reasoned that death with his friends would have been preferable, because soon he was running the gauntlet of the camp guards and being beaten with heavy sticks. All those involved in carrying the clothes were soon reduced to pulp.

Within a few hours, Rajzman's face was a bluish mass, his eyes bloodshot. What, he wondered bitterly, was Galewski up to? Was the man a favourite of the SS with the power of life and death, or had he attempted to save his friend in a sudden spasm of humanity?

When the two men met up again, Rajzman poured out all his pent-up fury and resentment. Galewski listened silently. Then in the barest whisper, at the same time carrying an unmistakable note of command, the engineer replied: 'You must live. You are now a member of a secret organisation. We are planning an uprising and you must live.'

Galewski, Rajzman soon learnt, had been instructed by the resistance leader, Dr Julian Chorazyski, to recruit prisoners with particular talents for disruption. What was being planned was nothing less than the systematic destruction of the entire camp, along with some of its more gruesome apparatus.

Chorazyski was well aware that this was likely to be something of a suicide mission. Plans went ahead; a target had been set for 21 April 1943.

Then, two days before, came disaster. One of Treblinka's prize bullies, Untersturmfuehrer Franz, struck Chorazyski full in the face with a riding whip for neglecting to return a salute fast enough.

The Pole, stung with rage and pain, reached for a knife. A thoroughly frightened Franz screamed for reinforcements. Chorazyski knew that he had sealed his own fate. Swiftly he swallowed a poison capsule.

At a single stroke, the resistance within Treblinka had lost its leader; the planned uprising, which had hinged on being able to seize ammunition and arms from the camp arsenal, had to be postponed.

But the groundwork had already been done. Months before, a Jewish locksmith had been sent to repair the lock of the arsenal's armoured door. An imprint of the key was secured, a copy laboriously made. Now there was nothing to do but await another suitable opportunity.

It did not come until the following August. Then, with a new leader, the conspirators acted. A prisoner was smuggled into the arsenal building at a time when one of the Unterscharfuehrers, who lived in a room adjoining the arsenal, was out of the way in his own quarters.

Outside was a pile of debris and bricks. One of the group arrived with a cart, ostensibly to clear the rubble. Under it, twenty hand-grenades, twenty rifles and a number of revolvers primed with bullets lay waiting. They were hastily taken to a ditch where lime and gravel was kept for construction work.

Success or failure was in the hands of one man – a prisoner to whom the Germans had given the job of disinfecting the camp. Another prisoner had to work out a way of somehow getting petrol from the trucks and tanks in the camp garage. The plan entailed changing the supplies of disinfectant for something infinitely more inflammable.

The routine job of disinfection went ahead – right under the noses of unsuspecting camp guards.

At 3.45 p.m. on 2 August, the resistance group received the long awaited signal. Hand-grenades were hurled at the previously 'disinfected' objects.

It seemed to observers that day as if the whole camp erupted in one magnificent roar; the entire arsenal was ripped apart.

172

Yankel Wiernick, another conspirator who survived the Treblinka uprising, later recalled:

> 'We had prepared everything for this moment. We had home-made weapons with which to kill and buckets of spare petrol for starting a succession of fires. All these were to be used under the full gaze of the watchtowers, which were armed to the teeth. At every turn there were either Germans or armed Ukrainians working for them.
>
> 'Without any compunction we killed everyone in our way. In a matter of minutes everything was burning.'

Wiernick found himself grappling with a single Ukrainian. 'I was armed with an axe and a file and with these I killed him.'

Of the 750 inmates of Treblinka, 150 to 200 managed to escape. The Nazis hunted them down one by one. Eventually only about twelve managed to make contact with the Polish underground outside the camp. Samuel Rajzman's own account of the uprising was used in 1946 when he appeared as a witness at the International Military Tribunal in Nuremberg.

Apart from destroying totally the Treblinka arsenal, the uprising had another important effect: the outside world was informed of what had been going on in Treblinka. The Polish government-in-exile in London received a full report. There was ample time to compile evidence with which the surviving camp overseers would one day be confronted.

Rumours of the horrors of the camps in the east were slow to reach the Allies. Countries slogging to defeat the Axis armies on the battlefield had little time or indeed inclination to believe many of the lurid accounts of what went on in the killing grounds.

In Auschwitz, it fell to the camp resistance to supply the necessary evidence.

Jozef Cyrankiewicz survived World War II to become Prime Minister of Poland, but in 1942 he was merely Prisoner No. 62933 at Auschwitz. The Germans were unaware that he was also something else – a leader of the camp's underground. He had decided to give himself the task of providing stark documentary evidence that Auschwitz was the most notorious extermination centre of them all.

Words, however graphic, were unlikely to be enough. The west was being bombarded with descriptions of atrocities. Cyrankiewicz decided to go one better. He would produce photographs of the crematoria and somehow smuggle them out. To fulfil the assignment, he detailed a Polish Jew and ultimate Auschwitz survivor named David Szmulewski. But how was the job to be done? At the time of Szmulewski's arrival in March 1942, the camp was still being built. Rudolf Hoess could scarcely contain his impatience to expand accommodation for the unending flow of new prisoners.

Szmulewski had only been in Auschwitz a few days when his totally unexpected opportunity came. A contingent of SS stormed into the barracks, yelling: 'Stand up those of you who are roofers.'

He recalled: 'I had never done any roofing in my life, but something made me get to my feet.'

One of the SS snapped at him: 'All right. But you had better be good.'

Szmulewski managed to bluff his way through searching questions about his proficiency. Slowly, he realised the amazing change in his fortunes. As a prisoner with a special skill he was no longer immediately expendable. And there were other advantages. He now had a permit which enabled him to move about the camp unguarded – and that included the area of Birkenau with its gas chambers and crematoria.

A more valuable link between the various underground groups scattered about the vast Auschwitz complex could scarcely be imagined. His alleged skill as a roofer and his mobility made him ideal for the scheme already beginning to form in his mind.

Fortunately, obtaining a camera was the very least of his problems. The daily transports which Eichmann despatched to Auschwitz from all parts of Europe inevitably contained whatever valuables the victims were able to take with them. Among these were any amount of cameras.

As soon as the new arrivals were herded out of the freight cars, their possessions were taken away to be sorted, stored and eventually shipped off to the Reich. Auschwitz had some thirty warehouses bulging with confiscated articles; members of the underground made up the sorting staff. By far the most serious problem was how to get a camera into the crematorium compound.

This enclosure, whose smoke-belching chimneys were visible to the scores of prisoners within the Birkenau barracks, was under the separate administration of Oberscharfuehrer Moll, a one-eyed sadist holding sway of the Sonderkommando. These were Jewish prisoners, in this case Jewish male inmates, who were promised their lives with adequate food in return for the job of burning the bodies of prisoners. Every few months, they themselves were marched off to the gas chambers and replaced. The Germans, after all, wanted no witnesses.

But the tentacles of the underground reached even there.

Szmulewski outlined his scheme to the underground and to sympathetic cadres within the Sonderkommando. One of their number, it was decided, would damage the roof of the compound. But, clearly, before Szmulewski could get down to work a suitable camera had to be available. There could be no question of his carrying it; rigid inspection by the guards would put paid to that.

An elaborate plan was evolved. Members of the underground swiftly sketched out a detailed map of the crematorium. The Sonderkommando, it was noted, did not have their own cooking facilities; they were fed from the central camp kitchen. To prevent contact with other prisoners, even during mealtimes, black ersatz coffee and the thin, tasteless liquid which passed for soup were brought into the compound in vast kettles. One of these would be infinitely suitable for storing a camera.

Mysteriously, one of the kettles was missing. It was promptly secreted in the cistern of the prison lavatory. At night, under cover of his single blanket, Auschwitz's resident tinsmith set to work.

After the false bottom had been made, the kettle was kept full of water for twenty-four hours to make sure that it was completely watertight. The test was successful. The camera was slipped into the false bottom and the rogue kettle returned to the kitchen.

When the Sonderkommando detail turned up for the next assignment of rations there was a swift exchange of kettles. The one with the camera was filled and soon was on its way to the compound.

Now it was up to Szmulewski. There was no problem in getting past the guards, who evinced scant interest in his tools and tar. The odious myopic Oberscharfuehrer Moll was a more formidable proposition. Characteristically, the German was determined to extract the maximum unpleasantness from the encounter.

He growled at Szmulewski: 'Do you know where you are?'

'*Jawohl*, Herr Kommandant.'

'I want you to stay at your job like a dog chained to his post. If you move away from there for one minute you will not come out of here alive. Is that understood, you *Schweinhund*?'

'*Jawohl*, Herr Kommandant.'

It now remained to make sure that Moll was out of the way long enough for the next stage. Fortunately that did not prove too difficult. The German had to leave the compound several times a day to meet the new transports arriving at Birkenau.

The moment came when one of the Sonderkommando was able to slip Szmulewski the camera. By now, he might have been a conspirator all his life. He had even remembered to enlarge the middle buttonhole of his prisoner's jacket so that it was large enough to push the lens through while keeping the rest of the camera concealed.

Then he climbed onto the roof of the crematorium and got to work.

Szmulewski choked down feelings of professional satisfaction. The material on which he focussed his lens could, in its terrible way, scarcely have been bettered.

He was able to snap three shots unobserved. One was of a group of naked women on the way to the gas chamber, while the others were of gassed bodies being burnt in open pits which were supplementing the work of the four crematoria.

As soon as he had finished, Szmulewski removed the film from the camera, wrapped it in a piece of rag and stuck it in the tar he had brought for the roof repair.

The camera by now was a dangerous hazard; it was quickly buried in the camp grounds. But before that, of course, it had been necessary to carry out the repairs as convincingly as possible.

The film was eventually passed to Cyrankiewicz. It found

its way by secret courier to the Cracow underground for processing. The world had its first pictures of Nazi atrocities inside Auschwitz.

Auschwitz also had its heroines. Rosa Robota was just eighteen when, three days after the invasion of Poland, the Germans came to her home town of Ciechanow. She was swept speedily into Hashomer Hatzair, a Socialist-orientated Zionist group, flourishing in the Ciechanow ghetto from the moment of its creation.

In November 1942, came mass liquidation for the Jews of the town. Some were deported to Treblinka, Rosa and others were sent to Auschwitz. For Rosa's parents at least there could be no more suffering: they had gone straight from the ghetto to the gas chambers.

Rosa was put to work in the camp's clothing supply section, the *Bekleidungstelle*. Other Ciechanow girls were assigned to the munitions factory, one of the Krupp slave labour plants at Auschwitz, operating on shift around the clock. All lived in the Birkenau barracks.

Somehow, news of Rosa's previous membership of Hashomer Hatzair had reached the three hundred-strong Jewish section of the Auschwitz underground.

Contact was made swiftly by a member, Noah Zabladowicz. As soon as the two were alone he told Rosa: 'The underground are planning a general uprising. It will include the blowing up of the gas chamber and the crematorium installations. For this we must have explosives and explosive charges.'

Zabladowicz went on to explain that Israel Gutman and Joshua Leifer, two members of the underground working on the shift among the munitions, had been given the task of establishing contact with the Jewish girls in the Pulver-Pavilion, the explosive section.

He explained: 'It's a virtually impossible task. The girls are under constant surveillance. Any contact between them and other workers, especially the men, is strictly forbidden. We desperately need an intermediary in Birkenau.'

Before long, Rosa had some twenty girls smuggling dynamite and explosive charges out of the munitions factory. The dynamite was shaped cunningly to look like buttons, which were inserted into small matchboxes. The girls hid them in their brassières or in special pockets sewn into the hems of their dresses.

Then would begin an elaborate chain, the seemingly harmless 'buttons' being passed from hand-to-hand until they reached the man who had indisputably the most important role of all in the underground.

The Russian prisoner Borodin was an expert bomb-maker. Equally important, he knew how to improvise. Empty sardine cans were pressed into service as bomb casings. The finished explosives rejoined the chain to reach various strategic hiding places throughout the camp. Near the crematorium compound nestled the cache of the Sonder-kommando.

Gutman and Leifer concealed their buttons in the false bottom of a specially made canister. They soon learnt that it was usual for prisoners to save a little of their food rations for later, so they made sure there were always some remnants of tea or soup when the time came for the usual SS inspection. A canister containing some liquid usually received only the most perfunctory glance.

Narrow shaves were inevitable. There was the day after work when they were standing in line during the SS inspection and Leifer was whispering urgently to his companion: 'I didn't have time to hide the stuff in the canister. It's in a matchbox in my pocket.'

It was news that made Gutman pale with fear; the SS were not above ripping matchboxes apart. Suddenly he could not control his shaking.

The guard could scarcely help being suspicious; Gutman was subjected to a thorough body-search. Throughout, Leifer stood by. He later recalled: 'Oddly enough, the longer that the examination of Gutman took, the calmer I became.'

It was just as well. The SS man, having found nothing, gave Leifer only a superficial inspection and eventually passed on to the next man. Gutman recounted ruefully: 'That was the one time when nervousness actually paid off.'

Rosa Robota was the direct link with the Sonder-kommando. Explosives which came to her were hidden in the handcarts on which the bodies of those who had died overnight in the barracks were taken to the crematorium.

It had been intended that the Sonderkommando would synchronise its revolt with the general uprising. Then came devastating intelligence reports: the days of that particular privilege squad were numbered. If elimination was indeed planned, there could be no further delay.

Thus on Saturday, 7 October 1944, a gigantic explosion shook the Birkenau barracks; one of the four crematoria exploded in one vast sea of flame.

Then there was a general onslaught on the hated guards, one of whom was pitched alive into a roaring oven. Four other SS men were killed and a number severely wounded. Then, their blood firmly up, the prisoners cut a barbed wire fence and released six hundred of their comrades. But the SS contingent was soon breathing down their necks. Liberty was brief; one by one, the fleeing hordes were hunted down and shot.

The revolt of the Sonderkommando, a desperate last-minute bid forced on it by circumstances, was the only significant revolt in Auschwitz. The grand plans of those who had dreamed of a total uprising which would spread throughout Poland and thence into Upper Silesia had crashed to disaster.

Worse, plans smuggled to underground supremos in Cracow had fallen into the hands of the Nazis. The courier had been shot by the SS and hauled off with his wounds to the camp hospital. Despite torture during interrogation, he betrayed no one. But the revolt had been robbed of any element of surprise and fizzled out.

Himmler personally ordered a thorough investigation. It was plainly necessary to discover the origin of the explosives and how they had reached the Sonderkommando.

Gestapo stool-pigeons were insinuated into the Pulver-Pavilion. Several girls were arrested and tortured. Then came the inevitable day when Rosa Robota was dragged to the notorious Block Two.

Gutman, Leifer and the others lived in daily fear of arrest. Ideas of suicide were prompted by what they knew of the interrogation methods of Block Two. Day after day, they watched from a distance as Rosa, her hair matted, her face swollen and bruised, was dragged by two female attendants for the day's ordeal.

For a time nothing happened. Both Gutman and Leifer

recognised that the Germans were playing a war of nerves. The prisoners decided to force the issue.

Yet another of the group, Moische Kulka, was detailed to put his head in the lion's mouth. He was known to be acquainted with Jacob, the Jewish kapo of Block Two. An appeal was made to Jacob: would Rosa be allowed a visit in her death cell?

Jacob shrugged: 'It will cost you a bottle of whisky.'

This was not, as it turned out, a crude bribe. When Noah Zabladowicz, who was also a native of Ciechanow and had therefore been assigned to make contact with Rosa, turned up complete with the bottle, the kapo promptly introduced him to the SS guard as a friend.

Jacob then proceeded to ply the German with the liquor. The two men took care to remain sober. As soon as the SS guard slipped to the floor in merciful unconsciousness, Jacob removed the man's keys and motioned Zabladowicz to follow.

Noah describes what happened next:

'I had the privilege to see Rosa for the last time several days before her execution. At night, when all the prisoners were asleep and all movement in camp was forbidden, I descended into a bunker of Block Two and saw the cells and the dark corridors. I heard the moaning of the condemned and was shaken to the core of my being. Jacob led me through the stairs to Rosa's cell. He opened the door and let me in. Then he closed the door behind me and disappeared.

'When I became accustomed to the dark I noticed a figure, wrapped in torn clothing, lying on the cold cement floor. She turned her head towards me. I hardly recognised her. After several minutes of silence, she began to speak. She told me of the sadistic methods the Germans employ during interrogations. It is impossible for a human being to endure them. She told me that she took all the blame upon herself and that she would be the last to go. She had betrayed no one.

'I tried to console her but she would not listen. "I know what I have done and what I am to expect," she said. She asked that the comrades continue with their work. "It is easier to die when one knows that the work is being carried on."

'I heard the door squeak. Jacob ordered me to come out. We took leave of each other. It was the last time I saw her.'

In a further attempt to thwart an uprising, the SS began transporting large contingents of Jews and other prisoners to work in various parts of Germany. The resistance movement was all but extinguished.

Meanwhile, a clutch of escapees from Auschwitz forwarded a heartfelt plea to the World Jewish Congress to bomb the extermination centres and their railway lines at Auschwitz and Birkenau.

But by now what had begun as a trickle of deportations by the Germans became a veritable flood. It was decided by the Allied governments to await the advancing Red Army. In the case of Auschwitz, three long months were to separate the Sonderkommando operation from eventual Russian liberation.

The gassings continued. But things were not quite the same for the Germans. One of the four crematoria had been put out of action entirely and was never rekindled. The essential underground role of Rosa Robota had crippled Auschwitz irreparably.

Meanwhile, outside Himmler's camps and the ghettos of the occupied territories of the east, the resistance movements were on the loose; organisers were flexing their muscles to bring a hitherto clandestine war directly onto the streets.

15

The Polish resistance had few better Nazi-haters than Lieutenant Jan Piwnik.

He was a native of ideal partisan country – the extensive woods and forests south of Warsaw where he had assembled a force of some three hundred. But the main stumbling-block to their effectiveness was one common to all such groups: shortage of arms.

More than once, Piwnik had reflected how he could easily double his manpower overnight, but what was the use of hands, however eager, if there were no weapons to put in them?

He reasoned early on that large-scale theft from the Germans was the only answer. An attack on the Warsaw-Cracow express had produced a gratifyingly rich haul of arms and money on one occasion. But the cost had been terrible. In retaliation for the raid, the Germans razed an entire village, slaughtering most of the two hundred inhabitants.

Polish guerrilla leaders swiftly ordered Piwnik to cease his arms-snatching forays and prepare for one big job.

His instructions came early in 1942 from the highest echelons of the Polish Home Army (Armia Krajova, AK), which had been formed before the end of 1939 as a centrally organised resistance movement loyal to the Polish government, which had settled in London after the fall of France with General Wladyslaw Sikorski as both Prime Minister and Commander-in-Chief. The Home Army received the support of the bulk of the Polish people and the main political parties, save the Communists and an extreme right-wing nationalist group. At its height, the Army numbered about four hundred thousand including full-time partisan units living in the forests.

Its commanders had heard of the almost legendary exploits of Piwnik – the man everyone called 'Ponury' ('Gloomy') because of a perpetually grim expression, accentuated by a dark band of eyebrow running unbroken across his face.

Certainly, the mission now proposed was scarcely likely to raise a smile from anyone.

The order was terse: 'A four-man partisan group who have carried out a successful series of sabotage acts, have been arrested near Pinsk. One had died under interrogation, the other three have been imprisoned. Your job is to get them out.'

Piwnik had grumbled previously about lack of arms; the formidable strike-group of sixteen that he had hastily formed could have anything that it wanted – plus a car and a couple of lorries. Just as valuable was a contact within the prison, an AK man employed as a guard.

Piwnik decided on a head-on attack. Of course, there could be nothing so crude as the party merely roaring up to the prison, shooting its way in and snatching its haul under the noses of the Germans. Such an approach might appeal to the tearaway elements of the group, but something more subtle was clearly indicated.

There was no reason for the guard to look particularly closely at the Opel which drew up at the Pinsk jail late on the afternoon of 18 January. Besides, the guard had no stomach for being officious with a haranguing driver wearing SS uniform. He signalled the car through, not paying particular attention to the lorry containing troops behind him. That was a mistake, because somebody in the lorry immediately opened fire.

Car and lorry trundled through to the inner gate. The trick worked again and the second guard was despatched. Then Piwnik's men were tumbling out of the lorry and scaling the wall. One group dashed to the commandant's office. A few short, sharp bursts of machine-gun fire were enough to secure the prison keys.

Piwnik had reserved for himself the task of actually releasing the prisoners. In all, he sprang some fifty men from their cells, including several Soviet partisans in addition to the three men who had been the original object of the raid.

The Opel roared off into the night, the main body of the attackers leaping into the waiting lorry, which sped away. Barbs were scattered in the road to pierce the tyres of any pursuing vehicle.

Jan 'Ponury' Piwnik seemingly led a charmed life; inevitably it could not last. In the summer of 1943, the Germans burst in on his main base, tucked away in the remote hills, and destroyed it.

It would have been impossible for such an attack to be launched without good intelligence. Someone, somewhere, had turned traitor. The explanation was devastating. An agent of the Nazis turned out to be a young officer known as 'Motor', who had shared the back seat of the Opel with Piwnik during the Pinsk adventure and was one of his closest friends.

In vain 'Motor' pleaded that the Gestapo had his mother in custody and had blackmailed him. The partisans condemned him to death.

Piwnik was forced to retreat further into his forests and marshes. On 15 June 1944, the Germans rooted him out and killed him.

There was, however, no shortage of willing replacements.

The girl had saucer-sized cornflower-blue eyes and long blonde plaits, which hung down on milk-white shoulders.

Her beauty was frail and demure, evoking in most men open admiration coupled with a desire to protect her from the buffets of a cruel world.

So even the SS automaton stationed outside Warsaw Gestapo headquarters melted when the girl stared at him soulfully, lowered wonderful eyes and whispered the name of a senior officer, adding: 'I *have* to see him. It's a personal matter.'

She was let into the building and given the number of a room. She entered and remained staring hesitantly.

The officer in his elegant SS uniform stood looking at her for one long moment, eventually gasping in genuine wonderment: *'Gibt es bei euch auch eine Lorelei?'* (Do you also have a Lorelei here?').

She made a gesture of embarrassment, mumbling something. Then she opened her handbag. It needed just one shot to kill her quarry. Then she walked back casually towards the exit, flashing the guards that high-octane smile.

Unhurriedly Nieuta Teitelboim – underground name 'Wanda' – disappeared into the crowds.

It was by no means the only death sentence she had carried out. There had been the particular ardent Gestapo officer who had awakened in the morning to find his beguiling bedfellow with a revolver pointing straight at him. He had attempted to dive under the quilt, but Wanda had shot him just the same.

She operated mostly in the Warsaw area but she became a legend throughout Poland, and in Gestapo circles they called her *'Die kleine Wanda mit den Zoepfen'* ('little Wanda with the plaits'). She was high on the list of wanted bandits and the price on her head stood at 150,000 zlotys.

Wanda had been born in Lodz in 1918 of a strictly Orthodox Jewish family. Her bid to earn a living in the gentile world, plus radical activities in the left-wing student movement of the Polish Gymnasium, had been abruptly halted when the Wehrmacht marched into Poland.

A year later she was one of half a million Polish Jews herded into the Warsaw ghetto.

There she organised a women's detachment. The underground was divided into cells of five; in one of them Wanda was an instructor in weapons. She had entered the ghetto with no knowledge whatever of firearms. Seasoned veterans of resistance watched in astonishment as she swiftly grasped technicalities and became a proficient instructor.

The hearts of German guards melted as Wanda distributed meals inside the ghetto from large covered baskets, bristling with hand-grenades. The People's Guard, the partisan arm of the Communist Polish Workers Party, had, however, rather more demanding work for her.

Wanda was promoted deputy commander of the special Warsaw task force whose speciality was sabotage.

On 16 October, 50 active members of the Polish Workers Party were publicly hanged. Their bodies swung from the gallows all day; the Jewish community had to pay a fine of one million zlotys.

Eight days later came the riposte of the People's Guard. Wanda was in the forefront of the faction whose bombs tore into Warsaw's exclusive Café-Club, a popular rendezvous for Wehrmacht and Gestapo.

At the same time, another group attacked the coffee house in the main railway station of the capital. Grenades were also lobbed into the editorial offices of the *New Warsaw Courier*.

The attacks left thirty German officers dead. Later the People's Guard distributed leaflets which informed Warsaw that with these acts the fifty hanged Poles had been avenged.

It was by no means the end of retaliation. There was one final act which had a touch of ruthless artistry in which many connoisseurs of partisan warfare seemed to detect the personal hand of Wanda.

On 30 November, the task force turned its attention to the Communal Bank. It was stormed in a commando-style assault; one million zlotys were stolen. This sum was, according to the later announcement, merely a repayment for the amount confiscated from the people of Warsaw.

In the early hours of 19 April 1943, came the Nazis' march

into the Warsaw ghetto to liquidate the last remnants of Jewry there. That evening at a secret address in the Warsaw suburb of Praga, the leaders of the People's Guard met to discuss how best they could help the fighters of the ghettos.

Attention focussed on a German artillery emplacement in Nowiniarska Street which was bombarding the ghetto.

Less than twenty-four hours after the target had been chosen, a special group, Wanda among them, opened fire. The artillery was silent; the bodies of two Germans and two Polish policemen lay nearby.

By now the Gestapo was hot on the trail of Little Wanda with the Plaits. Conscious that the net was tightening, her comrades in the underground begged her to lie low. She refused.

Then came the day in July 1943 when she came home and found the Gestapo agents waiting in her room. They took her to the cellars and tortured her; a note finally reached the underground after her death that she had not talked.

In the spring of 1945, on the second anniversary of the Warsaw ghetto uprising, the Polish Government post-humously awarded Nieuta Tietelboim (Wanda) the Gürnwald Cross, Poland's high battle decoration.

By 1943, events on the war front in the east pointed to a new dawn; total victory for the Germans was obviously impossible. But for the Poles the year was to bring a succession of disasters. Betrayal of leaders of the underground movement in Warsaw came thick and fast. Among those rounded up was General Grot-Rowecki, commander of the Home Army, who was sent to Germany and a year later, during the Warsaw Rising, shot on the personal orders of Hitler.

Then shortly afterwards, came the news of a flying accident at Gibraltar in which General Sikorski was killed.

By the start of the following year acute anxiety had gripped the forces of Polish resistance. Everywhere else, it seemed, the Germans were on the run. There was the successful landing by General Eisenhower's Anglo-American armies on the Normandy beaches. General Patton – 'Old Blood and Guts' Patton – had begun a dramatic breakthrough at Avranches. As for the Russians, General Zhukov had at last flung the Germans out of the Soviet Union.

And Poland? Seemingly, the country was to be stuck with the enemy until the last. Because of its geographical position, Poland was the steel door between the advancing Red Army and the Reich. Hitler was determined to keep it slammed. Above all, the grip must be maintained on Warsaw.

The Home Army anticipated the Fuehrer's reasoning; henceforth the bulk of the resistance would be concentrated on the capital.

Defeat of Germany was not the only consideration. Increasingly the Poles were asking themselves what sort of future they could expect after the eventual inevitable arrival of the Russians. Lieutenant-General Bor-Komorowski (dubbed by common consent 'Bor'), the new Commander of the Home Army, was among those who believed that if the Poles were able to gain possession of their capital and set up at least a skeletal administration, they would be able to receive the Russians as hosts. It would then be difficult, it was further reasoned, for the Communists to enforce their own authority.

There was good reason to fear the Russian legions, and not just those sections of it making up the Red Army. The dreaded NKVD had been active, joining the front-line troops as punishment battalions in a fashion which sometimes recalled the Einsatzgruppen. Polish partisans had been compelled to disarm. Then they were either forcibly enrolled in Soviet-controlled units or shot.

Bor attempted to invite Soviet military co-operation in any possible uprising. Stalin ignored the plea.

If there had been any doubt about launching Operation Tempest – code name for the uprising – one event removed the final scruple. It happened, not in Poland but in the Fuehrer's headquarters. On 20 July 1944, a group of Army officers, with the defeat of Germany looming, attempted to assassinate Hitler with a bomb placed under the conference table of his headquarters in Rastenburg, East Prussia.

The bid failed. But it seemed to give some pointer to the mood of Germany. Defeat was in the air; it was known that German civilians in Warsaw had already fled in terror. Victory over the Nazis was feasible. Besides, Bor pointed out, the Russian advance was so fast that there was good reason to think that it could reach Warsaw in a little less than a week. The omens were good.

Five days after the attempt on Hitler's life and in a buoyant mood, Bor flashed to London the message: *'We are ready to fight for Warsaw at any moment . . .'*

Still in a mood of euphoria, Bor added a few requests. He asked for the Polish Parachute Brigade to be dropped on Warsaw and for German airfields nearby to be bombed.

The requests were, to say the least, naive. The only aircraft that would have been capable of transporting the Parachute Brigade was the slab-sided, shoulder-winged B-24, the Liberator. Around two hundred and fifty of them would have been required for such an airlift. Rather more pressing use for the Liberator could be found in Europe, where D-Day was engaging Allied attentions. What was more, all the Liberators in the world would have been useless without landing facilities, which could only have been supplied by the Russians. Stalin flatly refused to be so accommodating.

Bor had the task of mobilising an army of around forty thousand men in an occupied city; there was no other country either able or prepared to help him.

The weapon situation was nothing short of dire, according to the Warsaw area commander Colonel Chrusciel. But he put a brave face on it, maintaining that his armoury of almost exclusively light weapons would be enough to hold out for a while, even without Russian help.

Bor's confident mood began running through Warsaw like a bush fire.

Germany's Army Group Centre had collapsed on the eastern front during June. The tattered remnants of the German 9th Army streamed eastwards through Poland in utter disarray. On Saturday 25 July, the tatterdemalion rabble passed through Warsaw. The sight of the disbanded units in full retreat provided the sort of spectacle that the Poles had never dreamt was possible. Five years before, proud arrogant victors had stridden through those same streets. The fruits of victory, it was widely believed, were fit for plucking.

Bor drafted a message to the soldiers of the Home Army:

'Soldiers of Warsaw

'Today I gave the long-awaited order for open
warfare against the age-long enemy of Poland,
the German invader. After nearly five years of a hard
and continuous fight underground, today you stand in
the open, arms in hand, to regain liberty for our
country . . .

Bor, Commander Polish Home Army.'

On 31 July in Warsaw, the decision was taken, spurred on
by news from Chrusciel that Russian tanks were in the
suburb of Praga, stretching along the right bank of the river
Vistula.

Chrusciel begged Bor: 'We must rise at once. Otherwise it
will be too late and the Russians will take over.'

The die was cast. The uprising was set to begin twenty-
four hours later, on 1 August at 1700 hours.

But there was one serious drawback to Colonel Chrusciel's
intelligence: it happened not to be true. There were no
Russian tanks in Praga. Indeed, they were some miles off and
all the signs were that they had halted.

Had the halt been ordered by Stalin? Or was German
resistance, as the Russians later claimed, so strong that a
move forward was, for the time being, impossible?

The only sure fact was that the Russians made little effort
to help the rising. Bor reflected helplessly that things would
have been a lot different if the armies at the gates of Warsaw
had been American or British.

Allied help for Warsaw was probably the best possible in
the circumstances. The RAF made a few supply-dropping
sorties, but the casualty rate was so appalling that Air
Marshal John Slessor, commander of RAF forces, had to call
off the flights. By the time they were renewed, it was too late.
Weapons and food dropped without parachutes by the
Russians were worse than useless. The Americans fared
scarcely better.

All was set for one of the major tragedies of the entire war.
Poland, the small country whose subjugation had ignited the
conflict in the first place, was destined for further suffering.
The Poles mounted their rising without first making sure

either of substantial help from the Allies or co-operation with the Russians. They were to go down outnumbered and outgunned.

Yet nothing, it seemed, could stop Warsaw smiling. For hours before the scheduled uprising, the Polish flag flew from the top of Warsaw's highest building. Before darkness conspired with the smoke of battle to obliterate the scene, more flags were unfurled proudly on the city hall, the post office and other public buildings.

Under covering mortar-fire from rooftops, the triumphant rebels hurled themselves at strategic German strong points and police, SS, Wehrmacht and administrative offices. Bullets and shells crashed into hostels, barracks, depots, bases and military hospitals.

Pistols and small-arms fire cracked and echoed around the city. There were the explosions of grenades and the shattering of glass. Unavoidably, the first victims were innocent passers-by, unaware that any revolt had been planned at all.

After the initial mortar-fire, AK units emerged from doorways, cellars and ruins. The idea was to storm German strongholds and take them by surprise. But they had reckoned without Nazi precautions. Administrative offices and military depots had long since become fortresses. The Poles came up against concrete pillboxes in doorways. Steel screens had been bolted onto windows from inside and fitted with rifle and grenade slits.

Soon tanks were rumbling on the streets. Elaborate plans were made by the Poles for immobilisation; a favourite was a bottle of petrol corked with explosive. A good job of disablement could be done by throwing bunches of home-made grenades under a caterpillar track. Several were captured and their guns turned on the Germans.

It was a minor triumph for the Poles, but tangible. Molotov cocktails manufactured in primitive workshops were excellent anti-tank weapons. All that was needed was to fill bottles with petrol or diesel oil, add a couple of spoonfuls of sulphuric acid and stick a small amount of calcium chloride onto the side of each bottle with a strip of paper. The bottles shattered on impact and the mixture inside, reacting with the chloride, exploded instantaneously.

Faced with crews who were forced to leap out and become

easy prey for Polish snipers, a frustrated Gruppenfuehrer Heinz Reinefarth was forced to admit that tanks were of help only in the suburbs and not in densely built-up city areas.

Reinefarth reported:

> 'Even in this short time our tanks have shown themselves to be unsuited for city warfare. Tanks cannot reverse and turn in the streets which are already covered in rubble and debris. Apart from this, they are too wide and difficult to manoeuvre.'

It was not merely the Home Army whose members sprang from doors and cells to claw at the Germans. Soon every man, woman and child was anxious to help, including the Communists. But there was not one of them who did not experience the chill of fear when waking on the morning of 4 August, to miss a hitherto reassuring sound. The angry murmur of Russian guns across the Vistula had ceased.

Soviet aircraft had disappeared from the skies; the Luftwaffe was back. A wave of Junkers swooped down on the district of Wola, location of Home Army headquarters.

Bor was forced to issue an urgent warning about wasting ammunition; the Home Army went on the defensive. True, there had been two Halifaxes over Warsaw, and the partisans had picked up the stores that had been parachuted in. But these were the only two aircraft to fulfil the mission, fourteen had set out.

Improvisation by the Poles became steadily more ingenious. Certain areas were marked *'Beware of Mines!'* That kept the Tiger tanks away for a while, even though there were no mines.

One group managed to scare off advancing tanks by rolling barrels down a slope towards them. The tank crews did not know that the barrels were empty and did not stay around long enough to find out. A simple clothes-line with bottles attached, strung across a street, looked appropriately sinister and made more than one tiger turn back.

The Germans began a push into Wola to establish an east-west link with the river. In they came, driving in wedges, punching their way street by street. They began first with bombs and incendiaries, then with tanks and infantry carrying bomb-throwers and grenades.

Barricades began crumbling; headquarters had to be moved to the Old Town. German sharp-shooters, installed in a high church tower, were annihilated by a blast from one of the captured tanks. But the ground held by the Home Army was shrinking visibly. German firepower was merciless. The Luftwaffe, which the Poles had thought crippled beyond repair, redoubled its raids. There were heavy guns, mortars, miniature robot tanks crammed with explosives that made short work of the flimsy barricades.

And there was something else. Into Warsaw, there now stepped a familiar bespectacled figure – SS-Obergruppen-fuehrer Erich von dem Bach-Zelewski, veteran of many a killing ground.

Von dem Bach was a man with a special mission; one entrusted to him personally by Reichsfuehrer-SS Heinrich Himmler. He picked as his lieutenants two of the more exotic characters in the sinister gallery of Nazi degenerates. The outfits of which the couple were in charge were equally bizarre – the Kaminski and Dirlewanger brigades.

Both groups were curiosities, even by the standards of the Third Reich. The full title of SS-Brigadefuehrer Mizieslaw Kaminski's group was the Russian SS Assault Brigade Rona (Russkaya Oswoboditeljnaja Narodnaja Armya – the Russian National Liberation Army).

Rona had sprung into existence because one German general had refused to implement Nazi policy in occupied Russia and had set up a large autonomous Russian district. The first Russian volunteer sections had sprung up there, consisting largely of fanatically anti-Soviet peasants.

The unpromising rabble had been knocked into shape as a sort of auxiliary army for Germany. When its Russian commander fell during a skirmish with partisans, Kaminski, an engineer, took over and was appointed by Himmler to head the 29th Division of the Waffen-SS Rona (Russian).

Here indeed was a strange mongrel! Kaminski's army was inexperienced, adventurous, impulsive and, in textbook military terms, a total disaster.

But there was a positive benevolence about it when compared with Oskar Dirlewanger's Police Regiment (Brigade).

As a Doctor of Political Science at Frankfurt University,

Dirlewanger might well have had a promising career if he had not been removed and imprisoned for molesting a minor. Luckily for him, however, he had good friends in the SS. Even the prissy Himmler had been able to find it within himself to like the tooth-brush moustached pederast, calling him 'a good Swabian fellow, wounded ten times, a real character – bit of an oddity, I suppose.'

Dirlewanger had a talent for low company. As early as June 1940, he had assembled a group of some two thousand poachers from Oranienburg concentration camp. The rabble took to its new work with enthusiasm – crushing partisan groups in Poland and later in White Russia.

Their conduct had been so atrocious that it could not be stomached, even by some senior members of the SS. Kruger, Police Commandant of Cracow, had been particularly vehement, bellowing at Dirlewanger: 'If this bunch of criminals has not disappeared from this area within one week, I'll jail them personally!' Himmler's promising acolyte had merely shrugged and moved on with richer pickings in the Soviet Union.

But now he was back with sixteen officers and 865 men in Warsaw. Since at this stage of the war it was necessary to scrape barrels assiduously, Dirlewanger managed to swell his numbers with assorted Muslims, Cossacks, Turkomens, Hungarians, Galicians and Ukrainians whose hatred of the Poles was notorious.

As far as the Ukrainians were concerned, the Poles return-ed the detestation with interest. Distinctive treatment was afforded the renegade Russians. A large *U* was painted on their bare backs before they went to their deaths forcibly erecting barricades under fire from both sides.

Nothing that the soldiers from the east could do was right. One side detested them cordially, the other distrusted their military prowess – and with good reason. As for Kaminski's contingents, they refused to accept even the most elementary discipline and only showed interest in fighting when they were assured that they could loot and plunder to their hearts' content.

The German commanders were reluctant to entrust Kaminiski's rabble with the new heavy weapons that were brought up, including a new kind of flame thrower.

In numerical terms, both sides were reckoned to be fairly even for most of the struggle. The Poles never lost their optimism, even cabling to London at one point: '*The initiative is in our hands.*'

It was a brave statement but ultimately futile. For in the suburbs of Warsaw there prowled the sinister legions of Reinefarth, Dirlewanger and Kaminski. The Warsaw Rising's most terrible day – Black Friday – lay ahead.

It was a clear, hot summer day that 5 August, not at all a time to be thinking of death, let alone of the sort of hideous slaughter awaiting the innocents of Warsaw.

The units of Reinefarth and Dirlewanger had begun assembling for their first major counter-attack in the early hours of that sultry morning. The target was the Wola district of the city; Dirlewanger's 1st Battalion took up a position south of the main street, Wolska Street (or Litzmannstadterstrasse, according to the German maps). In the north, the police companies of Reinfarth moved up. Heavy supporting fire was the responsibility of a number of tanks of the Hermann Goering Brigade.

But the Germans were putting their greatest faith in the large-calibre assault guns of the Tank Destroyer Unit. These, it was confidently felt, would snap the Poles' flimsy barricades like matchwood.

Reinefarth himself was in a confident mood. That morning he had moved his operations room, a staff bus, to a cross roads in Wola. His intention was to make a narrow breach in the Polish defences. Through it he would advance to the city centre, past the Saxon Gardens and as far as the Vistula bridges.

The distance was some three miles; about an hour's walking time. Reinefarth's soldiers were to take three days and in the process reduce whole streets to ashes.

But his progress was not quite as smooth as he had hoped. In the central sector he could muster around 2,500 men. He fretted after Dirlewanger's Second Battalion. But that was still being brought up; mobilisation even by telephone was out of the question before 6 August.

Admittedly, the numbers of the Home Army, of the AK, facing Reinefarth were somewhat smaller. But they were no mere partisans with more zeal than fighting experience. They belonged to the crack, well-equipped Kedyw-Radeslaw unit. They were kitted out in useful German uniforms – camouflaged SS combat outfits captured from a Waffen-SS depot. Both sides were indistinguishable except for the AK armbands and berets.

But the time for fighting was not quite yet. The pause before Reinefarth's attack rasped on the nerves of the beleaguered would-be saviours of Warsaw. Nevertheless, vigilance remained tight behind the Wolska Street barricades and in the cemeteries on the outskirts of the ghetto ruins.

Meanwhile in Ochota – the southern area of Wola – some 300-400 Polish soldiers were to face 1,700 of Kaminski's men under the command of Major Frolov, a turncoat Russian.

The fact that the Poles stood firm and prevented Kaminski from moving more than three hundred yards was not due solely to Polish battle skill. For SS-Brigadefuehrer Kaminski was making a perfect job of displaying precisely what a military incompetent he was.

Reinefarth had fixed the attack deadline for 0800 hours. It proved quite beyond Kaminski to keep it; indeed he was not ready for another ninety minutes.

The German Supreme Command observed such behaviour with a mixture of bewilderment and fury. There was a suitably withering entry in the War Diary: *'Kaminsky's troops engaged, as planned. Two hours later than anticipated.'*

It was but a small delay for Warsaw. What happened once Kaminski teamed up with the forces of Dirlewanger should perhaps surprise or shock no one. It was as if the subordinates of Himmler and Eichmann had actually stayed their hand until then, waiting to unleash against their hated eastern foes a vast holocaust of terror and cruelty, the ferocity of which had been kept in cold storage.

Himmler's two morally abysmal executioners went to work forthwith. On 5 August, Dirlewanger's SS convicts managed to advance about one thousand yards. Their concern was not solely getting to grips with the Home Army. Like men demented, they stormed into the houses they passed on or near the battle-line.

Inhabitants were ordered to leave. There were promises of 'evacuation'. But the fate that awaited them was to be herded into cemeteries, gardens, backyards, factory forecourts and squares. Then the murder squads set to work on men and women and children, often assembled in their nightclothes and with no time to remove the sleep from their eyes.

The corpses were piled in large heaps, petrol was poured over them and they were set on fire. With a strange delicacy, the killers covered over ashes and bones with the rubble of the ruined houses. Such buildings as remained were invariably burnt down.

On the evening of that terrible 5 August, arguably the worst in Poland's long calendar of suffering down the generations, the AK signalled London: *'The Germans are burning Warsaw methodically. Many and large fires. Attempts by the civil population to extinguish them are frustrated by the Germans.'*

Nor was this the end of the hideous catalogue of suffering.

Dirlewanger's cohorts – those fondly called 'good fellows' by Himmler – stormed into the hospitals in the Wola and Ochota area. The sick and wounded were shot in their beds. Sadism walked tall that day and it was turned on nuns, nurses, doctors and voluntary helpers.

The Curie-Skiodowska Radium Institute, containing women suffering from cancer, suffered the worse. The patients were dragged from their beds. They and their nurses were raped by the drunken mercenaries. Russian and German uniforms ran amok in an orgy of murder, pillage and the 'collection' of rings and jewels, watches and gold. Police and SS units joined in the general dance of death.

When it was all over, Reinefarth reported his own losses. On the German side, they amounted to six dead, twenty-four badly wounded and twelve slightly wounded. When questioned on Polish losses, Reinefarth shrugged: 'Ten thousand including those shot.'

Nonetheless, Warsaw was far from being subdued. Killing had been carried out to terrible effect, but actual military advances had been meagre. Contact between the German troops advancing from Vistula bridges could have been achieved with one concentrated thrust. But time had been lost in sadistic self-indulgence.

The will to resist by the Poles was absolute and increased in intensity once the horrors of 5 August became apparent. The

Home Army was to hold out in the vital sector until the following month.

Erich von dem Bach-Zelewski, who was in overall command, desperately tried to get the advance moving again. He ordered that the mass execution of the civilian populace should cease at once, along with the looting. The job of soldiers, after all, was to fight.

But mobs such as those of Dirlewanger and Kaminski could not by now be stopped so easily. What had they to lose? They had been told: 'If you retreat or fail, you will be taken from the probationary unit and sent back to the concentration camp. If you are captured, the Poles will shoot you.'

As for those Poles, they defended every street, every house and even every floor to the bitter end. But gradually they were forced to give up one building after another. The Germans were now on the move again and they were lavishly equipped with ammunition, while every bullet was precious to the Poles.

The Luftwaffe was hastily marshalled to press the new advantage. Out of the skies roared the Stukas whose one thousand pound bombs swept away entire barricades and blew vast gaps in the Polish pillbox lines. The Poles' communications were shattered and their defences reduced to chaos.

Idealism among sections of the Home Army gradually became tempered with sometimes horrifying ruthlessness. A favourite trick of the Germans was to use civilians as cover for their troops, advancing up a street behind a ladder to which Polish citizens had been tied. At first there had been scruples at retaliation under such circumstances. Now there were none, and the hostages were slaughtered along with the rest.

By 19 August, the Germans were moving in on the Old Town of Warsaw in overwhelming force. Among their artillery now was a 600 mm battery, but it was a sledgehammer to crack a pathetically puny nut. The old houses collapsed; the inhabitants, invariably taking shelter in the cellars, were buried beyond all hope of rescue. The more resourceful of them took to quitting their homes ahead of the advance, finding momentary shelter in already ruined houses.

Intense efforts were made to establish contact between the

Old Town and the district of Zoliborz to the north, which was separated by German-held territory. The Home Army sent a young boy with a message strapped to a goat, but when he attempted the journey on the next day he did not arrive.

Then two men managed to get through from Zoliborz. Their progress had been underground: via the sewers. It was a final act of macabre desperation. As the situation grew steadily worse, the sewers were pressed into service for communication and even transport of food and supplies.

Conditions were appalling above ground, but amid the subterranean filth they were terrible almost beyond imagining. It was a question of groping in total blackness through a network of tunnels constructed in the previous century. Invariably, the tunnels were round, the floor never level. The bottom was littered with all manner of rubbish, some of it so sharp that to use hands was to invite serious laceration and, worse, blood-poisoning.

Main routes through this maze of hell were marked with a string. Missing the marker was the ultimate terror: anyone who lost their way in the sewers of Warsaw was as good as dead.

The routes were first worked out by volunteers, many of them *Kanalarki* (sewer women) who frequently never returned from the tunnels they had explored.

And throughout, the sewers continued to perform the original function for which they had been built. Men and women waded chest-high through the sticky flood; one slip was quite enough for the current to sweep a victim off his feet to a death by drowning in that terrible swift tide.

Travel in such conditions was painfully slow, especially when the going was against the current, which flowed west to east across the river.

There was one sewer route which ran from the besieged Old Town to the city centre. It was no more than a mile long, but took a full nine hours to negotiate. Along the narrow tunnels, progress was made with the aid of short sticks held in each hand, used like crutches for hops of only a few inches.

From such a journey, strong men emerged at the point of collapse, and so often the enemy was waiting for them.

It took the Germans some time to realise that an entire transport and communications system had come into being under their very feet. But with the knowledge came the unleashing of new horrors.

Barricades and booby traps were set up. There were grenades hanging from the roofs of tunnels which exploded when bumped into. A barricade would act as a dam; when it was removed, a sudden flood would drown those in the tunnel. Sentries posted at manholes lobbed in grenades or poured down petrol, which was then set ablaze.

The sewers of Warsaw provided the Germans with some good opportunities to try out new weapons. One of the more refined was the *Taifun* (Typhoon) system, whereby an explosive gas was blown down into the sewers by special engineer units. When it was ignited, the resulting explosion set off a chain-reaction not unlike the damp-fire explosions in coal mines.

Dr Ludwig Hahn, Chief of Warsaw's Security Police, after the war described an inspection of the sewers with other officers a few days after the end of the uprising:

'Wherever "Typhoon" had been used we could still see the effects: numbers of dead rats and cats. The pressure from the explosion had plastered them onto the walls of the shafts like postage-stamps . . .'

German troops were despatched into the cellars, and there were hand-to-hand fights: two men ripping each other to pieces among the oozing excrement of the shattered city above.

And in the city, worn down inexorably by the renewed vigour of the enemy, conditions of everyday life deteriorated rapidly both for military and civilians.

Major Wardejn-Zagorski of the 'Polnoc' (Northern) Group wrote in his diary at the end of August:

'Field kitchens dish out food to the soldiers, sick and wounded fairly regularly, but its nutritional value is falling fast. Every day we have the same thin soup with oats, pieces of potato, now and again a few peas or noodles. There is little coffee left. Because the military and public kitchens use it so sparingly the people have no choice but to drink plain water (sometimes from ruined wells). This is causing stomach complaints on an epidemic scale.

'There is no sign of the operation to construct public wells which the civilian authorities have demanded. There are also very few places where something like that could be done, because as more and more houses in the Old Town are destroyed, the wells keep being buried and any work would be useless.'

It would be less than fair to the Germans, or truth, to say that the whole of Warsaw became the plaything of Kaminski and Dirlewanger. The incompetence and ultimately the brutality of Himmler's precious duo were altogether too much for senior officers in the Wehrmacht.

Above all, it disgusted a certain General Rohr, who was not only one of the Germans' most skilful tacticians, but a Prussian of the old school, a ruthless, merciless fighter who was at the same time utterly opposed to everything Himmler stood for.

His first act was to demand the withdrawal of Dirlewanger, Kaminski and their brigades from the front and their replacement by regular troops. Nothing happened.

Rohr then took matters into his own hands. An order was swiftly published which forthwith forbade any further looting and emphasised that all AK prisoners should be treated as regular prisoners of war. He even organised several tanks to patrol the streets specifically to protect the civilian population.

But above all, he wanted the head of Kaminski on a plate. He got it. Himmler, the last man to stand by a friend when the going was hard, promptly dropped the former engineer. His fate was sealed. To kill him in Warsaw, where he was surrounded constantly by an SS bodyguard, was patently impossible. So Kaminski was bundled to Lodz on some pretext and hauled before an SS military court for insubordination and theft. He was despatched by firing-squad two hours later.

Dirlewanger, however, was a different proposition. He still had powerful friends in the SS. Besides, since his brigade could, if coerced, fight as a military formation, it was still needed by von dem Bach-Zelewski.

Bor-Komorowski now had to face the unpalatable truth that

he could no longer guarantee to continue the uprising without outside help.

He seriously considered offering unconditional surrender, despite opposition from some Polish NCOs. The German Ninth Army had made it clear that there would be an absolute guarantee to treat the rebels as regular prisoners of war.

Predictably, Hitler and Himmler opened their mouths to protest at such misplaced humanity, and then promptly shut them again. The reason was a public declaration of British Foreign Secretary Anthony Eden that the Allies would not hesitate to carry out reprisals against German prisoners in England if the Poles were not treated in accordance with the Geneva Convention.

Meanwhile, the battle of Warsaw continued. On 10 September, a major attack on Praga was launched. Bor, still hoping vainly for some form of Allied aid, tried to stem the enemy advance. The Germans, predictably, called off all negotiations. As for the Russians, it was patently clear that they would settle for nothing less than a Communist regime once the war was over; in the meantime they were quite prepared to let the Home Army bleed to death.

Stalin twisted the knife even further. The entire rising was blamed on 'émigré circles in London'. Furthermore, the enterprise was dubbed 'criminal'.

The situation was plainly hopeless. On 4 September, at 18.15 hours General Bor signalled London from Zoliborz: *'Our struggle is in its last agonising stage . . . I shall be compelled to capitulate.'*

As the Old Town collapsed into rubble, Bor and his staff, including two officials who were over sixty, were forced to take to the sewers, where it was hoped to hold out a little longer. The familiar nine-hour route through three-foot high tunnels proved impossible for men of that age. Another had to be found. Even an alternative route seemed impassable, but by adjusting dams in other tunnels, the flow of water was reduced to knee height. The party left what just a month before had been a beautiful old city with its churches and medieval cathedral. It was now virtually unrecognisable.

They descended a manhole in Krasinski Square, under the shadow of the German guns. Behind them they left mounting misery as the refugee problem became steadily more acute. Hospitals tried vainly to deal with the mounting list of casualties as the enemy moved in. Soon there was no bread and no water. Electricity was provided by a few petrol-driven generators; ammunition was down to a dozen rounds per man. Basement taps coaxed the last precious drops of water and the starving took to the wholesale slaughter of dogs and cats.

A giant American supply drop was well-intentioned but ultimately useless: the tinned food was damaged and the ammunition did not fit the motley collection of weapons still in the hands of the Home Army.

By 27 September, the Poles were in command of only two shrinking areas of the city. Bor-Komorowski took the decision to cease resistance. Warsaw laid down its arms after sixty-three days of fighting. At 20.20 hours the surrender treaty was signed.

It must be recorded that Bach-Zelewski seemed to feel a genuine respect for the fighting spirit of the Poles. A meal was politely offered to Bor's officers but refused. Von dem Bach went further, even suggesting that the Poles and the Germans join forces and fight together against their common enemy, the Russians. Realism may have dictated the offer rather than humanity. But it made no difference: there was precious little of the Home Army capable of fighting.

The spirit of chivalry, for whatever reason, did exist – and was perhaps unique in the entire history of the war in the east.

Three Polish infantry regiments quit the battle area in close formations and fully armed. Only later did they lay down their weapons; officers were allowed to keep their small arms.

One of Bor's greatest anxieties was removed by a German guarantee that no foreign troops would be detailed to guard the Poles. Even civilian evacuees were treated with consideration, with female prisoners being put in officers' camps.

On 4 October there took place one of the most moving episodes in Poland's long Gethsemene. Companies of the First Regiment congregated behind the Technical University, from where the barricades had already been 'symbolically' removed.

The Poles were old and young, men and women. Many were clad in torn and blood-bespattered uniforms, on the caps of which were the Polish Eagles. But the miracle was that despite the destruction and lack of water the men had somehow managed to shave. Decorations were pinned proudly to chests.

German officers and soldiers lined the streets for the parade. Weapons were lowered; the proceedings were watched in silence. Salutes of respect were gladly given.

More than 9,000 of the AK were taken prisoners. Approximately 3,500 preferred to go underground, but they were not harassed by the Germans. About 16,000 of the Home Army had perished or had been reported 'missing, presumed dead'. The wounded numbered 6,000. But the greatest casualties of the rising were civilians: almost 200,000 perished.

The operation cost the Germans 2,000 killed and 9,000 wounded. General Bor-Komorowski was sent to the notorious escape-proof Colditz castle and liberated at the end of the war.

The Russians eventually liberated a dead city; what had remained after the rising had been razed by the Germans. Once the Nazis had quit, the power passed to the Kremlin.

One of the most striking – and, as later Polish history in the twentieth century was to show, prophetic – tributes to Poland came in a moving peroration from a totally unexpected source:

'Poland is such a glowing example! Throughout history it has forever been occupied, dismembered, split up, its boundaries dissolved, and all national life suppressed.

'Despite all this, its national spirit has been preserved throughout the centuries so that its flames always burn up again from the charred ruins and rekindle themselves – the stormier things are, the better the blaze!'

The tribute was made by the Reich Minister of Propaganda, Joseph Goebbels.

16

Something very close to fear gripped Hitler's Secretary of State in Czechoslovakia Karl Hermann Frank as he watched the tide of fortune change against the Third Reich with ever-increasing speed.

It seemed another world away, the year 1938 when the forces of Germany had trundled with such arrogant confidence into the Czech lands seemingly offered to the Fuehrer on a plate by the scarcely protesting democracies.

Czechoslovakia had not simply been a country conquered: it had put in Hitler's hand what amounted to a weapon of war. Whoever held the Prague-Berlin-Warsaw triangle was in a strong position to control the Balkans. Through Prague flowed civilian and military traffic – and, more to the point, arms shipments.

In the second year of the war and two and a half years after its union with the Reich, Bohemia was, second to the Ruhr, nothing less than the most vital centre for the German armaments industry. There were the Skoda works in Pilsen and the arms factories at Brno, two of the largest and most prestigious armaments manufacturers in the control of Adolf Hitler. From the conveyor belts of Bohemia there had flowed a third of German tanks, a quarter of the lorries of the Wehrmacht and forty per cent of light machine-guns.

As for Prague, it had grown to resemble a German suburb as vast numbers of German officials and executives, together with their families, had flooded in.

Until the end of April 1945, Frank's kingdom of Bohemia, Moravia and the Sudetenland lay quiet, almost as if possessed by a charmed life, while the tempests raged around.

There seemed to be a comforting stability about the Army Group commanded by Generalfeldmarschall Ferdinand Schoerner which was holding a line running south-easterly and approximately parallel with Czechoslovakia's northern boundary from Dresden in Saxony to near Cracow in Poland.

Then the Russians had hurled themselves at the First Tank Army, knifing through to Brno in the very heart of Czechoslovakia, cutting him off from the forces of the south.

Reinforcements were needed desperately. A flight by Schoerner to Berlin to plead for more armour was hopeless; there was none to spare for the Silesian front.

Fresh disasters followed swiftly. Soon the entire northern front of Army Group Schoerner had collapsed. Nothing could stop the advance of the Russians now.

Frank was a man indelibly stained with Czech blood. Unless he threw in his lot with the most powerful anti-German faction in the Protectorate, he knew he was finished.

His idea was to turn his government over to a Czech national body that would have been predominantly anti-Communist and composed mainly of Czech right-wingers who hated the Russians as much as the Nazis. He would then face the Western powers as a patriot, as head of a country which had been liberated from the Germans and now desperately needed protection from a new threat in the east.

Frank reasoned that such a scheme might save not only his own skin, but Hitler's as well. He flew to Berlin with his plan.

The half-crazed Fuehrer was deaf to all reason. Furthermore, he refused to accept the defeat staring him in the face.

Coldly, he told Frank: 'I have no intention of giving up the Protectorate. It is the arsenal of Germany and the German armies. Bohemia will be held at any price until the war is won.'

Frank was constitutionally incapable of questioning Hitler's judgement on anything. His plan had been turned down by the Fuehrer and that was enough. He was content to wait for the turn of fortune his master had promised.

If a waiting game seemed to suit Frank, it was very far from being to the taste of Czech resistance.

But then it never had been – right from 27 September 1941, when for the very first time the black-and-white flags of the SS had fluttered from the Hradcany castle alongside the red flags of the party. For on that day, Reinhard Tristan Eugen Heydrich, the disgraced former naval officer, had added

Deputy Reich Protector of Bohemia and Moravia to his already impressive clutch of titles.

Hitler had appointed him to replace the diplomat Baron von Neurath, whom the Fuehrer had regarded as 'too soft' and who was summarily sent on sick leave.

Karl Hermann Frank had been passed over for the post. Hitler had long been aware of how important Czechoslovakia was to Germany, economically and militarily. A certain amount of co-operation from the Czechs themselves was necessary; sheer brutality of the kind practised in Poland and Russia would be counter-productive.

Few men were hated more in Czechoslovakia than the Sudeten-German Frank. Heydrich, a man whose ruthless organising abilities had built up the Gestapo and the SD, was barely known by most of the Czech population. Hitler reasoned that this would make the job of diplomacy easier. Nevertheless, those who studied Heydrich's career felt a twinge of anxiety: they were sure that his appointment would mean a general tightening up of German policy.

Out of deference to Frank, Heydrich was careful to take the title of 'Deputy' Reich Protector. But there had been no doubt who was the master in Prague.

It was early in the morning of 27 September 1941 that Heydrich arrived. He was greeted with guards of honour composed of the Army, the Waffen-SS, police and units of the SD. There was a reception of small and carefully selected future colleagues, German dignitaries and journalists.

A statement issued by Heydrich was sharp and to the point:

'It is to be clear at the outset I am interested in one goal only: that this area should exploit its economic potential for war. Anything which endangers this aim I will suppress, whatever its origin or source. Anything which furthers it I will support.'

There also echoed in Heydrich's ears, a command which had come from Hitler during their interview before Heydrich's departure.

The Fuehrer had said: 'I want instant order throughout the Protectorate.'

He got it. Among Heydrich's immediate measures was a

merciless campaign against both nationalist and communist resistance movements, intimidation of the Czech population and the government of the Protectorate.

It was not, however, achieved by the sort of crude brutality which Karl Hermann Frank would have understood. Heydrich was contemplating a seemingly attractive package of social measures which would keep the workers happy and busy. While that was being enjoyed, Heydrich would be free to launch himself against the enemies of the Protectorate – including those Germans who were making a fat living out of corruption.

The citizens of Prague who switched on their radio at 8 a.m. on the very morning of Heydrich's arrival heard the announcement of a state of emergency to deal with (euphemism had not been abandoned) 'unusual incidents'. Anything which threatened or could threaten public life and security, or economic and industrial peace, became subject to martial law. Included was the illegal possession of weapons, ammunition or explosives and any act of sabotage.

News of Heydrich's new broom in Prague reached the government-in-exile in London. Reports in the first weeks revealed wholesale arrests of resistance workers, many of them shot for following the pleas of the BBC to put sand and broken glass in the axle-boxes of goods wagons. Savagely decimated was the Obrana Naroda resistance group, which had been formed at the time of the occupation of the Protectorate and which was still being guided from London.

A wide-reaching dragnet of arrests enabled Heydrich to eliminate one chain of organised resistance fighters after another; the number of arrests in October and November stood at between four thousand and five thousand.

Ahead of Heydrich, of course, had gone the Gestapo, observing and penetrating over the months. Heydrich himself lost no time in sending in the heavy squads.

Blow upon blow fell upon the Czech resistance. Communication with London became even more precarious. At the beginning of October, an agent, Pavelka, who had parachuted into Prague with new encoding keys for the resistance, fell into the hands of the Gestapo.

Heydrich left the majority of uninvolved Czechs alone. It was, after all, scarcely necessary to touch them. News of arrests of tiresome dissidents made the broad masses much more amenable.

There was soon a general reluctance to join the resistance, followed by wide surrender of weapons – in October the Gestapo found five hundred alone discarded.

Nazi thugs who could only see power in the very crudest terms were not Heydrich's style. In Prague there were no screeching cars disgorging sinister men in black and silver uniforms or public arrests and beatings up. Arrests were done discreetly and at night. Terror there was, but the policy was to keep it low key. Above all, it was necessary to gain some form of co-operation from the Czech people.

The way Heydrich chose was via their stomachs. Food shortages in the country were far above what was necessary even in wartime. Tough measures were not slow in coming: 169 of 404 sentences passed by the emergency courts struck not at political resistance, but against economic crimes.

From the gallows there now dangled racketeers and black marketeers. Those responsible for supplying poor foodstuffs were strung up after the briefest of trials. In a single day, 10 October, no less than twenty-two cattle-dealers and butchers were hanged. The newspapers, whose editors naturally had little choice in the matter, were soon screaming such headlines as 'FOURTEEN BLACK MARKETEERS HANGED, GERMAN AND CZECHS'; 'THE FIGHT AGAINST BLACK MARKETEERS AND COMMUNISTS'.

The next stage in Heydrich's strategy was to pose as the friend of the workers. Trades union leaders and workers' delegations were received in some splendour in the Emperor's Hall of the Hradcany. They received a flattering peroration from Heydrich, who addressed his audience as 'comrades at work' and proceeded to pour scorn and venom on 'racketeers and war-profiteers, the black marketeers and usurers'.

Heydrich's devilish energy would never have allowed him merely to sit behind a desk and distribute largesse. He concerned himself with details of wage levels; he toured shop floors and sat in on union meetings.

He reasoned that it was not enough to punish the enemy of the state; victims of sabotage must be rewarded as well. Thus when a policeman was severely injured by a bomb planted by the resistance, Heydrich made sure that the injured man's family received immediate aid and an increased pension.

These cynical measures to placate the Czech population were viewed with alarm by agents in London; the resistance was deliberately being softened up.

And that was why less than a year after his arrival, Reinhard Heydrich was to die.

The task of killing him was entrusted to two highly trained agents flown into Prague from England. Joseph Gabcik and Jan Kubis threw a specially designed bomb into Heydrich's open car, which had already been slowed with shots from a Sten. Heydrich was mortally wounded but only collapsed after he had given chase to the would-be killers, brandishing a pistol. He died unexpectedly a week later of blood-poisoning.

A revenge of unparalleled barbarism was unleashed on the Czechs. Martial law was proclaimed within hours of the assassination bid. The summary courts worked overtime. Executions of entire families were carried out on the vaguest of pretexts.

After Heydrich's death and with the full approval of Hitler, the village of Lidice, whose name was to become a symbol of the worst kind of atrocity, was destroyed completely. Male inhabitants were all shot. One was in hospital with a broken leg; the Germans waited till he came out and then shot him.

On 24 June, the hamlet of Lezaky was also destroyed and all adult inhabitants were shot. The pretext this time was that a Captain Bartos, a radio operator for the resistance, had been seized there, together with his equipment, and because two contact points for Czech exiles dropped by parachute had been discovered.

This was far from being enough for Hitler and Himmler. As an obscene but somehow apposite memorial to Heydrich, Aktion Reinhard was put in motion. One of its aims was to collect the property of deported Jews. And the deportations themselves were stepped up, especially from the ghetto in Theresiendstadt to the extermination camps in the east.

In the Protectorate, 3,118 Czechs were arrested and 1,357 sentenced to death by courts in Prague and Brno.

The assassins of Heydrich were eventually betrayed. What

remained of the Czech underground was virtually wiped out; the Czech Communist Party also disappeared, while the carefully nurtured Special Operations Executive network, the Commando group of British Intelligence, with agents working in Czechoslovakia, all but collapsed.

Reinhard Heydrich's violent and painful exit from the world stage was met with an orgy of death and vengeance.

Because of the scale of terror instigated by Heydrich's successors, the Czechs seemed for a while to have lost the will to resist. But the paralysis did not last.

In the course of time Frank's own secret service was reporting a build-up of preparations for a large-scale revolt – not only among the Communists, who received weapons from Russia by air, but from nationalist groups hoping for liberation from the Americans.

Frank, abandoning all efforts to be conciliatory, broadcast a bombastic speech over Radio Prague to an accompaniment of drums and bugles. He warned that any revolt would be smothered 'in a sea of blood'. It was a prospect which was greeted with no enthusiasm whatever by the still-considerable German civil population who had made a life for themselves and their families in the Protectorate.

Neither Frank nor the German settlers knew then of an exchange of radio messages between General Dwight D. Eisenhower and General Alexei Antonov, Deputy Chief of the General Staff of the Red Army.

Antonov, a particularly favoured protégé of Stalin, was carrying out his master's instructions. He was to do all he could to prevent the Americans from occupying a large portion of Czech territory. Stalin had reasoned that a Communist Czechoslovakia could be brought about only if the entire country was liberated by the Red Army. But, meanwhile, the advance of the Soviet troops was being held up by the troops of Generalfeldmarschall Schoerner.

On 4 May Eisenhower radioed to Moscow that the US Third Army stood ready to move into Czechoslovakia and Prague and 'to clean up the entire territory west of the the Elbe and Moldau Rivers'. On the same day Antonov requested Eisenhower 'not to advance beyond a line approximately 50 miles inside Czech territory, roughly parallel with Czechoslovakia's eastern border'.

Eisenhower ordered his troops to stop along the line laid down by the Russians.

Now the fates crowded in to destroy Karl Hermann Frank. The first sledgehammer blow came just after midnight on 1 May 1945. Hitler was dead. Every newspaper in the city, both Germans and Czech, appeared with black borders and featured long eulogies of the man who 'had died fighting to the last'.

Frank decided on one last desperate throw. He flew to meet Grossadmiral Karl Doenitz, Hitler's designated successor as Reich President.

But Doenitz, presiding over a rump government, had no desire to be associated with the more thuggish elements of the old regime. Frank was merely told to keep order in Prague as long as he could and to declare it an open city. If Frank revised his ideas of negotiation, there is no evidence that Doenitz evinced any enthusiasm.

Revolt was spreading everywhere. In eastern Czechoslovakia, with the Russians imminent, national and red flags were unfurled in every town and village.

German refugees, desperately trying to flee home, were left stranded in tightly packed trains because railway workers simply abandoned them. Those in wagons on the roads fared little better; the partisans stole the horses.

Czech industry came to a complete halt, with masses of workers roaming the streets, removing German inscriptions from shops with a hasty coat of paint.

Apathy seemed to attack the Germans. Even the SS, not slow at brutality when it was required, seemed to have lost all interest in their work. The civil police stood idly on street corners.

In a frenzy of desperation, Frank ordered a curfew to be slapped on the population; Prague would remain in a state of siege. The proclamation was received with a shrug. It seemed as if everyone, German and Czech, was caught in an enervating vice of total indifference.

Frank's control of Czechoslovakia slipped away. Early in May, the Czech Government of the Protectorate and a newly constituted National Council, representing anti-Communists, had urged that the full power of government should be turned over to them. They undertook in return to guarantee the safe-conduct of all German troops and all German civilians wishing to leave.

Frank could not bring himself to act. The initiative passed to the Communists. Their campaign was skilful and ruthless. Soon a rumour swept through Prague that American tanks were on the outskirts. It was a manufactured rumour; no Americans were in the area at all. Then the word went around that the Americans had demanded immediate surrender and the Germans had agreed.

It was a cue for still more Czech and red flags to decorate countless windows. Crowds turned out in their hundreds along the routes where it was fondly expected that the American liberators would pass. There was almost a festive air with street parties and patriotic national songs.

The Germans, not surprisingly, were thrown into utter confusion. Frank panicked, and played right into the hands of the Communists. He ordered the streets to be cleared. Obedience was fragmentary but some sections of the SS turned out and opened fire on demonstrators. Field-pieces and machine-guns rumbled menacingly through the streets.

The crowd seethed with fury. The Communists pressed the advantage. A truckload of supporters seized Prague radio station and saw off German attempts to recapture it. At the same time, clothing and arms depots were wrested from the Nazis.

By now Radio Prague was calling: *'Czech policemen, members of the Czech Army! Rise up against your oppressors, come to our aid. The following roads to Prague are open . . .'* Then followed a catalogue of atrocities which it was claimed had been committed by the SS. There was a demand for revenge.

By the evening of 5 May, most of the German administrative offices had fallen to the Czechs. The SS were deserting in droves, particularly the youngest members who had been drafted from the civilian population and who now feared for the safety of their families.

And with good reason. Germans on the streets were no longer safe; roving gangs of Czechs butchered them on the pavements. The rounding up of civilians began. Transports of men, women and even small children were paraded through the streets of Prague. They were stoned, spat on and beaten up.

Petrified groups, their arms clutched around their heads in terror, ran the gauntlet to reach prison gates under a hail of blows and kicks.

A particular humiliation was reserved for German women; whether they were innocent or guilty of any crime scarcely mattered. They were dragged from the groups, their heads shaved, their faces daubed with paint. Blouses were ripped off and swastikas daubed on naked breasts.

All the time, Frank remained sealed in Hradcany Castle, shunning all contact with the Czech National Council or the Protectorate Government.

Meanwhile, the dark drama of the Prague revolt had been distinguished by the strange enigma of one of the Soviet Union's brightest military talents, General Andrei Andreyevich Vlasov.

Talent, however, was of dubious use in the Soviet Union if the possessor lacked the ability to survive. Vlasov, the son of a peasant, had not only managed the considerable achievement of avoiding a firing-squad in the notorious purges of the 1930s, but had gained his master's respect sufficiently to receive the Order of Lenin and command of the LV Armoured Corps in Lvov.

At the defence of Moscow, Vlasov had distinguished himself even further, and within a year he was made Lieutenant-General and awarded the Order of the Red Banner.

A new command, the Second Shock Army, had taken him to the front at Volkhov. Here even his formidable gifts could not reverse a disastrous encirclement; he and most of his troops were taken prisoner.

Vlasov may have been an obedient and conscientious soldier, but he certainly had no love for Stalin. The brutal methods of the collectivisation of farming and the ruthless purges of the Soviet Union's top military talent had long left him disgusted and disillusioned with Communism. He began to reason that with Hitler's help it might be possible to remove Stalin and Bolshevism, thus creating a new truly Socialist Russia.

The idea caught the imagination of the German High Command. Vlasov was persuaded to become the voice of the

Russian Army of Liberation, which he and other former Soviet soldiers and civilians fondly hoped might become the nucleus of a free Russian army and government.

Millions, he believed, would flock to such colours: all Russians who loved their country but could not extend the same devotion to Stalin.

The knowledge of the very existence of someone like Vlasov threw Hitler into a towering rage. There could be no possible common ground between the predestined masters of Europe and the Slavic slave caste.

Vlasov's main champion within Germany indicated only too clearly the way things were going in the Reich. Heinrich Himmler, the once-ardent advocate of a German colonial empire in the east, was now persuaded that the promise of a free Russia could even at this late stage move large numbers of Russian soldiers to leave the Soviet ranks.

Himmler's opportunism eventually permitted Vlasov on 14 November 1944 to read a proclamation in Prague and to form an impressively sounding 'Committee for the Liberation of the Peoples of Russia' under Chief of Staff Trukhin, himself a former Soviet general.

There was a seemingly promising beginning with the setting up of an officers' training school, air corps and several special units. Two divisions were trained by two other Soviet Generals, Bunichenko and Saitsev.

An anti-Bolshevik crusade might have had some chance two years before, when the Soviets had been cowed by Nazi cruelties. But it was now too late to change the course of world history with a bunch of adventurers in Prague, however dedicated.

In the March of 1945, Vlasov, in a mood of highly mistaken optimism, despatched secret envoys to the British and American headquarters in France and Belgium. The suggestion was that they could all get together to build a new Russia. Vlasov's political naivety received a distinct jolt when he learnt that the emissaries were regarded as traitors to the Allies and turned over to Stalin, who promptly ordered them to be hanged.

The men of Vlasov's divisions were decked out in German uniforms but displaying on their shoulder patches and banners a blue St Andrew's cross on a white shield. Their reception was delirious. Prague took to its strange new champions instantly. Vlasov's men became the salvation of German civilians, prisoners and wounded. The mounting bloodthirst cooled.

That very same evening Prague was welcoming other visitors into the seething city – a small American patrol rumbled in. A relieved General Bunichenko assumed that it was an advanced patrol of the forces which would eventually occupy the capital.

Then came a shock, which was shortly replaced by cold fear. The patrol commander told Bunichenko: 'Our orders are to root out German resistance. There doesn't seem to be much. Your best plan is to maintain order and wait for the Russians.'

The artless piece of advice meant nothing less than a sentence of death.

Bunichenko was desperate. Swiftly, he ordered his men to cease fighting at once and take refuge in Vlasov's head-quarters.

News there was all gloom. The situation reports revealed that Soviet tanks were rapidly approaching Prague from the north-west.

The great trek began. Vlasov's forces retreated west, inevitably becoming entangled in the tragic chaos of war: the straggling remnants of German troops and spiritless refugees, desperate to reach the American lines before the arrival of the Russians.

Three of Vlasov's generals travelling separately were pounced upon by Czech partisans, who lost no time in turning them over to the Soviets. The First Division, however, had an easier passage, surrendering to the US Third Army.

Vlasov's grip on reality became increasingly unsure. Incapable of realising that he was now prisoner, he persisted in behaving like an honoured guest of the Americans, continuing to outline what he believed could be the destiny of a Russia shorn of Stalin's Communism.

He remained blissfully unaware that those of his forces still fighting were gradually being surrounded by American tank forces. As for the Soviet commissars, they pressed for the extradition of the men they had been instructed to regard as traitors.

At eleven o'clock on the morning of 13 May, Bunichenko was informed by the American commander that the armoured American enclosure around the First Division would be opened to the east and that the division would march out that afternoon. Bunichenko and his men realised all too well what that would mean.

A few of the troops tried to hide, while the bulk of them steamed east in the vain hope of getting beyond the American enclosure before the Russians. But Allied solidarity was absolute; US forces closed ranks and drove the renegades straight into the Red Army lines.

Vlasov's Second Division and various separate units stationed in Bavaria and Austria were also prisoners of the Americans and were held in a string of camps. There were mass suicides. But most were secured by the Russians.

Vlasov and his staff were now at the total mercy of the US Third Army. The final act opened with deceptive mildness. Vlasov was invited cordially to go with his staff for a parley.

They were led unsuspectingly through a wooded lane. On cue, Russian troops suddenly appeared. The party was overpowered almost before anyone knew what was happening.

A year and a half later, there was a secret trial. At the end of it Vlasov and twelve of his officers were taken to Moscow and hanged.

17

If the mood of Vlasov's followers had been one of mounting desperation and fear as their enemies closed in, no such emotion was felt by Ferdinand Schoerner.

At his headquarters, he was trembling with rage, holding in his hands orders from the Supreme Command of the German armed forces that all fighting would cease on all fronts at midnight on 9 May.

With Schoerner, and as white as a sheet, was von Natzmer, Chief of Staff. Such an order ended all his hopes that German troops would be spared Russian prison camps. It was simply impossible for all forces from the eastern front to be disengaged at the required hour.

Schoerner, purple with fury, was bent on prolonging the agony of the Czechs for as long as possible.

He yelled: 'I have no intention of respecting such an order. I shall tell all my Group Commanders that it has been received, of course. But we'll ignore it and go on fighting.'

Senior officers, conscious that the war was lost and that they could lose little by insubordination, violently disagreed and were prepared to say so. An intentional violation of the surrender agreement, they pointed out, would mean the destruction of the very last remnants of legal relations with the Allies. Any German soldier who fought on and had the dubious luck not to be killed would fall into the hands of the Russians, and would die after all.

To the onlookers, it appeared as if Schoerner would have apoplexy at this evidence of wholesale rebellion. In fact, he was thinking furiously. He realised that unless he acted quickly, he himself could expect no mercy from the Russians. He had no intention of falling into their hands – or, come to that, into the hands of the Americans, either.

It was von Natzmer who came up with a seemingly ideal solution. He suggested that the northern wing of the Fourth Tank Army should be ordered to continue resistance against Russian bids to break through in the north. All other units should be given permission for 'an organised flight to the west'. That some units would fall into the hands of the Russians was inevitable, but there was a good chance most would escape.

Here was the opening Schoerner needed. If he ordered his troops to flee west, he could shake off all personal responsibility and look to his own safety. He made little attempt to conceal his eagerness.

Von Natzmer was an honest man, unable at first to probe his chief's motives. He took Schoerner's orders to go ahead meekly enough. Then Schoerner told him he wanted several small aircraft to be at the airport of Saaz, some sixty miles north-west of Prague.

As preparations went ahead, Schoerner moved like a whirlwind. In his private quarters, he sped through the rooms, gathering together a few possessions. Then he snatched up a briefcase, crammed it full with all the money he could find and sped to seek out von Natzmer.

At first there were platitudes. The Generalfeldmarschall poured out his thanks to his Chief of Staff for loyal services and co-operation.

Then he changed the subject abruptly. He said: 'I'm going to take one of the planes at Saaz and make for Bavaria. I've got a secret mountain cabin there. It's obviously sensible to lie low just now. Around Christmas I'll emerge and size up the situation.'

He shuffled the money, pushing some notes in von Natzmer's direction. He noticed the other man's hesitation and with a trace of impatience said: 'Here, take it. It'll come in handy.'

The Chief of Staff had recovered himself. At first he had turned pale with disbelief. Now he was boiling with anger.

He exploded: 'Does not the Generalfeldmarschall realise that tomorrow the Army Group will be marching for its life? You can't desert at this time when a central command is absolutely essential. Your rank will count a great deal with the Americans.'

Schoerner snapped: 'And none at all with the Russians. I've authorised troops to flee west. Why shouldn't I do the same thing? You're perfectly capable of handling what's left of command.'

Then he snapped the briefcase shut and departed into a night bright with the fires of burning documents and papers.

Early next morning the convoy pulled out, with Schoerner's car leading. Von Natzmer followed, along with the radio truck and a clutch of other vehicles.

Schoerner lashed his driver into even greater speed. Soon the rest of the column, with the exception of von Natzmer, was dropping far behind. The cars streaked towards the airport. Schoerner's stomach lurched sickeningly as he surveyed the empty runway. Where the hell were the aircraft? There was no time to find out and the radio truck was way behind.

Suddenly, Schoerner spotted a tell-tale fog of dust on the far side. And there was a rumble, which all at once became a mighty roar. Russian tanks!

Schoerner leapt back to the car and streaked off westward. Despite himself, von Natzmer stuck behind, hoping desperately for the appearance of the radio truck so that he could keep in touch with his units.

Fatigue knocked relentlessly at Schoerner's brain. Ahead loomed the town of Podersam, close to the German border. Thankfully, Schoerner pulled in, only to be told that one of the aircraft which had failed to turn up at Saaz had been downed in a nearby meadow.

Schoerner brightened; there was still hope. An aide was despatched forthwith to secure the plane for the Generalfeld-marschall's immediate use. Schoerner then thrust his way through the crowd of wounded stragglers and made for the offices of the town commander.

Even at this stage of the war, a Generalfeldmarschall's uniform was still capable of inspiring awe. But Schoerner ignored the salutes of a crowd which respectfully stood back for him. A sharp order was issued to the town's Nazi Party chief. Two suits, one of them a Bavarian costume, were to be found immediately.

Not even bothering to conceal the action from the troops still watching him, he wearily unpinned his Ritterkreuz with its cluster of oak leaves and diamonds and thrust it into his pocket. Then he slipped into an adjoining room and changed into the Bavarian costume. When he emerged again it was to demand champagne and cigars. A couple of close cronies were invited to drown their sorrows in style. For a few hours, reasoned Generalfeldmarschall Schoerner, what was left of the war could go to hell.

A nagging sense of duty would not allow von Natzmer to relax, with or without champagne. He choked down his anger at the blatant opportunism of his superior as he searched through the dark town for a radio post to contact the Army Group. It was all in vain. The only means of communication now was the aircraft in the meadow. And there was not much time. The appearance of Russian tanks at Saaz could only mean that Soviet forces were threatening to stem the escape of the Army Group to the west.

He decided to turn back and face his superior. He would ask for the use of the plane.

By now Schoerner was thoroughly fuzzled with

champagne. He stared glassily at his Chief of Staff and coldly refused the request. Instead, he indicated the bottle and slurred: 'Forget it all. Join me in a drink.'

Von Natzmer stood his ground, only to receive a belligerent 'No.' This he countered by saying he would place a guard over the aircraft until the next morning.

The guard who was posted had instructions to allow no one but von Natzmer to approach the machine. But the few elderly Volkssturm (Militia) who were left had no stomach to quarrel with the tall, broad-shouldered man in civilian clothes who appeared in the meadow next morning.

The troops raised their rifles, only to receive the bellow: 'Don't you see who I am? I'm Generalfeldmarschall Schoerner!' In complete confusion they dropped their weapons and stood by while Schoerner clambered into the aircraft and flew off.

The plane made south-west for Austria but it was out of fuel and before long was forced into a crash landing. Schoerner drifted around the country for a few days. Then, around 15 May, he reported to the former staff of the German First Army, now in the hands of the Americans.

If he fondly expected mercy from them, he was out of luck. The Russian Commissars had his name as a wanted man and he was turned over to them.

It was a radiant May day in Czechoslovakia when the German forces obeyed the order of Doenitz, their new President and Commander-in-Chief and laid down their arms in final defeat.

Something like one million soldiers clogged the roads of western Czechoslovakia and the Sudetenland in that great trek west. They were driven ever onwards by the hope and belief that the Americans would accept them as prisoners.

Four hundred thousand men in the First Tank Army were completely isolated from the other units and had barely escaped Russian encirclement.

The sun beat down and the trees beside the roads were in full luxuriant bloom. It all helped to fuel the optimism of hardened troops, to whom a march of 110 miles to the

American position was certainly not the world's greatest hardship.

Some units, travelling on foot or horseback, fell victim to Russian sorties. But the bulk of the Army stuck together and strode out with confidence.

First to reach the Americans were the rear echelons and the hospital units. They were immediately taken prisoner. Optimism surged through the approaching combat troops.

General Walter Nehring, last commander of First Tank Army, set up his command post some five miles east of the lines of Fifth US Infantry Division. From here he aimed to direct the final stages of the surrender. Nehring knew in his heart that his men were doomed either to Russian firing-squads or to long empty years in the labour camps. But even as American aircraft landed on the roads ahead of the advancing columns to block their progress, he made one more bid.

His Chief of Staff, Oberst von Weitershausen, was despatched for an audience with the commander of the US Fifth Infantry Division.

He was received with courtesy but little help. An American staff officer told the German: 'The troops of the First Tank Army fought against the Russians and will have to be their prisoners.'

Von Weitershausen returned to his car in silence. The American extended his hand, saying with conviction: 'We respect the Russians as very fair fighters. I have no doubt you will be treated according to international law, and get home soon.'

Von Weitershausen allowed himself a bleak smile. Then he shook his head.

'You can deal with the Soviets only with a gun in hand,' he sighed. 'If you have no gun, you are their slave.'

It was true. Every single German prisoner taken by the Americans passed into Russian hands. Troops still on the march were scooped up in a series of Soviet dragnets.

Now the vast masses of the armies formed in columns and marched east. Few were ever to return.

In Prague, too, the fear of a Soviet nemesis raged like a fever.

As soon as he got wind of the surrender, German forces commander General Toussaint sought out the Czech National Council. He offered immediate capitulation – provided his troops and the German civilians were given safe conduct out of the city.

The Communist faction within the Council, however, would have none of it. It demanded that fighting should go on until the Soviet troops had marched into Prague. Then the way would be open for a Socialist revolution. The former masters of the Czechs now found themselves reduced to mere pawns in a political game.

Moderate elements in the Council eventually forced through a compromise solution which was the best in the circumstances – the Germans would be allowed to withdraw until the Russians actually approached. Then negotiations would begin in earnest.

Late in the afternoon of 8 May, the march began. Among the mechanised columns was the car of Karl-Hermann Frank who, throughout the negotiations, had maintained a resolute silence. Now he hoped vainly that he might be overlooked in the general confusion.

Long rows of soldiers and civilians shuffled through the barricaded streets of Prague towards the west, their progress slowed by the occasional tank. Soldiers carrying bazookas had no spirit to use them; the wounded hobbled on canes and crutches.

The exodus lasted throughout the night. There were unavoidable hold-ups. Around two o'clock in the morning a German battery opened up – diehard SS units had refused to take part in the surrender. Communist partisans retaliated by opening fire on the marchers. It was well into the next day before the columns could move again.

Troops and civilians who had held Masaryk Railway Station surrendered to the Czechs and were allowed to leave on their long march, making a slow progress past the tall, ancient walls of the Hradcany.

All at once there were shouts. Soviet infantry broke through with an almighty cheer at the prospect of such easy pickings. Machine-guns sliced their bullets straight into the defenceless ranks. Those who were not killed by the fire were literally torn to pieces.

Some German civilians who had been herded into Ruzyn prison were released from their overcrowded cells and told that the war was over: It was now their duty to help repair damage and dismantle the barricades. But even before they had left the compound they were treated to a spectacle that was only too clear a warning of what was to happen to them.

Several trucks loaded with Germans and medical personnel lumbered into the forecourt. Russian troops and Czech partisans could barely wait for the doctors, nurses and wounded to climb out. Soon the helpless Germans had their crutches, canes and bandages torn away.

Then they were knocked to the ground and beaten to a bloody pulp by a hail of clubs, poles and hammers.

There is nothing more addictive than mass violence. A hitherto-peaceful crowd watched in silence as the prisoners of Ruzyn were marched out to remove the barricades. Those wearing SS uniforms were seized and drenched with petrol. Hot tar was thrown indiscriminately. Bodies were tied together with barbed wire and rolled down into the Moldau River. There was no escape even for the children; the smallest ones were thrown into the street water-troughs and drowned.

A favourite sport was to force naked women to remove the barricades. Then their tendons were sliced and they were left writhing where they were.

Several hundred children who attended the Adolf Hitler School in Prague were lined up in the playground and shot. It was a comparatively merciful death amid the orgy of murder, torture and rape which had turned Prague into nothing less than a battleground.

There were Czechs that day who turned their eyes away from the atrocities or merely watched passively. If they had raised a single word of protest their fate would have been the same as the rest.

A bid for a peaceful evacuation of the conquerors had failed. Bloody revolution spread through Prague like flames in the wind.

18

The great wave of Soviet armies on the northern front drove across the Polish plain, forced its way through the Carpathians, invaded Slovakia by the gorges of the Upper San Valley and in an autumn of heady triumph rolled inexorably west with Hungary as the next enticing triumph.

Simultaneously, sweeping southward between Moldavia and the Black Sea, the tanks of General Rodion Malinovsky and the Cossacks of General Fedor Tolkbukhin, who had already played a leading role in the encirclement of the German Sixth Army inside Stalingrad in early 1943, engulfed Rumania and seized Bucharest.

After a six-day assault, Bulgaria also capitulated. The Russians stopped only long enough to arm their new Rumanian allies, then the advance rolled on. By the beginning of October, they had reached the endless forests of the Tisza valley in Hungary.

Now it was the task of the Soviet High Command to concentrate three Army Groups for the massive assault on Budapest, the final bastion before Austria.

In March 1944, Hitler's troops occupied the whole of Hungary in a dawn invasion. It was a step that had been forced on the Reich out of sheer military necessity; the Russian army's advance was already threatening south-eastern Europe.

Ankara Radio first gave the world news of Hitler's dramatic step. Later a report from Algiers Radio stated:

> 'Berlin decided to occupy all strategically important points in Hungary because the Hungarian government refused to offer resistance in the event of a Russian invasion.'

Hitler summoned to Germany senior members of the

Hungarian government. True to form, the Nazi war lord presented them with an ultimatum. The Red Army's offensive in south Russia, he declared, had cut the Lvov-Odessa trunk railway so seriously that the lines of communication of Generalfeldmarschall von Manstein – soon to be relieved of his command by Hitler – had become severely embarrassed.

Hitler had already envisaged the nightmare of a Russian breakthrough into Rumania and the Balkans and Central Europe.

Sternly, Hungary was reminded of her obligations as a member of the Axis. She must take an active part in the war against Russia and must allow the German army forthwith to take over the entire Hungarian transport system.

Those members of the delegation ill-advised enough to demur were promptly placed under arrest. Their objections made no difference: the occupation went ahead.

German resistance, though desperate, was to prove everywhere quite incapable of checking the mighty tide of men and guns surging westward.

On 14 December 1944, there had begun a terrible pounding of German positions in Budapest on both sides of the Danube. That very night twelve thousand guns angled at forty-five degrees and amassed all round the Hungarian capital, were fired simultaneously.

The darkness dissolved in apocalyptic flashes as the twelve thousand guns began to pulverise the city in a deluge of steel.

Then at dawn on 22 December, the Cossack cavalry struck. Three thousand heavy tanks and fifteen infantry divisions hurled themselves at Budapest.

A terrible battle raged for a full forty hours. Each district, street and building were fought for beneath a shower of high explosives and incendiaries. The ubiquitous von dem Bach-Zelewski's SS troops were in there, backed by the German-Hungarian forces under General von Friessner.

Fruitless opposition was waged from a succession of ruined houses; Soviet troops enjoyed a numerical superiority of fifteen to one. Wave after wave of Stormovik assault aircraft all but scraped the roof tops.

Explosive bullets and phosphorus tumbled onto the defenders, who refused even to contemplate defeat. The Russians eventually had little to do but mop up the bodies.

It was only on 12 February 1945 that the guns ceased firing in Budapest. The Hungarians were fleeing in their thousands towards the frontiers of Austria.

For train-loads of refugees there was a grisly fate. Hauptsturmfuehrer Peter Neumann of SS Regiment Viking later wrote:

> 'Terrible scenes take place each time these refugee trains are attacked by Stormoviks, YAKs or TU70s.
>
> 'The planes fly very low and with a tremendous roar they pitilessly machine-gun the mass of people, who scream and scream. Instead of lying down, they remain stupidly on their feet. When they are hit, the men's faces assume a sort of surprised look. As for the women, they nearly always fall with their arms raised, screaming horribly.
>
> 'When the planes with the deadly stars on their wings have flown away, the dead bodies are tossed over the side, to provide room for the thousands of men, women and children who have been tramping along for hours on both sides of the railway track, waiting for others to die so that they may have a chance to live.'

At dawn on 29 March 1945, the German army lashed into retreat by Soviet forces was forced into Austria. Neumann reflected bitterly:

> 'How come that we the warriors who were going to chase the Red Army beyond the Urals, have not even succeeded in stopping the Bolsheviks' advance, or at least in holding them beyond the frontiers of the fatherland?
>
> 'Well, we have failed. And we are still failing.'

On 6 April, an urgent, frightened voice interrupted the seemingly endless diet of aggressively popular music which had been clogging the airwaves of Radio Vienna.

The announcer declared:

> 'Heavy street fighting is going on just outside the centre of the city.'

As if to underline the point, a burst of Russian gunfire could be clearly heard.

226

The broadcast went on:

'At this very moment, shells are howling over our head, over the ancient tower of St Stephen, the heavily damaged Burgtheater, and the castle of Schoenbrunn. Our men are firing simultaneously from all barrels.

'Vienna Volkssturm formations have been deployed on a square. They are going into battle at any minute now to support the soldiers of the Wehrmacht, fighting on a few kilometres away.

'We can see the bombs and shells crashing. The Russians are trying to enter the bulwark of the German south-east. The thunder of battle is enveloping the front-line town of Vienna!'

Then a new voice was saying:

'The enemy's onslaught with huge masses of troops and material is increasing in ferocity. Earlier in the day our alarm units and Volkssturm formations halted the Russians in fierce house-to-house and street fighting on the southern fringes of the city.'

The station fell silent after ten o'clock, only to resume thirty-six minutes later with chimes from St Stephen's Cathedral. There was then a heavily accented Prussian voice calling for a back-to-the-wall defence.

Those who had greeted Hitler at the time of the Anschluss and had literally strewn flowers in his path preserved a sullen silence. But that was by no means everyone's mood.

Three days after the broadcast, the Red Army was closin in through the Penzing and Favoriten regions of Vienna passing the electric power station and the gasworks on the edge of the Prater.

Bands of workmen and students rushed to greet the Soviets. Unfurled at last were the red flags which had lain in hiding since their display had been proscribed. In country districts the colours of the Austrian national flag flew with pride.

But Hitler retained a tenacious grasp on the city he had known as a penniless student and which he secretly hated.

A representative of Q5, the Austrian resistance movement, who had managed to leave Vienna the previous March and had reported to the Austrian Socialist leaders in London, revealed that in the Peoples Court in Vienna between three and four hundred Austrians were being sent to their deaths each month for active resistance.

The Observer newspaper of 1 May 1945 carried the representative's report that he had been present in court when in twenty minutes a total of thirty-eight defendants had been judged; twenty-two of them were sentenced to death.

Courts worked day and night dispensing draconian sentences. *The Observer* reported:

> 'Courts in other parts of Austria bring the total death sentences to about 1000 monthly. In addition, three large concentration camps are overcrowded with political prisoners. About 120,000 Austrians are at present serving sentences for political offences.'

It was all done in a mood of spite borne of fear.

If it had not been for war, that spring of 1945 could have been one of exceptional beauty for Vienna. The sharp vivid blue of the sky shone defiantly through palls of smoke from burning incendiaries.

Nature, however, was not allowed to complete its work with those trees which had already begun to blossom. Bombs, shells and shrapnel stripped them of their branches and reduced them to bare trunks.

The trees which Peter Neumann noticed were those in the gardens of the Military General Hospital, against which the Russians had launched their tanks in groups of twenty or thirty.

The previous night Red Army troops had advanced through the tunnels of the subway systems. The Germans had fought blind, never knowing precisely where their enemy was. Down there, dull explosions with frightening blast effects had boomed and echoed.

Neumann's men held the hospital buildings – at least for the time being. He recorded:

> 'In the hospital corridors, hundreds of wounded lying on the bare floor wait for someone to come and attend to them. Some have horrible wounds, with blackish puffy edges, wrapped any old how in paper bandages.

Gauze and absorbent cotton have been unobtainable for a long time.

'In the operating rooms they are cutting, suturing, amputating. It is all without anaesthetics, for the last bottles of chloroform and ether have been used up.

'A terrible smell of blood, gangrene and ethyl chloride hangs over everything and clings to the walls.'

A Fuehrer decree of 25 September 1944 had created the Volkssturm, the People's Militia, units of which had already fought on both the eastern and the western fronts and were to figure even more prominently in the final battle for Berlin. They consisted largely of Austrian men well into middle age; a choice specimen of contemporary gallows humour declared that if a person called up for the Volkssturm could prove that he had a father already serving then he would qualify for exemption.

The Volkssturm was essentially an ill-trained, badly equipped last-ditch force. Above all, it consisted of men unblooded in battle and desperately afraid.

It was fear that had made these particular Austrians turn and flee from the din of the Russian fire in the subway tunnels. Now they were to pay the supreme penalty. The verdict handed out at the hastily convened court martial had been 'guilty of desertion in the face of the enemy'.

The SS, toting their machine pistols, lined up some dozen Volkssturm. The men knew that they had only a few minutes to live.

The word of command sliced through the morning cold.

'Squad! Ready!'

The Oberscharfuehrer in charge of the execution stared coldly at the whimpering line of Volkssturm. A few stood ramrod straight in a pathetic bid for dignity.

'Aim!' shouted the Oberscharfuehrer suddenly, lifting his arm.

The silence stretched for an eternity.

'Fire!'

The old men spun like dolls, some of the bodies crashing back into the shattered wall. Others slumped forward into the rubble.

It was pointless now. Street by street, alley by alley, the Russians continued their inexorable advance.

Come the night, the sinister glow of the fires was reflected in the dirty, grey waters of the Danube. And, overhead, where once the Luftwaffe ruled the skies, the drone was now from the Stormoviks, the Tupulevs and the gigantic Lavotchkin bombers. These and the MIGs and the YAKs were the lords of the air. The short machine-gun bursts along the ancient Elisabeth Promenade of the canal reminded the Germans that the Red gunners were awake.

Hunger gnawed at the defenders and was at its most acute among the SS, to whom the civilian population would not give as much as a twist of black bread.

Almost like an alarm clock, the sirens of the next morning as usual ejected the Viennese from their beds and sent them scurrying to the shelters.

The bombers homed in unerringly on the old town district. Gas, electricity and water installations had long gone. Bread was short and all stocks of food long exhausted. The coming of the Russians was to prove little consolation: the provisions they would bring would be sparse indeed.

Throughout the last days of the fighting, surrender talks went on between the Russians and the Austrian Provisional National Committee, hastily assembled as a negotiating body.

For the legions of SS who had run Austria at Himmler's behest, there was awareness that they were members of a criminal band who could expect little mercy. Those of the SS who were rounded up were frequently shot out of hand.

Fear of that fate explained why Vienna's canal was sluggish and filthy, and not just full of refuse and Russian and German corpses. For floating down with the current towards the Danube were also the silver eagles and the insignia of the SS torn hastily from uniforms.

It was a galling sensation, fear of your own uniform in defeat. Worse still was the ripping off of decorations – memories of triumphs at Kharkov, of the burning oil wells of the Caucasus, of the hell that had been Stalingrad. All were removed. And all military papers were torn to shreds and scattered in the water.

To remain on the run was foolhardy now, but still there were those willing to risk the machine-guns of the tanks grouped at the far end of Wiesingerstrasse, facing across the canal.

230

The guns opened up in a furious barrage at vague shapes swimming or running in the direction of the ruins of the Aspern Bridge. To fire back was merely a waste of time; the Russians were secure in their armour.

Besides, from the far side of the Untere Donaustrasse, the self-propelled machine-guns also joined in. Tracer bullets were soon making lacy patterns against the night sky, every fiery line the track of a murderous cone of flying steel.

But it was the Russian searchlights, blinding figures piercing the darkness, which made easy the final kill. The Germans were torn to shreds, floating down the Danube, which was now red with their blood, joining the many thousands more who had already fallen in the struggle to hold Vienna.

The T-34s advanced from the Stubenring and the Radetzky-strasse. They were joined by tanks from the other side of the bridge. A ring of steel was complete.

On 13 April 1945, the Russians finally captured Vienna, a tired city with all its gaiety gone. Crowds gathered to stare in sad disbelief at the charred ruins of the twelfth century St Stephen's Cathedral, which the Germans had destroyed almost as a final act. Then there was the Opera House, crumbled beneath the bombs of the Allies, the battered state buildings and the wrecked homes.

Gaunt walls stood out against the sky in the streets now strewn with crumbled stones. There were no trains, lorries or even horse-drawn carts to bring in food from the farms.

As the Russians removed the Schwarzenbergplatz sign and nailed to the wall instead one reading Stalin Square, many of the people of Vienna went about their business not just with empty bellies, but with ashamed faces.

This may have been the city of emperors, of the Café Mozart, of the wine gardens of the Grinzing Mills and the woods of Strauss, but it was also the city which had welcomed Adolf Hitler deliriously in 1938.

The first penalty had been the attention of Allied bombers; now there were the Russians as sinister conquerors.

The last occupation forces, under a Four-Power Allied Control Council, were not to leave Austria for a full ten years.

19

The sound of distant artillery rumbled over the bleak wastes around Auschwitz. The Red Army was drawing ever nearer. A desperate scramble to destroy evidence of the most notorious extermination centre of them all began in earnest.

At the end of the first week of January 1945, the SS organised the evacuation of more than 65,000 Jewish prisoners. Throughout the month, enormous columns, some with as many as 2,500 prisoners, set off on foot in the freezing weather, westwards towards the Silesian cities.

This was literally a death march. In one column of 800 men, only 200 survived the eighteen days of marching. In another column of 2,500, a total of 71 were shot during the first day. Anyone who stumbled and could not rise fell to the bullet.

Himmler and his lieutenants abandoned their policy of mass murder only reluctantly. Clear warnings of what would be in store for the guilty were at first ignored.

As early as 10 October 1944, a joint American-British Declaration was broadcast from Washington. It referred to German plans for mass execution at Oswiecim (Auschwitz). At this, and other camps, *'thousands of people from many European camps are imprisoned'*. The declaration continued with the warning that if plans for mass execution were carried out, the British government *'will hold responsible all those who are in any way involved, from the highest to the lowest. In full co-operation and agreement from the Allies, they would spare no effort to bring the guilty to justice.'*

To the considerable surprise of the Allies, there was a response from Berlin – albeit terse. The statement said: *'These reports are false from beginning to end.'* It sounded like a panic denial; the Foreign Office felt the declaration had been eminently worthwhile.

But for a long time it made no difference to the level of slaughter; on 12 October, three days after the warning, three thousand Jewish women were 'selected' from the barracks at Birkenau and gassed in Crematorium II.

The British tried again. Names of seven top SS were read out on the radio. There was a pressing reason to keep up the pressure: information had reached the Polish government-in-exile in London that the Germans at Auschwitz had killed 12,400 civilians driven from Warsaw after the rising.

The broadcast was unambiguous and ended:

'Let all the other people concerned be warned. These atrocities are capital crimes which will be punished. Let all those concerned in them whether as initiators or as executives or in any other way, reflect whether they are wise to behave like this at the end of an already lost war.

'And let the German people remember that the men who are now calling on it to commit national suicide on their behalf are the men who are directly responsible for a series of crimes which have left an indelible stain on the honour of their country.'

Allied bombing raids were stepped up on industrial plants in the area of Auschwitz. In one attack, a cluster of bombs fell by mistake on the SS sick bay.

One of the witnesses, Erich Kulka, looked upon the event as a welcome diversion:

'I and a colleague working on the maintenance squad had been called to the SS sick bay . . . because the central heating pipes had been damaged by frost over Christmas. We were ordered to repair it, and hurried across to the SS room. In the room we found oranges, figs and chocolates, things I had not seen for five years. Being left alone for a few moments to do the repairs, we took the food and hid it under our jackets, then we began the repairs.

'Suddenly we heard the sirens. The SS took us into the heating cellar. As we hid in the cellar we heard the sound of bombs falling. There were about five bombs. One of the bombs crashed near this heating building. We were covered with rubble and ashes . . .'

But Auschwitz was too grim a place for there to be much

rejoicing when at 3 p.m. on 27 January 1945, Soviet troops eventually reached the camp.

They found 648 corpses, and 7,600 survivors: 1,200 survivors in Auschwitz Main Camp, 5,800 at Birkenau, including 4,000 women and 650 survivors at nearby Monowitz.

Since the first gas camp had begun operations more than two and a half years earlier, a minimum of two million Jews had been killed there, along with two million Soviet prisoners-of-war, Polish political prisoners, gypsies and non-Jews from all over Europe.

The outside world by now was not entirely unprepared for the horrors. Earlier, the Red Army had reached Lublin, and had published photographs of corpses and skeletons piled up in the courtyard of Majdanek.

The atrocities had been difficult to take in. Captain D. MacLaren, of the US Psychological Warfare Division wrote on 3 January:

'The British and American people are still not as a whole willing to believe that German atrocities abroad and the Gestapo reign of terror at home, has been anything like it is.'

They were soon to learn.

There was a burning thirst for revenge on those who had executed Hitler's notorious eastern policy. But it could not be slaked immediately. In the case of Rudolf Hoess, Commandant of Auschwitz, it was to take over a year from the war's end.

There had been many fugitive Nazis who had burnt their uniforms, dug up the family jewels and sped to cattle ranches in Argentina. For those who stayed in Germany there was a general exodus north; Schleswig-Holstein, an agricultural area which was to remain fanatically pro-Nazi for years, was a favourite spot. Here, it was reasoned, a man might be protected until the worst of the hunt was over. There could then be a bid for a fresh set of papers, a new identity and skilful dodging of the various denazification courts.

It was the latter course which appealed to that intensely sentimental family man, Obersturmbannfuehrer Rudolf

Franz Ferdinand Hoess, Kommandant of Auschwitz from May 1940 until December 1943, when he had been promoted by Himmler to a desk job at the SS Central Economic and Administrative Office. Before that, he had returned briefly to Auschwitz as commander of the SS garrison there.

Hoess had first been arrested in May 1945, along with hundreds of thousands of other Germans. But he had not been recognised and was soon released to go and work on a farm. Not that he was in any way forgotten. Britain's Field Security section of Counter Intelligence stepped up the search. Soon its personnel were showing close interest in one particular apartment block in the Schleswig-Holstein town of Heide.

Bernard Clarke, a British Jew and a sergeant in 92 Field Security Section who had already been involved in a fruitless search for the elusive former Nazi Party Secretary Martin Bormann and is today a successful businessman working in the south of England, explains:

> 'We knew that Frau Hannah Hoess, her son and daughter had an upstairs apartment in this block, furthermore that Hoess was in the habit of sneaking in once a month to see them. A round-the-clock watch, however, produced not so much as a shadow of him.
>
> 'Nonetheless, Hoess had somehow got in and somehow seen his family. The news came from the army of informers at our disposal – wretched Germans who were keen to keep on the right side of the occupation authorities and were quite prepared to betray neighbours and friends for a few tins of bully-beef and a packet of cigarettes.
>
> 'The time to act had obviously arrived . . .'

At 5 pm on 11 March 1946, Frau Hoess opened her front door to six intelligence specialists in British uniform, most of them tall and menacing and all of them practised in the more sophisticated techniques of sustained and merciless investigation.

No physical violence was used on the family: it was scarcely necessary. Wife and children were separated and guarded. Clarke's tone was deliberately low-key and conversational.

He began mildly: 'I understand your husband came to see you as recently as last night.'

235

Frau Hoess merely replied: 'I haven't seen him since he absconded months ago.'

Clarke tried once more, saying gently but with a tone of reproach: 'You know that isn't true.' Then all at once his manner had changed and he was shouting: 'If you don't tell us we'll turn you over to the Russians and they'll put you before a firing-squad. Your son will go to Siberia.'

It proved more than enough. Eventually, a broken Frau Hoess betrayed the whereabouts of the former Auschwitz Kommandant, the man who now called himself Franz Lang. Suitable intimidation of the son and daughter produced precisely identical information.

A heavy snowstorm carpeted the roads out of Heide as around midnight the convoy of some thirty men, comprising officers of the military government, reinforced with medical personnel and troops, began the journey to the lonely farm-house standing in its own grounds at Gottrupel.

The convoy slowed to a halt; then came the order to douse lights and extinguish cigarettes.

Clarke and a Captain Cross edged forward, the sergeant cocking his service revolver as the silence was fractured by repeated knockings on the front door.

The elderly black-clad woman who eventually answered was soon denying that anyone else was in the house. The troops moved in, firmly placing her under arrest. The search began.

Examination of every room, cupboard and alcove produced nothing. It was now around 2 am; Cross was getting impatient.

He sighed: 'Maybe this is another of your Bormann escapades. There's certainly no one here and I'm getting tired.'

Clarke insisted: 'We haven't tried the stable block.'

It included the slaughter room for cattle with its enormous benches. The troops fanned out and began a methodical search, which ended in one of the numerous alcoves.

Clarke recalls vividly: 'He was lying on top of a three-tier bunker wearing a new pair of silk pyjamas. We discovered later that he had lost the cyanide pill most of them carried. Not that he would have had much chance to use it because we had rammed a torch into his mouth.'

Hoess screamed in terror at the mere sight of British uniforms.

Clarke yelled: 'What is your name?'

With each answer of 'Franz Lang', Clarke's hand crashed into the face of his prisoner. The fourth time that happened, Hoess broke and admitted who he was.

The admission suddenly unleashed the loathing of the Jewish sergeants in the arresting party whose parents had died in Auschwitz following an order signed by Hoess.

The prisoner was torn from the top bunk, the pyjamas ripped from his body. He was then dragged naked to one of the slaughter tables, where it seemed to Clarke the blows and screams were endless.

Eventually, the Medical Officer urged the Captain: 'Call them off, unless you want to take back a corpse.'

A blanket was thrown over Hoess and he was dragged to Clarke's car, where the sergeant poured a substantial slug of whisky down his throat. Then Hoess tried to sleep.

Clarke thrust his service stick under the man's eyelids and ordered in German: 'Keep your pig eyes open, you swine.'

For the first time Hoess trotted out his oft-repeated justification: 'I took my orders from Himmler. I am a soldier in the same way as you are a soldier and we had to obey orders.'

The party arrived back at Heide around three in the morning. The snow was swirling still, but the blanket was torn from Hoess and he was made to walk completely nude through the prison yard to his cell.

It took three days to get a coherent statement out of him. But once he started talking, there was no holding him.

The man who suffered most during the interrogation, however, was not the prisoner but Bernard Clarke.

He recalls:

'Prior to the capture, my hair was jet black. After the three days, a white streak suddenly appeared in the centre, which stayed there until the rest of my hair went white as well.

'It was not due to the strain of events. I could cope with that. But Hoess had repeated with pride the instructions that he had given to prisoners to dig pits in which they were subsequently shot. He revealed how the bodies were ignited and how oozing fat from them was poured over others.

'He admitted without a trace of remorse that he had been responsible for around two million deaths and that killings had frequently been carried out at the rate of 10,000 a day.

'And yet this was the man whose letters to his wife and children I had the job of censoring. Sometimes a lump came to my throat. There were two different men in that one man. One was brutal with no regard for human life. The other was soft and affectionate.'

Never once did Hoess attempt to evade responsibility or deny what he had done.

He was left seemingly unmoved by the death sentence following his trial before a special Polish people's court. He reasoned that Allies had their orders and that there could be absolutely no question of these not being carried out.

Rudolf Hoess was hanged on 7 April 1947 next to the house inside the Auschwitz camp where he had lived with his wife and children.

Hans Frank, former Governor-General of Poland, Reichsleiter of the Nazi Party and President of the Academy of German Law, was in May 1945 just one of two thousand prisoners held in a camp of huts at Berchtesgaden. He did not bother to nurse hopes that he might pass unrecognised; indeed, considerably before the end of the war he had taken a perverted pleasure at the prospect of being one of the more celebrated of the war criminals.

At a secret session in Warsaw the previous January, he had proclaimed:

'We must not be squeamish when we learn that a total of 17,000 people have been shot . . . We must remember that we, who are gathered here, figure on Mr Roosevelt's list of war criminals. I have the honour of being number one.'

Celebrity status of any kind singularly failed to impress the two coloured GIs who arrested him and made sure he was transported to the municipal prison in Miesbach only after he had been savagely beaten up and flung into a lorry.

A tarpaulin had been thrown over him to hide the more obvious signs of ill-treatment; Frank found the cover useful when he attempted to slash an artery in his left arm.

Clearly, no such easy way out could be permitted; a US army medical officer saved his life and he stood trial at the International Military Tribunal at Nuremberg.

Frank's language had always been forcible, whether in support of Hitler or not. In December 1941, he had declared:

> 'I ask nothing of the Jews except that they should disappear. They will have to go . . . We must destroy the Jews wherever we meet them and whenever opportunity offers so that we can maintain the whole structure of the Reich here . . . We can't shoot these 3.5 million Jews, and we can't poison them, but we can take steps which, one way or another, will lead to extermination, in conjunction with the large scale measures under discussion in the Reich.'

Defendants at Nuremberg may have been given the impression that a display of penitence and a confession of guilt in front of the Tribunal would result in a lenient sentence. This was Frank's hope. But for a convinced Nazi who had been head of a party's legal department as early as 1929 it was plainly clutching at straws.

Nevertheless, as befitted a lawyer, his defence was adroit and vigorous. Its main theme was that he had not really been responsible for the crimes with which he was charged but, in Poland, had merely given instructions for 'essential pacification measures'. He ascribed his crimes – somewhat generously described at Nuremberg as 'excesses' – to the activities of the police whom, he pointed out, he had not controlled.

Hitler, he complained somewhat plaintively, had double-crossed him – Hitler

> '. . . who outwardly had appointed me as his representative but secretly had handed the area over to the crazy tyranny of Himmler and his minions.
> 'All my complaints to Hitler over their activities, against

which I was in effect powerless and which I frequently tried to counter by the most desperate measures, were met in silence . . .'

It was all useless. With a dry detachment that was deadly in its effectiveness, Sir Hartley Shawcross, Britain's Chief Prosecutor at Nuremberg, described Frank as

'. . . a willing and knowing participant in the use of terrorism in Poland; in the economic exploitation of Poland in a way which led to the death by starvation of a large number of people; in the deportation to Germany as slave labourers of over a million Poles.'

The judgment also pronounced:

'The evidence establishes that . . . occupation policy was based on the complete destruction of Poland as a national entity and a ruthless exploitation of its human and economic resources for the German war effort.

'All opposition was crushed with the utmost harshness. A reign of terror was instituted, backed by summary police courts which ordered such actions as the public shootings of groups of 20 to 200 Poles and widespread shootings of hostages.

'The concentration camp was introduced in the Government General by the establishment of the notorious Treblinka and Majdanek camps.'

Frank mounted the gallows in the gymnasium of Nuremberg prison on 16 October 1946, leaving behind him a typically striking piece of rhetoric: *'A thousand years will pass and the guilt of Germany will not be erased.'*

It is not recorded that the failed former bookseller Karl-Hermann Frank, who had been Minister of State and virtual ruler of the Czech Protectorate, made any such pronouncement when he was hanged publicly in Prague.

A crowd of seven thousand gathered to see Lidice avenged; photographs of Frank's dangling body, clad in an ill-fitting, faded uniform were circulated to the world press.

Justice, however, was not yet to net that perfect model of an SS bureaucrat, the desk man of death, Adolf Eichmann.

At the war's end, Eichmann, armed with suitably concocted civilian papers, had decamped with his family for Argentina.

Israeli intelligence was biding its time.

20

Jerusalem was electric with rumours on that May day in 1960; Prime Minister David Ben-Gurion, it was whispered, would be making a major announcement in the Knesset, the Israeli Parliament.

Every available space in the chamber was crammed at 4 p.m. There was a sudden hush as Ben-Gurion rose for his brief statement. It was couched in deliberately unemotional language; even so he could not stifle the break in his voice.

He said:

'I have to announce to the Knesset that a short time ago, one of the greatest Nazi criminals was found by the Israeli Security Services. Adolf Eichmann, who was responsible together with the Nazi leaders for what they called the "Final Solution of the Jewish Problem" – that is, the extermination of six million Jews of Europe. Adolf Eichmann is already under arrest in Israel, and he will shortly be brought to trial in Israel under the Nazis and Nazi Collaborators (Punishment) Law of 1950.'

There was a single sob from one of the Knesset members. But that was not the reaction of the rest. There was a brief pause while the news sunk in; then there was wild cheering and clapping. Adolf Eichmann, ex-chief of Sub-section VI of the Reichssicherheitshauptamt, the main security department of Nazi Germany, was now in the hands of the people he had deliberately and coldly sought to exterminate.

That afternoon in the Knesset was remarkable in itself, but there also occurred that day an event totally unprecedented in the history of the still-infant state of Israel.

A few minutes before Ben-Gurion made his statement, a

48-year-old, affable, large-eared man had slipped into a seat in the Knesset normally reserved for senior officials behind the cabinet ministers' table.

His name was Isser Harel, and to those relatively few citizens of Israel who had heard of him, he was generally assumed to be a senior civil servant more than content to remain anonymous, buried away among mountains of paper in a government office.

But now the man who was never photographed and whose name never appeared in the press, was out in the open. For Isser Harel was head of Mossad, Israeli secret intelligence.

To Mossad had been entrusted one of the classic covert intelligence operations of all time – the kidnapping of Adolf Eichmann. Mossad agents, operating thousands of miles from home, had travelled on forged documentation and relied on superb professionalism to activate the project which became known as Operation Iyar, after the month in the Hebrew lunar calendar when Eichmann was to be captured.

The hunt had begun in earnest as far back as 1953 when Simon Wiesenthal, a survivor from the notorious Death Block at Mauthausen who was to become the world's most famous Nazi hunter, heard almost by chance that Eichmann was living near Buenos Aires and working for a water-supply company.

The interest of the Israelis was immediate, and to them was shipped Wiesenthal's entire collection of documents on Eichmann, including his original SS file.

Mossad got to work. By the end of September 1959 agents had discovered the whereabouts in Buenos Aires of Veronika Eichmann, reportedly living with a strange man, to whom she was not married but whose name she used.

It was this shadowy figure who daily became the object of interest to the members of the Mossad team whom Isser Harel had despatched to Argentina.

It was revealed that he called himself Ricardo Klement and now worked, not for a water-supply company, but for the Mercedes-Benz factory in Suareze San Jarosto. He was – and the choice of job seemed grotesquely apt – employed by the factory as an administrative clerk.

Mossad agents were skilled at shadowing a man without being spotted; through various ruses photographs were obtained of the man calling himself Klement.

There was always an agent on the buses which he used; one of the agents was invariably in the cheap restaurant where the quarry lunched alone every day. A room was rented across the way from Veronika Eichmann's house. During the 24-hour-a-day surveillance, Klement's every move was photographed by hidden cameras. Later, the prints were checked against those already in the possession of the Israelis.

The procedure involved in actually placing Mossad agents in Argentina was an elaborate and as seemingly melodramatic as any passage from a spy thriller.

But the mission – the Eichmann team actually called itself 'The Avengers' – was carried out in deadly earnest, not the least because it was essential that the Argentine authorities should have no knowledge of what was contemplated. In the strict terms of international law, it was to be an illegal snatch.

Long before the operation itself, three Israeli investigators had flown to Argentina for preliminary reconnaissance. As a result, a special office was set up within Mossad. Its sole job was to collect material on Adolf Eichmann.

A sub-section had the task of getting the Israeli team into the country and also bringing it out. By the time that the head of the sub-section had finished work, he had assembled a thousand-page manual reckoned to cover just about every eventuality.

One man was put in charge of the travel arrangements. It was decided that at least a dozen people, including Harel, would be necessary for the actual snatch. All of them would have to travel on different flights, from different corners of the world, and have forged passports and a variety of visas. No one traveller could have any traceable connection with another.

To maintain absolute security called for a Byzantine talent for intrigue. The documentation with which agents entered the country was frequently different from the documentation with which they left.

Agents had made elaborate journeys around South America, posing as travellers on a package tour who would be calling at Argentina merely as part of an itinerary.

To fly his precious cargo out of the country once it had been secured, Isser Harel hit on a scheme of impudent ingenuity which represented what was perhaps the most elaborate of all those involved in Operation Iyer.

But first it was necessary to capture Ricardo Klement.

The man who engaged the full attention of the Mossad agents lived with the woman and three sons on Calle Garibaldi in the San Fernando suburb of Buenos Aires.

Klement had his counterpart in modest, unambitious commuters throughout the world. His home was unassuming. He had built it himself and augmented an adequate but by no means ostentatious income by running a small chicken farm.

His life was as regular and as predictable as the tram lines he used every weekday morning. He would walk two blocks to the stop at exactly six a.m. The tram journey took twenty minutes and it dropped him in the Liniares section of the city, where he changed to bus No. 195 bound for San Jarosto.

Passengers on this route were also workers for Mercedes-Benz.

There was little conversation between Klement and his fellow commuters at that hour. The thin, unsmiling man had the reputation of speaking seldom even to the clerks with whom he worked.

What solely distinguished Klement from other Buenos Aires commuters was that every single move was watched and followed over a succession of weeks. Indeed, there was little that his shadowers did not know about their greying, 54-year-old target.

He was known to speak Spanish fairly well, if with a slight German accent. The single grocery store which he patronised was also pinpointed. Here, in addition to ordering food, he invariably bought several bottles of beer and wine.

Beyond a brief nod he seldom had anything to do with his neighbours. Friends were few. Those who did call at the primitive stone house which lacked gas, electricity or water were members of the strong Buenos Aires German population.

At five o'clock on the evening of 11 May 1960, Señor Klement went to a meeting of factory workers which lasted around an hour. After it, he caught the six o'clock tram from the factory and made for home.

It was a day like any other for Ricardo Klement. That is, until 7 p.m., when his life was suddenly jerked out of its dull, predictable routine.

244

On that particular day, he had left the tram at the city line on Liniares Avenue, heading for the intersection of Coriantes and Dorgunal Avenues, where he invariably took the small green and yellow tram for the final lap of the trip home. On that particular evening, however, he did vary the routine slightly. He stepped off to buy a packet of cigarettes, and it was then that the black sedan pulled up beside him.

A man leapt from the car and seized Ricardo Klement. He was too surprised to resist. Before he knew what had happened, he was pushed into the back of the already moving car.

The two men made no answer to the question in Spanish: 'Who are you?'

By now, the car was heading for a suburb on the other side of the city. It was doubtful whether Klement was any more nervous than the man at the wheel. It was true that the Mossad agent had rehearsed the trip several times. Nevertheless, he drove with extreme caution, keeping well below the authorised speed limit. An officious traffic policeman could well ruin everything.

The driver knew that there were three traffic lights that could present difficulties. He might well be forced to stop at intersections invariably manned by police.

As it turned out, the first light was red. As the car slowed to a stop the two men in the back felt their prisoner stiffen. A revolver was shoved into his ribs.

The threat was in German: 'One shout from you and you're dead.'

Klement saw a policeman a mere twenty feet away, but by then he was too terrified to call out. A bank of other lights slowed progress even further, but Klement was only conscious of the hard metal pressing into his ribs.

Soon the car had quit the crowded main streets and was well into the quieter suburbs.

Klement tried again: 'Where are you taking me?'

None of his captors replied.

The car was soon pulling up at a two-storey white house and Ricardo Klement was being pulled out and ushered up the stairs into a small low-ceilinged room containing nothing but two chairs and a small bed.

One of the captors was a large blond with blue eyes and he was snapping, 'Sit down!'

245

The next instruction followed swiftly. Klement was ordered to undress and lift up his left arm. The trio of abductors stared at the large scar under Klement's armpit.

It was at this precise moment that the elaborately contrived persona of Ricardo Klement collapsed irrevocably.

Each SS commander had sported the insignia of his organisation and his blood group in a tattoo under the left armpit. It was clear from the ugly scar that Klement had not removed the tell-tale signs through surgery. He had gouged them out himself.

One of the captors now produced a military cap of the type which SS officers had worn. He placed it on the prisoner's head, looking closely at the photograph he held in his hand.

Silently, the picture was passed to others. Up to that point, Klement had managed to keep his nerve. What shattered him was the sudden appearance of yet another Israeli. He was carrying a couple of X-ray plates, one of which showed a broken collar-bone. The other was of a fractured skull.

The man said: 'There is evidence of two old fractures in the places shown by the X-rays.'

Then came the pronouncement: 'You are Karl Adolf Eichmann.'

Trained physician's fingers were now running over the head, then over the upper chest. All the prisoner said was: 'Are you Americans?'

There had been a slight suggestion of hope in the man's tone, but it soon dissolved into despair as the question was repeated.

Klement said almost with resignation: 'You must be Israelis.' Fear showed in his eyes. 'The others are not interested in me.'

The strain under which he had lived for fifteen years was now manifest. The mask had dropped forever.

The man who up till now had resolutely stuck to the cover identity of Ricardo Klement was muttering: *'Ich habe die ganze Zeit gezittert, dass es so kommen wuerde.'* (I have always feared that this is how it would happen . . .)

One of the interrogators told him coldly: 'If you co-operate and don't try anything foolish, you will be given a fair trial and the benefit of legal council.'

All the spirit seemed to go out of Adolf Eichmann. He responded wearily: 'All right, I'll co-operate.'

Later that night in his own handwriting he produced a statement:

'I, the undersigned, Adolf Eichmann, declare of my own free will that since my true identity has been revealed, it has become clear to me that there is no point in hiding any more from justice. I declare that I am willing to go to Israel and face there an authorised court. I understand that I will be given legal aid, and I will do everything possible to give an explanation of the facts of my last years of service in Germany, in order that a true picture of the facts will be described for the coming generation.

'I make this declaration of my own free will. I was not promised a thing and I was not threatened. I only want to gain at last some peace of mind. Since I do not remember many details, and it happens that certain things are mixed up in my mind, I hereby ask to be assisted by having access to documents and testimonies, for I have made up my mind to help reveal the whole truth.

(Signed) Adolf Eichmann, Buenos Aires,
May 1960.'

The most elaborate search for one of the most notorious of Hitler's lieutenants operating in the vassal territories of the east had reached the end of its first phase.

By a remarkable and useful coincidence Argentina was celebrating the 150th anniversary of her independence on 19 May.

The date was of particular interest to Isser Harel. True, Israel was a far younger nation, but this was surely no reason why due respect should not be paid to Argentina by a new country.

What could be more natural than the Prime Minister David Ben-Gurion should despatch one of his cabinet ministers, Abba Eban, together with several high ranking foreign office and military officials to Buenos Aires as a mark of celebratory respect?

Harel reasoned that it would be both good public relations and good manners. The fact that certain unfinished and secret business which Israel had in Argentina could be completed at the same time was, of course, of only incidental interest to the Israeli secret service.

On 1 May 1960, Israeli newspapers carried prominent advertisements by the national airline, El Al. They proclaimed that an air service direct from Israel to Argentina would be inaugurated during the next few days. What could be more suitable than that those aboard the very first flight on the new route should be Abba Eban and distinguished colleagues?

There were a few raised eyebrows around the airline business. Hitherto, El Al had been doing capacity business to New York, Rome, Paris, Zurich and other European capitals. What on earth, it was asked, was the point of adding a new route that would plainly be a loss-maker?

Nevertheless, on the afternoon of 18 May a powerful turbo-jet warmed up at Lydda Airport outside Tel Aviv. The gleaming white Bristol Britannia lifted off from the tarmac and became an accomplice in one of the century's most brilliant manhunts.

The two first pilots aboard were not altogether happy at having been downgraded to co-pilots without warning for this particular flight. In overall charge and making absolutely certain that everyone knew it was El Al's chief pilot, Zvi Tohar.

But, of course, his aggrieved colleagues knew nothing of the interview chief pilot Tohar had attended some weeks before. He had received very specific instructions, not least of which was a reminder of his responsibility for a number of extra passengers on the inaugural flight who were not listed on the manifest but merely put down as 'crew members'.

It was those particular Mossad agents who would ultimately decide whether at the end of the day Zvi Tohar would be allowed to keep his job and draw his pension.

For all his seeming close attention, however, Tohar's mind was not fully engaged on the outward flight.

It was the return journey which was worrying him.

At about the same time that the Britannia was leaving Lydda, a young Israeli named Rafael Arnon, who just happened to be in Buenos Aires, was telling a hospital doctor that he was suffering from vertigo following a motor accident.

Arnon was remarkably convincing, which was hardly surprising since he had been well instructed by a Mossad medico who had provided him with some remarkably convincing symptoms. They would ensure his release from hospital, together with a certificate showing that he required further treatment back in his own country.

Arnon would then be required to hand over the certificate to a third party and bow out promptly, his work done.

At some ten minutes before midnight on 21 May 1960, the car containing the El Al crew who would fly the Britannia back home were waved on cheerily. No one paid any attention to one particular figure in uniform slumped on the back seat. If the airport authorities had stopped the car and asked about him, the drugged Adolf Eichmann would not have been able to reply.

His captors would have handed over a perfectly genuine medical certificate stating that the crew member was in need of medical attention, which he was going to receive at home.

Mossad had thought of everything. Even that highly professional organiser, Adolf Eichmann himself, was impressed – and later said so.

Pilot Zvi Tohar carried out his strict instructions to quit Argentina airspace as quickly as he decently could without arousing suspicion. Soon the Britannia was heading for Tel Aviv, with one stop at Dakar to refuel. It landed at Lydda Airport at dawn on Sunday 22 May.

Eichmann, the mindless petty bureaucrat who had so efficiently helped to organise the murder of six million Jews, was one step nearer the gallows.

21

The years had not been kind to Adolf Eichmann. The arrogance and the twisted charm which had once lulled the unwary seemed strangely muted. He looked considerably older than fifty-four; his face was shrunken and weary.

It was not just the fact of capture which seemed to have robbed him of the formidable energies he had displayed in the heady times of power. The years of running had taken their toll. After reaching South America in 1952, Eichmann had wandered for three years in Argentina, Brazil, Paraguay and Bolivia, before finally settling in Buenos Aires. Since then he had sedulously cultivated the civil status of Ricardo Klement, the peaceful small-time employee.

But now that was shattered as he stood to ramrod attention before Emanuel Yedid-Halevi, chief justice of the district of Tel Aviv and heard the charge:

> 'Adolf Eichmann, you are accused of causing the death of millions of Jews in Germany and occupied countries between the years of 1938 and 1945, with the intention of exterminating European Jewry while you were commanding SS units in Germany, and while you were in charge of the deportation of Jews in Germany and German-occupied territory.'

Eichmann, the man in the glass cage in the Tel Aviv courtroom, did manage to regain a good deal of his old bounce and assurance, but confidence was swiftly squashed the moment it welled up.

The formula answer to the prosecutor, Attorney-General Gideon Hausner, became an automatic: 'I don't remember – it was so long ago.'

Eichmann's counsel, the German Dr Robert Servatius, had a nightmarish task, not made much easier by Eichmann's burst of arrogance and threats to take over his own defence. Servatius managed to persuade Eichmann to stick to his original confession 'that he was merely a small cog in a large machine'.

The trouble was that nobody believed him. The line of defence was so transparently false that Eichmann himself came perilously near to losing complete faith in it.

The mild-mannered Judge Moshe Landau broke in at one point to ask: 'Is it correct that you were the head of the Office of Jewish affairs in Berlin?'

There was an impulse to tell the truth. Eichmann said: 'Yes, I . . .' then turned ashen when he realised what he had said. Hastily he reverted to the formula answer 'I was not responsible.'

At times this rigid line evoked the laughter of disbelief. There was Eichmann's plaintive declaration: 'In the entire operation, I was only concerned with the timetable of the trains and other technical aspects of transportation of the Jews.'

In other words, he had only been a transport official. The deliberations of Bureau 06 suggested otherwise. One document among hundreds was representative. Hauser submitted two copies of 1942 orders from Gestapo headquarters for executions of Jews in Ciechanow.

One order read: *'The Jews should be executed in the presence of members of their own race. I ask to be notified of the implementation of this order.'*

It carried the personal signature of Adolf Eichmann.

The trial's ponderous legalistic course was occasionally shattered by moments of drama.

All witnesses testified to the extremes of Eichmann's character: hysterical at one moment, cold as ice the other.

Dr Heinrich Karl Grueber, a Lutheran pastor, had been one of those actually inside Germany who had dared to help the Jews. He had hidden them, organised an underground movement to smuggle them out of the country and provided food and medicine which saved their lives. He had frequently sought audiences with Eichmann to plea for lives.

Grueber, facing the accused in the dock, said: 'The answer was always negative. I never got a positive reply. He sat there in his office like a piece of marble or ice. Nothing ever touched his heart.

'He never showed any compassion for the sufferings of others. Once he tried to persuade me from my endeavours, saying it wouldn't do me any good.'

In court, it proved a hard task quelling Eichmann's verbosity. He spent an entire day explaining the Nazi organisation – an organisation, he explained, of which he was little more than a bureaucrat blindly following orders. As for the extermination of Jews, that had been in the hands of his superiors, who had gone ahead without informing him.

To a question from Servatius on feelings of personal guilt, Eichmann replied with characterisitc opacity.

He proclaimed: 'The guilt is to be borne by those responsible for the political decisions to order deportations. Ethically, in one's attitude towards one's self, there is a sense of guilt applied to concepts which are above the law.

'Here, I condemn myself. In conclusion, I beg to say that I have regrets and condemnation for the extermination of the Jewish people ordered by the Nazi rulers.'

His statement concluded, Eichmann rose and bowed with military stiffness to the court. Dr Servatius had rested his case.

The tireless Hausner had cut ruthlessly through Eichmann's waffle, snapping: 'In your own heart, don't you find yourself guilty as an accomplice in the murder of millions of Jews? Answer yes or no.'

Eichmann's eyes slid in frightened appeal towards Servatius. But his counsel could do nothing; the question was a perfectly proper one.

Eichmann stammered weakly: 'That I do admit. I do not consider myself guilty legally. I merely received and carried out orders.'

Hausner's summing up took thirteen hours, knitting together the loose ends in the damning documents which formed the indictment.

Rhetoric was eschewed for as long as possible, but the very nature of the trial was such that it could not help breaking in eventually.

The three judges and the crowded courtroom heard the peroration: 'The onus of proving wrong the documented evidence against the accused lies with the accused. He has said that the documents lie, that he is telling the truth. But this had been the devious path of Nazism since it was started, and Eichmann is no different from the others – if they have regret in their hearts, it is the regret that their loathsome work was never finished . . .

'Eichmann was far from being a cog in the machine of destruction. He was in the middle of the destruction of people and in charge of the practical implementation of the crime already described here. The Jewish problem was his to solve, and his system for speeding up the extermination of the Jews was copied throughout the Reich.

'I request, your honours, that you rule Eichmann to have been involved in the conspiracy to commit the crimes against the Jewish people and against humanity, that he held a central position in the executive stages of this conspiracy and that he is responsible for all of its consequences.

'I ask you, oh judges of Israel, to render a just and truthful verdict!'

Eichmann never appeared to grasp the real nature of the indictment. He had been charged with crimes against the Jewish people and against humanity, with war crimes and with service at different times in the SS, SD and Gestapo, all of which had been proclaimed criminal organisations at the Nuremberg trials.

In addition to reiterating, 'I was not responsible', he claimed again and again that he had never personally killed anyone.

That was probably true. But it was not the point of the charges. He ignored resolutely proven evidence that he had been in overall command of the Einsatzgruppen, protesting that the actual killings had been carried out by men of the stamp of Otto Ohlendorf.

On Eichmann's desk there had been a teleprinter from Auschwitz which had stuttered out its ghastly messages of extermination.

Even Himmler had admitted that watching gassing through peepholes, even if there was an abundance of alcohol for the spectators afterwards, was 'hard' work. Eichmann had been absolutely indifferent. Conscientiously and efficiently, he had the clothes, hair, watches and gold teeth of the victims sifted, accounted, bundled and despatched. For being such a proficient sorting officer, he was rewarded with the rank of SS-Obersturmbannfuehrer.

One charge alone would have found Adolf Eichmann guilty under the indictment. This was Number Four, which accused him of ordering the 'sterilisation of Jews with a view to prevent birth, and with intent to destroy the Jewish people.'

This indictment left Eichmann equally indifferent. He had not witnessed the operations personally, not so much out of squeamishness, but because of lack of time in a busy schedule. Reports from Buchenwald, Ravensbrueck and Dachau were studied eagerly. Himmler was informed that the experiments were progressing with utmost efficiency.

Gideon Hausner had no need to go further than Tel Aviv or

Haifa for many of his witnesses against Eichmann on Count Number Four. The witnesses, scarred in body and in memory, had brought the exhibits with them into that Jerusalem courtroom.

There had been such witnesses as Polish-born Yaacov Gurfein, possibly the only survivor of 1,300 Jews who, herded into a locked goods train, had peered anxiously through a slit to see whether the train would turn right or left at a junction ahead. For they had known that if the train had turned left, they were heading for the labour camp and the slim chance of survival.

But the train had turned right and Gurfein, twenty-one in January 1943, recalled at Eichmann's trial: 'We managed to break open the window and some of the people in the train jumped out.

'We heard shots. There were sentries with machine-guns on top of the wagon. At about two in the morning, my mother pushed me out of the window. I left her and my brother behind. I crossed the tracks leading into the snow and stayed there for two hours.'

Gurfein said that after escaping he wandered through Poland, at times passing himself off as a Christian and receiving shelter from Christian families. 'I never saw my mother or anyone else from my family again.'

It was the sheer weight of documentation which eventually convicted Adolf Eichmann. A lot of it was lost, of course, burnt in the carpet bombing of German cities or ripped away by wind on muddy roads, slipping from gutted tracks in the endlessly retreating convoys.

Yet the files were so voluminous that more than enough fell into the hands of the conquerors. Indeed, many of the files had to take the place at Eichmann's trial of those most important witnesses who could neither be seen nor heard.

They were the six million Jews whose death and destruction Eichmann and others had decreed.

They had been in that courtroom in Israel nonetheless. Their ghosts had haunted the trial, pointing with unseen fingers, providing in death the line-by-line evidence required by the indictment.

Adolf Eichmann was hanged at Eamleh prison on 1 June 1962. He was accompanied to the execution chamber by the

Reverend William Hull, pastor of Jerusalem's Zion Christian Mission. At no time, he recorded, did the prisoner show the slightest sign of remorse: 'He is the hardest man I ever saw.'

The last great architect of Hitler's planned annihilation of the vassal states of the east had suffered a people's revenge.

1 The German invasion and annexation of Austria in March 1938 was accompanied by deliberate harassment and humiliation of the Jews of Vienna. Elderly Jews were forced to scrub the capital's sidewalks under the gaze of smirking Nazis and their willing sympathisers.

2
Reichsfuehrer-SS Heinrich Himmler was in 1939 chief of the entire police machinery of the Third Reich. At the outbreak of war he supervised the work of his SS (Schutzstaffel, Protection Department) in eastern Europe and the other occupied territories. He preached ruthlessness in achieving racial purity, urged the use of slave labour and stressed the frequent need for extermination.

3 Reinhard Heydrich in the uniform of an SS-Obergruppenfuehrer.
Himmler's deputy as head of the SS and Gestapo, Heydrich was also in
charge of the Einsatzgruppen (Action Groups), responsible for the
mass murder of Jews and political officials undertaken in the wake of
the German advance into Russia in June 1941.

4

SS-Sturmbannfuehrer Adolf
Eichmann, desk man of death.
Present at the Wannsee
Conference in January 1942,
which planned the pattern of
persecution in the occupied
countries, he was given charge of
the Jewish section of the Gestapo
and the RSHA (Reich Security
Office). One of the key activities
of this former travelling salesman
as Head of the Office of Jewish
Emigration in Vienna, was to
bring about the emigration
during 1938-1939 of 100,000
Jews,who left their wealth as
plunder for the Nazis.

5

The Nazi invasion of Czechoslovakia in March 1939 was followed by Hitler's triumphant legions marching into the Hradcany, the historic castle of ancient Bohemian kings in Prague.

6 SS-Brigadefuehrer Karl Hermann Frank was made Secretary of State for the Protectorate of Bohemia and Moravia. He was sentenced to death by a postwar Czech court and publicly hanged near Prague on 22 May 1946.

7 Polish civilians being rounded up by the German authorities. Jews were herded mercilessly into ghettoes and camps which by 1941 were established for extermination as well as slave labour.

8

Former legal adviser to Adolf Hitler, Baden-born Hans Frank was, in 1939, appointed Governor General of the central Polish territory known as the Government General. With headquarters at Wavel Castle, Krakow, Frank's punitive rule aimed at the enslavement of the Poles and the extermination of the Jews.

9 Jewish women and child prisoners in the key Nazi concentration camp of the east – Auschwitz-Birkenau. Situated outside the little Polish town of Oswiecim, about 160 miles south-west of Warsaw, it was to be the scene of the murder by gassing and other means of not less than three million men, women and children.

10 Jews sweeping the streets of Riga, the capital of Latvia and the most important naval base on the Baltic. Latvia was first overrun by the Red Army and then by the Nazis. Hitler's Reich Minister for the Occupied Territories, Alfred Rosenberg, decreed that racially assimilable Balts would have to be subject to "banishment on a large scale", while "the Baltic must become a Germanic inland sea".

General Tadeusz Komorovski who, in 1943, took command of the underground Armia Krajowa (Home Army) in Poland. He was known by his countrymen by the pseudonym "General Bor", hence his subsequent designation as "General Bor-Komorovski". In August 1941 he launched the heroic Warsaw uprising.

12 The Luftwaffe has dive-bombed this Soviet partisan hideout. The Russians systematically organised, trained and equipped partisan bands which eventually numbered some 200,000 men, women and even small children. Originally ill-organised bands, Russian partisans were brought eventually under the rigid control of the military machine.

13 On the Russian battlefront and from a concealed position, an anti-tank weapon to be used against the Germans is demonstrated by Soviet militia.

14 Insurgents during the Warsaw Uprising. There were two such acts of resistance during Nazi occupation, both heroic failures. The first involved the city's ghettoes, while the second saw the rising of the Polish underground forces and the denial by the Russians of a helping hand across the Vistula while the Germans strangled the revolt.

15 The Third US Army exposes the horrors of Buchenwald concentration camp in April 1945. These were mature inmates, but emaciation made them appear like youths. The camps had, in addition to Jews, anti-Nazi Germans and non-Jews from German-occupied countries. They died from starvation, general brutality and, in particular, medical experimentation.

Josef Terboven and SS-Obergruppenfuehrer Wilhelm Rediess
are met by Vidkun Quisling at Oslo Airport. (Courtesy
Historical Research Unit.)

Vidkun Quisling inspects men of the naval branch of the
Hird. (Courtesy Historical Research Unit.)

Joseph Terboven on a tour of inspection in Norway. (Courtesy Historical Research Unit.)

Memorial service held in Copenhagen on 17 December 1943 for members of the Danish Free Corps killed on the eastern front. Right: SS-Gruppenfuehrer Dr Werner Best. (Courtesy Historical Research Unit.)

French Chasseurs Alpins wearing their traditional blue berets. (Courtesy Historical Research Unit.)

Members of the Jeunesse Europe Nouvelle, a branch of the Milice, on parade in Grenoble. (Courtesy Historical Research Unit.)

Hanns Rauter (left) and Anton Mussert inspect Waffen-SS unit in Holland. (Courtesy Historical Research Unit.)

A unit of the French Milice on parade in Vichy, June 1944.
(Courtesy Historical Research Unit.)

Generalmajor Dietrich von Choltitz, Commandant of Paris.
(Courtesy Historical Research Unit.)

SS-Obersturmbannfuehrer Leon Degrelle and his adjutant
Lucien Lippert return in triumph from the eastern front.
(Courtesy Historical Research Unit.)

Maréchal Pétain at his trial. (Courtesy Historical Research Unit.)

Felix Plottier of the Haute-Savoie Maquis. (Courtesy Felix
Plottier.)

CROSS
OF IRON

The Nazi Enslavement of Western Europe

Cross of Iron

The Nazi Enslavement of Western Europe

Rupert Butler

PEN & SWORD MILITARY CLASSICS

TO JOYCE

ACKNOWLEDGEMENTS

In the preparation of this book I am greatly indebted, as always to the staff of the Department of Printed Books at the Imperial War Museum, London, for its patience in supplying material, in many cases books on World War Two resistance which have long been out of print. The store of newspaper cuttings and eyewitness accounts of occupation in various western countries made available by the Institute of Contemporary History and the Wiener Library, London, were of particular value, and I would also like to thank Mrs Edda Tasiemka for allowing me to consult her unique private collection of wartime newspapers and magazines. The special collection of World War Two books held by Wandsworth Public Library was also useful. Felix Plottier, doughty survivor of the maquis of Haute-Savoie, eastern France, and his wife Joan gave me limitless hospitality and kindness at their delightful house in Bonneville and a treasure store of memories of life under Italian, Vichy and German repression. Translation from the French on this and other occasions was the difficult task of Joyce Rackham, to whom I extend my love and respect. Squadron-leader Frank Griffiths, DFC, AFC, ('Cromwell'), who crashed near Annecy and was looked after by the local maquis, supplied a vivid account of life in those days. Indispensable editorial assistance was provided with all her usual faithfulness by Vicky Clayton. I am also indebted to Peter Elliott and Gordon Leith of the Royal Air Force Museum, Hendon, and the staffs of the Luxembourg National Trade and Tourist Office and the Netherlands Board of Tourism. Acknowledgements are also due to Jean Bourgaux, Terry Charman, Robin Cross, Professor M. R. D. Foot, Andrew Mollo and Joe Rose.

'Jetzt es kein Kriegsspiel aber ein grausamer Krieg.'
(This is now no game, but war in all its cruelty.)
—warning given at the outbreak of World War Two
to Henri Frenay, leading figure of the French
resistance

SELECTED BIBLIOGRAPHY

After the Battle, No 56 (Battle of Britain Prints International Ltd, 1988)

Bird, Michael J., *The Secret Battalion*. (Frederick Muller, 1965)

Collins, Larry, and LaPierre, Dominique, *Is Paris Burning?* (Gollancz, 1974)

Dank, Milton, *The French Against the French*. (Cassell, 1978)

Deighton, Len, *Blitzkrieg: From the Rise of Hitler to the Fall of Dunkirk*. (Cape, 1979)

De Jong, L., and Stoppelman, Joseph W. F., *The Lion Rampant: The Story of Holland's Resistance to the Nazis*. (Querido, New York, 1943)

Dourlein, Peter, *Inside North Pole*. (William Kimber, 1953)

De Vomecourt, Phillipe, *Who Lived to See the Day: France in Arms 1940–1945*. (Hutchinson, 1961)

Flender, Harold, *Rescue in Denmark*. (W. H. Allen, 1963)

Foot, M. R. D., *SOE in France*. (Her Majesty's Stationery Office, 1966)

Foot, M. R. D., *SOE: The Special Operations Executive 1940–46*. (British Broadcasting Corporation, 1984)

Frenay, Henri, *La Nuit Finera*. (Opera Mundi, 1973)

Griffiths, Frank, *Winged Hours*. (William Kimber, 1981)

Gudme, Sten, *Denmark: Hitler's 'Model Protectorate'*. (Gollancz, 1942)

Hambro, Carl J., *I Saw it Happen in Norway*. (Hodder & Stoughton, 1940)

Haukelid, Captain Knut, *Skis Against the Atom*. (William Kimber, 1954)

Hayes, Paul, *Quisling*. (David & Charles, 1971)

7

History of the Second World War. (Purnell & Sons, 1966)

Hoffman, Percy, *Hitler's Personal Security*. (Macmillan, 1979)

Irving, David, *The Virus House*. (William Kimber, 1966)

Jackson, Robert, *The Fall of France, May–June 1940*. (Arthur Barker, 1975)

Jones, R. V., *Most Secret War: British Scientific Intelligence 1939–1945*. (Hamish Hamilton, 1978)

Lampe, David, *Savage Canary*. (Cassell, 1957)

Littlejohn, David, *The Patriotic Traitors*. (Heinemann, 1972)

Lottmann, Herbert, *The People's Anger*. (Heinemann, 1986)

Mabire, Jean, *Chasseurs Alpins: Des Vosges aux Djebels*. (Press de la Cité, 1984)

Moen, Lars, *Under the Iron Heel*. (Robert Hale, 1941)

Motz, Roger, *Belgium Unvanquished*. (Lindsay Drummond, 1942)

Myklebost, Tor, *They Came as Friends*. (Gollancz, 1943)

Neave, Airey, *Saturday at M19*. (Hodder & Stoughton, 1969)

Petrow, Richard, *The Bitter Years: The Invasion and Occupation of Denmark and Norway*. (Hodder & Stoughton, 1974)

Pool, James and Suzanne, *Who Financed Hitler: The Secret Funding of Hitler's Rise to Power, 1919–1933*. (Futura, 1980)

Rickard, Charles, *La Savoie dans La Resistance*. (Ouest-France, 1986)

Schoenbrun, David, *Soldiers of the Night*. (Robert Hale, 1980)

Simon, Paul, *One Enemy Only – The Invader*. (Hodder & Stoughton, 1942)

Wiggan, Richard, *Operation Freshman*. (William Kimber, 1986)

1

The thick icy fog of a bitter dawn broke over the airfield at Muenster-Loddenheide on the morning of 10 January 1940.

Major Helmuth Reinberger of the Luftwaffe was only too conscious that the party he had attended the night before had been a particularly hectic affair. That would scarcely have mattered if, as parachute liaison officer at the headquarters of Luftflotte 2 under the command of General der Flieger Helmuth Felmy, he had not been due to attend a staff conference in Cologne.

Reinberger had intended to make the dreary journey by train but his sympathetic station commander, Reserve Major Erich Hoenmanns, suggested that he should be flown to Cologne instead. There could be no question of the severely hungover Reinberger piloting an aircraft himself. Hoenmanns agreed to do the flying. He had been a pilot during World War One and still held a current licence. Furthermore, there just happened to be the little Messerschmitt 108 communications aircraft available. True, there was no authorisation for such a trip but, since no one was likely to discover so trivial a bending of the regulations, that was not important.

As the aircraft snaked above the airport in that freezing January dawn, Reinberger shivered and attempted desperately to control waves of nausea. The only consolation appeared to be that the visibility, apart from a ground mist, seemed good. But what if anything should go wrong? For reassurance, he clasped the bulky yellow pigskin briefcase that lay on his knees and which was his special responsibility.

Surely, it now only remained for the weather to hold.

On 3 March 1939, in defiance of an agreement between Britain, France and Germany a few months earlier, the German Fuehrer, Adolf Hitler, set out to conquer Czechoslovakia. There had been two previous spectacular coups which amounted to blatant aggression: the first on 7 March 1936, when the Wehrmacht, ripping up the appropriate clauses of the Versailles and Locarno treaties, marched into the Rhineland. Then came the annexation of Austria, and when Hitler entered the country of his birth, the crowds strewed flowers in his path.

In all his adventures in the east, Hitler had enjoyed the indispensable neutrality of the Soviet Union, but the Fuehrer was under no illusions. On 9 October 1939, the generals were warned in a memorandum: 'We cannot count on Stalin leaving us to our own devices indefinitely. We must have freedom in the west.'

As for the people who lived in the west, it had been up till now a strange sort of war, one in which there was no fighting on land, while in the air, bombers carried nothing more lethal than crude propaganda leaflets. Only at sea was there any activity: U-boats prowled balefully amid British and neutral shipping in the icy immensity of the northern Atlantic.

But, in fact, Europe was sitting on a slow-burning fuse, even though Hitler had remained somewhat indecisive as to when he would apply a match to it. The German people were little wiser at the turn of the year. They had spent a miserable Christmas, with spartan food and absent menfolk; there was to be little warmth. A characteristic harangue from their Fuehrer was prefaced by a diatribe against 'the Jewish and capitalist warmongers'. He had gone on with vintage bombast to proclaim: 'United within the country, economically prepared and militarily armed to the highest degree, we enter this most decisive year in German history . . . May the year 1940 bring the decision. It will, whatever happens, be our victory.'

But even the seemingly unstoppable Adolf Hitler could not control the weather, which continued to be unrelievedly vile. On 27 December he had again postponed *Fall Gelb* (Case Yellow, the codename for the attack in the west) 'by at least a fortnight'. On 10 January the attack was set for precisely a week ahead; the onslaught would be at 'fifteen minutes before sunrise – 8.16 a.m.' Four days before that, it was intended that the Luftwaffe of Hermann Goering should have its moment of glory – in France. Belgium and the Netherlands would be left to sweat over their ultimate fate.

Plainly, Hitler meant business at last. German forces had moved up to their jump-off positions; unit commanders assembled at their respective headquarters for final briefings.

Then it was called off yet again. And the reason had lain in that yellow pigskin briefcase clutched so firmly by Major Helmuth Reinberger of 22nd Airborne.

For it contained nothing less than dossiers marked *Streng Geheime* (Top Secret). Their contents spelt out in chilling detail the intended destinies of a clutch of nations – France, the Netherlands, Belgium, Denmark, Norway and Luxembourg.

The Messerschmitt 108 carried aboard the proposed blueprint for the invasion of the west.

Any optimism felt by Major Reinberger did not last long. The weather had got worse. Furthermore, it was obvious that Major Hoenmanns was losing his bearings. Visibility narrowed by the minute and it was not long before Hoenmanns was admitting he was hopelessly off course. Without knowing it, he had been driven across the Rhine by the sharp easterly wind. The Me 108 was now in hostile territory.

The only possible lifeline would be a sighting of the Rhine, lying to the east. Hoenmanns struggled feverishly with the controls, but it proved useless, the engine was cutting out; there was nothing for it but a forced landing.

A swift decision was indicated. Hoenmanns selected a large snow-covered field, and there looming up was a dangerously solid-looking line of poplars. It was far too

11

late to avoid them; all that could be done was to kick the rudder frantically and steer for what appeared to be a sizeable gap. A second later, the Me 108 was juddering violently, the trees slicing into the wingtips. Mercifully, the landing was successful. The plane came to rest just short of the far hedge.

The two men, suffering from little more than a severe shaking, had only one thought now. Those all-important documents must be destroyed, and at once. Precious moments were spent studying a map which showed that they had landed near Mechelen-sur-Meuse, just north of Maastricht, in Belgian territory.

Reinberger sought shelter behind the hedge, struggling with his cigarette lighter in a desperate bid to burn the incriminating papers. What happened next had a strong element of comedy. The landing had been witnessed by a Belgian peasant, who gravely handed Reinberger a box of matches. To the relief of both Germans, the papers were soon alight.

But the vital act of destruction was not to proceed uninterrupted. A knot of shouting Belgian soldiers arrowed towards the crippled aircraft. The quick-thinking Hoenmanns, conscious that Reinberger must complete his task, walked away from his colleague towards the approaching troops, his hands raised. With a bit of luck, they might be persuaded that there had only been one man aboard the aircraft. The ruse failed. One sharp-eyed Belgian had spotted the ribbon of smoke behind the hedge. Both men were promptly arrested by two Belgian privates, Rubens and Habets, who fired warning shots.

To make matters worse, the documents did not burn as rapidly as Reinberger had hoped. Most of them were captured intact.

At a nearby police post, they were questioned by a Belgian intelligence officer. To protect the men from the cold, a cast-iron stove glowed warmly in the room. During a pause in the questioning, Reinberger feigned exhaustion and appeared to be asleep. But he was watching his guard

12

closely and noted, furthermore, that the precious documents lay unattended on a table. With a surge of hope, he leapt from his chair, grabbed the papers and attempted to stuff them into the stove. Captain Rodrigue, who was in charge of the command post, hastily put out the fire, burning his hand. He exclaimed furiously: 'It's always the same with you Germans. We treat you correctly and you play a dirty trick like this!'

Rodrigue's next action was to place his revolver on top of the papers. But Reinberger was not giving up yet. In a frenzy, he threw himself at the Belgian; Rodrigue had to tear the revolver away.

Reinberger had abandoned all reason and screamed hysterically: 'I have committed an unforgivable crime! I wanted your revolver so that I could kill myself.' Hoenmanns, who had remained docile throughout, attempted to explain his colleague's behaviour: 'You must excuse him. He's in real trouble. He's an officer in the regular army.'

But it is doubtful whether Rodrigue heard him. He was staring in open disbelief at some of the uncharred papers. Then he dashed from the room to contact his regimental staff.

The two Germans knew then that the last hope had gone.

Reinberger, soon in a state of terror, took refuge in lies. He reported to Luftwaffe headquarters through the German embassy in Brussels that he had succeeded in burning the papers to insignificant fragments, the size of the palm of his hand. It was a hollow move; the next day, 13 January, Belgium's German Ambassador alerted Berlin to considerable Belgium troop movements 'as a result of alarming reports received by the Belgian general staff'.

Any lingering doubts that the incident might be explained away were finally dashed at an icy interview between the German ambassador and the Belgian Foreign

Minister, Paul Henri Spaak, who proclaimed: 'The plane which made an emergency landing on 10 January has put into Belgian hands a document of the most extraordinarily serious nature, which contained clear proof of an intention to attack. It was not just an operations plan but an attack order worked out in every detail, in which only the time remained to be inserted.'

Such almost incredible carelessness by the Germans was viewed with suspicion by many of the Allied countries. Could the Nazis really have been so very lax? Could it be that the whole thing was a not particularly subtle plant to mislead them as to the date and place of an invasion?

Nevertheless, the documents, charred but still legible, were passed to the Dutch and French governments. Their representatives had more than a passing interest in them, particularly when they read 'General Orders of Luftflotte 2'. The document was, of course, incomplete, but enough survived to give a clear pointer to German intentions:

The German army in the west will . . . out its offensive between the North Sea and the Moselle, aided by the air force, through the Belgian-Luxembourg territory in order to . . . the most important parts of the French army and its . . . The area around Liège and . . . surrounded . . . Besides, our intention is to take over Dutch territory, with the exception of *Festing Holland*, with a grouping of troops . . . The 8th Air Corps and some of its troops must support a disembarkation operation made by 7th Airborne Division on the first day of attack. In close cooperation with the 6th Army (mainly positioned close to and west of Maastricht), it must support the progress of the ground force attacking the defence lines covering the Meuse basin and destroy the Belgian army west of that area . . . The fighter planes must gain air supremacy over the 6th Army's zone of attack.

The combined battle formation of the Luftflotte 3 shall take on the French air bases to prevent them from intervening in any battles fought on land. Next, the Luftflotte shall prevent French armies in the north from advancing towards the northeast . . . The 10th Air Corps, to get here with the Kriegsmarine, will concentrate on fighting the British naval forces.

The instructions for this operation were scheduled for Wednesday 17 January.

Hitler's reaction to the turn of events was predictable to anyone familiar with the towering rages of the would-be warlord. Even so, Hitler's anger surpassed anyone's worst fears.

Generalfeldmarschall Wilhelm Keitel of the Wehrmacht related after the war at the Nuremberg trials, where he was arraigned as a war criminal: 'When he was told about the incident, Hitler flew into a frenzied rage, the worst outbreak I have ever seen. The Fuehrer went into a trance, he was frothing at the mouth, he struck the wall with his fists, vowed he would have the guilty parties executed, and roared terrible oaths about the incompetence and treachery among the general staff. Goering, forced to bear the brunt of his fury, had not even recovered from it the next day . . .'

The hapless wives of Major Reinberger and Major Hoenmanns, who were in no way connected with what had happened, were both arrested and thrown into jail. General der Flieger Helmuth Felmy, commander of Luftflotte 2, was dismissed for the errors of subordinates.

The forced landing and the bad weather meant a postponement of Hitler's plans. The order went out: 'All movements to stop.' The Germans were hard at work, nonetheless. To the north were two other little neutral states: Denmark and Norway. These, it was reasoned, were plums ripe for picking.

15

2

Jens Lillilund was not by inclination a violent man. Reserved almost to the point of taciturnity, he was scarcely the type of which resistance heroes were made. But on the morning of 9 April 1940, he was fuelled by a novel emotion: a deep, smouldering anger at the sight of German troops in his native Copenhagen.

News had already reached him that Denmark had been rapidly overrun. He decided to have a look for himself. Indeed, there were the Germans looking remarkably relaxed on Langeline Pier, nonchalantly guarding the waterfront.

With difficulty, Lillilund kept control and peddled furiously away. But those Germans he saw striding arrogantly on the streets proved altogether too much. In what he was later to admit was a futile gesture, he aimed his bicycle at a knot of them. His response to the gutteral order '*Halt*' was to spit at the feet of the conquerors.

He was promptly arrested but, fortunately for him, turned over to the Danish police. The nervous authorities were not willing to antagonise their new conquerors needlessly. Lillilund was eventually released, with a stern warning not to provoke the Germans.

It was an injunction he forthwith resolved to ignore.

But *how*? A patient soul, he bided his time, studiously keeping out of trouble for as long as he could bear to. Then he saw the truck which the Germans had been ill-advised to leave unattended in Kongensgade Square. It contained hay for their barracks.

Jens Lillilund set fire to it. He had begun his resistance war.

In the early hours of the same day, the news editor of the *New York Times* was staring at a telegram which had just come in from the paper's Copenhagen correspondent.

It read: 'GERMAN TROOPS CROSSED THE DANISH FRONTIER AT DAWN AND TOOK POSSESSION OF COPENHAGEN. AT A CABINET MEETING IN THE SMALL HOURS KING CHRISTIAN AND THE GOVERNMENT AGREED TO YIELD BEFORE SUPERIOR FORCE.'

There was still time enough to rush out an extra edition and the news editor splashed over the whole eight-column front page a stark heading in thick type:

'DENMARK MURDERED'

The report was one of the first indications to the outside world of Hitler's assault in the west.

For six months it had seemed that the mighty German war machine had slumbered after the campaign in Poland. The Danes, in particular, were more than content at German inactivity. Memories went back to August 1914. Then Denmark had readily caved in to German pressure, mining the waters of the Great Belt, which had been within Danish jurisdiction and constituted one of the major nautical entrances to the Baltic. Denmark, by mining the Belt, had provided protection for Germany's naval base at Kiel until the war was over. King Christian X had justified the action by proclaiming: 'Denmark at the moment is in such a serious condition that one cannot play banque with one's country.'

The result was precisely as hoped: throughout the four years of World War One, Denmark remained neutral and untouched by battle. Now, twenty-two years later, this pleasant little country of four million, small and flat and therefore a gift to panzer armies, hoped desperately that it would be left alone.

Adolf Hitler also had his eyes elsewhere.

Norway would be the next objective. By gaining bases there, the British blockade line across the North Sea would be broken. Even more to the point, during the cold months iron ore from Sweden, vital to Germany's very existence, had to be switched to the Norwegian port of Narvik and brought down the coast by ship to Germany. German ore vessels would be sailing within Norway's territorial waters; their progress had to be assured.

But first there was the little question of Denmark.

The plans incorporated under the innocent-sounding codename of *Weseruebung* (Weser Exercise) became grim reality when German units fell upon Denmark on 9 April, exactly as scheduled. Simultaneously timed attacks were directed against Jutland, Copenhagen and the strategic island of Fyn. In Jutland, advance elements of the 11th Motorised Rifle Brigade and the 170th Infantry Division smashed across the border on a broad front. Resistance was feeble. No preparation had been made to block roads or mine bridges; in any case, Danish troops had little appetite for combat.

All too often, the pickings for the Germans turned out to be shamefully easy. The German advance had been greeted with blatant eagerness by pro-German Danes. They stationed themselves at crossroads, waving on the advancing German units. The allegiance of these particular Danes was not in doubt: many wore swastika armbands and greeted their conquerors with shouts of '*Heil Hitler!*'

Hitler showed himself the supreme realist. He needed the lands of Scandinavia, which is why the Germans were instructed to behave like liberators. There were harsh exceptions. Guards keeping watch over the frontier crossing at Krusaa in Slesvig were overpowered by men dressed as civilians. Three of them were killed; there were suggestions that the Germans were infiltrating fifth columnists. Local police, unwise enough to mount an investigation once the invasion was over, were told sharply to mind their own business.

Troops who garrisoned the Citadel, the ancient fortress

overlooking the harbour at Copenhagen and the site of the Danish General Staff headquarters, had been courteous to the German businessman who showed close interest in their activities, five days before the invasion. Indeed, a considerate Danish sergeant had escorted this personable tourist around the Citadel grounds. The visitor had been shown the General Staff headquarters and had been particularly interested in the two main gates leading to the fortress itself.

Generalmajor Kurt Himer, the German commander who had been given the responsibility of capturing Copenhagen, returned to Germany eminently satisfied with what he had seen.

The Danes, he was convinced, would be a soft target. And he was right.

When the German troopship *Hansestadt Danzig* arrived off Copenhagen, its progress was almost stately, as if the vessel was on an official visit. But vessels on official visits were not in the habit of carrying an assault battalion. Three combat companies were soon edging towards the Citadel, their progress barely noticed along dawn streets.

The only reported violence involved a hefty bricklayer who, on the way to work in the very early morning, encountered a solitary German, rifle in hand. He extended a burly fist; the German measured his length on the pavement. But the gesture of defiance was ignored.

The gates of the Citadel were unguarded; there were only two sentries. The entire Danish garrison surrendered without a shot.

With the Citadel secured, German troops closed in on the residence of King Christian X. Inside the castle, Premier Thorvald Stauning and Foreign Minister Peter Munch conferred. They urged swift capitulation. But General Wain Pryor, commander in chief of the Danish Army, argued stoutly that the fight must go on. The king, he urged, must leave with his ministers while there was yet still time. The struggle could be continued from the nearest military camp.

19

The seventy-year-old king, weary and confused, pleaded with General Pryor: 'Have not our troops fought long enough?' The swift riposte was indignant: 'They have not.'

Suddenly it all seemed sadly academic. The quiet skies were rudely shattered by bombers of the Luftwaffe screaming above the city.

Journalist Sten Gudme of *Politiken*, the country's largest daily paper, caught the sudden mood of fear: 'Are they going to lay the whole city in ruins? Will their bombload rain down on us the next moment? We had no idea then whether the Cabinet had decided to fight or surrender.'

What few in Denmark knew was that the German Minister to Denmark, Cecil von Renthe-Fink, acting on the instructions of Generalmajor Himer, had delivered an ultimatum. It acknowledged that German troops moving across the border into Jutland were landing on the principal Danish islands on the excuse that it was necessary to 'forestall a British invasion'. There had been a call on the Danes to capitulate immediately. And now leaflets from the aircraft were ramming home the point.

Anthony Mann, the correspondent of the *Daily Telegraph*, recalled:

The blow fell on me personally at 5.50 a.m. when I was still in bed in my Copenhagen flat. We were awakened by a mighty roar of engines: wave after wave of bombers, bearing sinister black crosses and swastikas, were flying in formation past our windows, almost at rooftop height. We could see the faces of the crew-members, peering down through the plexiglass. At intervals of a few seconds, handfuls of pale green leaflets burst from each plane and floated lazily down to almost deserted streets.

Printed in extremely bad Danish, they informed the Danish people that Germany had forestalled an attack on Denmark and Norway by Churchill 'the greatest warmonger of the century', and had assumed the duty of protecting Scandinavia. Everyone should go quietly about his business and do what he was told.

At two o'clock that same afternoon, Himer and Renthe-

Fink called on the king. The elderly monarch, although inwardly shattered, rigidly maintained his dignity. Barely able to conceal his emotion, he proclaimed: 'The king and government will do everything possible to keep peace and order. Any friction between the German troops and Denmark must be eliminated. The country must be spared misfortune and misery.'

Himer was determined to match the king in dignity. He was, he explained smoothly, only doing his duty as a soldier. The Germans had come solely as friends.

Christian suddenly became embarrassingly servile, begging to be allowed to keep his bodyguard.

No objection was raised and the king noticeably relaxed. His last words to Himer were almost pathetically conciliatory: 'General, may I, as an old soldier, tell you something? As soldier to soldier? You Germans have done the incredible again! One must admit that it is magnificent work.'

Hunched at his desk in the editorial offices of *Politiken*, Sten Gudme anxiously grabbed the jangling telephone. The voice said: 'This is the German Legation. Press Attaché Frielitz speaking. Who is that?'

Gudme gave his name. Frielitz adopted a deliberately friendly tone; it might have been a conventionally social call.

'Good morning, Herr Gudme. I'm afraid that there can't be any more issues of *Politiken* or other papers until I let you know. I'm sure you understand. Will you please tell the other editors in your building?'

Then the line went dead.

Aksel Lannoe of the Danish Air Force was in the thick of events at Vaerloese airfield, Denmark's pitiably inadequate main point of resistance against the might of the German Luftwaffe. On that morning of 9 April, the airfield could

21

boast 21 obsolescent fighters, 27 spotter aircraft, one helicopter and 19 trainers.

Lannoe recalled:

'We had repeated "stand-bys" during the night and we were not certain whether it was serious trouble or just an exercise. Our planes were lined up in neat rows on the perimeter.

One aircraft, which had been ordered on a mission, began taking off. At that moment, German aircraft came in at hedge-hopping level and shot down the Danish plane at a height of a few feet. Then they crossed and recrossed the airfield, firing incendiary into our planes, which burst into flames. Our anti-aircraft guns were useless because we had no ammunition.

When we tried to get into a brand-new shelter, we found that the door was locked and the key had been removed. We threw ourselves flat in the surrounding fields. A little later we received a message telling us to "cease resistance".

There had been a time when the Danes were a warlike people. Long ago in their history, they had battled their way south into Italy and east into Estonia. They had over-run England and tightened their hold on Norway and Sweden and the north. But that was some 400 years before. Denmark had mellowed down the generations, and the language had evolved a word to describe its people: *hyggelig*, which signifies cosiness and comfort.

And now into the *hyggelig* country stalked the German Wehrmacht.

It all seemed, at first, deceptively pleasant. The German conquerors were prepared to be reasonable. What had changed? Very little, if you judged by externals. There was no German Reichskommissar in Denmark. King Christian continued to live at Amalienborg Palace in Copenhagen. The royal standard floated and Danish sentries in their bearskins kept guard.

But Copenhagen had also become the city where police cars careered through the streets in the small hours. Their quarry, it was whispered, were English and French immigrants. Those rounded up were questioned, not by the

Germans, but by the Danes. It was reassuring to learn that prisoners were being sent to Danish jails and not to Nazi ones with their ominous reputation.

The king's appeal for order – 'an absolutely quiet and dignified demeanour' – had a tranquillising effect. The German troops who were chosen for the occupation certainly seemed to be an elite bunch; many could speak fluent Danish. They came either from Schleswig Holstein on the boundaries of Denmark, where Danish was an accepted language, or else from Austria. The Austrians had always been conspicuously friendly to Danes, and the tradition seemed to be maintained. The German supreme command issued a number of guidelines to the troops.

These indicated that seeking to educate the Danes in the tenets of National Socialism was a waste of time. The troops were told:

The Dane is freedom-loving and self-reliant. He has no idea of military discipline and authority.

Therefore: Give few orders, don't shout. It arouses in him a desire for opposition and is useless. Explain clearly and convince him. A humorous tone proves most effective. Unnecessary severity is wounding to self-respect and must be avoided.

The Dane loves a homely, comfortable existence. He may be won over by friendliness, small attentions and personal recognition.

The Danish businessman has a leaning to England. He abhors wars. Of Germany's National Socialist aims there is, except in a very few instances, no understanding.

Therefore avoid political discussions. The German language is understood by many Danes.

This document caused a certain amusement among a naturally humorous people. Yet another, entitled *Manual of Instruction in the Danish Language* also had its comic side:

Be so kind as to direct me to the mayor of the city.

'Good day, Mr Mayor! Will you show me the municipal cash box?

'If you do not hand over the cash box willingly, Mr Mayor, you will be shot.'

The tactics of Danish resistance in the early months of Nazi occupation were deceptively mild, ranging from gentle ridicule to studied indifference.

At first, the Germans were slow to get the message. An eager band of German musicians, smiling like young puppies desperately anxious to be liked, turned up to play in one of Copenhagen's main squares. The trouble was that their arrival always seemed to coincide with a parade of the Danish Guard, who insisted on playing loudly in the square since it was on the customary route to the royal palace.

Crowds became expert at turning up initially to hear the Germans, then teasingly peeling off to follow the Danes. Sten Gudme reported: 'There is always an empty space gaping in front of the German military bands when they turn up to play. It is a little ray of brightness in a hard and wretched year.'

Those who encountered their German conquerors on the streets were prepared to be polite, or even friendly. But a close look at shoulder lapels told a rather different story. Danes had taken to wearing a variety of buttonhole badges. These could consist of the king's portrait, the Danish flag, the Union Jack, the colours of the RAF or, most tellingly of all, the initials DKS.

They stood for *Den Kolde Skulder* (the cold shoulder).

News of DKS filtered through to London, and *The Times* reported: 'To the Danes belongs the credit of inventing a new order, unthought of by Hitler – the Order of the Cold Shoulder . . . and it expresses the feelings towards the Germans of about 90 per cent of the Danish population.'

Overtures of friendship were at first accepted, then spurned. The Germans, that summer of occupation, set up an academy for their own scientists and prominent Danish ones. It seemed a harmless form of collaboration;

24

the National Museum of Copenhagen received the German organisers civilly enough. Minister Renthe-Fink was installed to make the necessary arrangements.

He strode out smilingly to greet the guests for the opening ceremony. He did not smile for long. The Danish flag was ostentatiously flown at half-mast. In vain, museum officials were berated. Blandly, someone pointed out that one of the museum's oldest and most distinguished officials had died that morning. Surely the minister would not approve of any lack of respect?

The ceremony proceeded. Observers noted that Herr Renthe-Fink's smile looked as if it had been nailed on.

It was good fun, this German-baiting. Good fun for schoolboys in Elsinore who, when the Wehrmacht marched through the narrow streets singing '*Wir fahren gegen Engelland*' (We're marching against England), riposted with '*It's a Long Way to Tipperary*'.

But the humour, even for the naturally humorous Danes, had an air of desperation. On the surface, life did not seem too bad under the shadow of the jackboot. But elsewhere in the west the Wehrmacht and the SS prepared to scythe through Europe with the slash of iron.

3

That fatal 9 April had turned out cold and cheerless in Norway. Even so, the husky blond man with the bulging eyes and the shiny blue suit had spent most of the day sweating. He had to wait until evening before he could reach the studios of the Oslo broadcasting station and deliver his bombshell.

In a hoarse, guttural voice he proclaimed from the hastily scrawled text: 'Norwegian men and women! England has violated the neutrality of Norway by laying mines in Norwegian territorial waters . . . The German government has offered the Norwegian government its help, accompanied by a solemn assurance respecting our national independence and Norwegian lives and property.'

Norwegians were urged to desist from further resistance; furthermore, Vidkun Quisling informed his listeners that he had 'deposed' the country's legal government and now presented himself as the Prime Minister of Norway.

He continued: 'All Norwegians are hereby called upon to keep the peace of the realm and to preserve their presence of mind in this difficult situation. By united exertions and the goodwill of all, we will bring Norway free and safe through this serious crisis.'

Hitherto, the language had been bland. But now came the clear threat: 'I add that resistance is not merely useless in the situation which has now developed but directly synonymous with criminal destruction of life and property. Every official and every municipal employee . . . is in duty bound to obey orders from the new National Government. Any deviation from this will involve the utmost personal responsibility on the part of the offender and will be proceeded against according to the principles of justice and with the same consideration towards all citizens.'

With this single address, Major Vidkun Abraham Lauritz Jonsson Quisling made his mark on history; the epithet 'quisling' was given to collaborators throughout all the countries of occupied Europe.

But that lay in the future. Right now, Quisling sensed the whiff of power which he considered to be within the gift of his Nazi masters.

The man's background was respectable enough. He sprang from good solid yeoman stock in Fyresdal, a scattered village in the mountains of Telemark in southwest Norway. The family had been respected as pastors, farmers and professional men for six centuries.

He graduated first in his class at the Norwegian Military Academy and in his early twenties was posted to Petrograd as military attaché. The Russian Revolution of 1917 loomed; Quisling's sympathies then were pro-Bolshevik. Back home in Oslo he offered his services to the Labour Party, at that time a Comintern member.

His offer to set up a 'Red Guard' was spurned. Very well, he would form a party of his own. There was an ideal model to hand. In 1933, Adolf Hitler had come to power in Germany, his strident nationalism bolstered by strong-armed SS lieutenants within the National Socialist Party.

Quisling, with Hitler as inspiration, set about fashioning the Nasjonal Samling – the party of National Unity. But a bid to enter candidates in the Storting (the Norwegian parliament) turned out to be a humiliating failure. Only a scant two per cent of the votes cast went Quisling's way; even with Norway's system of proportional representation, he failed to place a single one of his followers in the Storting.

In a general election, Quisling stormed the country in a car built like a tank and equipped with a loud speaker.

Incensed voters, not caring for his particular brand of nationalism, broke up his meetings, clashing in the streets with the bullyboys of the Hird, Quisling's answer to the stormtroopers of Munich and Berlin.

By 1937, support had dwindled to a mere shadow. The figures were grotesque: in the local elections, fifteen-one-hundredths of one per cent of the votes cast in rural districts and six-one-hundredths of one per cent of those cast in towns. The Nasjonal Samling had become a thoroughly bad joke.

But in Nazi Germany no one laughed.

It was true that Hitler did not like rival fascist organisations on his doorstep; the mere whisper of challenge to his authority made him uncomfortable. But the Fuehrer had his own special plans for Norway. Quisling, the faintly ridiculous little man who looked like a provincial shopkeeper, was too important a potential ally to be disregarded.

Nazi Germany began courting Vidkun Quisling.

For the role of chief suitor, Hitler assigned Estonian-born shoemaker's son Alfred Rosenberg, who combined being adviser to the Fuehrer on foreign policy with an industrious, all-consuming hatred of Jews and Bolsheviks.

One of Rosenberg's racial fixations was particularly attractive to Vidkun Quisling. He dreamed of the establishment of a great Nordic empire which would exclude the Jews and other 'impure' races. Rosenberg, firmly in the grip of his fantasies, bombarded the Norwegian with Nazi propaganda and weighty philosophical treatises.

Rosenberg found his overtures falling on sympathetic ears. He sent an enthusiastic memo to Hitler: 'Of all the political groupings in Scandinavia only Nasjonal Samling, led by Vidkun Quisling, deserves serious attention.'

Mutual admiration was all very well. But Quisling was after a great deal more.

Reports had been reaching him from contacts in London that there were British fears that the Soviet Union, having attacked and subjugated Finland, might move into Sweden and Norway. Furthermore, there was a case for cutting off those vital iron ore supplies to Germany. There could therefore be no delay – Germany must occupy Norway.

Quisling told Rosenberg confidently: 'I have many supporters among top officers in the Norwegian Army.' Anxious to press his advantage, he outlined a bold plan which amounted to nothing less than staging a coup within Norway. He proposed that a number of hand-picked Hird members should be hurriedly trained in the Reich under the command of 'experienced and diehard National Socialists who are practised in such operations'.

The stormtroopers, safely back in Norway, would seize some of Oslo's strategic points. At the same time, the German Navy, with contingents of the German Army, would be on hand at a selected bay outside Oslo to answer a special summons from the new Norwegian government, of which Quisling, naturally, would be Prime Minister.

It was all very well, however, working out paper schemes. They would prove a waste of time if they did not find favour with Hitler. And they did not. The Fuehrer was in a cautious mood. Two interviews with the German Chancellor brought Quisling something decidedly less dramatic than a blessing for a coup: the leader of the Norwegian fascists would be provided with funds to combat British propaganda and strengthen his own pro-German movement.

Rosenberg also preferred to proceed by stealth. A special agent, Hans Wilhelm Scheidt, was assigned to Norway to work with Quisling. A small security-screened knot of officers of the Oberkommando der Wehrmacht (OKW) began work on what at first was called Study North.

The project's name was later changed to *Weseruebung* (Weser Exercise).

Hitler's summons went out on 21 February to the commander of 21st Corps, General der Infantrie Nicholas von Falkenhorst, a professional, nonpolitical soldier who had earned his spurs in the assault on Poland a year before.

Hitler fixed 9 April for the attack. It was a formidable

proposition. Norway's terrain was heavily mountainous. The internal communications were poor, which did not augur well for a rapid advance. A study of the country's history, however, put Hitler in a more cheerful frame of mind.

It was true that Norwegians had fought bitter border wars against the Swedes, but that was back in 1814. In the remaining years of the nineteenth century, the country had gone soft and antimilitaristic. In the 1930s, with Norway crippled with economic depression, sympathy for what was regarded as a stuffy military caste sank still further. There would, the Fuehrer was convinced, be little military resistance in 1940.

For an invasion fleet, however, it was a different matter; there was the very real threat of interception and destruction by heavier units of the Royal Navy. Strictly in terms of strength, Britain had the power to crush the German invasion even before the first Wehrmacht soldier set foot in Norway.

The first battle was, inevitably, a sea engagement between British and German fleets. In the balance hung the fate of Norway.

Narvik is an attractive town, sitting in a stubby peninsula flanked by the waters of two fjords. It is also the port and railhead to receive essential iron ore from Sweden. Elderly Konrad Sundlo, a Quisling sympathiser in command of the local garrison, faced an impossible situation.

Norwegian units had been charged to resist any invasion to the last bullet, but bad training, poor leadership and weak morale had left them with little stomach to fight. Sundlo had only 400 troops to man the town's perimeters and the key machine-gun and antiaircraft emplacements. The harbour itself was doomed when torpedoes smashed into the hull of the defending ship *Eidsvold*. It had split in two and sank immediately. Then German destroyers moved into Narvik's inner harbour. The *Eidsvold's* sister ship, *Norge*, opened fire; it was quickly sent to the bottom by torpedo attack.

Generalleutnant Eduard Dietl, a Bavarian crony of Hitler since the early brawling Brownshirt days, was able to walk ashore unopposed after he and his men tied up their launches along Narvik's waterfront.

His greeting to Colonel Sundlo was cordial. Admission of honourable defeat, he argued, was the only course. What would be the point of further bloodshed? After all, the rest of Norway were welcoming German troops as friends and protectors.

The last statement was patently a gigantic bluff, but it made Sundlo hesitate. Certainly, his orders had been plain enough: the Norwegian High Command had ordered him to fight and throw the Nazis into the sea. But now he hesitated. The situation had, after all, changed. Germans seemed to be ashore and digging in.

Eventually, he capitulated, saying: 'I hand over the town.' Not a shot at that stage had been fired. But, as it turned out, Germany's hold on Narvik was precarious; the British counterattacked fiercely later.

As early as noon, five principal Norwegian cities and ports and the big airfield along the west and south coasts – which run for 1,500 miles from the Skagerrak to the Arctic – were in German hands.

It was idle to pretend that the supremely successful invasion of Norway had not been a remarkable triumph for German arms. Hitler was ecstatic, proclaiming: 'The campaign was not only bold, but one of the sauciest undertakings in the history of warfare.'

In dizzy euphoria, the Nazi warlord instructed that Quisling was to receive full support and, in all negotiations with Norway's King Haakon, he was to remain the country's Prime Minister.

As for the capital, its inhabitants read in the newspaper of heavy fighting in the Oslo fjord. German aircraft streaked over the city at agonisingly low level. Plainly, Oslo was going to be blitzed. The population were told on the radio to evacuate forthwith.

The Dutch newspaper *Nieuwe Rotterdamsche Courant* reported:

At the entrance to the underground the people were struggling madly to get down into the tunnel; there are no other public shelters in Oslo. Some people sought shelter in the park near the Palace, all were distracted with fear, dismay and doubt. Others, again, fled or tried to flee from the town, trundling prams, on trucks, storming the stations, where every bit of rolling stock was loaded to the limit and sent away from the town, to the country.

Oslo fell to little more than a phantom German force dropped from the air at the local undefended airport.

Despite Hitler's endorsement, Vidkun Quisling was not altogether happy. By no means was he favoured by everyone in the Third Reich. He was known to be Rosenberg's man, and the party 'philosopher' had plenty of enemies within the Nazi hierarchy. There was a very real risk that Hitler could be persuaded to change his mind over the appointment.

It galled Quisling that his Nazi friends had not seen fit to give him advance notice of the invasion. But the important thing was that Hitler was firmly in control. He decided to take a look at the situation in Oslo. At the War Office, some old army cronies received him warmly. Encouraged, he moved on to the offices of his own Nasjonal Samling party. There things were even more promising: assurances were received that Germany would be delighted if Quisling, as saviour of Norway, was to form his own government.

It was enough encouragement. The radio address to the Norwegian people was drafted hastily. Its effect was nothing less than devastating. The supreme failure among the country's politicians, a man popularly regarded as a pompous windbag given to ludicrous nationalist vapourings, was taking upon himself the mantle of dictatorship. To the Norwegians, the very idea was as grotesque as it was shaming. They were not alone in regarding Quisling's new role with dismay. The German Foreign Ministry representative in Oslo, Dr Curt Brauer, a punctilious, old-fashioned diplomat, was in a painful quandary. Quisling, a man apparently without popular support, was the self-proclaimed Prime Minister of Norway. But what was to be done about the previous Premier, Johan Nygaardsvold? The only way of solving the matter, Brauer reasoned, was to discuss it around a table in the approved manner. A call was put through to Quisling's secretary, suggesting a meeting in Brauer's office.

Quisling now showed his greatest weaknesses; rank arrogance and a lack of tact. In a sudden flush of anger, he snapped at his secretary: 'Tell the German Minister that if he wishes to see the Norwegian Prime Minister he must call on me.'

Brauer obeyed meekly enough. He found Quisling and his underlings comfortably installed in the luxurious Continental Hotel. Quisling's effect on the veteran German diplomat was electric. Brauer, for once abandoning the niceties of diplomacy, rang German Foreign Minister Joachim von Ribbentrop in Berlin.

There was no mincing of words. Brauer reported: 'The man is incompetent, has no political sense – and, far worse no support!'

Ribbentrop's first reaction was delight. Here was a golden opportunity to score off Rosenberg, whom he detested. Even so, it would not do to disown Quisling without Hitler's blessing.

To Ribbentrop's dismay, Hitler, still flushed with the success of his engagement in Norway, would have none of it. All reservations were brushed aside and Hitler demanded: 'Why not Quisling?'

Further support from Ribbentrop was now out of the question. The Foreign Minister was Hitler's mouthpiece; if the Fuehrer said so, then of course Quisling must stay. Brauer reflected bitterly that he might just as well have held his breath.

Quisling, with his bumptious conceit, had previously been bad enough. Now he became intolerable. Flanked by his supporters he descended on the Storting building, demanding that the German troops occupying it should move out; space was needed for the new Norwegian government. As a move, it could scarcely have been more tactless. The swastika had already been raised over the building, and Hitler's bust reposed in the front entrance. The Germans were plainly the masters.

Quisling's little group was studiously ignored; the self-proclaimed Prime Minister stalked off in a huff. Consolation came from a whirlwind of activity as he set up a series of meetings with Norwegian businessmen, trade union leaders and public officials.

In vain, Quisling tried to interest them in the merits of a Nasjonal Samling government with, naturally, himself as the head. Everywhere he met rebuff and ridicule and, most serious of all, downright hostility from the army he had tried so assiduously to court.

King Haakon, who had fled from Oslo and was with his ministers outside Elverum, to the northeast, flatly refused the German demand for capitulation and his return to Oslo under a government led by Quisling. The alternative had been spelt out brutally. The weight of the mighty Wehrmacht would crush the face of Norway.

Haakon was deaf to threats and he proclaimed: '. . . I find that I cannot appoint Quisling Prime Minister, a man I do not know and in whom neither the people nor its representatives, the Storting, have any confidence at all.'

Quisling's reaction was to go ahead and announce a cabinet. His reward was a blunt judgement by General-major Bruno Uthman, German military attaché in Oslo:

'Quisling's proposed cabinet is a gangster government. Quisling is nothing more than a common criminal.'

Berlin had its first nagging doubts, and took a fresh look at the Nasjonal Samling party. It was soon discovered that Quisling's much vaunted movement could boast no members in parliament and drew such support as it had from malcontents with ill-defined dreams of a European new order. Moreover, a heavy percentage of supporters were still at school.

Frantically, Quisling tried to repair the damage. But it was too late. Hitler had been brought to realise that such an obviously detested ally would do Germany's standing no good at all. The Third Reich, it would be thought, had been duped all too easily by a charlatan.

After only six days as Prime Minister of Norway, Vidkun Quisling was sacked by his German masters. And, furthermore, sacked unceremoniously. The comfortable life at the Continental Hotel was over. Quisling's hefty bulk and outraged dignity found themselves literally dumped on the pavement, along with his Nasjonal Samling supporters.

Curt Brauer was not normally a vindictive man, but he relished offering a new job to Quisling by way of a sop. The post of Commissioner of Demobilisation was completely meaningless.

A wave of relief swept through Norway. But for Adolf Hitler, there was a fresh problem: there was now no Norwegian government with which to deal. It seemed a case for rather more drastic measures of the kind traditionally associated with the Third Reich.

As for Quisling, he was very far from regarding himself as a spent force. He skulked hopefully in the wings.

4

Josef Terboven was a tall, slim individual who in his youth had worn his hair slicked back to look like Rudolf Valentino.

This former bank clerk, whose job in Germany had been swept away in the economic blizzard of the 1920s, was a consummate main-chancer. He wangled an introduction to one of the country's most prominent industrialists, Emil Kirdorf, who in turn was courted by Hitler and the Nazis.

Kirdorf saw the personable Terboven as a likely front man to persuade the country's big-business brains to support the National Socialists. Funds for the purpose, some supplied by Kirdorf himself and the rest by a coal mine owner's wealthy widow who was also Terboven's mistress, suddenly ceased to be a problem.

Otto Strasser, editor of the newspaper *Berliner Arbeiterzeitung*, and one of Hitler's earliest allies, wrote of Terboven with a distinct trace of envy: 'I remember him as a rather hard-working party member who seemed to have a good deal of spending money on his person at all times. Since most of our members were poor, his frequent small gifts to them were not without effect – and at the first election he was voted leader of the Essen district. From this new position as one of the leaders in the Nazi party, Terboven did much to bring Hitler and the industrialists together.'

Before he became Gauleiter for Essen, Terboven had been appointed to the Prussian State Council and elected to the Reichstag as a National Socialist Deputy.

But Terboven wanted more than that. As was his wont,

he began cultivating senior influential figures, this time within Ribbentrop's ministry. Before long, Ribbentrop came to regard him as his protégé and set about finding him a suitable job.

This time there would be no nonsense from Rosenberg and his cronies. Terboven's brief was terse: 'The Fuehrer wants you to knock Norway into shape.'

Josef Terboven saw no reason why this process should not be carried out in the most comfortable circumstances possible. The money from Emil Kirdorf and his former mistress had given him a taste for the good things of life. He saw his new job in terms of a viceroyalty; what could be more natural than having his living quarters as Reichskommissar in the king's summer palace, with his working offices in the Norwegian parliamentary building?

The title of Reichskommissar signified that Terboven enjoyed the full backing both of the German state and the Nazi party. He lost no time in exercising his power to the full.

As in Denmark, the press was soon receiving a slap from the iron fist.

The existing staff of the Norwegian Telegraph Bureau, the agency which handled news from abroad, was summarily dismissed and replaced by Nazi journalists.

The guidelines for newspapers were rigid: there were to be no reports of German losses or British victories. Speeches by the king or members of the previous government were to go unreported. Foreign news was to be commented upon in a 'German spirit'; economic matters must be reported in 'progressive' terms, and there was to be much talk of 'improved conditions'.

It was time for the next step. On 14 June 1940, Terboven summoned representatives of the major Norwegian political parties to his office.

There the Reichskommissar proclaimed: 'A government must be formed that is sympathetic to Germany.' This seemed, at first, mild language to describe the proposed imposition of a puppet administration. But soon Terboven was shedding mildness for belligerence. He snapped: 'If Norwegians are not cooperative, then Germany will impose a government of commissars who will rush at you like bulls.'

Most of those who had to deal directly with the Reichskommissar had already judged him pompous and humourless. Now he was shown to be brutal as well.

Furthermore, he was just getting into his stride. It was the monarchy's turn next.

It was true that King Haakon and his government were in exile in England, but the continued existence of a royal house, even one in limbo, was an irritating reminder of the old order. It could not be tolerated.

Within a week, the newly established Riksrad (State Council) had decreed that the previous government of Prime Minister Johan Nygaardsvold could no longer be regarded as in power. The decree added: 'As the king is resident outside the frontiers of the country, he is unable to exert his constititional function.'

It was a touchpaper for resistance.

First to catch the mood was King Haakon himself. Although he was now resident in England, he had been able to follow every twist and turn of the negotiations, thanks to sympathetic channels in the Swedish capital. Then came the demand from the Riksrad for the king to abdicate 'in consideration of the welfare of the nation and the future of the country'.

The response was swift. Over the BBC from London, the king stated: 'If I was persuaded that at this time I could serve best by abdicating, or if I was certain that at the back of the request stood a majority of the Norwegian people, I would, deeply as it would hurt me to separate myself from Norway, grant the request you present me.'

Then came the sting in the tail for the conqueror. The request, said the king, had been drafted under pressure from a foreign power and was therefore unconstitutional.

The press – Terboven's press – were forbidden to print

the text of the king's reply. Instead, there was condemnation: Haakon had failed his country in the hour of need.

Although there seemed to be no concerted campaign, the mood of anti-German defiance smouldered. Those with radios who had heard the king's message passed it on to their neighbours. It spread through cafés and bars and, by some bizarre quirk, gave a new lease of life to a game which had been highly popular in Norway a whole decade earlier – the sending of chain letters. It was the perfect method for mobilising opposition to any suggestion of collaboration. One such letter began:

Thou shalt obey King Haakon . . . thou shalt detest Hitler . . . thou shalt regard as a traitor every Norwegian who keeps company with Germans or Quislings at home . . . thou shalt despise treason and remember that its punishment is death.

Hatred was reserved particularly for Quisling's Nasjonal Samling party. Although Quisling was not now in the government, he remained a figurehead whom Hitler could not entirely bring himself to disown. The fascist-style party remained in existence; along with a strong, ruthless Gestapo and 330,000 German troops, it was a handy tool of repression.

Terboven's twin attack on monarchy and the political parties was quickly followed by moves against the clergy of the established Lutheran church. The order went out that the Norwegian state radio was to lard its regular religious programmes with 'sympathetic sermons' and talks by the clergy friendly to the regime. The confessional meetings of the Lutherans were protected by rigid privacy. Plainly, such heresy could not be permitted. Terboven moved to abolish this tradition. Any priest who rebelled against the edict would be imprisoned.

There were a number of clerics who bowed to the pressure, if only to the extent of praising Quisling at the start of their sermons and then blithely ignoring the Nazi threat. But this latest edict by Terboven was something different. January 1941 opened with a protest by the Lutheran bishops, who cited acts of terrorism by the Gestapo and Quisling's Hird.

It was no mere outburst of moral indignation. The bishops went into details. There had been an incident of Hird youths smashing their way into the Oslo school of business and beating up teachers and students with fists and clubs.

A sixteen-year-old Oslo youth had dared to appear on the streets sporting a paperclip in his lapel – the adopted symbol of Norway's solidarity against oppression. He had been hauled off to the Hird cellars, where he was stripped and lashed.

And there had been the case of the head of a students' organisation in Trondheim who had dared to refuse to post placards for the Nasjonal Samling party. The result was a sound beating.

The focus of hatred became Oslo university, where groups of dissenting students meeting in their favourite cafés ran the gauntlet of hustling and catcalls.

Students who forcibly ejected the Hird bullyboys were not allowed to enjoy their minor victory for long. The troublemakers, their uniform brown shirts torn to shreds, staged a march on University Square off Karl Johan Street, near the National Theatre and the main clutch of university buildings.

At first, the students watched the procession in contemptuous silence. Then came the sharp order in German: 'Attack!' The marchers tore into the crowd. Shoulder belts were removed, blackjacks swung. The students were all at once fuelled with a fury that overcame the vicious lashing from the blackjacks. They fought back and, within minutes, a number of Hird lay stunned and bleeding on the pavement.

Nor were the students the only defenders. It was early evening; the rush-hour was at its height and the opportunity for a scrap proved irresistible. Workers joined in with gusto, fists flying. The pent-up fury showed no signs of abating as a posse of police tumbled into the square.

To the astonishment of the students, the police made no attempt to protect them; instead, they formed a protective circle around the Quislings, who were swiftly marched out of the square.

There was a final insult to the decamping Nasjonal Samling members, when they broke into the Norwegian national anthem. The sound was soon drowned by one vast jeer from the crowd, rising into a roar.

After that, there was nothing the disconsolate students could do beyond dispersing.

But by the dawn of Norway's second spring of occupation it was clear that a new spirit stalked abroad. Throughout the country, a rash of duplicated leaflets appeared on city and village streets and in letter boxes. They were thrust into the pockets of workers on their way to work in trains and buses.

The forces of resistance were determined that the anniversary of German conquest was not to be forgotten.

The leaflets read:

Norwegians! On 9 April you must devote a full half-hour from 2 to 2.30 p.m. to thoughts about the fall of Norway. Spend this half-hour in your homes. Let not a single person appear at that hour in street, restaurant, store or any other public place. Surround with hatred and contempt those who would dare to disturb this half-hour vow of silence and thereby desecrate the memory of our fallen fighters.

The half-hour of silence was by no means the only form of passive resistance, even though the leaflets continued to pass from hand to hand, multiplied on typewriters and duplicators.

Germans who used trams in Oslo made the journey alone. As if in response to a single order, passengers stood up and left at the first available stop.

The Communist paper, *Ny Dag*, published in Sweden, proclaimed:

Persons who join Quisling's party are immediately cut off from

41

their friends as if by a magic rod, and they are everywhere met by unconcealed hatred and contempt. So great is the popular hatred for the stormtroopers that the latter hesitate to venture on to the street except in compact groups.

Such defiance, although a puny affair compared to what was to develop later, threw Josef Terboven into a paroxysm of fury. His anger only intensified the opposition. Terboven felt that some public and civic workers might be promising recruiting material. After all, this was the group that still had to run the country, and some form of cooperation might reasonably be expected. Most of these people presumably wished to go on doing their jobs.

But even here there was little comfort for the Reichskommissar. A special bureau set up to check political attitudes among civil servants produced a clear slap in the face – twenty-two organisations protested against Nazi enslavement.

Such form of anti-Nazi solidarity was bad enough. What was far worse was that the text of their protest was broadcast from London by the BBC even before it had reached Terboven's desk.

Now fury was replaced by something like fear. He knew that unless there was action, Berlin would step in and the palmy days of the viceroyalty would come to an abrupt and bloody end.

Gestapo agents instituted a dragnet, swooping down on the homes of dissidents. Those lucky enough not to disappear into Gestapo headquarters in Oslo were marched at short notice to the parliament building and treated to a harangue, while German guards, armed to the teeth, lined the walls. There were more arrests; those known dissidents who were left at liberty were warned 'not to create trouble'.

But all this, Terboven realised, was mere tinkering with the problem. Something far more dramatic was needed.

Meanwhile, the resistance organisations would be deliberately lulled into a false sense of security.

Far worse was to come.

5

An isolated corner of Rodert, near Muenstereifel, some forty miles southwest of Bonn, was a gloomy barely accessible spot, distinguished at the outbreak of war only by a knot of troop huts and antiaircraft gun emplacements.

Military maps at first designated the spot as 'Installation R' and then, equally anonymously, 'Installation F'. The final name, however, was to carry a suggestion of Wagnerian melodrama. As a tightly secure military headquarters for Adolf Hitler, this gloomy spot became known as '*Felsennest*' (Rock Nest).

At dawn on 10 May 1940, Hitler, flanked by his closest military confidants, strode to his own personal quarters, which consisted of a tiny bunker with one office, one bedroom, a few small rooms for aides and a kitchen and bathroom.

An air of tension had gripped *Felsennest* days before. A codename for the Fuehrer's arrival had been arranged: 'Whitsuntide leave approved'. It meant that Hitler's special train had arrived at Euskirchen station, where it would be met by the headquarters motor convoy.

At 4.38 p.m. on the day of departure the train pulled out of Berlin. A Fuehrer-Begleit-Bataillon (escort battalion) marshalled under cover near Euskirchen station shortly before 1 a.m. moving out to the square in front at 4.25 a.m. – the exact moment of Hitler's arrival. Five minutes later, the party was on its way to *Felsennest*. By 5 a.m. the Fuehrer was touring the entire installation, his keen eyes taking in every detail.

It is reasonable to hazard, however, that at least part of his mind was elsewhere. The codename *Danzig* had been

44

flashed to all posts; at 5.35 a.m. on 10 May 1940, the German armies attacked in the west. A mere twenty-five miles away, the awesome machine of the Wehrmacht hurried over the Belgian frontier.

Along a front of 175 miles, from the North Sea to the Maginot Line, Nazi troops smashed across the borders of three small neutral states: the Netherlands, Belgium and Luxembourg.

Three days before, General der Artillerie Alfred Jodl, chief operations officer of OKW (Oberkommando der Wehrmacht) had written in his diary that Hitler, who had previously postponed the attack because of uncertain weather, had consented 'to postponement until 10 May, which he says is against his intuition. But not one day longer . . .'

Part of Hitler's anxieties, Jodl revealed, had been due to alarming reports from the Netherlands. News had filtered through of leave cancellations, evacuations, roadblocks and various forms of mobilisation.

As it turned out, there had been no need to worry.

Hitler had been able to spare only one division of panzers for the conquest of the Netherlands. But it had been buttressed to deadly effect by parachutists and troops landing behind flooded water lines which cautious souls in Berlin had believed would hold up the Germans for weeks.

The campaign in the Netherlands carried the distinction of being the first large-scale airborne attack in the history of warfare.

The aim of the Germans was the same as in Norway – seize the capital, together with monarch and government. But now there was a stumbling block: Dutch infantry, supported by artillery, ejected two German regiments from the airfields encircling The Hague. This certainly took the pressure off the capital, but it meant a severe haemorrhaging of reserve troops.

General der Artillerie Georg von Kuechler's 18th Army

had a formidable task. The drive from the German border was nearly a hundred miles and meant crossing bridges over two estuaries at Dordrecht and Moerdijk.

But first the bridges had to be seized. Airborne units – including one company landing on the river at Rotterdam in antiquated seaplanes – swooped down on the bridges before their Dutch defenders realised what had happened. Units were hastily improvised; for a time it looked as if the invaders were getting the worst of it. The Germans held on with the tenacity of a razor-fanged dog. All depended on one armoured division promised to Kuechler and which even now was smashing through the Grebbe-Feel Line, a fortified front to the east where there were a number of water barriers.

The Dutch pinned hope on French 7th Army, under General Henri Giraud, which had raced up from the Channel and reached Tilburg on the afternoon of 11 May. The Germans, however, luxuriated in air support and sophisticated armour; Giraud was pushed back. German 9th Panzer Division plugged the gap. Its forces poured across the bridges at Moerdijk and Dordrecht, arriving at the Bieuwe Maas across from Rotterdam. And, there, the German airborne forces held the bridges.

But the defence of Rotterdam held tenaciously. In The Hague, to the northwest, airborne forces were getting a bloody nose. With ill-concealed impatience, Hitler issued Directive No. 11: 'The power of resistance of the Dutch Army has proved to be stronger than was anticipated. Political as well as military considerations require that the resistance be broken *speedily*.'

A swift order was issued. Detachments of the Luftwaffe would be snatched from the 6th Army front in Belgium 'to facilitate the rapid conquest of Fortress Holland'.

Hitler went on to be even more specific: Rotterdam was to be obliterated as Warsaw had been during the Polish campaign of the previous year.

Rotterdam had been looking forward to 1940, but the expectation had nothing whatever to do with the Germans. Precisely 600 years before, the port had been granted its city rights, and it had been in a mood to celebrate. The Dutch are not generally associated with vivacity; Rotterdam is an exception, with crowded cinemas, theatres and nightclubs, the little waterfront cafés known to sailors the world over, added to the sights and smells of a rich and vital city.

On a bright summer's day the Germans set out to murder it.

A German staff officer from 39th Corps crossed the bridge at Rotterdam under a white flag and with a demand for the surrender of the city. Unless there was capitulation it would be bombed. The raid began as negotiations were under way.

For years, the Rotterdam raid was hailed as representing Nazi wantonness and terrorism at its worse. Yet, after the war, the tragedy was revealed as a direct result of confusion and error. Dutch commander Peter Scharoo protested to his German opposite number, General der Panzer Truppen Rudolf Schmidt, that the Nazi ultimatum carried no proper signature. Schmidt obliged willingly enough. But vital time was lost; the German's order to delay the raid disappeared along the chain of command. Schmidt had given Scharoo until 4.20 p.m. to surrender, but at three o'clock, the 100 Heinkel HE IIIs, the glazed-nose standard-level bombers of the Luftwaffe, were in the air. The pilots carried clear instructions that the mission was to be aborted if red Very lights were shot over Noorder Island.

Certainly General Schmidt had no stomach for the bombing of Rotterdam. Within minutes of his signing the ultimatum with his name and rank and the addition of *Kommandierender General eines Armee-Korps* (Commanding General of an Army Corps), the bombers roared in.

Schmidt cried out in horror: 'God Almighty! What will happen? It will be another Warsaw.'

And all at once he was acting like a man possessed, screaming for the Very lights to shoot into the air. Then he was frantically clawing at some bales of white cotton hastily seized from a department store and unfurled in the street.

But it was too late, far too late.

The leader of the German bomber wave which was approaching from the south spotted the Very lights and veered away. But the first three aircraft had already relinquished their lethal cargoes. The greater part of the bombing force proceeded with their mission. People fled to the cellars or flung themselves down on street pavements.

The howl of the sirens cut through the warning drone of the bombers, then there was the scream of falling explosives.

Water mains were fractured, gas pipes, the power network and the telephone system were annihilated. In one cellar under a small shop at the Oostplein more than thirty men, women and children were jammed so tightly that when the rear of the cellar was hit by a bomb, even those who had survived were powerless to help the wounded; their groaning was punctuated by the sound of still further explosions.

It was conceivable that fire appliances might have got through – but for the fact that the brigade building itself was a charred ruin. The efforts of individual firemen were valiant but hopeless. Splinters of burning wood and sparks drifted into the air. They set fire to curtains waving in the wind through shattered windows.

And there was the added cruelty of a strong west wind, which was soon spreading the flames like a whirlwind.

For the people of Rotterdam there were terrors beyond imagining. In front of one house, six corpses were scattered over the pavement like rag dolls. They consisted of an entire family. In another ruin, a small boy's head hung down, clamped between fallen beams; he had not been able to free himself. Elsewhere, a child's hand protruded from the rubble. Witnesses spoke of seeing a body plastered against the surface of a door, while another hung from a window.

There was a butcher who had sought shelter in his refrigerator, and three women who had taken refuge in a vault. The doors had buckled and they had all suffocated. Those who survived confronted fresh horrors. In a cellar beneath a shop at Oostplein the stairs had been cleared of larger debris. Something soft was encountered: the squashed head of a young girl.

At Bremen, the aircraft were loaded for a second strike. It never happened; Rotterdam surrendered and the aircraft were recalled.

For years after the war, it was believed that 30,000 people had perished in the raid. Total casualties were in fact around 900. But there were other statistics to spell out the tragedy: several thousand injured, 78,000 made homeless. Twenty-one churches and four hospitals were destroyed. Rotterdam surrendered, and then the Dutch armed forces. Queen Wilhelmina and government ministers had fled to London.

There was now an added threat. Utrecht, the Germans said, would share the same fate as Rotterdam. But the destruction of a second large city was more than General Hentl Winkelman could stomach. At 4.50 p.m. he issued the order to all commanding officers:

Germany has bombed Rotterdam today, and Utrecht is threatened with destruction. To save the civilian population and prevent further bloodshed, I believe it to be justified to order the troops under your command to stop fighting.

If the bombing of Rotterdam had indeed been due to an administrative muddle, that, predictably enough, was not something that OKW was prepared to admit. On 14 May, the German radio issued a special communiqué:

Under the tremendous impression of the attacks of German dive bombers and the imminent attack of German tanks, the city of Rotterdam has capitulated and thus saved itself from destruction.

49

The visitor to Rotterdam today will scarcely be able to ignore the powerful sculpture by Zakine which is called 'Destroyed City'. It is a powerful, jagged work, showing the figure of a man extending powerful arms to clutch at the sky as a symbol of defiance. But it is not just this affirmation of survival which strikes the spectator. For the stomach of Zakine's figure has been ripped out: the heart of a city raped and vandalised.

The surrender signed by Winkelman and Kuechler virtually ended the fighting in the Netherlands, which had lasted just five days.

The occupation of the Netherlands, however, was to last five years.

6

The freedom of the Dutch was slowly chipped away. On the surface, at least, little seemed to change during the first few months of occupation. Newspapers continued to appear. Amsterdam's main newspaper, *De Telegraaf*, was slow to change, except for the prominently displayed exchange rate between the Reichsmark and the Dutch guilder.

Neither, at first, was there undue worry at the appointment of Dr Arthur Seyss-Inquart as Reichskommissar for Occupied Holland.

It seemed hard to equate this mild, bespectacled young Viennese lawyer with what was known of the worst of the Nazi excesses. His manner was pleasant and cordial; he was known to be a diligent churchgoer, his service in World War One in a Tyrolean Kaiserjaeger regiment had been exemplary. The fact that he was Austrian was deemed the most favourable portent of all; the Austrians were noted, after all, for Tyrolean yodelling and the Strauss family. Plainly, there was nothing to be afraid of here.

Reaction might have been rather different if the Dutch people had known that Seyss-Inquart, as Reichstaffhalter (governor) of Nazi-occupied Austria, had made a speech urging the Austrians to respect the swastika, sacred symbol of the Third Reich.

More ominous were Seyss-Inquart's remarks at the time of Hitler's incursion into Austria in 1938:

We do not wish to plunge Jewish human beings and Jewish families into any material misfortune. In following our unchange-

51

able course, we neither wish nor enjoy individual hardships which it may involve. But neither do we seek to avoid their infliction.

During a visit to Linz at the time of the Anschluss – the union movement in Germany and Austria – he had proclaimed:

Austria is German and only German. The only guarantee for Austria's independence can be one given only by the German people. The spiritual Great German Reich is already a fact.

There could be no doubt about his first loyalty.

The dust of destruction had barely settled above Rotterdam before Seyss-Inquart was in full command in the Netherlands. The mailed fist would be kept wrapped in velvet for a while; a little flattery to the Dutch would not come amiss. Seyss-Inquart was determined, however, that his honeyed approach would be stage-managed in a manner appropriate to a conqueror: the people would be in no doubt as to who was master.

Of course, there would be full inaugural rites fit for a paladin of the Third Reich. The choice backcloth displayed a crashing lack of tact; the Germans opted for the ancient Ridderzaal (Hall of the Knights) at The Hague, where Queen Wilhelmina in happier days had opened the winter session of the States-General in solemn ceremony. Seyss-Inquart hoped that this would be interpreted as displaying a respect for Dutch traditions. Instead, right from the start it raised the ire of the Netherlands.

One detail in particular did not escape them: instead of Netherlands musicians in attendance at the Reichskommissar's inauguration, the entire orchestra of the Cologne Broadcasting System was transported to The Hague. The air hung heavy with Wagner.

In his speech, Seyss-Inquart declared that the Germans had come as the Netherlands' friends. And he added reassuringly:

We do not come here to suppress and annihilate a people, or to take away from it its liberty . . . The Germans do not wish to subjugate imperialistically this country and its population. Nor do they desire to force upon them their political convictions. Their activities will be limited by the necessities resulting from the state of war.

We are to build a new Europe based upon the foundations of honour and common labour. We all know that the ultimate purpose of our Fuehrer is: peace and order for all who are of goodwill.

If parts of the Netherlands was lulled into something like acceptance, the people of Rotterdam were not. Evidence of the ruined streets and shopping centre could not be smoothed away with conciliatory words. It was true that by the spring of 1941 German troops were no longer singing about invading England, and the subjugated Dutch could occasionally hear the encouraging note of English bombers passing overhead to attack the Reich. But it took an optimistic nature to believe in an Allied victory in the near future.

Yet there *were* stirrings of resistance, however tentative. They began as early as 29 June 1940 with the birthday of Princess Juliana's consort, Prince Bernhard, who often wore a white carnation in his lapel. All at once, white carnations flourished in the streets.

It was not much, but it was something. If it had only been the Germans whom the Dutch had cause to fear, resistance might have flowered earlier and more forcibly.

But the enemy was also within.

The rhythmic tramping of heavy high boots sported by black-shirted legions echoed through the sparsely populated streets of Amsterdam, watched by a small, sullen crowd.

At first, it seemed a mere token show of strength. Then all at once the procession wheeled away from the main thoroughfares, making for the Jewish quarter, which lay to the north. Jews on the streets were savagely beaten up, their homes attacked and looted.

The black-shirt cohorts then turned their attention to the trams, forcibly evacuating and ill-treating passengers. Other groups smashed and destroyed cafés and restaurants.

But the bullies responsible for similar incidents in a score of Dutch towns were not Germans. Anton Adriaan Mussert, ardent disciple of Adolf Hitler and Benito Mussolini, and leader of the Nationaal-Socialistiche Beweging – the NSB – had crawled out of the woodwork.

If it had not been for the war, there might well have been no moment of glory for this thick-set, balding municipal engineer from Utrecht who had plodded conscientiously up the ladder of the Dutch civil service. As with Vidkun Quisling in Norway, no one had taken his muddled political pretensions over-seriously; the NSB was a small right-wing party with a decidedly pedestrian chief and a caucus of disgruntled intellectuals.

At first, the German's reaction to Mussert had been condescending. The NSB had only 30,000 members; it by no means engaged the hearts and minds of the Dutch. Mussert's proposition to Seyss-Inquart that a Dutch government should be formed to consist of members of the NSB was politely declined.

As might be expected, Seyss-Inquart had no intention of submitting to a situation that might weaken his own power base. The hint of such a possibility kept him awake at night. He wrote hastily to Himmler: 'Mussert's political capabilities do not compare favourably with those of an average German gauleiter.'

Heinrich Himmler, as Reichsfuehrer SS and supremo of the German police, was also worried, but for another reason. He had kept an eye on the Netherlands as a source of racial material. If there was such potential it should be controlled by the SS, not by any pale, home-grown copy.

54

In the summer of 1940, Himmler had established at Munich an SS regiment, Standarte Westland, seeking volunteers from the Netherlands and Flanders. The level of interest had proved gratifying. Himmler looked forward to raising more Dutch and Flemish volunteers for the SS. But no one in the Netherlands, sympathetic or otherwise, was to have any ridiculous ideas of independence. Plainly, a truly reliable subordinate was needed to watch the situation on the spot.

Himmler's gift to the Netherlands was another Austrian, SS-Obergruppenfuehrer Hanns Albin Rauter.

The old Austro-Hungarian Empire that went to war in 1914 was an unwieldy structure of separate nationalities which crumbled to dust with the onset of an uneasy peace. Klagenfurt-born Hanns Rauter had served it as an officer in the Gebirge-Schuetzen-Regiment I in the Imperial Army. By the time he returned to Graz in 1918, Austria was a country in turmoil, seething with revolutionary unrest. There was the threat of invasion from annexationist armies of Yugoslavia, Poland and Hungary.

The burning spirit of nationalism was fuelled by a succession of student riots masterminded by the numerous 'free corps' (Freikorps) who fought off the intruders with a campaign of frenzied street violence. One of the most vicious and fanatical was the Styrian Home Guard (Steierische Heimatschutz), a paramilitary corps to whom Rauter had given total allegiance.

Throughout the 1920s, it stormed the streets with provocative marches and sustained violence against the hated Socialists. Above all, the Styrian Home Guard, from whose rank Rauter sprang as a prominent figure, was fanatically pan-German and anti-Semitic, dedicated to a last-ditch struggle for German supremacy amid the entrails of the ramshackle, doomed former empire of the Hapsburg rulers.

Its ideological platform moulded the future of Hanns Rauter.

55

In addition, one of its most ardent observers was the young Adolf Hitler, who had eked out a miserable existence as a third-rate commercial artist in Vienna and was nursing his own crude, ill-formed nationalistic and political ambitions. Hitler was to write of that time in his testament *Mein Kampf:* 'I achieved an . . . understanding of the importance of physical terror toward the individuals and the masses.'

As a practitioner of bullyboy violence on the streets of Austrian towns and cities, Hanns Rauter was absorbing the same lesson.

By the late 1920s, links were forged between the Styrian Home Guard and the Austrian branch of Hitler's National Socialist German Workers' Party.

On 30 January 1933 the Third Reich, which Hitler boasted was to endure for a thousand years, was born in Germany. And Hanns Rauter was there, busily organising the total absorption of his Heimatschutz into the Nazi apparatus.

If if had not been for the outbreak of war in 1939, Rauter might well have become an obscure backroom figure, a mere technician of dictatorship. As it turned out, on 22 May 1940, Rauter was sent to the Netherlands as Hoehere SS und Polizeifuehrer Nordwest (HSSPF, Higher SS and Police leader) – 'Nordwest' being the pan-Germanic designation for the Netherlands.

An ardent casting director seeking a model to symbolise SS brutality in all its crudity and terror might well have chosen Rauter on appearance alone. Here was a tall, tough-looking butcher with an aquiline nose and a brutal countenance fractured by a vicious slash of a scar.

The title of HSSPF was no mere ornament; Hanns Rauter was Heinrich Himmler's personal lieutenant and that, in SS matters, meant total power. Rauter was to command all SS organisations in the Netherlands. These included the Ordnungspolizei (the ordinary German police force), the Sicherheitspolizei and Sicherheitsdienst (SIP and SD, Secret Police and Security Service), and all Waffen-SS units stationed there. He also commanded the entire Dutch police force.

Of course, it could be argued that Rauter's writ was limited. After all, Arthur Seyss-Inquart was his senior in the Netherlands; all orders would naturally have to be cleared with him. But behind Seyss-Inquart towered the infinitely more sinister figure of Heinrich Himmler, the erstwhile chicken farmer wielding absolute power in the police states of the occupied countries.

No one – and certainly not Arthur Seyss-Inquart or Anton Mussert – had much doubt of Rauter's main task. The Jews greeted his arrival in Amsterdam with suspicion and fear – suspicion in no way lessened by a period of ominous inactivity. In Germany there were the Nuremberg Laws of 1935, which deprived the Jews of citizenship, confining them contemptuously to the status of 'subjects', and which eventually went on to outlaw them so completely that shops, hotels, beer gardens and places of public entertainment invariably carried signs indicating that Jews were not welcome. But nothing of the kind happened, at first, for the Dutch Jews.

Their gradual disinheritance was being planned, nonetheless; the campaign, when it came, was launched with a direct assault on a fundamental tenet of Jewish belief.

On 7 August 1940 the Germans peremptorily prohibited the ritual slaughter of animals. No longer were cattle to be killed by severing of the arteries or bleeding. The generally accepted methods of stunning or shooting would have to be adopted. The first stirrings of discrimination had begun, and they grew apace.

The next stage was for Aryan and Jewish butchers to be separated. The Jews would no longer be permitted to serve gentiles; overnight, Jewish butchers lost eighty-five per cent of their trade.

It was, predictably, only a matter of time before *all* Jewish tradesmen came under the edict. By as early as

57

October 1940, the campaign had struck even deeper: entry into the civil service was completely banned to Jews and to gentiles married to Jews. Those who already had jobs could expect no further promotion. Then, at the end of one working week, came the next stage – a bald announcement under the signature of Seyss-Inquart: 'No Jews are expected to return on Monday.'

Into the decree were swept all Jewish professors, teachers, doctors and clerks.

That final Saturday which spelt the end of a livelihood for so many, certainly brought mass protest of a kind, but it was protest wearing a gentle face and expressed with flowers. Clinics, classrooms and workshops throughout the country were a riot of colours, decorated by non-Jews as tributes to those colleagues who had been forcibly removed. Children came with their parents to take grave, formal leave of their teachers.

Beyond the odd skirmish, blood had not yet spilt on to the streets. Rauter and his SS contingents, nominally responsible to Seyss-Inquart, held their fire.

But progressively the persecution worsened. Economic privation was the next stage. Mrs Alfred B. Spanjaard, a Jew from Amsterdam who survived two years' imprisonment in German concentration camps, recalled at the end of the war:

New decrees were issued daily. We were not allowed on certain streets. We couldn't ride in streetcars, our telephones and radios were taken away, we could shop only between 3 and 5 p.m., and we had to be in our homes at 8 p.m.

All Jews were ordered to bring their money, jewels and insurance policies to the Lippmann and Rosenthal Bank in the Sarphati Street, which the Nazis had taken over. There we had to make a complete accounting of our funds and valuables. We were allowed to keep 250 guilders and were told we couldn't spend more than 100 guilders a month for rent, clothing, food and medical expenses. It didn't matter whether rent alone amounted to more than that figure – that was the order. After the 250 guilders were spent, we had to draw on what was left of our funds at the bank. If we had nothing left, we were either supported by the Jewish community's pooled resources, or we died.

Then the so-called 'Koco Affair' burst on a shocked Amsterdam.

The two ice-cream parlours collectively called 'Koco' were popular meeting places for both Jews and gentiles in the non-Jewish quarter of south Amsterdam. What was worrying was not so much that the owners, Cahn and Kohn, were Jews, but that they were refugees from Germany. It was obvious that it could only be a matter of time before the establishments gained the close attention of the Nazis. Some form of protection was clearly needed.

Unfortunately, fledgling resistance groups at this time consisted largely of enthusiastic young amateurs. Some of them proceeded to deck out the parlours with a variety of primitive weapons, consisting largely of gas pipes encased in straps. One of the owners was encouraged to fix a special twenty-inch flask of ammonia to the wall.

The results were greeted with enthusiasm. After a few unsuccessful forays, the Germans left the 'Koco' alone. Encouraged, the resisters reinforced the parlours with fresh weapons. Here was something of an adventure, a game that had all the best elements of a Hollywood Western.

In a frenzy, the Germans returned to the attack. On 19 February 1941, a police patrol swept down on the parlours, only to be greeted by a bombardment of ammonia. The two owners, together with other Jews, were arrested.

Ernst Cahn endured a month of torture but refused to reveal which 'conspirator' had fixed the bottle to his shop. On 3 March 1941, he gained a tragic niche in the history of the German occupation of the Netherlands: he was the first in the country to be shot by a Nazi firing squad.

Dutifully, Hanns Rauter turned in a report on the incident to Himmler. The account was made deliberately lurid. Here, argued Rauter, was a fine example of the disorderly behaviour and lack of discipline prevailing among the Jews. There were graphic descriptions of a Jew 'gnawing through an Aryan's artery and then sucking out his blood', another had squirted 'poisonous fluids at policemen pursuing their duty'.

Such Jewish treachery cried out for retribution. It was the pretext for which the Germans had been waiting.

Within a few days, a series of lightning terror raids were unleashed. Enthusiastically assisted by Anton Mussert, around 200 Jewish men were snatched on 22 February and herded into synagogues which were promptly put to the torch.

Those who survived a little longer were sent to the concentration camp at Mauthausen, near Linz, which had been built by Himmler with the original intention of housing Austrians.

Three weeks after the men had been rounded up, their relatives received identical letters telling them that the prisoners had been 'killed trying to escape'.

The raids were to go on for the rest of the year and well into 1942. Jews, under the constant fear of arrest and deportation, killed themselves by the score.

Mrs Alfred Spanjaard was able to watch the raiders at work.

She related:

... I was approaching the Jewish Institute of the Blind on Amsteldyk, when I saw several trucks drive to the kerb. Gruene Polizei got out and dashed into the building. They came out dragging the blind, young and old. I stood there, I couldn't help looking. I retained my senses sufficiently to hold my bag so it would cover the *Jood* star over my heart. Otherwise the Nazis might have seized me too.

... The Nazis began throwing – literally throwing – the blind into trucks ...

A few days later I was passing the maternity hospital on Nieuwe Keizersgracht, when I saw the scene repeated. Nazis were dragging out mothers, some of whom had given birth only a few hours before, and throwing them into the trucks. Many of the women haemorrhaged and the blood began to drip through the wooden boards of the vehicles.

Opposition to the Nazis in the Netherlands began at a low murmur. Gradually it changed into the harsh clamour of sabotage and resistance. But there was still the long hard night of Nazi barbarism.

7

For a few short moments, the bewildered men of Belgium's 7th Infantry Division defending the eleven-mile front along the Albert Canal thought the bright lights cascading to the sea were meteorites.

Bewilderment was understandable: the perspex of the cockpits had caught and magnified the rays of the sun. The contours of the attacking force seem blurred from below.

The Luftwaffe aircraft were flying too high for the attention of the antiaircraft guns; nothing, it seemed, could stop the onward progress of the attackers, trailing behind them long parallel streams of whitish vapour.

Like a flock of starlings scattering at some mysterious signal, the planes dispersed momentarily then tipped their wings and wheeled towards their target.

That was how the Belgian infantrymen saw the German invasion of the west. It was a little after 4.15 a.m. on Friday 10 May 1940.

By the time the Dutch surrendered, the fate of Belgium, France and the defenders of the British Expeditionary Force had been sealed. After the bombers screamed their destruction of the Albert Canal, the avalanche broke. Its force was a vast, swiftly moving concentration of armour which had cut through the forest of the Ardennes that day and stretched back in three columns for a hundred miles, far beyond the Rhine. It had smashed through the French 9th and 2nd Armies, and was heading swiftly for the Channel.

Indisputably, the greatest and the most spectacular prize was the capture of Fort Eben Emael, which commanded the junction of the Meuse and the Albert Canal, Belgium's frontier with the Netherlands. The triangular-shaped fortress, resembling a giant segment of pie and constructed in a series of steel and concrete galleries set deep underground, its gun turrets protected by heavy armour, was fondly considered a formidable obstacle.

It did not take long for the Germans to shatter the illusion, for the entire structure was fatally flawed. It did not command the surrounding landscape, and its gun positions could offer no protection to the bridges of the canal.

Into the attack went the Koch Storm Detachment, formed at Hildesheim. The unit consisted of the 1st Company of the 1st Parachute Regiment, the Parachute Sapper Detachment of the 7th Flying Division, the Freight Glider Unit, a beacon and searchlight detachment and an airfield ground staff. These were buttressed by a towing unit of Junker 52s. To the parachute company went the responsibility for the capture of the high bridges of Vroenhaven and Veltwezelt.

The sapper detachment was under the command of Oberst Rudolf Witzig, a Westphalian veteran of the Wehrmacht from World War One. Oberst Witzig later wrote:

We were the only parachute unit comprised entirely of sappers, and all were volunteers. Among us were the best amateur glider-pilots from pre-war days when Germans already excelled in the sport of gliding. During the two years of the unit's existence, it had grown into a sturdy, close-knit community in which each man had confidence in his fellows.

So it was that in a light ground mist, through which the attackers could dimly make out the outlines of the fortification, nine gliders – two out of the total force of eleven were lost during the flight – actually landed on the fort, crippling the rooftop gun emplacements and periscopes.

Then it was the turn of the flame-throwers, with Belgian

troops becoming human torches. Charges were fixed to steel cupolas, to the guns of the casemates and even in the barrels of the big guns.

An almost mystic faith had been placed in Fort Eben Emael; it had mesmerised the Belgians into fatal neglect. The fort lacked mines or barbed wire; the garrison was deprived of infantry training; and there were no trenches round the casemates.

Attempts by Belgian infantry to dislodge the attackers were set at naught by waves of Stuka bombings and further parachute attacks. At noon on 11 May, after a bout of hand-to-hand fighting in the underground tunnels, a white flag was hoisted. One thousand two hundred dazed and demoralised defenders filed out and surrendered.

Gleefully, the propaganda machinery of Josef Goebbels went immediately into action. Hitler was later photographed with these bemedalled heroes of the Reich, who sported their battle smocks and paratroop helmets rather than the customary ceremonial dress.

As a moral blow to the Belgians, the loss of Fort Eben Emael proved devastating.

But the process of humiliation began on 10 May itself, some two hours after the start of the invasion. The windows of the foreign ministry in Brussels rattled from the explosion of bombs in nearby airfields and the air was rent with the constant roar of the Luftwaffe, as Vicco Buelow-Schwante, the German ambassador, solemnly intoned from a document: 'I am instructed by the government of the German Reich to make the following declaration: in order to forestall the invasion of Belgium, Holland and Luxembourg, for which Great Britain and France have been making preparations clearly aimed at Germany . . .'

The farce of diplomatic niceties in such circumstances proved altogether too much for the Belgian Foreign Prime Minister, Paul-Henri Spaak. He cut into Buelow-

Schwante's litany by saying: 'Hand me the document. I should like to spare you so painful a task . . .'

By the morning of 19 May, the mighty wedge of seven armoured divisions had driven westward north of the Somme; there was a mere seven miles separating the Germans from the Channel.

Hitler was delirious with undreamed of success; the 2nd Panzer Division had reached Abbeville at the mouth of the Somme. Generalleutnant Erich von Manstein, chief of staff at Hitler's Army Group A, had previously persuaded the Army High Command (Oberkommando Des Heeres or OKH) that a frontal conflict with the Allied armies on the flat land of Belgium would lead to a war of attrition like that of 1914–18. There was, Manstein believed, an enticing alternative.

Massive armour could thread its way through the Ardennes forest and over the Meuse. Ahead would be flat open country that was nothing short of a gift for tank warfare. Furthermore, terrain like this could be found all the way to Paris and the Channel. Manstein was a detached, icy professional, but he allowed his imagination to soar at the prospect of vast armoured thrusts, with panzer and motorised forces far outstripping all other transport.

The Manstein Plan, as it turned out, was no dream. By 13 May, a mere five days into *Fall Gelb*, German armour had secured four bridgeheads across the steep-banked Meuse from Dinant to Sedan.

The plan to hold the river was abandoned under the relentless pressure of the German advance; even so, the Belgians held out for seventeen days. On 13 and 14 May, the Germans broke through the French lines north of Dinant in Belgium and at Mézières in France. For the French 9th Army it was wholesale debacle; General Maurice Gamelin, the Allied supreme commander, ordered a general retreat. On Monday 27 May, messages from the French liaison officer at Belgian HQ reported that they had 'abandoned the struggle'.

King Leopold III sent an envoy to the Germans, proposing a ceasefire at midnight. Back came the reply: 'The Fuehrer demands that arms be laid down unconditionally.' They were.

Unlike the crowned heads of the Netherlands and Norway, the king refused to contemplate setting up a government-in-exile. He declared: 'I have decided to stay. The cause of the Allies is lost.'

In a speech full of bitterness, Premier Paul Reynaud of France went on radio to declaim: 'I must announce to the French people a grave event... France can no longer count on the Belgian Army... King Leopold III without a word to the French and British soldiers... laid down his arms. It is a fact without precedent in history.'

Supporters of the king argued that he had taken a perfectly legitimate decision, not as head of state, but as Allied Ground Chief. General Maxine Weygand, who became the king's superior commander and Allied Ground Commander-in-Chief, professed himself stunned by the lack of consultation: 'It was like a bolt from the blue. There had been no warning...'

The French rubbed salt into the Belgians' wounds, regarding them as a defaulting ally. A British war correspondent, Gordon Waterfield, listening to Reynaud's broadcast in a bistro, saw two women burst into tears, crying *Les salauds! Les salauds!* Parisians threw innocent Belgian refugees out of their homes or set fire to their wrecked carts. They had to endure heckling and intimidation.

The progress of the conqueror coincided with days which slipped past under blue skies and bright sun, and the perpetual starry nights. May and June would normally have been smiling times for the people of this rich, proud land. But in 1940, the heat of the Belgian summer served only to mock the endless columns of men and women bowed down with fatigue and an overwhelming sense of loss.

Ahead of the distracted columns on the traffic-choked

roads lay France, already in sight and in its death agonies. The provinces of the centre and south were in no position to receive a large influx of Belgian refugees. In stark statistical terms two million Belgians became homeless and the French had five million refugees of their own from the north.

The capitulation by Leopold III had been bad enough; the material privations were even worse. Belgium had previously snuggled within a cocoon of prosperity and comfort; the events of September 1939 to May 1940 had not bothered the country particularly. Within a few short days all complacency was shed: a reassuring daily routine was no more, the future for thousands appeared to be an endless walk over congested roads where there was little prospect of a roof or a bed or, indeed, the means to pay for either.

The German columns marching into Brussels encountered virtually a ghost town. There was barely a transport service worth considering; bridges had been destroyed by the Allies in their retreat.

The capital lacked water, gas or coal; barges sunk by Belgian troops blocked the main canals. Without the bridges, there was nothing for it but to cross the canals by lock gates not sufficiently wide for two-way traffic. Thus pedestrians were only allowed to cross for five minutes in each direction alternately.

Yet there were rich pickings for the country's new German masters. It was true that the country only covered an area of 12,000 square miles with a population of 8.5 million. Yet in the league table of foreign trade, Belgium occupied fifth place in the world, with exports that could touch £250 million and gold holdings estimated at £200 million.

All this, the Germans reasoned, pointed to the existence of vast reserves. Just how vast they made it their business to discover with maximum speed.

The swastika barely had time to cast its baleful shadow over Antwerp before a fleet of German trucks roared in

67

to seize everything that was either edible or remotely of industrial value to the Reich. Under the sullen murmur of the guns, bills were posted throughout the port proclaiming:

All foodstuffs, raw materials and half-finished products are of primary importance to the economic life of the occupied countries. The British blockade will render these stocks insufficient; therefore, in the interest of the occupied territories, all goods enumerated below are to be requisitioned: foodstuffs, raw materials, half-finished products and all other commodities which are scarce or of which there are insufficient quantities.

By 3 p.m. on 18 May 1940 in Antwerp huge army trucks had been backed up to the warehouses, which were swiftly stripped of all merchandise. The contents of cases and bales were unchecked; the trucks sped off towards the Reich.

It was not crude looting. Everything appropriated was paid for. The owner was required to put in a bill for the confiscated merchandise. He received a bond for the entire value of the goods – to be redeemed, of course, by the Germans from Belgian coffers. The exchange rate was pegged at a level which made everything available at virtually half-price for the conquerors.

The Wehrmacht troops could scarcely be blamed for believing they had landed in paradise. By the time the first cold wave of winter arrived, woollen goods had become virtually unobtainable; the Germans had seized them all. Lars Moen, an American journalist working in Belgium, wrote in *Under The Iron Heel*:

They had rushed to buy warm woollen underclothing. . . . Women's stockings are equally scarce; every German soldier bought a few pairs of silk stockings for his wife, sister or girlfriend, not to mention silk underclothing of every description. When I left, two Belgian women out of three were going barelegged. . . .

The German soldiers bought anything and everything, and

then purchased expensive leather luggage to carry what they did not send home via the army postal service. It was years since most of them had seen shops stocked with so much merchandise – some never had – and they made the most of the opportunity.

Many of them not only spent their entire accumulation of army pay in the shops, but wrote home for every bit of money the family could scrape together . . .

As for the 90,000 Jews in Belgium, life before the occupation seemed secure. There was flourishing employment in the clothing trade and other small businesses. Antwerp was also the focus of the diamond trade, largely in Jewish hands. The illusions of security were swiftly stripped away; within six months of the arrival of the Germans, the Belgian tragedy of deportation had begun.

For the Gestapo it was a triumph of organisation. Hermann Goering, when the Nazis seized power in Germany, had lost no time in securing control of the Prussian State Police, the forerunner of the Gestapo. He had an ardent disciple in Hamburg University graduate Rudolf Diels, who had hitherto been solely interested in carousing in Berlin beer halls.

The dissolute Diels now swiftly became intent on making a name for himself. The fate of the Jews was of the keenest interest to his superiors; plainly, there was profitable work to be done. Within four months of Hitler gaining power, Diels had helped fashion a draft law to regulate status of Jews throughout the Reich. This law would, it was proposed, be administered by the creation of a Jewish council, composed of the Jews themselves and answerable to the Gestapo.

Desperately, the leader of the council in Belgium played for time, seeking to negotiate the release of individual Jews. At first, the Gestapo seemed remarkably conciliatory, indicating that it might be possible to do business – at a price, of course. Jews could be allowed, at 25,000 francs a time, to make for Switzerland, transported by the Belgian

69

Red Cross. Reassuring letters were produced from Dutch Jews who had made similar journeys.

The council yielded up scores of Jews who, full of hope, prepared for the journeys. Most of them got no further than the deportation centre at Mechelen, staging post for a final journey to the concentration camps of the east. The Dutch letters had been faked by the Gestapo or written under duress.

The Gestapo found a healthy supply of collaborators who were prepared to act as intermediaries for the Jews. A fee of 25,000 francs was common. Those Jews who did succeed in fleeing the sinister shadow of the Gestapo in Belgium frequently turned over their jewels and possessions. Even so, there was always the risk of finding a Gestapo reception committee at the border with France.

The Jews who remained were easier prey. Wave after wave of Gestapo raids was launched on the Jewish quarters.

Tos Hakker, a Jew living in Antwerp, wrote:

The Jewish inhabitants were dragged outside and ill-treated. Ten minutes were granted to collect some clothes. Many of them, almost dead with fear, suffered themselves to be taken away without saying a word. . . . Vehicle after vehicle was loaded and driven away. No distinction was made: old and young, whether ill or healthy, everybody was dragged outside, many of them half-dressed. First the victims were taken by the Gestapo. They remained a full day without food or drink. Then came large closed furniture vans. . . . The human cattle were heaped up on them. . . . The raids went on regularly. Carts traversed the Jewish quarters and many a cowardly compatriot was willing to point out houses where Jews were living or places where many of them were hidden.

Many a cowardly compatriot. . . . Along with the other occupied countries of western Europe, the story of occupation was not just one of stoicism in defeat and defiance in resistance.

Collaboration was an ever present reality.

8

In the dark of the early morning of 10 May 1940, the Wehrmacht poured into the Grand Duchy of Luxembourg, the pathetically small postage stamp of territory at the back door of the mighty German Reich.

The complexion of the land constituted an irresistible gift to the invader. On the German side of the three rivers constituting its border with Luxembourg, the land rises swiftly to heights of hill and escarpment, growing wilder and steeper towards the north. There are thick forests with villages dotting the edge of streams crossed by some bridges. Direct routes from Aachen, Cologne and Koblenz to the north and northeast, from Mainz, Frankfurt and Mannheim to the east, Saarbruecken and Strasbourg to the southeast converge on the bridges. On the east bank of the rivers, roads course from village to village; along these roads and on top of the ridges the invader dug in his commanding concrete gun emplacements.

The previous night, around 11.45 p.m., the first messages had started arriving from the frontier: 'Important troop movements are to be seen on the German-Luxembourg frontier especially at Palzem on the extreme southeast.'

An eyewitness account, published after the war in *La Resistance du Peuple Luxembourgeois*, recorded:

As if by chance, one began to see groups of armed men wearing armbands with swastikas on them. They were members of the fifth column who had finally come out in the open and were awaiting their master. At the German legation, all the windows were lit up, as if an important meeting was taking place. Everything indicated that the Germans were on the road ready for action. The messages from the frontier bore out events in the capital.

Invasion was imminent.

The people of Luxembourg had long learned to live with the threat. A decade earlier the smaller countries of western Europe had banded together to form the Oslo Group – Norway, Sweden, Denmark, Finland, the Netherlands and Luxembourg. It aimed to forge economic links and agree on some form of political consensus under the daunting shadow of its powerful neighbour.

By 1936, Luxembourg had already caught the scent of danger – Nazi Germany had reoccupied the hitherto demilitarised Rhineland. Two years later, Hitler had walked virtually unopposed into Austria and in 1938, after the notorious Munich agreement, had seized the Sudetenland of Czechoslovakia.

The threat seemed so palpable that Belgium had made ready to receive the entire Luxembourg population retreating from invasion.

And now it had happened. From its industrial southwest 47,000 Luxembourgers streamed into France, inevitably entangling with the hosts of French fleeing to the south. Another 50,000 sought refuge in the Ardennes; a third of the nation was on the move.

On the move also from his job as Gauleiter of Trier, conveniently placed for the Luxembourg border, was Gustav Simon, the Fuehrer's gift to Luxembourg.

It would have been a mistake to underestimate the little man with the soup-bowl haircut and an old-fashioned bank clerk's deference. The same colourless qualities, after all, were shared with Reichsfuehrer-SS Heinrich Himmler and, in terms of acquiring power within the Nazi hierarchy, they had done him no harm.

Simon was not simply a traditional bureaucrat. There

was a restless energy, fuelled by a fanatical devotion to the interests of his Fuehrer, one of whose more bullying tenets he was never tired of echoing: 'We can go to the limit of humanity if we restore happiness to the German people.'

The bustling little Gauleiter did far more than merely mouth the utterances of his master; within three months of the occupation, he had approved an order proclaiming that 'the language of Luxembourg and its inhabitants is, and always has been German. . . . The German language shall be the exclusive official language.'

With that single utterance Simon had railroaded the centuries-old Luxembourg tradition whereby the Grand Duchy had been bilingual in both German and French. Sturdy, independent Luxembourgers were not unduly worried; they were determined to continue with their old ways, no matter what the Germans said.

For his part, Simon reckoned it was time for the iron fist. He rushed out a shoal of decrees on what were termed 'measures of Penal Law'. The fourth of these, published in *Nationalblatt*, was couched in language of unambiguous pomposity:

. . . Any person undertaking any action calculated to interfere with the planned return of Luxembourg to the German Reich, either by the restoration of Luxembourg or its inclusion in a foreign state, likewise forfeits his life for this dishonourable offence against the nationhood.

Furthermore, the plotting of the above-mentioned crimes and any offer or invitation to participate in such treasonable activity is punishable by death, as also is the furthering of any such attempts of high treason and any communication with foreign governments with the object of preparing any such undertaking. . . .

The death penalty is also applied to any person who, whether at home or abroad, undertakes to assist an enemy power in any way or to hinder the war effort of the Reich and all its Allies. . . .

Simon also thundered in *Nationalblatt:* 'It is forbidden to use non-Germanic accents (i.e. acute, grave and circum-

73

flex) when writing in the language of Luxembourg. Offences will be punishable by a fine of 150 Reichmarks or imprisonment.'

In addition, the use of 'Monsieur' and 'Bonjour' was outlawed, as well as such French names as 'François' and 'Camille', consigned to oblivion, along with 'Jacques' and 'Dupont'.

The Gauleiter, who after these measures pronounced himself satisfied, proclaimed: 'Luxembourgers are Germans by race and language, and only by vicissitudes of history, the intrigues of the Great Powers and separatist movements, have they been torn from the German fatherland. They now wish to return.'

Such reassurances would doubtless satisfy Reichsfuehrer Himmler, who announced that absorption in Germany was a historical necessity, since Luxembourgers had become 'racially degenerated by their ancient contact with Belgium'.

The Luxembourgers, however, had no wish to 'return' to Germany and no stomach for Nazi occupation. Gustav Simon was prepared to meet their defiance with cold cruelty.

The unstoppable mobile columns on 10 May had continued their deep thrust into the very entrails of France. In the west Generalmajor Erwin Rommel's forces occupied Le Havre; after two days' rest came the order to slice through to Cherbourg on the Contentin peninsula. Hitler's forces had encircled the British Expeditionary Force, compelling it to evacuate by sea. The much vaunted Maginot line – the concrete and steel fortifications stretching from Luxembourg to Switzerland along the French border with Germany – had been bypassed with contemptuous ease.

But it was the loss of Paris which was the most bitter blow of all. Until the Germans reached the capital, the weather had been perfect; on 13 June, the leaves along the Champs Élysées had been a tender green. The majestic dome of the Invalides, containing the tomb of Napoleon, glistened in gold, and through the gateways of the Louvre could be glimpsed the vivid flowerbeds of the Tuileries Gardens.

Anyone seeking reassurance had only to glance at the tricolour flags waving serenely above the Chamber of Deputies and the Ministry of Foreign Affairs. Since the July day twenty-one years before, at the end of another war, when with a thunderous roll of drums and fanfare of trumpets a squadron of the magnificent Gardes Republicains rode through the Arc de Triomphe in front of France's two heroic Maréchals, Joffre and Foch – Paris had enjoyed its freedom.

On 14 June 1940, a single armed German policeman stood outside the Invalides. He wore a green uniform with helmet and jackboots, directing nonexistent traffic with a small stick. At the Place de la Concorde were massed tanks, guns, lorries, and ambulances. Two cameramen were filming Paris firemen busy on a high ladder, hoisting a Nazi flag on the facade of the Ministry of Marine.

As the Germans approached Paris, the fine weather gave way to drizzle and sullen skies. Early on the morning of that same 14 June, Oberstleutnant Dr Hans Spiedel, an officer on the staff of the 18th Army of General der Artillerie Georg von Kuechler, received two French officers who had come under a flag of truce. Their instructions were to give up the French capital. The bloodless and orderly entry into Paris was made by troops of the German 87th Infantry Division, led by an anti-tank detachment which speedily occupied the Hôtel de Ville and the Invalides.

There was no denying that the first troops to enter Paris had an impressive bearing. There was an element of stage management about it all; the Wehrmacht had deliberately prepared itself. The men were spruce and smartly polished, and could easily have been models for a recruiting poster. Soon, troops were drilling in the public squares and mounted bands were practising on the Champs de

Mars, and there was the bizarre spectacle of soldiers clad in shorts kicking a football in the Tuileries Gardens.

There was heavy emphasis on correct behaviour; officers were saluted by their men with scrupulous rectitude.

The politeness extended to the people of Paris. For a while, the Parisians allowed themselves to relax and even stopped groups of German troops in the street to ask what was happening. The Germans answered all questions with grave courtesy before getting on with what seemed to be their main leisure activity – taking snaps of the Arc de Triomphe or Notre Dame.

But there were ominous portents. 'Occupation money' was soon issued – notes which were legal tender, circulating only in France. Their value was set at four times the value of the franc; any shopkeeper unwise enough to refuse them found himself severely penalised. The 'occupation money' was spent lavishly with soldiers buying everything in sight. A Paris journalist, Paul Simon, who was to edit the clandestine newspaper *Valmy*, saw the unemployed at Vaugirard packing a Berlin-bound train with goods that had been gathered from every part of France.

Inevitably, there were those who later made conspicuous profits from the victory celebrations to the new conqueror. One of the first objectives of the Germans was Montmartre and the promise of 'Les Girls'. An estimated 4,000 troops swilled champagne in their victory; the first French fortunes of the occupation were made that night. One restaurant owner swiftly converted a three-roomed apartment into a 'furnished hotel' for the German troops and their girl friends. There was no coyness in proclaiming the riches of such instant collaboration; certainly not from a fashionable restaurant which sold nearly a thousand pounds' worth of champagne on victory night, and there were tireless whores whose weekly takings from then on averaged three hundred pounds.

Those who had decided to quit the city in the wake of the German advance could not believe it would be long before they were back to the old life. The scenes on the congested roads frequently resembled a holiday outing rather than evacuation from a potentially lethal foe.

An eyewitness wrote:

... The queue of traffic which our car joined at the Barrière d'Italie contained vehicles of every description – delivery vans, touring cars, heavy lorries, and even antique horse-drawn cabs. Big lorries contained whole families, who were passing round sausage and wine. Every time a queue stopped – about every 100 yards – people would scatter to the roadside and go into houses, returning with a hunk of bread or a bottle of water. The hot sun blazed down on the happy crowd – a paid holiday.

Paris, with its stone bridges arching above the clear waters of the Seine, was serenely beautiful under the pale blue of the summer sky. But it was also a city under the heel of the conqueror. There was a visit from the Nazi warlord; a gloating Adolf Hitler smirked like a gargoyle on the Palais de Chaillot.

Clearly, life would never be quite the same again, although it was hard to believe it at the smart racecourses of Longchamps and Auteuil. Here the women seemed as attractive and as fashionably dressed as ever. Only their escorts had changed. The men wore the well-cut field grey officers' uniform of the Wehrmacht or the blue of the Luftwaffe.

But the majority of the five million Parisians settling down to what was to be four years of occupation did not welcome the Germans. Least of all those with memories of just twenty-one years earlier.

One man above all stood out during the deliriously triumphant victory parade through Paris in July 1919. Maréchal Henri Philippe Pétain, Commander-in-Chief, rode through the Arc de Triomphe on a white horse, tall and magnificent in his uniform of horizon blue. For him, the crowds gave more than applause. Here was veneration for a national hero who had led his *poilus* through the sublime ten-month nightmare of the battle of Verdun and who had nursed and restored French morale after an army mutiny in 1917.

These achievements were indeed remarkable for a man who had sprung, not from an aristocratic or patrician background, but from peasant stock.

Such a background, it was said, denied him promotion for something like forty years. It took World War One, to change all that. Henri Philippe Pétain rose to be a Maréchal of France, a national father figure, drawing affection and admiration even from political opponents.

And now, not a generation later, here he was, head of the French government, sitting apprehensively in Bordeaux waiting for a telephone call that would bring him news of the German terms for an armistice.

The presentation of the terms, it turned out, was to be no mere formality across a green baize table; Adolf Hitler was determined to make the most of the occasion with a bold piece of theatre.

He chose for the setting the forest of Compiègne, where a delegation of Germans in November 1918, in a railway carriage, had signed an armistice dictated by Ferdinand Foch. Now the roles were reversed; France was to quaff the cup of humiliation to the last drop.

Hitler gave precise orders for the staging of the new armistice; the old railway carriage No. 2419D was to be taken from a museum and returned to the exact spot where it had stood in 1918. Hitler took the seat formerly occupied by Foch who had laid down the terms of the 1918 armistice to the Germans.

The Fuehrer had not finished with his elaborate theatre of revenge. Generaloberst Wilhelm Keitel explained that the site had been chosen 'as an act of reparatory justice'. The reading of the terms took fifteen minutes. Another of the historical parallels was rigidly adhered to.

In November 1918 Maréchal Foch had greeted the German delegation with *'Qu'est-ce que vous désirez, messieurs?*' The head of the German delegation, Matthias Erzberger, had replied that the group were there to receive the proposal of the Allied Powers for an armistice.

Foch had replied sharply: 'I have no proposal whatever to make.'

In other words, no discussion was permitted. In June 1940, in the same railway carriage, no discussion was allowed either. When Keitel had finished, Hitler threw a Nazi salute and left to the strains of 'Deutschland, Deutschland Ueber Alles'.

Pétain announced over the wireless on 17 June that France was asking for an armistice and that Hitler had drawn it up for signature on 22 June. This was greeted by the more optimistic French as a sign of possible reasonableness from the Germans. After all, where else had Hitler signed an armistice with a defeated foe? In all other occupied territories, conditions were dictated flatly on the basis of unconditional surrender.

Certainly, the terms of the armistice were harsh, but not, at first sight, humiliating. The country was to be spared total occupation. France was to be divided into occupied and unoccupied zones. But over *both* zones the French government's authority was to apply equally. No official text of the terms was published immediately, but in London the British produced a summary stating the main provisions.

Germany will occupy roughly all territory north and west of Tours in west-central France and will thus control Paris as well as all western seaports. All rights of occupation except local administration are to be maintained by the troops stationed there, with France to pay the costs of occupation.

These costs, as it turned out, were to be at a rate of four hundred million francs a day.

Despite earlier optimism, it soon became obvious that there was much about the German terms to stick in the craw. Even though there was no complete occupation, the

79

country was obliged to turn over to the Reich all the anti-Nazi refugees in France and her territories. This struck at one of France's most cherished traditions, the right of asylum.

In addition, the French accepted Article 20 of the armistice agreement, stating that French prisoners of war were to remain in captivity. It had been naively assumed that this stricture would no longer apply once the armistice terms were signed. The German conquerors did not see it that way at all; a million and a half Frenchmen were condemned to rot in prison camps for nearly five years.

The French government was free 'to choose its seat in the unoccupied territory or even, if it so desires, transfer to Paris'. The French government did not so choose; instead, it opted for the spa town of Vichy in the south-central part of the country. It had the major advantage of a central position, good communications, including its own airfield, and ample accommodation in its many hotels. But it was not simply a matter of administrative convenience. Vichy had figured on the contingency plans of the French government long before the war; it had been considered a suitable alternative to Paris, should the battle front threaten the capital.

On 10 July the French National Assembly, meeting at Vichy, buried the Third Republic, which had been the longest living government since the Revolution. Pierre Laval, the political figure who was to become most identified with the policy of collaboration and was now Deputy Prime Minister, informed the Assembly that a 'national revolution' was in the making. 'Liberty, Equality and Fraternity' were obsolete irrelevancies. From now on it would be 'Work, Family and the Fatherland'.

Democracy had patently failed; the time had come for autocratic government by decree. The matter was put to the vote. Of the 666 deputies present, a mere 80 voted 'no'. By an overwhelming affirmative vote of 569 (there were 17 abstentions) 'the Vichy regime' was launched into history.

Hitler's provision of an Unoccupied Zone for France was a shrewdly calculated move. Talk had reached the Germans of plans for a French government-in-exile with its seat in North Africa.

Now that scheme was set at naught, with the country divided both geographically and administratively.

By no means were all members of the Vichy government pro-Hitler. Nonetheless, there were enough useful enemies of democracy who might reasonably be expected to cooperate in the realisation of the Nazi New Order in Europe.

Adolf Hitler had good reason to express himself satisfied with the way things were going. France, unbeaten for four years in the previous war, had been knocked out in just six weeks. His troops were masters of most of Europe, from the North Cape above the Arctic Circle to Bordeaux, from the English Channel to the river Bug in eastern Poland. German hegemony in Europe seemed assured.

The Franco-Italian armistice was signed in Rome two days after the German one. The bellicose Benito Mussolini's attitude towards France had been recorded long before in the diary of the Duce's Foreign Minister, Count Galeazzo Ciano. On 13 May 1938, Mussolini was being described as 'more and more anti-French. He said they are a nation ruined by alcohol, syphilis, and journalism'. Four days later, Mussolini was noted to be 'very worked up against France'. When the Italian leader launched into a shrill anti-French speech in Genoa, the crowd hissed, and a rash of anti-French sentiment broke out all over Italy.

In terms of actual fighting, however, Italian efforts were puny. Some thirty-two Italian divisions were, after a week, unable to budge a scratch French force of six divisions on the Alpine front and further south along the Riviera.

After the armistice, signed at 7.35 p.m. on 24 June, Mussolini was able to occupy only a small portion of French territory.

Six hours after the Italian armistice, the guns in France fell silent.

9

Not everyone had left Paris. Even during the first few days of the occupation, scattered groups of dissidents, many of them ex-soldiers, congregated in the cafés. Over the coffee and the Pernod, bewilderment was soon being replaced by a slowly burning anger. The journalist Paul Simon translated it into a course of action which, recalled later, seemed puny indeed. But at least it had been a start.

He had managed to lay his hands on a small rubber printing set that was, in fact, little more than a child's toy. Soon, a group of fledgling resistants were composing each letter into what was hoped was a pithy slogan. The words '*Long live the Republic, in spite of everything*' seemed to strike the right belligerent note. It was printed on the most convenient material to hand: strips of gummed paper.

Simon later revealed: 'That night, returning home in the dark, we stuck our small slogans on maps at the metro stations, on lamp posts, and on shop-fronts. The next day, passing the same places, we each saw our handiwork being read. We mixed with the little groups of two or three and overheard some friendly comments. This encouraged us.'

A friend from northern Europe who had taken refuge in Simon's home brought some half a dozen rolls of the sticky papers. When those ran out, they used the kind of paper intended for protecting windows against bomb blast.

Soon, Simon's little group had expanded to five, each paying a monthly subscription of five francs, and, in true resistance tradition, adopting cover names.

One of the number, known as Boyau-Rouge, had a weakness for metro stations. He planned his campaign scrupulously, each day taking a different route and sticking slogans secretly on German posters and the handrails of escalators. Great satisfaction was to be gained from stuffing the slogans into the belts of German soldiers when the trains were crowded.

Another friend was responsible for a rash of adhesive labelling on the walls of cafés, on lamp posts, railings, trees and hoardings. People downing a quick drink in a bar suddenly spotted a label stuck to the bottom of the glass. Even a quiet stroll down the Champs Élysées or through the Bois de Boulogne provided no escape. There they were stuck on seats and on the barks of trees.

Many carried the blunt message *On les aura* (We shall get them).

But somehow these initiatives, although personally satisfying, lacked the sufficiently brazen touch. More spectacular acts of defiance were clearly necessary; Simon decided to extend his personal skills to the service of resistance.

Paris, he decided, would have its very own underground newspaper; its very title would breathe defiance in the face of humiliation.

Everyone in the group agreed on the excellence of the name *Valmy*, in recognition of a key victory during the French Revolution which had freed France of Prussians and royalists. A bow would thus be made to historic pride. Paris would go into battle with words – at this stage, the only weapon it possessed.

For such a newspaper to be printed in conventional form was obviously out of the question. It would have to be typed; reasonable enough if typewriters in Nazi-occupied Paris had not been as rare as printing presses. There were suitably sympathetic firms prepared to rent out machines in a good cause, but the business of making a smart profit could not be subordinated to patriotism. Almost overnight, prices from hire firms mysteriously multiplied. The rental was clearly beyond the slender resources of Simon and his group.

More direct methods were called for. An attractive sympathiser named Renée was employed as a secretary by a company doing business with the Germans. The solution was absurdly simple; at the end of one working day Renée strolled into a neighbouring office, lifted a machine and walked out with it.

The audacity of the move took the group's breath away. There was now sufficient encouragement to do something even more daring. By a stroke of luck an incredibly primitive duplicator had been secured, but stencils and ink were needed. Fortunately, Suzanne, also a resistant, worked for the Germans. Coolly, she and another member of the *Valmy* staff walked into the offices and collected the stencils. Simon confessed gleefully: 'We even took extra time to type the word *Valmy* on top of a stencil and we left smiling happily at the German officers we met in the corridors. But then Suzanne was an extremely pretty girl.'

Ownership of a typewriter and duplicator required a police permit. Production of each issue of *Valmy* was almost an open invitation to arrest; the clatter of machines could have alerted either collaborator or the police.

But *Valmy* survived and triumphed. In one of the earlier issues the paper was trumpeting:

CERTITUDES

Six months have elapsed since France laid down her arms and came to terms with the enemy, contrary to her pledged word. Today, one may assess from the unfinished history of the war some of the results.

To begin with, the armistice has not ended the state of war.

For the two million French prisoners it is still war; occupied France submits to a state of siege; the so-called free zone feels itself a military protectorate.

It has been claimed that to come to terms with the enemy was a necessity. Experience proves the contrary. Norway, Holland and Belgium, completely invaded, have continued the struggle to the seas or from vast colonial territories. Their lot is not harder than ours. If the French fleet and overseas armies had not abandoned the fight, under orders . . . the Italian vulture

85

would have its claws cut and Mussolini would be hiding in shame. Is that what it was desired to avoid? . . .

You, Frenchmen, have only this choice. To agree to uphold an order of life which is nothing but a welter of joyless misery, and to accept as final a defeat turned to surrender by men hating liberty and greedy for power. You do not want that.

You know that democracy still lives. It has known betrayal and besmirching, but it will not be attacked from now on without risk, for it is forging arms in the world's mightiest arsenal.

Valmy

For the time being, these arms were made only of paper. But the spirit of rebellion was contagious. It would spread further, to the other occupied countries of the west.

10

High above the battlements of Oslo's Akershus Castle the Norwegian flag fluttered in the winter breeze, but its presence had nothing to do with the defiance of a conquered people.

For on 1 February 1942, the unthinkable had become reality – Vidkun Quisling, whom many had thought still smarting under the contempt of his Nazi masters, was back in power, his new-found authority vested in the title of Minister President.

At the time of Quisling's ignominious dismissal as Prime Minister, Hitler, conscious that his much hated protégé might nevertheless be of future use, had insisted that Quisling be given an 'honourable position' and 'held in reserve'. The move by Kurt Brauer to give him the meaningless sinecure of Commissioner of Demobilisation had by no means drawn Quisling's fangs.

He had remained in firm control of his Nasjonal Samling party, a strong-armed ally that Josef Terboven realised he had need of. True, in 1940 it had been little more than a disreputable rabble, but the Nazis' hold on Norway had changed all that. Collaborators had crawled out of the woodwork in October 1940; by the end of that year membership of Nasjonal Samling had risen to 26,000, and it kept on increasing.

But with Quisling in the shadows, nominally at least, the credit for this could be attributed primarily to Terboven's icy presence. It was he who wielded ultimate power in Norway; his clout was far greater than that of General der Infanterie Falkenhorst or, indeed, even of the Nazi secret police.

87

It was not just a question of crude oppression or terror, although there was plenty of both. Terboven attacked Norway through its stomach. Germany looted Norway's larder; for the first time in living memory, beggars appeared on the streets of Oslo. In the land of the smorgasbord, it became impossible to buy an egg; milk was scarce; and there were acute shortages of poultry and cattle. As early as October 1940, Olaf Hansen, a Norwegian journalist who eventually escaped to London was reporting: 'Meat is not rationed, for the simple reason that there is not enough of it to ration ... You would have difficulty in buying a bar of chocolate in Oslo and there is practically no tobacco. All prices have increased by double since the German invasion.'

Newspapers in Oslo reported that only a flour substitute was available and that production of some form of powdered fish was expected. Even this was wishful thinking; the last supplies of fish were fast running out. Hansen reported: 'At the moment, Norway's great fishing industry is at a standstill because of the acute shortage of petrol. Nobody is allowed to use a private car in Norway. There are a few taxis left in Oslo, but the owners who have survived are permitted to run their vehicles on three days a week only.'

There were consolations of a kind. In the early months of the occupation, there were plenty of jobs, and all available labour was absorbed by the Germans' extensive building of aerodromes and barracks. Pay was more than adequate. But winter was soon casting its grey shadow and the employment figures plunged.

The effect on the middle classes was devastating. Long-established shipping firms shed their labour, along with import and export agencies. Scores of black-coated workers found themselves on the streets, and with the depression came the abolition of unemployment benefit.

Here was fertile ground indeed, for Quisling's Nasjonal Samling members moved in to fill vacant jobs.

Among the ranks of Hird youths there were plenty of

takers: fat wage packets could now be tucked into the pockets of crisp new uniforms.

Terboven, however, remained uneasy. This, after all, was a *Nazi* occupation of Norway. His masters in Berlin demanded a heavy injection of National Socialist ideology and expected him to supply it. The schools of Norway looked like fertile ground. The job was turned over to Ragnar Skancke, one of Quisling's close associates and an ardent Nazi.

Skancke's intention was to pull up Norway's education system by the roots and remodel it for the New Order. Revision of all textbooks on constitutional law and European history was demanded. German was to become the country's second language, in place of English. To discourage rebellion, pictures of Quisling glared down from classroom walls; anyone removing them was disciplined.

That was just a start; Terboven was determined that Quisling would earn his rehabilitation. Not that the architect of Nasjonal Samling had exactly been idle. With the improvement in the fortunes of his organisation he was soon looking to his friends in Berlin. But, as it turned out, there was no need to seek fresh favours. Hitler had begun looking fondly on Quisling once again, and there was an equally enthusiastic advocate in his old crony, Alfred Rosenberg.

Within Norway there was no such support for Quisling. Members of those organisations that had been absorbed by Nasjonal Samling retaliated by resigning or by dissolving their movements. These dissidents – known as B groups – were to form the nucleus of civilian resistance.

But they could not strike yet with any prospect of success. Furthermore, they were contending with a Quisling armed with awesome new powers.

Nobody was more astounded than the man himself when the summons came from Josef Terboven.

The Reichskommissar for Norway told Quisling: 'The time has come for you to have a public role in Norwegian politics. You will be allowed to form a new government.'

89

The words were carefully chosen. Terboven was implying that Quisling would not have a free hand to do precisely what he liked in Norway. He was to be first and last a tool in an overall scheme to consolidate pro-German appeal throughout the country.

It was necessary, Terboven realised, to feed Quisling's considerable vanity; a colourful ceremony to mark his latest elevation would not be out of place.

And so it was that on 1 February 1942 the Norwegian flag was raised over Akershus Castle and the parliament building to signify that now Norway had a government of its own, led by Vidkun Quisling, who, at the elaborate ceremony, stood to attention in his grey Hird uniform in the presence of an honour guard drawn from seven Norwegian regiments.

Hitler did Quisling proud. The Nazi hierarchy was represented by Martin Bormann, the Fuehrer's most trusted confidant, together with the German Kriegsmarine and Wehrmacht. The day reached a lavish climax at a sumptuous banquet in a mansion in the suburb of Bygdo.

Quisling was not averse to luxury. The Villa Grandi was considered eminently suited to his new-found eminence. It was promptly requisitioned. The name Villa Grandi, however, was not considered grand enough; Quisling had it changed to Villa Gimle (Home of the Gods). What title, after all, could be more suitable for Norway's undisputed new masters?

Terboven claimed to be suitably impressed, but he lost no time in telling Quisling that results in stamping out opposition must be speedy and effective.

Quisling made up his mind to intensify Terboven's relentless campaign against the teachers. Furthermore, he would step it up in such a fashion that no one would be left in the slightest doubt about the power of the Minister President.

A new organisation, the Teachers' Front, sprang into being. Quisling's newspaper *Fritt Folk* defined its purpose with unambiguous crudity. It would, the paper empha-

90

sised, 'serve as a straitjacket for all those who are unwilling to do their duty to the state and to Norwegian youth' .

Quisling's warning was orchestrated with silky menace by Orvar Saether, the former chief of staff of the detested Hird who became the Front's first leader. Saether warned in a speech that, while individual teachers would not be compelled to join Nasjonal Samling, they would in time 'no doubt find it appropriate to do so'.

Quisling was by no means finished yet. Hot on the establishment of the Teachers' Front came a fresh decree forming a Nasjonal Samling Youth Movement. Quisling's eyes, as usual, were on Berlin. The young people's movement, Hitler Jugend, had proved a conspicuous success in Germany; the Nasjonal Samling model would ape it assiduously. Such a movement in Norway, Quisling declared, 'gives us control of 400,000 young, from whom we shall select those who are to be trained for membership in our party'.

For the teachers there was now a clear, if uncomfortable, choice. They would either have to bow to the demands of the Norwegian Nazis, or reject membership and be hounded out of their jobs. For days, the underground B organisation agonised. Its eventual decision was courageous and fateful: the teachers would be mobilised throughout the country for a mass action that would decisively reject membership of the Teachers' Front.

By a method of secret communication bypassing the German censors, letters were sent to teachers in the towns and villages of Norway. They were ordered in their turn to mail their rejection. So that the defiance would have the maximum effect, the members of the B group ordered the teachers to write in identical terms on precisely the same day – 20 February.

The reaction surprised even the organisers. The Teachers' Front was spurned by 12,000 out of Norway's 14,000 teachers.

It was a direct challenge to Quisling's rule and could scarcely be ignored. It was not merely a question of rebellion by the teachers, serious though that was. Plainly, there was an organised civilian resistance at work.

Saether ordered a series of sweeping arrests in Oslo, Bergen and Trondheim, together with other dragnets in smaller towns and cities. By the end of March, Quisling had more than 13,000 teachers under arrest; many of them were sent to the Grini concentration camp outside Oslo.

For 700 of them, a special horror was reserved. Quisling decreed that they were to be sent to forced labour in the Arctic, alongside the prisoners from the war in Russia.

Their initial journey, packed in railway cattle trucks, was to the rural concentration camp at Jorstadmoen. Physical harassment – gymnastic exercises at the double, belly crawls through slush, and constant hard labour on meaningless tasks – accompanied total isolation. Conversation and the writing or receiving of letters were forbidden.

It might have been thought that men and women more at home in school classroom or university library would have cracked under such a harsh programme of physical and mental humiliation. As it turned out, the action of those so cruelly oppressed was nothing less than heroic.

The harsh regime was kept up for fourteen days and nights, with the camp officials dropping the hint that membership of the Teachers' Front would bring it to an end.

Only fifty teachers out of 687 at Jorstadmoen gave in. They were promptly freed. One hundred and fifty other broken and dispirited prisoners found themselves back at Grini. The rest were marched to unheated cattle trucks and transported to Trondheim, packed aboard the *SS Skjerstad*, a creaking wooden coastal steamer built at the turn of the century and intended to hold only 200.

The conditions were so appalling that they enraged the Nasjonal Samling doctor allowed on board. He sent a personal message to Quisling:

SS Skjerstad, with some 500 teachers and guards and crew, is due to leave Trondheim. Many cannot lie down at night but must stand, as the ship has only room for 200 persons. Many of the teachers are very ill with pneumonia, gastric ulcers, asthma, bronchitis, haemorrhage and mental derangement. There are only two toilets for everybody. . . .

As if sensing the likely reaction from Quisling, the doctor ended his message by stating: 'Several of the teachers are willing to join the Teachers' Front.'

Appeal was useless. Quisling thundered that the teachers had been given their last chance to repent at Jorstadmoen; the ship must sail as scheduled. The *Skjerstad* left on 14 April for the Arctic port of Kirkenes, near the Finnish border. There was no let-up in the appalling, crowded conditions, with prisoners receiving only one hot meal a day. One teacher, crammed with others in the hold, wrote: 'A tiny gleam of light shone from above, but there was no fresh air. There was a fearful stench and one heard the despairing moaning of the sick.'

But even the deportations did not break the spirit of the teachers and there were only a few defections.

For a few months, Quisling kept up the pretence that the Front had a future. With the schools bereft of teachers, the country's entire educational system looked like collapsing. He was forced to give in and reopen the schools.

Like a petulant child whose favourite toy has been taken away, he assembled a group of teachers and stormed: 'You have destroyed everything.' A little later, the prisoners from Kirkenes returned home, greeted as heroes.

But Vidkun Quisling did not allow himself the luxury of sulking for long. Instead, he turned his attention to the Norwegian Jews.

The Jews of Norway, never a large community, had settled comfortably enough in Norwegian cities after fleeing from the dark pogroms of Russia and Poland. By April 1940, at the time of the German invasion, the Jewish population was still only around 1,500 including some 350 political refugees from the Nazis.

Against this pathetically vulnerable minority, who asked only to be left in peace, the Germans moved with savagery and speed. Richard Petrow, in his book *The Bitter Years*, which covers the period of occupation in Denmark and Norway, records:

Within days of the invasion, German troops slashed out at visible signs of Jewish life. In Trondheim, German soldiers smashed into the synagogue, where they replaced Stars of David with Swastikas, demolished all holy objects, and pockmarked the interior walls with bullet holes after using the synagogue's large religious lamps for target practice.

Terboven, a spiteful anti-Semite, lashed Quisling into greater activity. Until the arrival of the Germans, the Nasjonal Samling party had not openly avowed anti-Semitism; getting its cohorts to change their minds was not that easy. If the rank and file had scruples, the police had none. Arrests of Jewish shopkeepers were stepped up, along with the confiscation of their businesses. The letter J was stamped on all identity papers held by Jews.

There was a rash of arbitrary arrests on the flimsiest of political charges. The Nasjonal Samling police were helped out with enthusiasm by a strong and ruthless Gestapo. It was not just a question of unpleasant imprisonment in Grini. There was large-scale deportation for Scandinavian prisoners to, among other places, Auschwitz in Poland, Bergen-Belsen near Hanover, and Ravensbrueck, the women's camp north of Berlin.

Of the 760 Norwegian Jews deported to Auschwitz, only twenty-four survived the war.

But among the Jews of Scandinavia were those who did not perish at Auschwitz or elsewhere. The Danes received advance intelligence of what was in store for them.

Resistance was mobilised for action.

11

On the morning of Friday 30 September 1943, the Jews of Copenhagen were a puzzled people. It was the day before Rosh Hashana, the Jewish New Year, and the 150-strong congregation gathered at the town's synagogue stood before the Holy Ark.

Rabbi Marcus Melchior was telling them bluntly: 'There will be no service this morning. Last night I received word that the Germans plan to raid Jewish homes throughout Copenhagen. They intend to arrest all Danish Jews for shipment to concentration camps. They know that tomorrow is Rosh Hashana and our families will be at home.'

He pressed on urgently: 'We must take immediate action. You must leave the synagogue now and contact all relatives, friends and neighbours whom you know are Jewish. They must pass on the word.

'You must also speak to all your Christian friends and tell them to warn the Jews. You must do this immediately, within the next few minutes, so that within two or three hours everyone will know what is happening. By nightfall we must all be in hiding.'

It was scarcely believable. Hitler, it had been widely supposed, was prepared to be kind almost indefinitely to his *Musterprotektorat*, his model protectorate.

It had seemed that the tenets of National Socialist philosophy allowed for the Danes being pure Nordics, descended from the stock that had inhabited the Danish islands before the Stone Age. The racial theorists of the Third Reich had been pleased to note that the Kimbric peninsula, Jutland, was the birthplace of the Teutons and the Gottons; the Danes, it was patent, were blood brothers of the Germans. Toleration was obviously called for, and this would even be extended to the Danish Jews. If Germany pursued so enlightened an attitude, it was suggested, then there was likely to be little trouble from possible resistance groups.

By no means everyone within Hitler's Germany was so tolerant. To the SS of Heinrich Himmler, Jews were Jews, wherever they might happen to be. How was it that 8,000 of them were allowed to live in peace in Denmark? Here was the ultimate in heresies.

Cecil von Renthe-Fink, the German plenipotentiary, was, above all, a diplomat. There was sense, he believed, in treading warily with the Jews. If they became incensed, if there was an attack on their civil rights, then there would plainly be violent upheaval. Why was it necessary to prejudice what appeared to be good relations between the two countries? Of course, there were the so-called 'Jewish experts' who insisted on bombarding him with memoranda from Berlin about the Jews. Renthe-Fink was prepared to meet them some of the way: he suggested that Jewish firms in Denmark be deprived of their allocations of coal and fuel from Germany.

Surely, in the name of common sense, such a measure would be sufficient. It was considered nothing of the sort. Berlin responded to Renthe-Fink's delicate approach by sending to Denmark one of Himmler's most assiduous disciples, Dr Werner Best. As a key man within the Gestapo, Best had impeccable credentials.

As early as 1935, the Prussian Supreme Court of Administration, which was answerable to Himmler, then deputy chief of the Prussian State Police, had ruled that the orders and actions of the Gestapo were not subject to judicial review. The courts were barred from interfering in any way with the activities of the Gestapo – a rule which received more than an approving nod at the time from Dr Best. Indeed, he had put Himmler's case well: 'As long as the police carry out the will of the leadership, it is acting legally.' Such a lack of scruple, it was considered, would stand him in good stead when it came to dealing with the hitherto feather-bedded Danish Jews.

But Best was not just a textbook Nazi. He had a fund of pragmatism and soon was telling his stupefied masters in Berlin that Renthe-Fink was right: Denmark was supplying Germany vast quantities of foodstuffs, far beyond the agreed quotas. From Danish factories there poured a seemingly endless stream of marine diesel engines, parts, aircraft and armoured vehicles. Ideology was all very well; the Reich had need of such hardware. Talk of the Fuehrer's plan to make Europe free of Jews did not allow for such practical considerations. Besides, this was 1942. A bitter and bloody war was being fought in the Soviet Union; the very future of the Reich was being determined. All reason suggested that the Danish Jews should be left alone.

For Foreign Minister Von Ribbentrop such ideas were abhorrent. The proposition that these Jews, unlike those of Poland, Slovakia and the Ukraine, were to remain inviolate could not be tolerated.

Plainly, both Renthe-Fink *and* Best needed a further lesson. An even grimmer mouthpiece of the Gestapo was despatched to Denmark. SS-Standartenfuehrer Rudolf Mildner was of far sterner stuff. Not only was he a proven anti-Semite, but he had done sinister work at Auschwitz, where he had introduced some novel methods of torture. Mildner was hastily snatched from Poland and despatched to Scandinavia.

The result served only to sting Von Ribbentrop and Himmler into fresh fury. Mildner reported: 'The fact has to be faced that hatred of anti-Semitism in Denmark is endemic. There is an atmosphere of racial and religious tolerance that cannot be denied. The deportation of the Jews will be politically unacceptable.'

The argument raged for nearly a year. Eventually, Hitler's patience snapped. Werner Best was summoned to Berlin. The Fuehrer stormed: 'The idea that Danish Jews

97

should walk around free is loathsome. I demand action.'
He went on to point out that, aside from the Jewish question, the Germans had been facing growing resistance from the Danes. There was now an admirable pretext for moving against the Jews.

Danish resistance, previously slumbering, grew steadily bolder. At first, Denmark had enjoyed the fruits of booming exports to Germany. But the occupying power had steadily drained the country dry. The Danes, legendary for eating abundantly and well, had suddenly been faced with serious shortages. They were in mutinous mood.

Even more serious for Germany, they were beginning to sense a change in the tide. The fortunes of the Reich had turned. There had been catastrophic defeats at Stalingrad and El Alamein. In the summer of 1943, Sicily was invaded by the Allies and Mussolini had been toppled from power. All Hitler's instincts were for retaliation.

To Best, Hitler added menacingly: 'If conditions get any worse, I will entrust the government to the military commander.'

Best returned to Denmark pale and shaken. He had good reasons. If Hitler turned over the initiative to the Wehrmacht and its commander, General der Infanterie von Hanneken, the Gestapo would plainly be in disgrace.

And that is what happened. Best was relieved of his job as plenipotentiary and replaced by the Wehrmacht commander. He clung desperately to his position within the Gestapo. He would seek salvation in action.

The pretext for moving against the resistance was ready to hand. Workers' groups, protesting at the food shortages, launched a rash of strikes in the Copenhagen and Odense shipyards. The initial response of the Germans could not have been more insulting to Danish pride – members of the Schalburg Corps, Danish pro-Nazis who had volunteered to fight in the east, were ordered home to turn against their own people. At first, the strikes had been contained and manageable; now they spread like a virus throughout the city. The inevitable violence was dramatic.

When a German officer opened fire on the strikers, the crowd turned on him in fury and beat him to death.

There were mass arrests of known or suspected dissidents. Best called a meeting of Danish newspaper editors and stormed: 'In this ridiculous little country, the press has inoculated the people with the idea that Germany is weak ... From now on, every editor will be responsible with his head for seeing that the people are no longer poisoned.'

The editors reacted by forming one of the most effective underground newspaper organisations to be found in any occupied country. Like other Danes, they were smarting from a proclamation issued by Hanneken and, at his insistence, broadcast incessantly over Danish radio:

'The latest events have shown that the Danish government is no longer capable of maintaining law and order in Denmark. The disturbances provoked by foreign agents are aimed directly at the Wehrmacht. Therefore in accordance with the articles Nos 42–56 of the Hague Convention of the laws and customs of war on land, I declare a military state of emergency in the whole of Denmark.'

Then followed a shoal of decrees. Crowds and gatherings were restricted to no more than five people, with a rigid curfew and a total ban on the use of mail services or the telephone. Inducements to strikes 'which would cause disadvantages to the Wehrmacht' were punishable by death.

The call to resistance placed the Jews in a hideous dilemma. There was widespread approval for protests against the occupation and the more obvious tyrannies. On the other hand, the Danish Jews reasoned that up till now they had led a charmed life. The Germans, hideously decisive in other countries, had been slow to move against them in Denmark. But for how much longer?

On 8 September 1943, Werner Best gave the answer. He dashed off a telegram to Berlin suggesting that the present state of emergency now amply justified the deportation of the Danish Jews. Sooner or later, the Jews would be sucked into the mainstream of resistance; diplomacy had patently failed.

Hitler was delighted; he promptly reinstated Best as plenipotentiary. A greatly angered Hanneken was instructed to take orders from Best. To Ribbentrop was given the task of ensuring that all Best's needs for the coming operation were met. The Reich's Foreigh Minister sent for Reichsfuehrer Himmler, and Best was telegraphed: 'The Reich Foreign Minister asks you to put forward concrete proposals with regard to the deportation of Jews decided upon, in order to determine how many policemen and how many SS should be detailed to the implementation of the operation in question.'

For Best, there could now be no turning back. On 11 September, he communicated his needs to Berlin. All were granted. Furthermore, Best was told that the men in charge of the coming raid would be SS-Standartenfuehrer Rudolf Mildner and SS-Gruppenfuehrer Guenther Pancke.

Best set about informing his lieutenants. Among them was his head of shipping operations, Georg Ferdinand Duckwitz. For the Jews, the choice of Duckwitz turned out to be highly significant. He had enjoyed a comfortable life in Denmark. He and his wife had gone there from Germany back in 1928, after he graduated from law school. He had secured a post with a Copenhagen coffee firm, followed by a job at the German Embassy as the head of shipping. Duckwitz liked the Danes and certainly had no stomach for delivering them into the hands of the SS.

The Duckwitzs had many friends in Danish political circles, notably in the Social Democratic Party; he was not to forget them in the wake of Werner Best's latest plans.

As for Best, he had not entirely swallowed his misgivings. In a gloomy mood he confided to Duckwitz that pressure from Berlin was rapidly becoming intolerable.

First, there had been Hitler's demands; then had come a request from Ribbentrop to submit plans for an operation that meant nothing less than shipping as many Danish Jews as possible to the concentration camps.

Duckwitz exploded: 'If you consent to this, then you are a disgrace to the German Embassy here.'

Best shrugged: 'I'm personally sympathetic to the treatment of Jews, but it is necessary to obey orders.'

It was too much for Duckwitz; he promptly turned his back on Best and began laying his own plans. The first move was to fly to Berlin and find out exactly what Ribbentrop was planning.

Of that there was little doubt. Ribbentrop had entrusted to Himmler all 'technical questions' involving the arrest and transportation of the Danish Jews to Theresienstadt concentration camp; all necessary troops, trucks and transport ships would be supplied.

It was now that Georg Ferdinand Duckwitz risked his life on behalf of the Danish Jews.

He picked an evening when he knew that his contacts in the Social Democrat party would be together at a meeting; it turned out to be just twenty-four hours before the raid was due.

Although fully aware that the shadow of the Gestapo loomed menacingly, Duckwitz calmly left his apartment and made for the meeting at 22 Roemer Street. Without ceremony, he marched straight into the building's main conference room and went over to Hans Hedtoft, the Social Democrat party chief. He told Hedtoft: 'Within a few hours ships will anchor in Copenhagen Harbour. Those of your poor Jewish countrymen who get caught will be dragged forcibly on board and transported. No one knows what will happen to them.'

Hedtoft barely had time to reply before Duckwitz melted away.

Clearly, there was more than hearsay evidence of German intentions. But to his dismay, Hedtoft came up against a wall of disbelief. Might not the whole thing, people reasoned, be an elaborate Gestapo plot to flush out Jews? Besides, Werner Best had informed the Jews countless times that no such action was contemplated; the Danish government had received his assurances. Hedtoft was pressed to reveal his source, but he could not bring himself to point the finger at Duckwitz.

With his warnings rejected, Hedtoft decided to act on his own. There could now be only one question: how could he warn the Danish Jews?

Time was not on his side. As early as mid-September, members of the Jewish Community Centre had complained to Best that their office had been raided by Germans in mufti: records of members' names and addresses had been seized.

Best seemed both penitent and embarrassed. He confessed: 'I'm aware of what happened. But in fact it is only a minor action' (*eine recht kleine aktion*). Best went on to explain that the quest had been merely a routine affair to root out saboteurs. There was no connection with 'the Jewish question'.

To Duckwitz, Best later told a different story. This was indeed the prelude to a planned raid. Duckwitz, as head of shipping, would have a crucial role to play and he would be kept informed. Even so, Best continued to be nagged by doubts. But there was little that he could do now to stem the plans of Ribbentrop and Himmler.

He made one more try. Could not, he suggested, the Jews be rounded up *after* the state of emergency in Denmark had been lifted? It would surely be possible for an edict to be presented whereby the Jews would be instructed to report for 'work' at the Wehrmacht offices. They could then be arrested and deported.

The suggestion reached the desk of SS-Sturmbannfuehrer Adolf Eichmann, who in January of the previous year had been assigned the task of the mass deportation of Jews to the extermination camps of the east. Eichmann was, in fact, the architect of the entire genocide operation. And he had no time for Best's pussyfooting. A special contingent of SS commandos under his direction was poised for work in Copenhagen.

Its mission was clearcut: to prepare for the transportation to Germany of 8,000 Jews. There would be no question of those Jews being lured into a trap; they would be arrested in a carefully planned 'lightning raid' on 1 October.

Hints of the dangers reached Rabbi Marcus Melchior. The rabbi pondered recent happenings, the state of military emergency, the seizing of the membership lists of the Jewish Community Centre.

No delay could be justified; he forthwith warned his congregation. They were stunned, disbelieving, even hostile. A few hours before, the very idea of ranting in his own synagogue, surrounded by the sacred scrolls of the Torah, the silver candelabra and the prayer books, would have been unthinkable. But now here he was shouting: 'You must do what I tell you.'

The traditional authority of the rabbi had its effect.

News of the planned German raid coursed through the Jewish community. Those who had been at the synagogue were soon telling everyone they knew of the vital need to go into hiding. Many risked the telephone, but, conscious that the Gestapo could well be listening in, word-of-mouth intelligence spread rapidly. Jews told not only other Jews, but Christians they felt they could trust.

No haphazard warnings, however well intentioned, would be enough. Melchior targeted his intelligence through known sympathisers who were able because of their jobs to move around Copenhagen without arousing suspicion.

Christian and Jewish policemen, postmen, taxi drivers, shopkeepers, doctors, teachers and students spread the word during their normal working day. One of Melchior's most able lieutenants was ambulance driver Jorgen Knudsen; the rabbi reasoned that the sight of an ambulance parked outside houses and blocks of flats would not be likely to cause comment. Knudsen promptly agreed to take the day off and, armed with a list of prominent Jews, drove round to spread the word. Those Jews who panicked, he instructed to play at being patients. Swiftly, he ferried them to the local hospital, where a friend, Dr Karl Henry Koster, was willing to hide them.

Jens Lillilund, who at the time of the Danish invasion had expressed his contempt for the Germans by spitting at them and who had been arrested and later released for a singularly fruitless act of resistance, had broadened his activities. He wandered the streets at night, slashing the tyres of cars belonging to the Germans. After that, it was remarkably easy to become a full-time saboteur, blowing up Danish factories in production for the Germans.

Such activities were personally satisfying and even effective, but they paled into significance with this new threat. Lillilund was not Jewish and did not feel that he had any exclusive loyalty towards the Jews. But they were being threatened by the Germans, and that was more than sufficient reason to help them. He saw no need, however, to alter his normally impulsive style. Very well, the Jews would be warned. But *which* Jews?

The family doctor, Max Rosenthal, was to hand. A telephone call would be madness; Lillilund burst in on the morning surgery.

Rosenthal snapped: 'What the hell is the matter with you? You know better than to break in like this. I've a room full of patients.'

Lillilund retorted: 'If I don't talk to you there won't be any patients. This is very definitely an emergency.'

Dr Rosenthal was to hold no more surgeries for a very long time to come. Within the hour he and his family were in hiding in Lillilund's own home.

Mogens Staffeldt was most people's idea of a bookseller. He was short, mild-mannered, unworldly. Not for one moment would he have dreamt of aiming his bicycle at German troops, let alone spitting at them. Neither was he the type who would willingly spend cold winter nights priming fuses for explosives aimed at enemy factory buildings.

For choice, he would have preferred to ignore the Germans. Unfortunately, they had other ideas. When they moved into Dagmarhaus, the building where his bookshop was located, he was forced to find new premises. In high dudgeon, he moved across the road and prepared to start his business all over again.

But he was not allowed to. The curb on his activities, however, came not from the Germans but from his old friend Jens Lillilund.

Within days, the bookish Staffeldt, torn away from his beloved catalogues and shelves of stock, had become a dedicated resistant. Just how he allowed himself to be persuaded was always a perpetual mystery to him. The bookshop became a secret headquarters for the underground; the cellar was given over to printing illegal resistance newspapers containing accounts of German atrocities against the Jews in other European counties.

Then came the word from Lillilund of the intended German roundup.

Staffeldt promptly told his clerks that he would be away for a while. He mounted his bicycle and rode throughout Copenhagen to pass the warning to a score of Jewish families. Soon he had built up a network of Jewish informers whose job was to spread the intelligence still further.

To his considerable astonishment, Mogens Staffeldt actually began to enjoy his new life of intrigue. Soon word was abroad that his bookshop was a collecting point for Jewish refugees. He welcomed them all without question. His new-found enthusiasm began to worry Lillilund.

He protested: 'The risk is enormous. There are a lot of Germans in this building, and sooner or later they'll see something.'

Staffeldt argued: 'But they are excellent customers and spend money. When the place is free of them I'll indicate it by putting a copy of Kaj Munk's poems in the window. It will mean that the coast is clear. The absence of the book will mean that it is dangerous for Jews to enter the store.'

It was a piece of melodrama straight out of the movies. Jens Lillilund remained uneasy; the Jews kept on coming.

Some ninety per cent of Danish Jews lived in Copenhagen; it was a statistic that made the work of the underground that much easier. The Jews were found hiding places everywhere – in the homes of their relatives, Christian friends and even total strangers. They were harboured in Protestant churches and Catholic cloisters. They found refuge in hotels, summer huts, cellars and warehouses.

Shortly before midnight on 29 September 1943, the Germans struck. Two German transport vessels, including the large freighter *Wartheland*, anchored in Copenhagen harbour. Then two days later, right on schedule, came the Eichmann commandos. All telephone communications throughout the country were severed. Into the offices of the Ritzau news agency flooded German troops; the teleprinters were swiftly disabled. The dragnet was under way. But most of the knocks on the front doors of Jewish homes went unanswered.

Inevitably, there were tragedies involving families for whom the warnings had come too late. They were dragged away to the waiting ships. One hundred and fifty German troops threw a cordon around an old people's home next to a synagogue. The residents, aged from sixty to ninety were dragged from their beds, including a paralysed elderly woman who had been bedridden for eleven years. Bound to a stretcher, she was carried to the synagogue, and later questioned about sabotage operations. The elderly were forced to watch the synagogue being looted of its treasures. German soldiers urinated in the sanctuary.

By the standards of the Nazis, the raid could only be rated a dismal failure. A total of 202 Jews had been arrested – far short of the number that could be accommodated in the transport ships. Throughout the country the number of seizures stood at 284 men, women and children. The bulk of the Jewish population had escaped.

For Werner Best, embarrassment was complete. In a mood of misguided optimism, he had sent a premature telegram to Hitler: 'It was my duty to clean Denmark of her Jews and this has been achieved. Denmark is *Judenrein* – [free of Jews] and completely purged.'

Adolf Eichmann, the ravings of Hitler and Himmler still ringing in his ears, arrived in Copenhagen three days later. The full blast of his fury was vented on Best and Mildner. Eichmann declared later: 'That small country caused us more problems than anywhere else.'

The transport vessels departed with their meagre cargo. Eichmann, with more pressing business and more promising quarry in the east, departed with the instruction that raids were to go on. After all, he argued, the Jews could not remain in hiding for ever.

But where were they to go next? The doors of neutral Sweden remained tight shut.

As it turned out, one man was to be the key figure in helping to prise them open. Only then could the exodus of the Jews begin.

12

Danish scientist and Nobel prizewinner Niels Bohr was, by common consent, the world's leading authority on nuclear physics after Albert Einstein. And in 1943 Bohr was wanted urgently in the United States for developing the atomic bomb.

Late in September, he was spirited by the Allies from Denmark to Sweden, where he was swiftly contacted by Professor Lord Cherwell, Winston Churchill's personal consultant on scientific matters. Cherwell outlined an elaborate scheme. It involved Bohr flying to London as the first stop on his way to America, where he would begin work immediately.

To the astonished Cherwell, Bohr announced that he wanted nothing to do with the plan – at least, at first. Instead he demanded an urgent meeting with Sweden's Foreign Minister, Christian Guenther.

He got it. His demand was uncompromising: 'Unless you offer refuge to all Danish Jews who are able to reach Sweden I have no intention of leaving the country.'

The explanation for Bohr's ultimatum lay in an earlier meeting held in Copenhagen with Hans Hedtoft in which the German plans for rounding up the Danish Jews had been revealed. Guenther, however, appeared lukewarm. Bohr had no intention of leaving matters there. His next request was a meeting with the Swedish king. This time, the response was far more positive; King Gustav came across with his offer the very next day. Sweden *would* accept the Danish Jews.

Allied agents in Stockholm breathed again; Bohr would now be available for his essential work in America. But the Danish scientist had by no means concluded his mission. The Jews, he insisted, must be informed at once of Sweden's offer, otherwise plans for escape could not be formulated.

The Allies sweated. If this awkward scientist was not spirited out of the country soon, there was the real possibility that he might be kidnapped or murdered by German agents. But Bohr held the trump card, and Cherwell and his cohorts knew it.

Within days, the Swedish press was carrying the offer of refuge on its front pages. Swedish radio relayed the vital message to Denmark; Bohr was soon on his way to London.

He left behind a burning question: how were those Jews trapped in Denmark to be spirited to Sweden, literally under the noses of the Germans?

Clearly, the only possible way was by boat. It was an obvious route for the Germans to plug; several days before the 1 October raid they had ordered that all Danish boats were to be confined to harbour. The exception to the new edict was fishing vessels: an obvious loophole the owners were not slow to exploit.

Several hundred Jews in hiding rushed to coastal towns such as Elsinore, Snekkersten and Dragør. There, they hoped, would be fishermen willing to make the dangerous journey across the sound to Sweden.

People living around the towns did not hesitate to put up the Jews in hotels, farms, private houses and even garages. Nevertheless, the flight was hasty and chaotic and the Germans took full advantage of this obvious weakness. Most of the Jews caught by the Germans were arrested before the escape boats could be properly organised.

The one-time reluctant resistant Mogens Staffeldt was soon cheerfully accepting that his bookshop had become far more than merely a precarious refuge and meeting place for itinerant Danish Jews. The shop was the collection point from which they would make for other hiding places near the docks. Jens Lillilund was now undisputed boss of the Holger Danske resistance organisation, which took its name from a legendary Danish hero who rose from his sleep whenever his country was threatened. At first, Holger Danske had engaged in active sabotage against the enemy. But from now on, everything would be concentrated on the safe transport of the Jews.

Lillilund, meeting in the bookshop with his fellow resistants, did not mince words. There had, he stressed, been too many individual escape attempts in fishing boats, which had only resulted in capture by the Gestapo. The time had come to organise the business properly. Fishermen prepared to do the job must be pinned down to a fixed price. The existing Fishermen's Association would be given the job of nominating those of their members who were considered absolutely trustworthy; freelancers and freebooters would be out. That Lillilund was capable of such organisation was proved beyond doubt after the operation was over, when it was discovered that Holger Danske had under its control as many as a dozen fishing vessels, which had carried around 1,000 Jews to Sweden by the end of October.

Behind each sailing lay appalling risks. There could be arrest, deportation, imprisonment and even execution. Even successful escapes had their moments of terror.

One Jewish woman related:

We were taken by taxi to the beach near a little fishing harbour. Each of the four passengers and the organiser were then hidden under a bush by the shore. The plan was that at a certain time we were to crawl along the beach to the harbour, where there was a watchtower manned by Germans. We lay a whole day waiting for darkness. Up on the road we could hear cars drive by and we shivered with fright . . . At seven o'clock in the evening, a strange sight revealed itself. From the bushes along the beach human forms crawled on their stomachs. We discovered that these were other passengers of whose presence we had been completely unaware. After a while we reached the fishing boat without mishap and were herded into the hold, like herrings in a barrel.

Frequently, there was not enough space below; passengers were wrapped in fishing nets and sacks on deck. The whipping-up of the wind brought seasickness, and the refugees were forced on deck to retch, away from the stench of the hold. Possible searchlights from a German patrol boat were a recurring nightmare. Then the engine was stopped and the Jews stood silently around the wheelhouse, whose weak light could well have given them away. A small boat would be blown off course by the gale and, in the light of early dawn, there was no way of gauging their position.

The Jewish woman's account went on:

Would we ever be saved? At seven in the morning, land was sighted. But what land? The boat approached the coast; we hoped that liberty was at hand. We were *really* in Swedish territorial waters. The Danish flag was raised and people threw their arms around one another and cried for joy. We were saved at last. The harbour we had sailed into was full of Swedish warships on whose decks sailors waved and shouted 'Valkommen'.

For Rabbi Melchior, bereft of any knowledge of boats, the escape to Sweden was an astounding experience.

It began promisingly enough. Arrangements were made by the Reverend Hans Kildelby, Lutheran pastor at Orselv, forty miles from Copenhagen, for a young fisherman to ferry the six members of the Melchior family. Although it was pitch-black when the party set out from the island of Falster, everyone was cheerful enough. After all, the journey would take a mere six hours.

Anxiety mounted, though, when the six hours became eight and eventually stretched to ten. And then came alarm, when the rabbi spotted land. It was the Danish town of Gedser, near the German mainland.

Melchior turned on the young fisherman, yelling for an explanation. It emerged that the man had lost his way, was terrified of running into German patrol boats and had wasted twelve hours cruising in a circle.

For the first time in his life, Rabbi Marcus Melchior hit a fellow human being.

The fisherman was left on the floor of the boat to nurse a swollen jaw. As for the rabbi, he never was able to explain how he had managed to grab the rudder and turn the boat around. He held it on course for six hours until he reached Swedish waters.

On the day that Germany invaded Denmark, Erling Kiaer's main reaction was one of intense irritation; the roar of aircraft had disturbed his sleep. Not that the arrival of the Germans came as any surprise; in Kiaer's view his government had been singularly spineless in standing up to the Nazi menace. He shrugged and went back to sleep again.

Later that afternoon, the young bookbinder, in common with many of his fellow townsmen in Elsinore, bicycled to the centre to find out what was going on. The number of Danish lives lost amounted to precisely thirteen and, in the face of that, the government had caved in. Kiaer settled down in some disgust to tolerating the enemy and getting on with his life.

It appeared remarkably easy to keep out of trouble; the secret was never to discuss politics. Then came the day when the Germans disturbed Kiaer's sleep for the second time. The disturbance now was not from aircraft, but from sporadic bursts of gunfire in the streets around his apartment. Soon the explanation was spreading through the neighbourhood. A number of Danish girls known to be sleeping with Germans had been dragged from their homes and paraded through the streets with their heads shaved.

Fraternisation had led to punishment for some of the German troops, who in turn had decided on a little revenge of their own. A number of them had gone on the rampage and fired at random into Danish homes.

Such an incident chipped away at Kiaer's conscience. If the war was to be brought to the streets, should he not be playing his part? Was his self-imposed isolation from resistance any longer acceptable?

Soon he was discussing his conscience with three friends, all of whom had previously been more than content to keep out of trouble with the Germans. Thomod Larsen was a solid police officer whose routine work was still necessary, Germans or no Germans. Ove Bruhn beavered away contentedly as a book-keeper, while Dr Jorgen Gesfelt had more than enough patients to keep him busy in the fishing village of Snekkersten.

The policeman obviously had to be handled carefully; Kiaer, feeling his way, suggested to Larsen that possibly he could extend his work a little. He was in an ideal position, after all, to gain access to confidential reports, possibly about refugees and underground groups. Part of his job was to be a good listener; now was the time to eavesdrop on both Gestapo and Wehrmacht.

Bruhn had talents for organisation that would prove useful. A doctor was frequently needed to administer sedatives to the children of refugees smuggled onto the boats; Dr Gesfelt's main attraction, of course, was that he practised in a fishing village.

The nucleus of the group was complete. The search was on for the most innocuous cover name; the Elsinore Sewing Club was born.

The world knows Elsinore above all for Kronberg Castle, setting for Shakespeare's *Hamlet*. But for hundreds of Danish Jews in 1943, Elsinore was the springboard to freedom: base of one of Denmark's most effective underground units.

As a crossing place, the main advantage of Elsinore is that at this point the sound separating Denmark and

Sweden is only two and a half miles wide. But it is narrow, and was therefore easy for the patrolling Germans. To make matters worse, there were not enough Danish fishermen sufficiently daring to cope with the volume of passengers.

At first, there was an attempt to use trains; there was an important ferry crossing at Elsinore for German rail traffic. On the trip from Sweden, the trains were piled high with iron ore and other key war materials. But on the journey out they were often empty.

Although the trucks were kept locked, there was enough of a wait at Elsinore before they were loaded on to the ferries: time for the Danes to open them and sneak Jewish refugees aboard. Unfortunately, Danish security was lax, the Gestapo moved in to guard the empty trains. Once again, the fishermen came into their own.

There were inevitably delays, dangers and tragedies. The Germans made a number of successful swoops; tragedy struck at the town of Gilleleje where arrangements had been made to take one hundred Jews to a large schooner in the harbour. Kiaer and another colleague, journalist Borge Ronne, set out on foot to check final details at a farm which was to be the rallying point for the escapees.

For Kiaer, the going was particularly hard; he was weighed down with four thousand pounds needed to pay the fishermen, sewn into his coat lining.

At long last, the two men were knocking at the door of their resistance contact at the farm. There was no answer. The same thought struck both: had the Gestapo got there first? Or had there been a breakdown in communications and they were not expected?

The door was opened a cautious few inches. In the gloom, Kiaer and Ronne made out a face chalk-white with fear.

The man gasped: 'The Gestapo have called. I think they've rumbled the entire set-up.' The door was slammed shut.

It was far too late to warn the escapees who were already on their way. As two of the key resistants, it was essential for Kiaer and Ronne to remain at liberty. Within seconds, the pair had vaulted the garden wall, leapt several hedges and were hurtling towards the open fields. Kiaer was only too conscious of the weight of the money stitched to his coat.

Fortunately, both men knew the area well enough to avoid the roads. For several hours, they moved gingerly through fields of mud and dirt. Nowhere was there any sign of Germans. They decided to chance returning to the farm. There they were greeted by badly scared refugees who had been brought from Snekkersten in a convoy of trucks and cars.

Kiaer was terse: 'You'll have to go back to Snekkersten. There can be no question of a sailing tonight. It's far too risky.'

The drivers of the trucks and cars caught the mood of fear and refused to budge. Kiaer began ripping at the lining of his coat, desperately handing out money to make the drivers change their minds. The bribe worked, but by now many of the refugees were on the edge of panic. A mother and her daughter resolutely refused to make the return journey.

Kiaer explained patiently: 'If the area really is thick with Gestapo, it'll only be a matter of time before they surround the farm. You've got to move.'

The persuasion worked with everyone – except the mother and daughter. There was no choice but to leave them behind. The drivers doused their headlights and set out with the remaining refugees on the return journey. Later, Kiaer learnt that the Gestapo had arrived soon after. Mother and daughter were both taken.

It was a hard blow, but the Elsinore Sewing Club continued its work, extending it to ferrying out saboteurs, Danes wanted for political crimes, and English and American airmen shot down over Denmark while on bombing missions to Germany.

Erling Kiaer carved his own legend in resistance folklore as the 'Danish Pimpernel', perpetually elusive and bearing a charmed life. He also had a considerable sense of style. To the rest of the club, he announced: 'We can't depend solely on the fishermen. We need our own boat full time.'

The very idea was dismissed as ridiculous. To procure a boat independent of the professional fishermen was no easy task and virtually impossible to keep secret from the Germans. But the next day Kiaer had his boat.

'Where did it come from?' someone asked.

Kiaer responded happily: 'I stole it.'

That same evening he made his first trip to Sweden, celebrating his success with a gastronomic dinner at Helsingborg's Grand Hotel. He returned to Denmark and made three more successful crossings.

A handy donation from a wealthy Jewish doctor provided the down payment on a new boat. With contributions from the local townspeople, a second, larger one was secured. The original purloined vessel was returned to its astonished owner, who had not even realised it was missing.

News of the steady exodus of the Jews was greeted with cold fury by Heinrich Himmler. His sacred SS and Gestapo were beginning to look foolish. The local Gestapo was reinforced; the Germans went out looking for informers.

They were successful. Thomod Larsen, on the beach at Snekkersten awaiting the arrival of a fishing boat, was shot down in cold blood by a waiting German patrol. They had obviously been tipped off. But Larsen managed to convince his captors that he was a police officer on normal duty. An ambulance rushed him to hospital in Elsinore. Members of the Sewing Club took over; he was smuggled to Copenhagen, and from there, still gravely ill from his wounds, to Sweden.

Gestapo officers tumbled into Borge Ronne's apartment. His brother answered the door, giving the journalist a chance to escape over the rooftops. The following day he went into hiding in the home of another Sewing Club member. Several days later he was smuggled to Sweden.

All the key members of the Elsinore Sewing Club survived the war, including the 'Danish Pimpernel' himself. But no matter how sweet revenge may have been, it did not save the Elsinore Sewing Club. It was forced into extinction, destroyed by betrayal.

Two of the informers were eventually unmasked – O. I. Madesen, a police colleague of Larsen, and a naturalised Dane known as the 'Vienna boy'.

An offer of passage to Sweden was made to the unsuspecting Madesen. Halfway on the boat journey, the informer was throttled and his body thrown overboard.

The 'Vienna boy' lived a little longer. Furthermore, he did so in lavish style, thanks to his German masters. He was tucking into an elaborate dinner in his apartment when the men with machine-guns broke in.

Any regrets they may have felt for the ensuing violence were reserved strictly for the building's landlord. The killers left a note among the carnage. It read: 'Sorry for the holes in the wall.'

13

Mogens Staffeldt was enjoying himself. The successful exodus of the Danish Jews had boosted the courage of all the resistants. The time had come, they all felt, to attempt something more daring. Staffeldt's new ambition was to turn his bookshop into nothing less than an assignment centre for saboteurs trained in England and parachuted back into Denmark.

There were, Staffeldt pointed out to his no less enthusiastic colleagues, plenty of factories and railways just waiting to be blown up, to say nothing of the necessary liquidation of informers and traitors.

Inevitably, there was the day when the Gestapo came: three men dragged Mogens Staffeldt off to headquarters. Only the day before, twelve highly skilled saboteurs had left the shop for the south of Denmark, on a key mission of destruction near the German border.

The Gestapo men were all studied politeness, and they gave the impression of having all the time in the world. Furthermore, they did not seem to show any interest in sabotage activities at all.

One of them asked casually: 'Have you helped with the escape of Danish Jews?'

Staffeldt decided on a calculated risk. To admit it would do little harm now: all the Jews were away and presumably safe. It would make no difference whether he admitted it or not; plainly, the Gestapo would not let him go. His arrest was serious enough. All he could do was limit the damage. In any case, if he talked about the Jews, it might divert his questioners from the bookshop's function of providing a haven for saboteurs.

It was a forlorn hope. The next moment, he turned pale as one of the Germans said: 'By the way, we have caught your saboteurs. We would like the name of any others, together with your underground contacts.'

Obstinately, Staffeldt went on talking about the escaping Jews. Anything to keep his listeners busy; the main worry now was that they would take it into their heads to search the shop for arms.

But it was only delaying the process. The search was made, anyway. Staffeldt was no less astonished than his tormentors when nothing was found. Staffeldt later understood why. A fellow resistant, Christian Kieling, had got wind of his arrest and took the considerable risk of moving everything from the shop ahead of the Gestapo raid.

From Gestapo headquarters, Staffeldt was moved to Denmark's Vestre Prison. He escaped extreme torture; his captives contented themselves by losing their tempers and hitting him occasionally. He told them nothing.

The Germans, though, had their own ways of trying to get him talking. In the next cell was a close friend and fellow resistant, Svend Otto Nielsen, a mathematics teacher turned saboteur.

The Germans let Staffeldt hear Nielsen's screams under torture.

In attempting to escape, Nielsen had been shot no less than eight times. Life was a lot easier for his torturers after that.

He had broken his thigh-bone, and it was a simple matter to allow the limb to heal and then break it again and rub the fractured ends together. He was denied all medical attention; even the dignity of washing himself. Over the weeks and months, Nielsen's mattress hardened with cakes of blood, faeces and pus.

Staffeldt realised that, whatever the outcome, release would be out of the question, either for him or his friend. Talking would be hardly likely to relieve Nielsen's sufferings. He kept quiet. The Gestapo realised that they were getting nowhere with Staffeldt; he was forthwith despatched to the concentration camp at Horserod. His death sentence was never carried out. He and Jens Lillilund both survived the war.

And Svend Otto Nielsen? Suddenly, all torture ceased and the thigh-bone healed. Then came the day when Nielsen had recovered so well that he was able to enjoy the coffee and cigar which his suddenly amiable jailers brought him.

They next took him out of bed, sat him in a chair and carried him to the courtyard of the prison. Then they shot him.

Reichskommissar Josef Terboven had, by the end of the second year of the occupation of Norway, good reason to feel satisfied. The high spot of his achievement had been in June 1941, soon after the Germans invaded the Soviet Union. He had given orders for all Jews in Tromso and other towns in northern Norway to be rounded up and deported to the Reich. There had been hundreds of arrests around Kristiansand: twenty-four resistants and the leaders of Milorg, the organisation for Norwegian military resistance, had been executed.

Just what deportation meant for Jews leaving Oslo for Germany was illustrated by an eyewitness account from a Norwegian seaman:

The Jews ... were taken in lorries or, in the case of very sick people, in buses down to the harbour near Filipstad, in Oslo. The Germans and Norwegian Nazi guards prevented the deportees from taking leave of their friends. The Jews were immediately driven on board where they were given numbered discs. Embarkation went on from seven in the morning till one o'clock the following night. The Jews were taken in groups down into the two foremost holds where straw mattresses were spread on the floor. Space was extremely restricted, because the number of Jews was 200, more than had been expected. The youngest was a little boy of six or seven and the oldest was over 80.

In the morning, the *SS Kiel* sailed. The sea was rough and

conditions in the holds which had already become very bad during the night grew far worse. There were very few prisoners who had not been seasick and the smell was indescribable. The extremely inadequate sanitary facilities were soon unusable. Only in exceptional circumstances was anyone allowed on deck... One young Jew tried to take his own life by cutting an artery with the lid of a tin can; another one tried to jump overboard. A woman gave birth to a child down in the hold and was allowed after trying to kill the child to move up into midships. The food was the most meagre imaginable.... The guards were very severe, and the slightest movement or the least word brought batons and fists into play.

In order to get permission to go on deck or to the lavatory, a prisoner would first have to kneel down and kiss the boots of the guard. Those who were seasick were hosed with water from the deck. The hose was also used to clean the holds. The straw mattresses and clothing became soaked and never dried throughout the voyage.

The ship cast anchor outside Copenhagen, and the woman with the baby together with a very sick old man and the young Jew who tried to commit suicide were taken away in a police boat – 'to hospital', it was said. On arrival in a German port, the Jewish prisoners were allowed to take with them only a few of their miserable possessions. The rest was thrown overboard or burnt.

Home-grown fascist movements fed on fertile ground with the advent of Nazi subjugation.

As for the Belgians, it was their lot during World War Two to suffer Leon Degrelle.

There had, admittedly, been a time when the Belgians seemed only too pleased to accommodate the strikingly handsome, fiercely nationalistic son of a prosperous Catholic brewer, who appeared to be equally mesmerised by Benito Mussolini and Adolf Hitler.

In the 1930s, making full use of an invaluable platform supplied by his directorship of a barely solvent publishing house called Christus Rex, the property of the Action Catholique de la Jeunesse Belge, Degrelle launched what he came to regard almost as a sacred mission. From a tiny office, he bombarded Belgium with pamphlets roundly denouncing corruption in high places – above all, politicians who were also financial manipulators. The country's powerful Catholic party cringed beneath the barrage of abuse and denunciation, and had to act; it forbade its parliamentary representatives from holding salaried directorships while they were members of Parliament.

It was not enough. Degrelle, far from deaf to the hoarse demagogy of the German and Italian dictators with their mass meetings and parades, bands and banners, desperately wanted a party of his own. From Christus Rex evolved a protest political group high on ideals but vague in aims. In a manifesto, called *Message of Rex*, Degrelle declared loftily: 'Rex is the realm of total souls . . . complete lack of selfishness and individualism; a cause which transcends the individual, demanding all, promising nothing.'

From Adolf Hitler, the new dictator of Germany, was to come unstinted admiration: 'If I had a son, I would want him to be like Degrelle.' Mussolini, however, provided a commodity far more valuable than praise: funds for the coffers of the severely stretched Rexists. All heady stuff. It was especially gratifying when the party, on an avowedly anti-Communist, anti-Socialist, anti-Semitic and anti-bourgeois programme, made a sensational showing at the 1936 polls.

A party which two years before had not even existed now swept into Parliament with twenty-one seats in the Lower House and eight in the Senate. People began talking about Degrelle as the coming man. The king sounded him out on his willingness to accept a cabinet post. It was arrogantly thrust aside: 'I desire power, complete power, not just a ministerial job for myself or one of my lieutenants.' Within three years, the dream had turned to dust.

Degrelle's courting of Flemish nationalists demanding autonomy, and a covert meeting with Hitler's propaganda minister Dr Josef Goebbels, chipped away at the popularity of the Rexists. In April 1939, when the movement again faced the electors, its slump was every bit as dramatic as its rise. Seventeen of its twenty-one seats melted away. The share of the poll fell from 271,491 in 1936 to 103,636. By the outbreak of World War Two, it looked as if the Rexists were a spent force.

The German advance towards Belgium not only changed all that, it quite probably saved the life of Leon Degrelle.

Inevitably, it triggered a panic over the activities of those likely to be sympathetic to the new conquerors. Degrelle was arrested and interned by the French at Vernet but eventually released by the Germans.

Revenge was to taste sweet indeed. After his return to Belgium, Degrelle had his former guards brought to trial. The officer who had been in charge was sentenced to fifteen years' hard labour.

Degrelle now gave himself wholeheartedly to Hitler. On a barnstorming tour of the country, he urged his audiences: 'Do not be afraid to shout Heil Hitler.'

The Rexist paper, *Pay Reel*, stormed at the clergy: 'Their passionate sermons, their continual interference in political matters, their insults to Hitler and Germany . . . the abuse of their clerical rights for provocative and aggressive ends, the atmosphere of rebellion which many priests and monks seem intent on spreading, all this is, quite frankly, unbearable.'

Any manifestations of resistance were dealt with harshly. On 30 April 1942, posters sprouted all over Brussels. They read:

On April 16, at nine o'clock in the evening, in a hall at the Grand Place, where Brussels Flemish SS-men were gathered, a bomb exploded under the platform. A few persons were injured, and considerable damage was done to to the hall. The criminals are certainly Communists. Ten Communist prisoners, some of them already under sentence for other crimes, have therefore been deported to the East. The population of Brussels is asked to help clear up this crime. If the criminals are not discovered by noon on May 5, an additional batch of Communists will be sent to the East.

The alternative often meant incarceration in Belgium's Breendonck concentration camp, where many of the guards were Rexist or Flemish men decked out in German uniforms. These men received special rates of pay, with superior food rations, free lodging, free food and – possibly the most attractive inducement of all – free fuel.

No such privileges were granted to those ordinary Belgians striving desperately to hold on to their pride and lead as normal a life as possible. Roger Motz, an exiled member of the Belgian Parliament, wrote in *Belgian Unvanquished*:

Poverty, hunger and the humiliation of foreign domination have cast a shadow of dismal gloom over the whole Belgian people. . . . As for the quality of the bread which is sold to the population – it is absolutely revolting. The bread contains about 30–50 per cent foreign matter; it is black and sticky; it is impossible to cut it with a knife and it can only be eaten in shapeless lumps. Needless to say it is completely indigestible and its nutritive value is practically non-existent. But for whole weeks there is none to be had, and the newspapers in Brussels frequently publish announcements advising the public not to get unduly upset on account of the total lack of flour, but of course it is the Germans who by their extensive requisitioning have disorganised the distribution of commodities. This is particularly so in the case of butcher's meat. The requisitions of the German army as far as slaughtered livestock is concerned have been so heavy that they have absorbed the whole national output. Recently the Nazis commandeered 8 million pounds of raisins for their wounded on the Russian front. . . . The population has kept alive mainly on bread, potatoes, milk.

People seldom received the full amount of their theoretical rations. Roger Motz commented dryly: '. . . It may be said that the only article which is plentiful in the system of food control in Belgium is the coupons. The products which they represent are to all intents and purposes almost non-existent.'

The Germans were swift to hit back at the black market with the ordinance: 'Anyone who counterfeits ration tickets will be condemned to death or, in less serious cases, to hard labour. An unsuccessful attempt will be punished in exactly the same way as a successful one.'

Anne Somerhausen, a Belgian woman who kept a diary throughout the occupation, wrote:

People read it, shrug, look more carefully at the ration tickets they buy – pay higher prices for them. . . . Blessed black market! On Saturdays and Sundays, before dawn, labourers and office workers pile into trains going to the provinces, tramp about the countryside in search of black market potatoes, wheat, butter and eggs and return at night bowed under suitcases and knapsacks in the blacked-out trains, tired but happy. They have black market food to sell at high prices to richer families, to war profiteers, even to Germans. They will feed themselves on the difference between farm and city black market prices.

They are however subject to nightmares of risk, for control officials inspect trains, stations, and street cars and fall upon these petty tradesmen. Black trading is not an easy calling. Yet, as I see it, it is the only one likely to save the little people of Belgium from German-imposed malnutrition.

The erosion of food supplies was far from being the only stranglehold exercised by the Germans. Even the simplest journeys within the country became virtually impossible. About 45,000 Belgian railways trucks were seized by the conquerors and sent as far as Italy and Romania; almost the whole of Belgium's stock of lorries had vanished. Private cars, even for doctors, had become merely a memory. But for those few fortunate enough still to have them, it was possible to get petrol – from the more enterprising Germans who were prepared to sell military stocks at rarefied prices.

And resistance? In Belgium, it seemed to many that the underground had, for a time at least, been cowed.

125

Elsewhere, too, there seemed little prospect of relief or release.

14

Gauleiter Gustav Simon's brutally direct methods of reversing recent Luxembourg history continued remorselessly. The Grand Duchy, he proclaimed, had always been German and, furthermore, would remain so.

True, Luxembourg had in 1815 formed part of the old Germanic Confederation; it was equally true, though, that in 1939 it had been declared neutral territory by the Treaty of London. Furthermore, at the Treaty of Versailles in 1919, Luxembourg, victim of an earlier German invasion in World War One, had been pronounced free of all German ties.

Such facts were both embarrassing and inconvenient; Simon decided, quite literally, to blast them out of existence.

The Monument du Souvenir, a proud, soaring spire in the centre of the capital, had been erected in memory of 3,000 Luxembourg volunteers killed during World War One. On 10 October 1940, the memorial was blown up by the Nazis.

Protests were ruthlessly put down by arrests and Gestapo beatings. There were any amount of German immigrants, their numbers stiffened by Luxembourg sympathisers, who, under the banner of Die Volksdeutsche Bewegung (the German People's Movement), were also more than willing to beat up anyone daring to demonstrate Belgian or French sympathies or unfurl the red, white and blue flag of Luxembourg.

Simon was set on a head-on attack on Luxembourg national pride. On 30 August 1942, the Gauleiter solemnly proclaimed the reunion of Luxembourg to the Reich as part of the 'Moselgau' (Moselle district).

In a public address he stated: 'The German Reich as a State has received you within its sphere of sovereignty. Thereby you accept all the duties entailed by Reich citizenship; at the same time you receive all the rights bound up with it. In this solemn hour I greet you as Reich citizens of Adolf Hitler's Greater German Reich.'

Compulsory military service was introduced; into the ranks of the Wehrmacht were sucked able-bodied men between the ages of eighteen and forty. As for racial and religious persecution, attacks on Luxembourg Jews were sadly predictable. There was confiscation of wealth, expulsion and deportation. But Simon reserved a special hatred for the Roman Catholics, the religious majority of the old Grand Duchy. For them he had special plans.

His SS descended on the ancient Benedictine monastery of Clervaux, timing their swoop with celebrations on 15 January 1942 for the feast of St Maurus, the patron saint.

Orders were terse: the monks were to leave within the hour. The Gestapo permitted the consecrated hosts in the tabernacle to be consumed. Each monk was allowed to take with him just two habits and a few devotional articles. The exodus was filmed by German newsreel cameramen for showing in Luxembourg cinemas.

The *Catholic Herald* newspaper, published in London, a few months later, reported:

After a minute and shameful search of each individual had been conducted, the monks left the monastic enclosure singing the Miserere and the Magnificat as a last farewell to the Blessed Mother. . . . With the temperature at minus 20 degrees Celsius the monks were forced to cover part of the way on foot; then they were taken across the Luxembourg-Belgian frontier in trains. There they were abandoned on the main highway after being given express command not to return to their own country.

Amid the terrible cold there were individual tragedies.

Forty-six-year-old French monk Joachim Bredoux, already seriously ill with a raging fever, died in Clervaux town. The local people defiantly gave him a spectacular funeral.

As for the monastery, Simon swiftly converted it into military barracks, ripping out the interior and destroying all religious insignia. The well of the church was then divided to take in a large swimming pool and gymnasium.

As an added insult, captured Jews had their bank accounts seized; 100,000 Reichsmarks of the money was used for the conversion of other monasteries into barracks.

The crucifix was forthwith banned from all courtrooms and public buildings. Similar treatment for the red, white and blue of the Luxembourg tricolour proved more difficult. The *Luxembourg Bulletin*, published be emigrés in the United States, reported, 'All over the country Luxembourgers empty eggs so that they can fill them with red, white and blue colours. At a given moment, they throw them at the walls; the Luxembourg colours appear in many patterns.'

At the small town of Rumelange, there was considerable entertainment value in the sight of a German Gefreiter baulked by a 150-foot factory chimney topped by the banned Luxembourg flag. The sergeant was detailed to remove it. A conscientious soul, he dutifully began scaling the chimney's iron rungs. But the individuals who had raised the flag had removed the rungs nearest the top. There was nothing else for it; the Gefreiter, to the delight of the crowd, was forced down. The flag was later despatched with several hundred rounds of machine-gun fire; the Luxembourgers reckoned they had won a sort of victory.

Among little Luxembourg's larger neighbours, however, moments for light relief were sparse.

In the Netherlands, Obergruppenfuehrer und General der

Polizei Hanns Rauter worked away as industriously as ever.

The veteran Freikorps warrior from Austria had never actually been noted for subtlety. The ideological baggage of National Socialism obviously required some lip service, but secretly Rauter regarded it all with contempt. He was a man who liked to think on his feet.

When the Dutch showed a distressing reluctance to listen to the rigidly controlled radio stations Hilversum 1 and 2 but preferred instead to bolt windows and doors and tune into the BBC and Radio Orange from London, Rauter's solution was simple. He confiscated radio sets by the hundred; the SS swooped on houses and blocks of flats. The haul was more than 800,000 sets. After that, having a radio became both illegal and dangerous throughout the Netherlands.

Under the relentless, efficient *Arbeitseinsatz* system, able-bodied men and women were mustered for work in the factories of the Reich. Those likely to be affected sped into hiding. Rauter made it his business to root them out; again, the methods were characteristic.

From as early as March 1941, everyone above the age of fifteen had been required to carry a personal identity card at all times – a regulation even applying to swimmers, who were expected to tuck their documentation into their costumes.

There was little taste for these measures; the Dutch evolved ingenious schemes for dodging them. But Rauter was ready. Orders were given for the existing ration card to be redesigned. It would be issued only to those who applied personally; without it, there would be no way of getting food or clothes.

Those stubborn enough to remain unregistered from July 1943 onwards became the victims of Rauter's manhunts. Whole villages or sections of cities were cordoned off for house-by-house dragnets. Those who fell into the net – Jews, ex-servicemen, escapees from forced labour, members of the underground – were deported.

The three largest organisations of the resistance – Armed Squads, Order Service and Council of Resistance – made plans to combine. The joint aim would be to deal with Hanns Rauter personally. But the effectiveness of Nazi oppression meant such plans were slow.

By contrast, in France resistance was already at white heat.

15

It seemed to many Parisians that the tone of the BBC broadcasts from London in the first October of occupation was disappointingly bland.

There was a reminder to French citizens that Armistice Day was approaching; everyone should be ready to demonstrate on this traditional holiday commemorating victory of France and the Allies over the Kaiser's Germany in World War One.

The broadcast suggested that this should be a peaceful affair. Patriots should gather at the Arc de Triomphe and merely lay flowers on the Tomb of the Unknown Soldier. A shade more aggressive, perhaps, might be the act of putting wreaths midway down the Champs Élysées at the foot of the statue of Georges Clemenceau, the 'Tiger of France', who, from the brink of defeat in that earlier war, had whipped the country to victory.

To Roger Langeron, the police prefect of the capital, this advice from London seemed unrealistic. He doubted if such conciliatory tactics would satisfy the Parisians. Demonstrations – and quite noisy ones at that – were highly likely on 11 November.

It was not just the appeal of the date. Already, Langeron had received reports from his men that students were especially incensed by a meeting between Henri Philippe Pétain and Adolf Hitler.

Hitler had flattered Pétain as a head of state. There had been elaborate courtesies for the old man: the salutes of three generals in full dress and the presenting of arms by a company of the Wehrmacht as he crossed the demarcation line into the Occupied Zone. Baron Alexander von

Doernberg, Germany's head of protocol, had done the Vichy leader proud. The strong handshake from the Fuehrer had been recorded by film and press cameras. After it, Pétain appealed for 'the acceptance of collaboration'.

But the new generation of students did not venerate an old man; it had its own hero in General Charles de Gaulle, who, ever since the armistice, had denounced all *rapprochement* in his own broadcasts from London.

And now Langeron was learning that an increasing number of de Gaulle stickers, handbills, pamphlets and suggested slogans (ideal for graffiti) were finding their way into the capital. It was not long before they were appearing on the Boulevard St Michel and all the streets surrounding the ancient university of the Sorbonne.

Potentially more serious, attacks were being made on German vehicles by dropping incendiary gas bottles from rooftops.

The Germans caught the mood. On 13 October German wall posters in Paris adopted an ominous new tone. From now on, anyone harbouring English soldiers would be shot. Parisians were informed that they must report to the German Kommandantur before 20 October with any information on sheltered English military personnel. If information was withheld after that date, then the penalty was also the firing squad.

Against this background, some form of rebellion looked increasingly likely. Then a single action by the Germans made it inevitable.

On 10 November, the Paris press carried the communiqué: 'Public administration offices and private establishments will work normally on 11 November in Paris and in the department of the Seine. Commemorative ceremonies will not take place. No public demonstration will be tolerated.'

For the students it was more than enough.

Early on the morning of the Armistice anniversary, a Citroën truck rumbled into the Place de la Concorde and turned into the Champs Élysées, making for Clemenceau's statue. Solemnly, the occupants of the truck unpacked its contents. These were not wreaths, which would have represented death and the past. Instead, there was a gigantic yard-long banner wrapped in a blue, white and red ribbon and bearing the legend in thick capitals 'Le Général de Gaulle'.

The police moved in to take away this prize piece of heresy. But not before it had been spotted by a number of Parisians, who gleefully spread the news. Soon the statue was steeply banked with flowers.

Within hours the Tomb of the Unknown Soldier had also attracted the crowds. Despite the order from his German masters, Langeron held off his men for as long as he could. The demonstrations, after all, were peaceful; if the Germans were prepared to turn a blind eye, little harm would be done.

It was a vain hope. German troops began patrolling the Champs Élysées; in the meantime, students from lycée and university poured out of the metro and up the Étoile.

The banner had been provocation enough; the tricolour ribbon was something else entirely. As it was unfurled, the first shots sliced into the students jammed into the Place de l'Étoile and the Arc de Triomphe. Then the troops went in, their batons flying. The screams of anger and terror were drowned by the shrill sirens of cars and trucks charging the mob. Other students attempted to rescue their fallen comrades; they were run down. The scene switched to further down the hill from the Étoile, where Paris witnessed an impressive meeting of the generations. The students there had the support of war veterans. All, massed together at the corner of the Avenue Georges V and the Champs Élysées, were chanting, *'Vive la France! A bas Pétain! A bas Hitler! Vive de Gaulle!'* Then came the singing of 'La Marseillaise'.

The Germans were not prepared to let it alone. Crack SS troops concealed in a nearby cinema were joined by convoys of military bunched in the side streets. As they hurled towards the mob, machine-gun crews peeled away to set up positions. At the sight of the crews, students and veterans scattered, and shots mingled with the screams. The Germans chased their quarry well into the night, arresting whoever they could. In fact, their haul was sparse; around 120 were seized, among them 90 lycée students and 14 university students. Many were eventually released.

But young engineer Jacques Bonsergent was not so fortunate.

The day before the protests, Bonsergent's main pre-occupation was not students, resistance, or even the Germans. Of infinitely more importance was the wedding of his closest friend, Robert Abadie. Sunday 10 November had been set aside for a little celebration: Bonsergent was to join the young couple and four other friends for a convivial evening.

When it was over, the companions lurched cheerfully down the rue St-Lazare towards the metro. The fact that Paris was in darkness and that there was an air-raid alert bothered them not at all.

That darkness was to prove particularly unfortunate; also in the rue St-Lazare that night, and belligerently drunk as distinct from merely merry, was a group of Wehrmacht troops.

At the sight of the revellers, a German waded in. One of the Frenchmen retaliated with a shove, sending the German flying. Furious at his injured dignity, the Wehrmacht man came out, fists flaying. In no time at all, there was a free-for-all on the darkened Paris streets, the blows and shouts punctuated by the screams of the women. For no particular reason, the arriving reinforcements pitched into Jacques Bonsergent, ignoring the rest. He was forthwith marched to the nearest military post.

Bonsergent's friends, when they eventually regrouped, were not unduly worried. It was bad luck for poor Jacques, certainly, but it was unlikely that much harm would befall him. It would mean a few months in the prison of Cherche Midi at most.

Bonsergent took the same view. From his cell, he calmly wrote to his older brother Gabriel, requesting that his employer be told what had happened and pleading for a razor, toothbrush and a change of clothing.

The next day the students of Paris marched. The German military command was in a mood to do something dramatic. To hand was a young Frenchman who had struck a German soldier.

There was now no holding the German court martial. Bonsergent, not sensing danger, took full responsibility for the event of the previous night. He refused to name any of his companions. On 5 December, he was condemned to death.

Bonsergent's defence counsel was reassuring. It was, he told his client, a mere formality. The Fuehrer would undoubtedly show leniency; indeed, the Germans had taken a fairly lenient view of the events of 11 November and there had been few serious recriminations.

But Hitler was not so easily placated. Another unrelated event was to seal Bonsergent's fate.

Hitler had previously conceived what he regarded as a magnanimous gesture towards the French. The Fuehrer had ordered that the ashes of Napoleon's son, l'Aiglon, should be returned to Paris from their resting place in the Capuchin Chapel in Vienna. The ceremony, with its heavy Teutonic trappings, was largely shunned by the people of Paris, who proved remarkably unimpressed by Hitler's gesture. Pétain shunned the ceremony for a different reason: he believed that his attendance and that of his entourage might be a cunning trap. The Maréchal had other problems as well. He had become highly suspicious of the activities of the vice-premier, Pierre Laval, whom he suspected of attempting a *coup d'état* within the Vichy government. Pétain demanded and received Laval's resignation, although Laval was later reinstated.

Here were unforgivable affronts to the power of Germany and the authority of Adolf Hitler. Clearly, these stubborn French were getting out of hand and must be taught a lesson.

Bonsergent's appeal for mercy was turned down. Jacques wrote to his brother Gabriel on 22 December:

They have just told me that my plea for pardon has been refused. I am to be executed tomorrow morning . . . I will die the victim of a mistake.

. . . I am accused of having struck some German soldiers on the tenth of November . . .

Above all, don't cry too much for me. I might have been killed at the front.

Votre petit
Jacques

The long drive to the rifle range at Vincennes was preceded by confession, heard by the German priest who stayed with the condemned man all night.

Bonsergent told the Abbé Stock: 'I would have preferred to die in battle.' At the moment of death he refused the blindfold. The Abbé later declared: 'He died, brave, pious and determined . . .'

The death sentence appeared in the local newspaper – 'condemned to death by military tribunal of the army of occupation in Paris and shot on 23 December 1940.'

A sympathetic German censor could not bring himself to refuse publication but was content merely to plead that it should be placed in a 'discreet' part of the paper. Gabriel Bonsergent countered bitterly: 'Did you shoot my brother discreetly?'

The student defiance had left German and Vichy authorities badly rattled. Radio broadcasts from London had enthusiastically fed reports to resistance groups on the spot. The bulletins were picked up by clandestine listeners in other parts of France and occupied Europe.

The lesson was now clear: in occupied France the hated German conquerors could expect to face the most determined resistance of all.

And as far as Paris went, the intellectual revolution,

typified by the students massing at the statue of Clemenceau and the Tomb of the Unknown Soldier, was just beginning.

16

With his striking fair good looks and clear blue eyes, it might have been thought that thirty-year-old gifted linguist Boris Vilde could be regarded proudly by the Nazis. Any sculptor seeking a model for 'a pure blond Aryan' need have gone no further.

The Germans might well have been further attracted to Vilde on learning that this bright, fair-skinned native of St Petersburg had previously served a sentence for anti-Soviet activity and had eventually decamped to Berlin.

His credentials for National Socialism seemed impeccable. He was a language expert on the staff of the Musée de l'Homme (the Museum of Man), which is situated on the broad esplanade of the Trocadero in Paris, and devoted to anthropology. A collaborator at the very centre of French academic circles who shared the Nazis' racial creed would have proved an ally indeed.

But Vilde was not for the Nazis. In fact, he might not have been for the resistance, either, if it had not been for tiny, dynamic Yvonne Oddon, chief librarian of the Musée de l'Homme.

Vilde had long been intrigued by Yvonne – intrigued, above all, by the stream of strangers who kept asking for her because she was giving them 'English lessons'. To the best of Vilde's knowledge, Yvonne had never done any teaching in her life.

What she was, as Vilde soon discovered, was an excellent hater of Germans. It had all begun with her friend Agnes Humbert, an historian working at one of the museum's offshoots, the Musée des Arts et Traditions

Populaires in the Palais Chaillot. Agnes's experiences there in the wake of the Nazi occupation were sickening.

First, there was the rape of the library. Books by Jewish scholars were literally torn from the shelves and destroyed. Their place was taken by crude tracts on National Socialism, together with anti-Semitic diatribes. The staff could probably have lived with those. But Agnes Humbert could not stomach her museum director's subservience to the Germans, or the constant parade of society ladies with their obvious worship of Pétain. And there were the German soldiers, who swarmed over the museum, attracted by nauseatingly fawning posters announcing that there would be no charges for Germans.

Agnes Humbert had taken a whirlwind of fury to Yvonne Oddon.

Launching an underground newspaper, to be called *Résistance*, seemed a reasonable start to the two women. There were other young academics prepared to launch a stream of propaganda tracts lambasting the Germans and Vichy with equal enthusiasm.

Vilde had long known of the existence of a mimeograph machine in the cellar of the Musée de l'Homme. Even before the occupation, it had put out diatribes against the far right in France. It had all seemed a bit of a game then, great fun calling yourselves the Vigilante Committee of the Anti-Fascist Intellectuals. In those days there had not been the Gestapo or the threat of the firing squad. It was different now.

Vilde made further enquiries about Yvonne Oddon. What he learned explained the English lessons and squared with her mysterious telephone calls and meetings, and her frequent absences.

There came the day when he asked the girl casually: 'Would you give me English lessons?'

Yvonne smiled broadly and held out her hands.

For hours, they discussed how it might be possible to contact General de Gaulle's Free French in London. The trickle of leaflets and pamphlets denouncing collaborators

140

and the Germans was destined to become an avalanche. From the talks, it was but a step to sounding out those on the staff of the Musée de l'Homme and other possibly sympathetic institutions.

One of Vilde's first actions was to seek out his close friend Anatole Lewitzky, chief of the European Asiatic Department of the Musée de l'Homme. Lewitzky, like Vilde, was Russian-born. When his family fled the Bolshevik revolution, he had made for Paris. For White Russians in those days it had been a question of scratching any living. In true tradition, he had become a cab driver. Almost killing himself with exhaustion, he drove by night and completed his university studies by day. It paid off: he gained his degrees with honours, completed his military service and became a French citizen. Like Vilde and Oddon, he hated the Germans and was an ideal recruit to a resistance movement that as yet could do little to nourish its dreams.

Indeed, it seemed to the trio as if they alone constituted the intellectual resistance. They were badly in need of friends.

René Creston, a colleague at the museum, proved among the most active. One of his earliest moves was to strike out for Brittany with the task of contacting London. Creston, it turned out, had valuable contacts at the German submarine base of St-Nazaire. Here was the chance to show London that the tiny group in the Paris museum possessed some muscle. Plans and maps of the port and base were drawn up, particularly of a water-locks system which would be agreeably vulnerable to British bombers. The documents went to London.

Vilde realised the full significance of Yvonne's parade of 'English students'. They served as excellent potential couriers for contacting the resistance on the ground: those agents willing to undergo all the risks of taking the St-Nazaire documents with them to England.

The little group which Vilde built up recruited more

agents, including a fisherman in Brittany able to sail the Channel.

Almost imperceptibly, the mood of the Musée de l'Homme group changed. Resistance ceased to be an intellectual abstraction; the chiefs were no longer simply known as Boris Vilde and Anatole Lewitzky. They were respectively codenamed Maurice and Chazalle. The men and women of Musée de l'Homme, scholars in arms, were going to war with a vengeance.

In London, the Musée de l'Homme network began to attract the attention – and the considerable respect – of General de Gaulle's movement for infiltrating agents into France. This was the Bureau Central de Renseignements et d'Action, the BCRA. During the late autumn of 1940, not the least of de Gaulle's problems was to snatch one of his most promising agents from under the shadow of the Gestapo. André Weil-Curiel, codenamed Dubois, had been on a key mission: to infiltrate occupied France, take the measure of Gaullist support and see how many patriots he might recruit.

The mission was a total failure. It was time to pull out. But how? Traversing the Channel was highly dangerous. A journey across Spain would depend on reliable contacts. At this point, it was time to turn to the Musée de l'Homme.

Boris Vilde's choice of a resistant able to arrange Weil-Curiel's departure fell on Albert Gaveau, a resourceful aviation mechanic.

It was true that Gaveau was an odd character, a loner without friends. Unlike most of the resistants, he seemed detached from politics, even from patriotism. That was not necessarily a drawback; emotional idealists could be a nuisance. And Weil-Curiel could not deny the man's courage; he was plainly willing to take risks. After numerous false starts on his journey to England, Weil-Curiel found himself shunted to Toulouse. There Gaveau told him confidently that their problems were almost over; he had wind of a departure for London the day after next from Nantes, which is east of St-Nazaire and on the Loire. It

142

would be necessary to meet up with another resistance group next morning in Tours, which lies to the east.

Weil-Curiel, with a mixture of elation and anxiety, began his packing. Gaveau might be a strange individual, but there was no doubting his efficiency. He made all resistance work appear to be simply a matter of pushing buttons. Gaveau explained that they were making for the demarcation line between occupied and unoccupied France. The farm which was their goal was in the Unoccupied Zone. There were other farms and buildings on the way which were situated on the German side. It was a matter of moving quietly and quickly from farm to farm. There would be no problem in crossing the line. A car would be waiting.

Weil-Curiel asked sceptically: 'What about guards?'

The other man was brisk: 'There won't be any.'

And so it proved. Gaveau seemed unflappable, even when, at the meeting at the farm, he revealed calmly that the car had broken down and had to be collected from the nearest garage. Weil-Curiel found such detachment difficult; it seemed to him that every delay made disaster more likely.

But, sure enough, the car was ready; evidently all that had been lost was a little time. Gaveau climbed into the front seat next to the young driver. Weil-Curiel got into the back, idly glancing at the driving mirror.

What he saw made his bowels turn to water. The low black Citroën of the kind used by the police slid to a halt immediately behind. But Weil-Curiel relaxed when he saw the occupants were a man and a woman.

Not that relief lasted very long. There was another Citroën in front now. Out tumbled the German police. Weil-Curiel was bundled into one car, Gaveau into the other. As they streaked towards Tours, Weil-Curiel stole a glance behind him.

The road was empty. Only later did it strike him as curious that there was no sign of the car from which he had been abducted.

143

From Tours, the Germans took Weil-Curiel to Paris – more specifically, to Gestapo headquarters in the rue de Saussaies. Its reputation was only too well known. It was said that the cooks, whose quarters were on the second floor, often complained that they were disturbed by the screams of the victims being interrogated on the fifth floor.

But there were to be no tortures that day, at least not for Weil-Curiel. SS-Hauptsturmfuehrer Doehring was all smooth courtesy. He explained: 'I am completing the file on the affair of the Musée de l'Homme. You could be of considerable help by telling me of your relationships with these people.'

Weil-Curiel kept his nerve. Blandly, he told the Hauptsturmfuehrer that, of course, he knew some of these people. As far as he was aware, Lewitzky and Agnes Humbert had directed their activities primarily against the government of Vichy.

It was a shrewd reply. Weil-Curiel knew that the SS had its own twisted code of conduct: it had no love for traitors. Doehring nodded as if in sympathy. Then he snapped: 'Come with me.'

Doehring led his prisoner to the glass door of an office, beckoning him to look through. Weil-Curiel mentally composed himself and peered in.

The office's sole occupant was Boris Vilde.

Doehring laughed confidently: 'That is the ringleader of the bandits of the Musée de l'Homme. The ring is broken. Soon we will have the rest.'

The next to be picked up was Agnes Humbert. Once they had seized Vilde, the link with Agnes was not difficult to establish; indeed, her fingerprints had been all over the stencils for *Résistance*. She was taken to the Cherche Midi prison.

Vilde had been seized while walking unsuspectingly across the Place Pigalle. Another member of the group, a Socialist Jew named Leon-Maurice Nordmann, who had been furnished with false papers by the ever willing Albert Gaveau, had been picked up before Weil-Curiel.

Nordmann and Gaveau were aboard a train leaving Paris when Gaveau slipped away to the toilet. As the train slid to a halt at Versailles station, the Germans broke into Nordmann's compartment and hustled him away. They did not think to check the toilet; as the train pulled out of Versailles, Gaveau leapt to safety.

René Creston, the agent with the St-Nazaire contacts, was picked up later but released. Even though his work had been crucial, there was little solid evidence against him and, sticking to a previous plan, Oddon and Lewitzky disparaged him to Doehring as an ineffectual pawn of resistance and of no importance whatever.

The Nazis contented themselves with hounding Creston out of his job at the museum and out of Paris. His role was long over: several copies of the St-Nazaire papers had reached London and the Allies were able to lay their plans for eventually destroying the harbour.

The Nazis decided they would have some sport with Nordmann, their prize Jewish prisoner. He had been arrested previously, charged with producing a clandestine newspaper. The penalty, much to his relief, was a mere two years in jail. For a Jew, it had been an incredibly lenient sentence. But with the seizure of the other leading figures of the Musée de l'Homme, Nordmann was arrested on a new charge and brought to trial.

He knew only one verdict was possible.

As they awaited trial, one question was uppermost in the minds of all the accused: just who had betrayed the resistants of the Musée de l'Homme? The truth, as it turned out, was to come from an unexpected source. The trial judge, Hauptmann Ernst Roskothen, a German lawyer who spoke fluent French and detested the job he had to do, saw no reason to protect a traitor. He confided to the defence attorney: 'The newspapers shouldn't be calling this trial the Vilde affair. It should be called the Gaveau affair.'

It was Gaveau who had arranged the ambush of Weil-Curiel at the demarcation line, and vanished so conveniently afterwards. And Gaveau had disappeared again, of course, by speeding to the train toilet when the Germans came for Nordmann. There had been other instances of his diligent service to Hauptsturmfuehrer Doehring of the Paris Gestapo; all were to help seal the fate of the brave patriots of the Musée de l'Homme.

The courage of the seven men who in the winter of 1942 were taken to their deaths at Fort Mont Valerien just outside Paris was sublime. They chatted and joked as they were tied to the execution posts.

For the condemned men there was one last agonising decision. Since there were only four posts, who would go first and who last? Boris Vilde volunteered to be the last to die, along with Anatole Lewitzky. Another of the resistants, Pierre Walter, codenamed 'Didier', had also stood trial and been condemned to die with the others.

All the men scorned blindfolds and broke proudly into 'La Marseillaise' above the crash of the bullets.

The death sentence on all of the women involved were later commuted to prison sentences, and they were deported. Most survived the war.

André Weil-Curiel, agent of General de Gaulle, was another of the lucky ones. For some reason, Hauptsturmfuehrer Doehring had taken a fancy to him; possibly the German had the idea of nurturing him as a double agent. In any event, he came up with a strange proposition: would Weil-Curiel be willing to travel to the Unoccupied Zone and return every fortnight with a review of what the local press was saying? Naturally, the distressing little matter of his involvement with the Musée de l'Homme could be forgotten. Furthermore, there would be a salary and expenses.

It was a handy way of getting out of Paris. Weil-Curiel took a chance and agreed.

Once in the Unoccupied Zone, Weil-Curiel set about asking questions. But not about local newspapers. Did anyone know the quickest way to Spain? In the meantime, it would seem rather churlish not to let his benefactor

146

Doehring have something. Diligently he filed reports of innocuous information.

Then came the day when Doehring's seemingly attentive acolyte was seen no more in Paris; he was on his way across the Pyrenees to London.

His mission had ended. And so had the resistance cell of the Musée de l'Homme.

17

From his modest suite of offices and bedrooms on the third floor of the Hôtel du Parc in Vichy, Maréchal Henri Philippe Pétain presided over the destiny of Unoccupied France. Its boundaries were not marked by fences, barbed wire or brutal slabs of concrete; the seemingly haphazard division would be marked at one place by a road and at another by a stream. There was nothing remotely haphazard, though, about the patrols of Germans and the vicious guard dogs on the northern side. Between one zone and another lay a hundred yards of no-man's-land, forming a hazardous trip for anyone brave enough or foolhardy enough to cross the line illicitly.

For those living in Vichy France but having a family or friends in the Occupied Zone, life was a mixture of fear and frustration. In the early days, means of communication were limited and letters illegal. Inevitably, ways were found of circumventing the letter ban. Plain one-sided postcards, known as 'Cartes Interzones', subject to the close attention of the Nazi censor, were allowed; it did not take long to realise that these could be made to serve as a letter simply by sending a number at a time and numbering them. On delivery they could be read in sequence.

But there were times when even more ingenuity was called for. The restaurant-car attendants on the Paris-Vichy express became adept at removing a panel in the dining saloon, popping a bundle of letters inside, and replacing the panel. At Vichy, the panel would once again be unscrewed and letters removed.

Equally, there was no shortage of helpers for those anxious to make the trip to the Occupied Zone. These were *passeurs*, willing, either for money or nothing, to operate on the Franco-Spanish frontier. Most of the help was extended to military personnel or to Jews fleeing from the ever present threat of deportation, torture and death.

The *passeurs* were skilled at gauging the intervals between German patrols. Some were fishermen who carried their passengers across rivers or provided ropes strung across banks. As the threat of the resistance increased, the Germans became more wary and stepped up their patrols. Many an illicit traveller knew what it was like to crouch fearfully in the mud while dogs growled and snarled above. Their German masters would turn up and the dogs would be allowed their fun. Then would come the beating, followed by a spell in jail.

But few disputed that the most dangerous German patrols were to be found in the railway stations. Illicit travellers – those lacking the coveted *Ausweis* – knew there was no prospect of escape as they huddled in the crowded carriages. The Germans did not look at a suspect's face – at least, not at first. Their concern was with dirty and mud-caked shoes, the telltale sign of the demarcation-line traveller.

Then would come the demand: *Your papers. . . .* Inevitably, troops or police would take their time, deliberately prolonging the comparison between photograph and bearer. With the removal of a suspect, those left behind on the train, packed so tightly together, sensed each other's slackening of tension. But, of course, the Germans would come back.

Your papers. . . . The nightmare would then start all over again.

The war began almost gently in the pleasant market town of Bonneville, which nestles below the mountains of Andy and Le Bugey with the Plateau de Cenise between. This part of eastern France, in the department of Haute-Savoie, close to Switzerland, came within the writ of Vichy.

Indeed, in June 1940 there was fighting and there was occupation: the Italians had moved in to secure their small toehold on this corner of France.

Felix Plottier, who had done his national service with the mountain troops of the 27th Battalion Chasseurs Alpins and who was eventually to play a key role in local maquis resistance, today runs the family business in Bonneville. He explains: 'We fought the Italians for something like fourteen days, but nobody's heart was really in it. After all, this had been the old kingdom of Savoy and there were a number of families who, while being good French patriots, were nevertheless of Italian origin. Few of the soldiers sent by Mussolini were dedicated Fascists. They must have wondered what they were doing.'

Certainly, no other parts of occupied Europe were favoured with such an obliging Italian officer as the one in Bonneville who wanted to take over the local school as barracks for his men. Recalls Plottier: 'We told him he couldn't have it because of the children, and would he put up with an old château that had once been a prison? He was quite happy.'

This, at least, was not a murderous war – not against Alpine troops who spoke perfect French and knew the mountains better than many Savoyards. The people of the region were not yet living under the threat of lightning arrests, torture and mass deportation.

Felix Plottier's English wife, Joan, explains: 'Resistance to the Italians probably didn't go beyond a little childish baiting. When they visited a café and hung up their distinctive plumed hats, it was a favourite sport to sneak up and cut off the feathers. It made the Italians cross but not much else.'

Opposition was of the sullen kind. When the Italians took it into their heads to march through Bonneville with a blaring military band, they would suddenly find the streets unaccountably empty, the shutters of shops and houses firmly bolted.

Silence was one of the less sharp weapons of resistance.

But in faraway Paris, repression had grown steadily harsher with the years of occupation, and the change of mood was contagious. Even Bonneville was not immune; all too soon, the demand for militant resistance was expressed, quite literally, in countless knocks on the front door of Felix Plottier himself.

It would only be a slight exaggeration to say that Capitaine Henri Frenay had been a soldier virtually from the moment of conception. He came from a family the length of whose military tradition no one could quite remember. His mother had worshipped Maréchal Pétain just this side of idolatry; his bedside stories had been an eternal retelling of the glory of French arms. In the hot August of 1939, he had stood proudly on the Maginot line.

That elaborate string of forts designed to protect the central part of northern France had been considered impregnable. This was the same Maginot line that was bypassed and enveloped, its defences forced to fall back in rout.

Stunned into disbelief by the disaster, Frenay recalled in his memoirs:

We, the defenders of the Maginot line, had received the incredible order to retreat. Nothing had prepared us for such a move, neither our individual equipment nor our permanent armoured emplacements, least of all our garrison's standing order to hold the line at all costs.

After the debacle, Maréchal Pétain was called to the highest post in France, while Henri Frenay was destined to become one of the most celebrated heroes of the resistance, architect of the militant Combat movement, which was ultimately absorbed into a single Armée Secrète (Secret Army).

The Armée Secrète flowered during the winter of 1942. As seemed only just, this coincided with a sharp downturn

151

in the fortunes of Adolf Hitler. Rommel, the 'Desert Fox' and darling of the German people, had escaped encirclement at the Battle of El Alamein and been forced to abandon Benghazi. At the same time as he was carrying out the evacuation of Egypt, Operation Torch was under way at the other end of North Africa with the landing of American forces. The anti-British Jean Darlan, Minister of Marine in the Vichy government and Vice Premier in 1941, had unexpectedly returned to North Africa two days before the invasion. Allied forces found themselves with an unforeseen opponent but, after fierce fighting, Darlan was persuaded to tell the French commanders to surrender.

Hitler now had the pretext he had long wanted. On 11 November, four days after Darlan's capitulation, the troops of Generalfeldmarschall Gerd von Rundstedt, in full battle array, crossed the demarcation line and occupied the whole of France. The French army was demobilised shortly afterwards.

The reinstated Pierre Laval, even more of a lackey of the Germans now, proceeded in Paris to rub salt in the wounds by instituting the STO, Service du Travail Obligatoire. This was a forced-labour conscription in which young Frenchmen would be obliged to work in German industry in return for the repatriation of French prisoners of war.

For potential victims of the STO this was to prove altogether too much.

Henri Frenay, however, relaxing with comrades on a snowy 31 December, found Laval's decree the best of all New Year presents. His evening celebration was interrupted by the arrival of a colleague, Marcel Pecl. Sections of Paris, he declared, were on the brink of revolt. Young Parisians had fled the capital ahead of conscription. They had made their way south and, armed with revolvers they were not afraid to use, were bent on resistance.

Michel Brault, chief of intelligence for Combat, commented thoughtfully: 'They've taken to the maquis.'

The word means scrub-wooded upland. At least, that was so at the dawn of 1943. Now it signified a new style of resistance – armed camps in the woods, ready for action.

18

The creation of the maquis was just the sort of adrenalin that the French resistance needed. In just one year the mood of the country changed miraculously.

But back in 1941 morale had plunged with the leaves of autumn. The onset of winter had been a spectre to dread, not just because of dwindling food supplies, but because of the chronic shortage of fuel for domestic heating. The resistance then seemed a lonely, abandoned force; German jamming of BBC broadcasts had become more sophisticated. Moreover, links with England were fragile.

There had been crumbs of comfort. The RAF had been able to bombard both Berlin and the still formidable Luftwaffe. British aircraft, it was said, were pounding the cities of northern Germany. But in the Soviet Union the stupefying victories of the Wehrmacht had become monotonous. True, the German armies had to be content with a glimpse of the towers of the Kremlin rather than conquest of Moscow. But still a self-confident Hitler could proclaim: 'The enemy on the eastern front will be crushed before the onset of winter.'

The despairing French, huddled in their now fraying prewar clothes, shivered in queues for shops and tramcars. Henri Frenay, recalling those days, wrote: 'I had the impression that for 90 per cent of the French people this was somebody else's war and that they believed Russia had already been beaten. Soon it would be England's turn.'

With the onset of 1943, the first cracks appeared in the Nazi facade of success: there was defeat at Stalingrad, followed by collapse at the Kursk salient, a hundred miles north of Kharkov.

A new mood swept through totally subjugated France: not least was the determination to frustrate the detested Service du Travail Obligatoire. Countless young people had been neither collaborators nor resistants. Above all, they had wanted a quiet life; that was now something the STO threatened to deny them. Previously, there had been an attitude that it was only worth attacking when attacked. All that had changed. The leaders of the resistance spelled out the new philosophy in the starkest terms: strike the Germans wherever and whenever possible.

But where to start?

An early choice of battlefield was the city of Montluçon, northwest of Vichy. Here on 27 November 1942, workers had been snatched from their homes and forced on to trains by police. Soon intelligence reached the resistance that another roundup was planned for the coming January.

Flying squads of painters, armed with pots of liquid tar, swarmed all over the town, daubing strike slogans and incitements to rebellion on the walls, particularly at the large Dunlop tyre factory.

But the organisers felt that one single act of defiance would be more effective than merely swabbing walls. Workers were told to turn up at the railway station at 1 p.m. for a protest meeting. The result was more successful than anyone had dared to hope. A crowd of around 6,000, consisting of young men and women who had already been conscripted, confronted the police in charge of herding the Reich's fresh labour force on to the trains.

At first, all was calm, but the solid police lines soon infuriated the crowd. Fights and scuffles broke out. The armed police force, the Garde Mobile, struck out with rifle butts, only to have their weapons seized by the demonstrators. Into the main station concourse they poured, singing 'La Marseillaise' and 'L'Internationale'. There were cries of *Vive de Gaulle! Vive L'Union Soviétique! A bas Laval!*

There were elements of comedy. As a number of young

men already herded on to the train jumped clear, the badly rattled stationmaster signalled for it to move. The engine pulled out alone; the demonstrators had uncoupled the locomotive.

Even when the train was recoupled and on its way, there was further trouble. Railway workers, bristling with wrenches and sledgehammers, had already mangled the track. The police, smarting under the jeers and shouts of triumph, withdrew. They were replaced by armed-to-the-teeth Wehrmacht troops, but the resistance was not giving up. They delayed the departure of the train until midnight; by then most of the intended victims of STO had melted away.

For the Germans, the operation was humiliating: out of 180 requisitioned young people, only around twenty made the journey to the Reich. A good number of those who escaped made for the strongholds of the maquis.

As the German fortunes changed in the east, so the Nazi grip tightened. The creation of maquisard cells intensified. In the south, strongholds were established in such places as the steep-hilled department of Corrèze, a prewar centre of Communist and Socialist dissent that seemed a natural habitat for hardened resistants. The steep, thickly wooded countryside became a crucible into which was poured a fair microcosm of dissenting France. Here came Jews on the run from Paris, Spanish fugitives fleeing the rule of General Franco, teenagers from half the departments of France and even deserters from the Wehrmacht.

In the north and east, expanses of wood and mountain soon cradled cadres of the maquis. In particular, two plateaux – the Vercors, in the southeastern Alps, and Les Glières, above Annecy in Haute Savoie – became settings for tragic clashes of arms in the unfolding saga of France's shadow army.

In Bonneville, Felix Plottier became virtually sole organiser of resistance under Colonel Vallette d'Osia, a notorious iron-nerved commander.

Plottier had formed the nucleus of a resistance cell as early as 1941. He declares: 'In those days probably only one per cent of local people were in favour of active resistance against the Germans. By the end of the war it was more like ninety-five per cent – but a lot happened in between.'

Not least in importance was the disarming of the French army. Plottier says: 'There were suddenly a lot of men without jobs and nothing to do. I wanted men who would make promising commanders. Unfortunately, leadership potential was not enough – resistants had to be for de Gaulle and against Pétain. That often created problems. There were, for example, men against the Germans but very much for Pétain. The conflict of loyalties was enormous.'

For Joan Plottier, some of the difficulties had to do with eager volunteers for the maquis with hair-raising disregard for even the most elementary security. She remembers: 'They used to turn up, little more than boys, banging at our front door or the family shop, brandishing identity papers and asking: "Where is Felix Plottier? We want to join the maquis." They even used to appear from behind trees in the garden.'

For the Plottiers, it meant living in perpetual fear that without warning either Germans or police would swoop down and seize those artless STO dodgers.

Madame Plottier had already made up her mind how she would receive unwelcome visitors. She explains: 'I worked out that I would be cosily in bed, keeping warm with aluminium hot-water bottles into which I planned to shove incriminating papers.'

From the same house, members of the maquis would be smuggled to refuges in the mountains in a variety of guises – anything from farm hands to priests. Madame Plottier says: 'The dressing up was accompanied by a lot

157

of laughter. They were like kids at a party and they only stopped laughing when they got outside.'

In Bonneville, statues and monuments were ripped down and melted for the war effort, along with the brass ornaments that every household was supposed to surrender. The Plottiers handed over the tyres of their treasured red and black Simca coupé. But not the car itself. They buried that under faggots of wood in a nearby barn and forced themselves to forget about it.

There was, after all, a greater priority. In a France now wholly occupied, resistance and the maquis had a new enemy to rival the Gestapo. What was more, it was home-grown.

On his restoration to power in April 1942 after his bitter dispute with Maréchal Pétain, Pierre Laval lost little time in stepping up the repressive profile of the Vichy regime.

During a visit to France, Fritz Sauckel, Hitler's shifty slit-eyed Reichsplenipoteniarie of Labour, whose orders at the war's end would result in the movement of five million people from occupied Europe to Germany, all but insisted on the establishment of STO. His immediate demand was for 350,000 French workers. 'You provide them, or we'll take them,' he snapped.

Laval, sensitive to German threats, went on in 1943 to create the French militia (Milice Française), under the tutelage of his German masters.

As the Praetorian Guard of the Vichy regime, it began life as the Service d'Orde Légionnaire, an organisation with more than a few of the trimmings of Heinrich Himmler's SS, including the unequivocal oath: 'I swear to fight against democracy, against Gaullist dissidents, and against the Jewish leprosy.'

This was ominous enough, but it was not until the 31 January 1943 issue of *Journal Official* that the true character of the organisation really emerged. The journal carried a new law, signed by Laval, establishing the Milice Française.

Article 2 of the statutes declared: 'The French Milice is composed of volunteers morally ready and physically capable, not only of supporting the new state by their action, but also of cooperating in the maintenance of order.' Article 3 went on to require that members of the Milice be French by birth, not Jewish, not belong to any secret society and be volunteers.

Control of the Milice was to shift from Pierre Laval to Joseph Darnand, Secretary of State for the Interior. It was rubber-stamped by Pétain himself as 'the advance guard for the maintenance of order inside French territory in cooperation with the police'.

On the Milice were lavished all the trappings, ceremonies and insignia so beloved of the Nazi stormtroopers. There was a uniform already to hand: the khaki shirt and black tie of the Service d'Ordre Légionnaire. To these were added dark blue trousers and jacket and the beret of the Chasseurs Alpins. Then came army shoes, leggings, and a wide military belt from which a gun holster was suspended. At the start, the holster was stuffed with paper; Vichy was not permitted to supply arms. However, that was one deficiency that the Germans were more than pleased to remedy.

From now on, the resistance had to become reconciled to new brutal enemies on French soil. Neither the maquis nor the other groups was equipped to fight it alone. In his memoirs, Henri Frenay wrote: 'We were as ill-armed as we were ill-financed. The key to the arms question was in London. . . .'

London, indeed, was to fuel the resistance movements. And not just for France.

19

The Hardanger Plateau, northwest of Vemork and deep in the mountains of southern Norway, is a desolate place.

Hosts of migrant reindeer alone survive in this cheerless wilderness of cruel winter blizzards. Anyone unwise enough to venture there with features exposed runs the risk of laceration by stinging hail. Even if a man is prepared for this assault he can still perish; sudden squalls can snatch him off his feet and dash him bodily against the ice.

To the planners of the Special Operations Executive (SOE) in London, however, the friendless Hardanger Plateau was regarded as an ally. From there, it was proposed to launch one of the most daring resistance coups of the war. The reward for success would be a prize unrivalled: the destruction of a key element in the Third Reich's effort to produce a German atomic bomb.

But, first, for the Norwegian resistance there was to be disillusion and tragedy.

In the spring of 1942, the Norwegian coastal steamer *Galtesund* was appropriated by a group of Norwegians, who successfully reached Scotland. Their exploit was applauded enthusiastically by Special Operations Executive, the British powerhouse for subversive activity in Nazi-occupied Europe. But SOE's main interest centred on one particular escapee – Einar Skinnarland.

The fact that Skinnarland was a hydroelectric engineer had a lot to do with it. Furthermore, interrogation revealed that he was also a remarkable skier, an amateur radio operator and, by no mean consideration, in the pink of health.

His job was at the Norsk Hydro heavy-water factory at Vemork. The place was being used by the Germans to produce heavy water, an element in the production of atomic energy.

Lieutenant Commander Eric Walsh, head of the Norwegian section of British Intelligence, told Skinnarland: 'We've had our eye on this place for some time. We need an agent to operate inside Vemork itself.'

Both Walsh and Skinnarland were only too aware that there was little time. The Norwegian had told neither family nor friends that he was going to Britain and had merely mentioned a skiing holiday. Such a cover, obviously, could not last indefinitely.

Organisation within SOE moved fast. After instruction on the intricacies of the radio set he would take back to Norway, Skinnarland was rushed through basic parachute training. Then came exhaustive briefing sessions with Leif Tronstad, a major with particular responsibility for Norwegian espionage operations. The two men studied the layout of the Vemork plant in detail.

A mere three weeks after his arrival in England, Einar Skinnarland was back in Norway – dropped from an RAF bomber in the early morning of 29 March 1942.

He arrived ravenously hungry. What more natural, therefore, than to ski straight home and enjoy a breakfast cooked by his mother? He told her that his holiday had been most enjoyable. His friends were puzzled that he looked a little pale for a man who had presumably had a vacation of bruising athleticism.

Fortunately, no one pressed the point. Skinnarland went back to work.

As soon as he could, he was radioing back to London. His information was devastating: orders had been received from Berlin to pack and ship to Germany the plant's entire stock of heavy water.

The War Cabinet turned to Lord Louis Mountbatten,

Chief of Combined Operations and the overseer of special forces, which included the commandos. Mountbatten and SOE decided to pool their talents; SOE would provide the manpower for the first operation.

This involved a four-man advance party dropping near Vemork. This party would prepare a landing area for a following volunteer assault force. That force would home in by glider near Vemork and then shoot its way into the plant, which it would proceed to destroy. The bleak expanse of Hardanger was earmarked as the landing place, despite SOE uneasiness at the prospect of giant boulders and deep-cut fissures being hosts to flimsy gliders.

There was no time for debate; the news from Norway was getting steadily worse. In September 1941, production at the Norsk Hydro plant had been stepped up, and it continued to rise. Dr Jomar Brun, the plant's chief engineer, who had escaped to London, added disturbing evidence of German progress towards making an atomic bomb.

For operations behind enemy lines, the Norwegians were able to draw on considerable home-grown talent. It consisted of Company Linge, the volunteer group of special action troops, rigorously trained in hand-to-hand combat, signalling, sabotage techniques, map reading, advanced weapon handling, silent killing and survival.

The attack on the heavy-water plant could not have come at a better time, for Company Linge was demoralised and unhappy. Its original leader, Captain Linge, had been killed in a previous action, and it had been given little to do since. From the ranks of Company Linge, the SOE chose a four-man advance party, codenamed Swallow.

The advance party, led by tall, lanky Lieutenant Jens Poulsson, parachuted into Norway at around midnight on 18 October 1942. Right from the start, the mission faced disaster. A glance at the map revealed that the four had landed a hundred miles off target; the trip to Vemork would have to be undertaken over some of the toughest terrain in southern Norway.

At first, the men took considerable consolation from the weather. True, there was a layer of fresh snow, but the sun shone through it cheerfully enough. However, at an altitude of 4,000 feet, it proved a vastly different story.

Here temperatures plunged to zero. The men, struggling under heavy equipment, buffeted by high winds and chilled by cruel cold, pushed ahead towards Vemork. Failure was out of the question. Unless they all got through, the succeeding phase of the operation would collapse; much of the equipment that the men carried was needed to light a landing zone for the assault gliders.

Even on arrival, Skinnarland, who had been forewarned of the Swallow mission, could offer little encouragement. The local German commander had recently reinforced the guard at Norsk Hydro; resistance would be strong.

London was also worried. Something was plainly wrong with Knut Haugland, the unit's radio operator. The men of SOE had long developed a sixth sense which alerted them to possible false messages. It was not unknown for a German radio specialist to substitute for captured agents and take over a sending key. Acting on a hunch, the SOE began sending Haugland prearranged check messages. To the further puzzlement of London, all were answered correctly. Had the Germans completely penetrated the mission? It seemed unlikely. The truth, when London eventually learnt it, was distressingly prosaic. The bitter cold had stiffened Haugland's fingers and changed his normal touch.

His reports scarcely augured well for the mission. Toughened protection for the Hydro of course meant increased firepower for the Germans. They could reinforce the guard of the Hydro at whim; there was no question of London lavishing limitless resources. Combined Operations, however, had no intention of aborting the venture.

Out went the go-ahead signal for the actual assault, codenamed Freshman. Thirty-four specially trained sapper volunteers, under the command of a British lieutenant, would leave within ten days.

The two Halifax bombers, each towing an Airspeed AS51 Horsa Mk 1 glider, roared above Wick Airfield in Scotland on 19 November. There had been some uneasiness over the wisdom of attempting the mission at all; the glider pilots had never made night take-offs with fully loaded gliders. Maps for the flight were not of the best, but it was reckoned that this deficiency could be more than made up by the highly skilled navigators. The use of Horsas by no means pleased everybody; their windscreens had only two small clear vision panels, and it was feared that buffeting would break the towropes.

The initial meteorological report had been excellent, but after reaching the Norwegian coast on correct bearings, the aircraft flew into a blizzard. To make matters worse, the telephone links between each glider and the towing aircraft did not work.

In addition, one of the Halifax's Rebecca radio units failed to make contact with the Eureka ground beacon. It was also later revealed that the briefing given to the Halifax pilots had been inadequate. Even allowing for the thick cloud curtain, the pilot on one bomber had insufficient knowledge of the Norwegian coast to prevent him coming in too low over the area of Egersund, southeast of Stavanger.

It proved fatal. Fuel was getting disastrously low; no more time could be spent scouring for the landing zone. It was then that the towrope snapped; the glider, by now smothered in snow, plunged into a mountain. For a few seconds, it looked as if the Halifax would escape. The pilot cleared the peak but smashed headlong into the next range. All the crew were killed; they had barely reached ten miles inland.

The other unit appeared to be faring rather better. The 10,000-foot altitude seemed safe enough, and progress towards the dropping zone seemed good. But where precisely was the zone? In vain, the pilot strained to pick up the welcoming pricks of light which should have been set out by the Swallow party. There was no margin for extra time; more to the point, there would soon be no fuel. The pilot of the Halifax prepared to turn for home.

Then it happened. The towline connecting glider and bomber broke apart. The Halifax began its slow descent to the sea.

The wreckage that had crashed near Egersund was found the following morning by German troops. From the position of the two wrecked aircraft, and the distance between them, it was evident that the bomber pilot had released the glider at the last minute in a bid to save his own aircraft. It had proved fruitless. All six crewmen of the Halifax were dead by the time the Germans arrived. Fourteen soldiers who had been in the glider survived the crash.

That they were on a sabotage mission was only too evident when explosives, small arms and radio transmitters were found among the wreckage.

What happened next was the direct outcome of events on 18 October 1942 when Adolf Hitler had issued what was termed a *Fuehrerbefehl* – a top-secret edict that spelt death for the Operation Freshman survivors from the moment that their gliders crashed in the snow-covered Norwegian countryside.

In the *Fuehrerbefehl*, Hitler accused Germany's opponents of using methods that did not conform with the Geneva Convention. Commandos were singled out for special mention; their behaviour was described as 'especially brutal and cunning'. Commandos, Hitler went on, were recruited partly from among hardened criminals who specialised in killing their prisoners. The order stipulated:

From now on all opponents captured by German troops in so-called commando operations in Europe or in Africa, even when it is outwardly a matter of soldiers in uniform or demolition parties with or without weapons, are to be exterminated to the

165

last man in battle or while in flight. In these cases it is immaterial whether they are landed for their operations by ship or aircraft or descend by parachute. Even should these individuals, on their being discovered, make as if to surrender, all quarter is to be denied them on principle. . . .

Furthermore, it was decreed that such 'opponents' should not be held in military custody, but handed over to the Sicherheitsdienst, the intelligence arm of the SS. The implication was clear: no prisoners were to be shot until, under the tender mercies of the SD, they had divulged sufficient information about their mission.

As it turned out, the German battalion commander in Egersund's enthusiasm for the *Fuehrerbefehl* was absolute. Hot on Hitler's commando order had come his own decree: 'On account of the increased number of cases in which aircraft are used for landing saboteurs, who do serious damage, I order that personnel from sabotage aircraft shall be immediately shot by the first persons who come into contact with them.'

The Wehrmacht took this responsibility on its own shoulders. The fourteen survivors were rushed to Egersund and, after perfunctory interrogation, all shot.

The news was greeted with incredulity and fury by Reichskommissar Josef Terboven. Here was a group of saboteurs who threatened the country's security. No attempt had been made to probe their mission in detail. Nobody could be certain what their target was; a valuable source of information had been thrown away.

Obergruppenfuehrer Wilhelm Rediess, Chief of Police and SS in Norway, was equally furious but for different reasons: the Wehrmacht had by implication undermined his authority by taking the law into its own hands. Rediess fired off a teleprinter message to Berlin marked 'Urgent'. He was careful to keep it bland until the very last sentence:

On 20 November around three o'clock in the morning a British aircraft towing a glider crashed near Egersund; cause of the crash as yet unknown. As far as has been ascertained, towing

166

aircraft's crew is military, including one Negro, all dead. There were 17 men in the glider, probably agents. Three of them dead, six gravely injured. Glider's crew was in possession of large quantities of Norwegian money. Unfortunately, the Wehrmacht executed the survivors so clarification is no longer possible.

As intended, the message caused consternation. General der Infanterie Nikolaus von Falkenhorst, the commander in chief in Norway, who was to be brought before a war crimes tribunal in 1945 for the murders, took steps to avoid the same happening again by ordering that in future the executions were to be delayed until the prisoners could be interrogated by the security police.

In the case of Operation Freshman, Feldwebel Kurt Hagedorn, in a statement to the court trying Falkenhorst, stated that troops had been awakened to capture English soldiers in the area covered by his battalion, which had its barracks at Slettebo. He was standing outside a barrack with a comrade when he saw the English soldiers being brought to the military hospital. They were carried under guard in the direction of the ammunition store. The Feldwebel stated:

At the same time I heard rifle fire. I went to the place from whence the shots had come and saw still more English soldiers at a distance of about a hundred metres bring brought to the shooting place. One English soldier was lying at the side of the road as he seemed to be hurt, and the others were standing up. Several German soldiers watched each English. Hauptmann Schrottberger, the battalion commander, was standing in front of the military hospital and gave orders as to which way the English had to go. "This way", and he pointed the direction out with his hand.

We went up the street and at the first ammunition store, I saw an English soldier being shot.

Wehrmacht troops, who had come from the ammunition store, lined up opposite the prisoner. An order was rapped out; the prisoner fell and was finished off with a pistol. The

167

body was carried to a hole by four Germans. Feldwebel Hagedorn witnessed some three English soldiers being mown down and tumbled into the same hole – shot, as he later learnt, for being 'saboteurs' by members of the Erschiessungskommando (firing squad).

Hagedorn was by no means the only witness of the event of that grim November afternoon. A Polish prisoner of war, Roman Zetelski, stated that ten of his comrades had been brought from the prisoner of war camp at Egersund to the barracks at Slettebo and sent to the place where fourteen dead soldiers lay. All were in English uniforms. The order went out to place in a truck the still warm bodies from which blood was flowing. The trucks were driven to a garage, where three more bodies, wrapped in sacks, were loaded. At a remote spot, the bodies were stripped naked and shovelled into a common grave.

Rediess, annoyed that he had been deprived of the custody of the dead bodies, had his pride salvaged by the discovery of the other British aircraft and glider. This time the Gestapo had its way. The British soldiers were subjected to a lengthy and brutal interrogation. Only when they revealed all they knew were they put out of their misery. They were executed in compliance with Hitler's commando order as amended and interpreted by General der Infanterie Falkenhorst, who pronounced himself pleased with the outcome. He proudly reported: 'The interrogation provided valuable admissions of the enemy's intentions.'

Jens Poulsson and his men, who waited for the gliders at the designated time, received what little information Combined Operations in London was able to pass on. He noted in his diary that it was 'a hard blow'. But to mourn the dead was a luxury no one could afford: his preoccupation now was keeping alive in the snow. As for food, it meant trapping the reindeer and devouring not only the animals, but also the contents of their stomachs.

This was to be a long winter, but the brutal truth was there: no matter what tragedies had been involved in Operation Freshman, the Vemork plant was still intact and still producing heavy water.

The men of Swallow would have to wait. London was planning its next assault, and all attention was on the Hardanger Plateau.

20

Lieutenant Joachim Ronneberg from Ålesund was an uncomplicated individual whose reason for fleeing Norway and arriving in Britain was, he disarmingly told interrogators, 'just to fight the Germans'.

For the men of SOE, who now had sole responsibility for bringing about the destruction of the Norsk Hydro, Ronneberg appeared to be the ideal leader. He had won his spurs as an officer instructor on other 'special actions'. He was itching for combat, and SOE was only too pleased to oblige him with its latest exploit, cloaked under the codename Gunnerside.

Ronneberg's initial order was to select five good skiers from the pool of talent within Company Linge and report for briefings in London. What Ronneberg learnt was scarcely encouraging. The element of surprise was clearly important in this sort of enterprise; that would be lacking because of what had happened to Freshman. The Germans would be armed to the teeth and waiting. Intelligence suggested that about a hundred guards would be on the alert, the majority of them Gestapo. Furthermore, that took no account of the unit stationed at Vemork itself.

By 15 December 1942, the 'most secret' order was ready. It instructed the Gunnerside force to 'attack the storage and producing plant at Vemork with high explosives so that present stocks and fluid in the course of productions are destroyed'.

Then followed another three weeks of training. A dummy plant duplicated the features of the real Norsk Hydro. Ronneberg was reassured by his team's progress; they could practically set explosive charges in the dark and identify the vital tanks and machinery purely by touch. Advance intelligence was so sophisticated that Ronneberg and his men knew where to locate a key which, if necessary, could be used to lock any prisoners in the plant's washroom.

Ahead of the 23 January deadline, Swallow force was alerted; the team moved from its building area near Cambridge to Scotland for the flight to Norway. Clerks at the SOE offices in London filed away last letters written to next of kin. They were all going on a highly dangerous mission; the possibility that they might not come back was very real. They boarded the RAF bomber carrying them over their dropping zone, each man clutching a small brown cyanide capsule. The instruction was to swallow it at the moment of capture.

All at once the grim spectre of the failure of Freshman rose to haunt the men of Gunnerside. The pilot could not make out the dropping zone, and spent two hours aimlessly cruising. Any prospect of flying above the Hardanger plateau was set at naught as German antiaircraft fire erupted in a vicious curtain of flame. Badly mauled and minus one engine, it limped back to Scotland.

The first attempt of Gunnerside had failed ignominiously; the next full moon was not until 15 February.

A different dropping zone was singled out for the second bid – Lake Skryken on the Hardanger plateau, thirty miles from the factory and chosen because it could be identified from the air, even without marker lights.

Steel rods of rain slashed into the faces of the six Norwegians as they again boarded the bomber, laden with demolition explosives, skis, provisions and white-camouflaged weapons and equipment. The dropping zone loomed up around midnight, the green signal lamp lighting up the fuselage hatch.

The clutch of parachutes separated. Six Norwegian soldiers and their drums of supplies drifted down to the smooth, level expanse of the frozen lake of the plateau a thousand feet below.

In a gale which lashed and screamed throughout the night, the party scrabbled around to salvage the parachute supply containers. These were dragged to a deserted hut on the shores of the lake. It was not until 4 a.m. that they finished burying their stores and a carpet of snow had obliterated all landing traces.

If they had cursed the weather previously, it was nothing to their feelings about the westerly wind which howled like a demented animal and drove them for two whole days into the welcome refuge of a hunting lodge.

The bad weather ultimately abated; its effects on the men remained. They had badly swollen neck glands; two of them looked like becoming seriously ill. When the party reached the original supply dump it was impossible to identify it. The snowdrifts had covered the marker stakes. Several hours of tiring work were wasted on the search for a single food container.

It took another forty-eight hours for the weather to be fine enough for Ronneberg to give the order for noon departure.

Fresh optimism swept the Gunnerside force. The vital task was to make contact with the men of Swallow, albeit six days behind schedule.

But Jens Poulsson felt little optimism. In such appalling weather, he reasoned, the men of Gunnerside must surely have perished.

Still, it seemed only reasonable that Sergeants Arne Kjelstrup and Claus Helberg should start the search for Ronneberg's unit on the slender chance that its members were still alive.

Ronneberg's men had skied southwestwards all night and all day, weighed down by their sixty-five-pound packs and the weight of two sledges heavy with two hundred-weight of supplies. At first, when they spotted the two bearded figures near Lake Kallungsja, fear gripped the men of Gunnerside. Might not these be Germans? But then Ronneberg heard wild yells of pleasure. Gunnerside and Swallow had at last linked up.

After they had reached the advance party's base hut at Sandvatn, some twenty miles from Rjukan, it was possible to pool joint rations and consider how to attack the plant at Vemork.

The hydrogen-electrolysis plant was built on a massive precipice. It was widely held to be impassable. On the other hand, aerial photographs had shown trees growing up the sides of the gorge. If trees could take root, then surely there was hope for men anxious to scale the rockface. Lieutenant (later Captain) Knut Haukelid wrote in his account of the raid:

The Germans no doubt considered that Vemork was so well protected by nature that it would be difficult for attackers to reach it. The works lie like an eagle's eyrie high up on the mountainside. In front the way is completely barred by a deep and sheer ravine cut by the river Maan. . . . Across this crack, the Germans thought, no one could make his way. A narrow suspension bridge, about seventy-five feet long, crosses the ravine at this point, and this was kept under constant guard.

Latest intelligence pointed to fifteen Germans in the barrack hut between the turbine hall and the electrolysis building. Two more sentries, changing every couple of hours, guarded the suspension bridge. There were three patrols inside the factory compound. There were known to be four Norwegian night watchmen. Only one door giving out to a yard was left unlocked.

A formidable proposition indeed!

The final approach to the plant was timed for 8 p.m. on Saturday 27 February. The schedule called for an attack thirty minutes after the changing of the guard at midnight. The choice was deliberate. On Saturday night, the mood at the Hydro would be more relaxed; it was traditionally the one night of the week when discipline was not so stringent and more leave passes were given. Those unfortunate enough to remain on duty might well be less alert than usual.

With the knowledge that they were at last on the home

173

stretch, the Norwegians moved quickly out of their final rendezvous hut, weighed down with the explosive charges. Although they carried rifles on their backs, Ronneberg had ordered that the weapons were not to be loaded until the very last moment. The temptation to become trigger-happy too early might prove impossible to resist; if the garrison was alerted that would spell the end of the mission.

The first 600 yards down the mountainside were dauntingly steep, but the party barely noticed it because their attention was caught by the sight ahead. The seven-storey factory loomed like some medieval castle, hemmed in by precipices and rivers. The hum of the machinery was clearly audible across the ravine.

The saboteurs reached the clutch of houses near the northern end of the suspension bridge and abandoned the road which snaked on in a series of hairpin bends down to Rjukan town.

It was now approaching ten o'clock.

Everyone knew that shifts would be changing, and confirmation came when a couple of buses laden with workers rumbled towards the plant. The men followed the course of the road for several hundred yards until they reached a spot where a wide cutting had been made through the woods for the Vemork power line. Now they were making for the reassuring dark woods to the right. Each man peeled off his white camouflage dress and donned the uniform of a British soldier. It was reasoned that this would give the Germans no excuse to blame civilians for the raid and thus take reprisals.

Pockets were filled with ammunition and hand grenades. Guns were seized, together with sets of explosives, some rope and pairs of armourer's shears. The final descent down the face of the rock had begun.

Because of the thaw, even the smallest move sent shoals of loose snow crashing into the valley. But the air was full of the low hum of the turbines to mask the noise.

The men streaked across the ice and started to climb

on the other side. Once they had made it, the Gunnerside force took shelter behind a small building a few hundred yards from the plant. Now there was a chance to regain strength and review the plans for the actual assault.

The sentries changed on the stroke of midnight; it was now just thirty minutes to zero hour. A five-man covering party was to advance towards the factory to force the gate and the fence, if necessary.

The two sentries who had been relieved were in no hurry to depart. Long experience had taught Ronneberg patience; a precipitate move could ruin everything. Even when the sentries moved off, he did nothing. It was worth waiting until they were securely in bed and out of action.

After what he considered a reasonable time, Ronneberg ordered Sergeant Kjelstrup to advance towards the factory fence. The sergeant crouched low, clutching his armourer's shears in one hand and his rifle in the other. He raced forward, snipping a man-sized hole in the wire-mesh fence. Then he waved the rest of the party into the compound.

The attacking force fanned outwards to designated positions. Lieutenant Haukelid, touting his pistol and hand grenades, and Lieutenant Poulsson, gripping his Thompson sub-machine-gun, stationed themselves within twenty yards of the German barracks. Both men were able to enjoy the luxury of conversation; more than once, the steady hum of the generators was to be an ally. If German troops approached, there could be only one possible response: the wooden barracks would be holed with the steady assault of small-arms fire. Haukelid would lose no time in lobbing his grenades.

Meanwhile, the demolition teams had moved speedily in the direction of the demolition plant. Ronneberg and Sergeant Frederick Kayser tried at first to get in through one of the doors on the ground floor. It would not yield. Then the pair somehow became separated, but they pressed on, eventually crawling into the building over a web of tangled pipes and cables. Through a vent in the

175

tunnel, they were able to catch the merest glimpse of the high-concentration room, where one man was working. Within minutes, the man was looking down a gun barrel and being pushed into a corner.

The prisoner watched, frozen with fear, as Ronneberg started laying the charges. The leader of Gunnerside had his attention distracted fleetingly by the sound of broken glass as two more of the party forced their way in. It seemed to everyone that the noise would betray them all, but the Germans had plainly heard nothing. Ronneberg pulled up his leather gloves, cursing the shards of glass that cut his hand, from which blood was trickling down.

His prisoner suddenly found his voice and pleaded urgently: 'Try not to short-circuit. If you do, there'll be an explosion.'

Frederick Kayser laughed harshly: 'Explosion! That's just what there's going to be.'

The fuses were set for two minutes. The reaction of the prisoner was so unexpected that Ronneberg and Kayser were briefly nonplussed. The man burst out: 'Where are my spectacles? I must have my spectacles.'

Ronneberg snapped: 'They're on your nose. Frederick, get him outside.'

The prisoner was told to run. The demolition team went on to complete the job of setting the explosive charges on the heavy-water tanks. Two-minute charges and a single thirty-second fuse were placed on each cell. There was thus a double backup system, ensuring that no cell would escape.

In all resistants there lurks something of the schoolboy, and now it was demonstrated. The Norwegian saboteurs had their own way of cocking a snook at the Germans; they scattered around the room unofficial calling cards deliberately calculated to confuse their enemies: authentic British parachute badges. When all was ready, Ronneberg ordered the fuses lit. The four-man-strong demolition team fled for cover; their Norwegian prisoner, curiosity overcoming fear, had suddenly rematerialised and was almost touchingly pleased to be dragged to safety. They only just made it before the charges went off with a dull rumble.

In his account of the raid, Ronneberg wrote that after the explosion he 'looked back down the line and listened. But except for the hum of machinery that we heard when we arrived, everything in the factory was quiet'.

Certainly, German reaction seemed remarkably muted. A lone, bareheaded Wehrmacht soldier was seen peering hesitantly out of the barracks. He reappeared, with a helmet thrust hastily on his head; he clutched a rifle and a flashlight which he circled uncertainly over the ground.

The action told him nothing. As he disappeared around the corner of the plant, Haukelid and Poulsson retreated from their posts, making for the previously earmarked assembly point. Ronneberg and the rest of the Gunnerside team were exultant. The job had been done; their task now was to look after themselves.

The explosion may have been muted, but the damage was all that could have been wished. The base had been knocked off every cell and the priceless fluid had flooded down the drains. Flying shrapnel had shattered the tubes of the cooling systems and the high-concentration room was awash with spraying jets of water. This particular water was of the ordinary type, but it had the effect of ruining the heavy variety.

Nor was this all. Eighteen cells had been completely drained of almost half a ton of heavy water. The Germans would have to face the fact that, even after the torn and twisted installation had been replaced, it would take weeks of full-power working before the contents of each cell were usable.

The Nazi uranium programme had been put out of action for months; the Germans could ill afford the delay.

It was time for the Gunnerside and Swallow forces to split up. If they considered that their movements had been fast on the way up, it was nothing to the speed of their retreat. The men hopped and slid down to the Maan river

177

and made their way across. The water had sharply risen by then; because of the thaw there was a good deal of water on the ice.

Knut Haukelid later wrote:

When we were down in the bottom of the valley, we heard the air-raid sirens. This was the Germans' signal for general mobilisation in the Rjukan area. They had at last collected their wits and found out what had happened. That did not matter much to us. To capture nine desperate, well-armed men in a dark wood at night would be difficult enough for people with local knowledge; for Wehrmacht men it should be quite impossible.

On the main roads, things began to get lively. Several cars, including a large vehicle with a gas generator in tow, scorched past. There was just time for the party to throw itself into a ditch. On the other side of the valley, away on the railway line, the lights of torches could be spotted. The German guards had discovered the line of the saboteurs' retreat.

Lieutenant Ronneberg led four members of his unit on a 400-mile trek to Sweden, a journey successfully accomplished within eighteen days.

Knowledge of the full extent of the damage inflicted by Gunnerside threw General der Infanterie Falkenhorst into a towering rage, which he vented on the unit's officers and men in the presence of a group of Norwegians – who considered it tactful to keep straight faces. When he had calmed down, the General conceded to a colleague: 'It's the best coup I've ever seen.' It was a remark that reached the delighted SOE planners in London.

Members of Norwegian resistance working outside their own country had dealt a crippling blow to the activities of the occupation forces within. The muscle in London was indispensable for fuelling the resources of the various 'secret armies'.

But there were no easy victories for the resistance.

There were also the traitors.

21

Slim, dark, grey-eyed Trix Terwendt experienced a sharp jab of pain as the final stages of her otherwise immaculate parachute jump into the Netherlands went badly awry.

A sudden snatch of wind knocked the former KLM hostess sideways; her jaw struck the ground with a violence that seemed to wrench her head from her body. The reception committee of Dutchmen were polite but formal. And, in the manner of resistants everywhere, one of their number grumbled: 'London doesn't understand our problems. We don't get all the backing we need. Communications are very bad.' Then he added with a touch of malice: 'Our chief will not be pleased that they sent a woman.'

If Trix had not been in pain from her fall she would probably have exploded, but she was too tired and there was too much to be done for argument. She shrugged and walked with her new friends across the field, away from the dropping zone.

The Allied information network in the Netherlands had long been infiltrated by the Abwehr (German Military Intelligence). It took two years for SOE to come anywhere near repairing the damage; by 1942, agents and radio sets were being poured into the area. But what was needed above all was the setting up of an escape line to Belgium organised by the Dutch from within.

And that, as it happened, was the speciality of the top-secret section of British Intelligence within M19, code-named LS9 (d). It was true that there had been a number of Dutch guides who had already brought would-be resistants to Belgian territory, but there were spies everywhere and it proved unwise to trust the guides too much.

Besides, the Germans – at any rate, for the moment – appeared to hold most of the trump cards. It was all due to the presence of a certain washing line dangling below a suburban block of flats in The Hague. It was to provide the Abwehr with one of its biggest coups.

The Abwehr radio-detection van, masterminded in a routine surveillance operation by Oberstleutnant Hermann Giskes, the senior intelligence officer responsible for the Netherlands, had long suspected the existence of one particular two-way set, being operated, as it turned out by, SOE wireless operator Hubertus Lauwers, codenamed Ebenezer.

The woman from whose flat Lauwers and an associate were working noticed the suspicious arrival of some plain-clothes men just a little too late. The only course of action was for her to throw the radio into a clump of bushes below. Unfortunately, it tangled with a washing line and was clearly visible. Both SOE men were seized.

A proposition was put to Lauwers: would he care to work for the Germans, operating his set to London? He was told: 'We are impressed by your expertise. We can find you plenty to do.'

Lauwers readily agreed. But not because he had decided to turn traitor. London, he assumed, would notice that he had deliberately omitted his vital security code.

Unfortunately, London did not. The absence of the security code went unnoticed. In desperation, Lauwers inserted the word CAUGHT into the coded message. London did not spot that either. All the information transmitted back to the Netherlands by SOE fell into the eager hands of the Abwehr.

A victim of this particular lapse in security by SOE Dutch section was Trix Terwendt, the agent with a special mission. Her task was to assemble a number of Dutch people prepared to shelter airmen on their way to Brussels. It was her intention, in fact, to create an escape line.

Advance information of Trix's mission was studied with the gravest attention by Oberstleutnant Giskes and SS-Sturmbannfuehrer Josef Schreyeder of the SD. Both men assured SOE in the most courteous of terms that all arrangements had been made to receive the new agent with containers of arms and a radio set.

At midnight on 14 February 1943, Trix donned her parachute harness and clutched her supply of Dutch currency and the papers which identified her as a hospital nurse. As she climbed into the Halifax, a group of Dutch and British intelligence officers stood saluting.

Promptly on her arrival came the message: 'We extend a welcome to a gallant woman comrade.'

Oberstleutnant Giskes of the Abwehr was enjoying himself.

Trix's instructions from SOE were to submit to the authority of her Dutch reception committee for twenty-four hours. Then she was to break contact before proceeding with her mission to establish the escape line.

Before leaving, Trix had been given the address of a man named Smit, who was to be found at the Bally shoe shop in The Hague. Smit had provided sanctuary for RAF evaders and his name had figured in M19 interrogation reports over the previous few weeks. The unsuspecting Trix could see no reason why this information should not be given to the Dutch reception committee.

Her escorts took Trix in driving rain to a wooden shed. One of them threw a blanket over her shoulders, explaining that the colour of her raincoat was light and conspicuous. Suddenly, the man who had been holding the blanket seized Trix's wrists, then yanked her hands behind her back.

She tried to fight down panic by laughing: 'Don't make

silly jokes. You think I'm frightened because I'm a woman?'

But even now she could not grasp what had happened. Possibly, she hoped, she had fallen into the hands of some Communist resistant louts who intended nothing beyond boisterous horseplay. There was no time to ponder over the puzzle; she was bundled roughly into a car, which sped to the Abwehr headquarters at Dreibergen.

On the way, she cursed that she could not swallow her poison pill, but her captors had wrenched handcuffs on her and she lay in the back of the car, trying to make sense of it all. Her tears were not those of fear: they were born of the knowledge that unwittingly she had sealed Smit's fate.

Her Dutch captors, judging by the way they talked, were clearly part of a highly efficient organisation that had thoroughly infiltrated SOE, most notably its wireless communication. One thing above all else was clear: she had been dropped straight into the hands of the enemy.

From his initial success at securing Lauwers, Oberstleutnant Giskes had gone on to capture more English wireless sets and organise a string of 'reception committees' for parachuted SOE agents. The deception had been given the codename of *Nordpol* (North Pole) and was also known as '*England Spiel*' (England Game).

From a purely technical view, Giskes was well pleased with his coup. But cooperation with the SD evoked his distaste. The rivalry between the Abwehr and all departments of Himmler's SS was notorious; the Reichsfuehrer was known to have been intriguing for years to remove Admiral Wilhelm Canaris, the Abwehr chief.

Giskes reflected that at least he would not have the distasteful task of interrogating a woman. That particular assignment had been appropriated by Sturmbannfuehrer Schreyeder.

The SS man was in an avuncular mood, greeting Trix

with the suspicion of a twinkle. He remarked: 'I see that Felix has landed safely in spite of the wind and rain. That's precisely the message I've sent to London.'

Trix really was frightened now: the Abwehr even had her SOE codename. . . .

Schreyeder maintained a silky courtesy throughout. It was almost as if the SD regarded her as one of themselves, that her arrest was an unfortunate necessity and it could only be a matter of time before things were put right.

Perhaps, Schreyeder suggested, they could all work together. It would be a lot more pleasant, he announced blandly, than a spell in a concentration camp.

Trix's interrogation stretched over four days and nights, with just one break for a bath and sleep. She was not tortured. It was scarcely necessary since her extreme tiredness was in itself a form of torture.

The moment she had dreaded most came when Schreyeder proclaimed: 'We would like you to go and find this man Smit in The Hague. After all, you gave us his contact address.'

Stung into fury, she riposted: 'I would weep for shame if I had to do that.'

The answer appeared to disconcert the SD man. For a few seconds, he stared at his prisoner with something like admiration. *After four days and nights*. . . . Then he was the cool professional again, summoning his subordinates and telling them to get the girl ready for transfer to the prison at Haaren. There, a horrified Trix learnt the extent of the damage *Nordpol* had done to SOE. The Germans possessed detailed knowledge of names and meeting places, even of the activities of the SOE training schools.

Trix Terwendt remained at Haaren in solitary confinement for six months. After that, the only relief was supplied by another female prisoner put in her cell. But the woman turned out to be an SD informer.

After that, Trix went to Ravensbrueck concentration camp, transferring to Mauthausen in January 1945. She reached Switzerland through the Red Cross at the end of the war.

Beatrice (Trix) Terwendt, alias Felix, was one of the few survivors from the *Nordpol* operation; she told her captors nothing.

Although the agent Smit was arrested and perished in a concentration camp, his escape line held. No justice came to the Dutch traitors who had lain in wait for Trix that night.

They escaped revenge. Others were not so fortunate.

By November 1943 the occupying forces in Denmark had conferred a dubious distinction on Jens Lillilund.

Only three years before, he had expressed his hatred of his country's enemies by literally spitting at their feet. But now, as head of the Holger Danske sabotage group, he was one of Denmark's most wanted men. One evening the warning had come: *Stay away from your apartment. The Germans are waiting.*

He and an agent whom the resistance knew only as John had returned to Copenhagen from a particularly tricky sabotage mission. And they had nowhere to sleep.

John suggested: 'There's Hedwig Delbo's apartment. She's an agent from Norway. It has been used more than once by our people.'

Lillilund was doubtful. 'Is she to be trusted?'

John was suitably reassuring, and the two men cycled out to the grubby, nondescript back street near the Trianglen traffic junction.

John pressed the bell of No. 4 in the drab brown hallway. A handsome blonde drew back the glass-panelled door a few inches, and John was asking: 'Mrs Delbo, can you put us up for the night?'

As if it was the most natural thing in the world, the woman led them into the apartment, down the narrow hallway and into a room that Lillilund noticed was cluttered with pieces of cloth, packets of pins, spools of thread, a sewing machine and women's garments.

John introduced Lillilund by his cover name: 'Hedwig Delbo, Mr Finsen.'

Plainly it was unnecessary. The woman raised an eyebrow in mild irony and said: *'Finsen?* The leader of Holger Danske?'

Despite himself, Lillilund shot a questioning glance at his companion. If Hedwig Delbo noticed, she gave no sign. She fed the two men, showed them beds and promised to wake them.

The two saboteurs were ready and dressed before eight o'clock and plainly anxious to be gone. But their hostess was in a chatty mood, urging breakfast. She pleaded: 'Let me get some milk from across the street.'

Her absence stretched to ten minutes; Lillilund felt a mounting anxiety. He snapped: 'We're moving. We're wasting time and it could be dangerous.'

Outside, they unlocked their bicycles and pushed them to the end of the street. It was only when they got to one of the bigger thoroughfares that they noticed the large black saloon parked in front of a newspaper shop. In Nazi-occupied Copenhagen, only the Germans or the police had large cars. No one else had any fuel.

Crouched over the handlebars and not daring to look round, they heard the whirr of the starter motor and the sound of tyres crunching asphalt. Lillilund was firmly in command: 'Don't look back. Go round the traffic island and sharp left down Osterbrogade.'

The presence of other people cycling to work was oddly comforting; the traffic lights favoured the two resistants, who were able to circle the traffic island without stopping. Within minutes, the car had caught up with them.

The two men put on a burst of speed, suddenly turning completely round and doubling back.

Behind them, they caught the sound of screeching tyres. There was just a chance they could lose them in the heavy cycle traffic. It was then that the occupants of the car began shooting. John's hand darted to his jacket, but Lillilund shouted: 'Don't waste time. You can't shoot from a bicycle. Let's get away.'

At the corner of Osterbrogade, he caught a final glimpse of John swerving off to the right. Lillilund kept on, steering straight through the traffic, making for Rosenvaengets Allé. It was there that he passed another black car, which swerved round and came up directly behind, and joined the chase.

All Lillilund's concentration was now on reaching the other side of Rosenvaengets Allé because he knew that past the apartment blocks and the large town houses was a short path which could take a cycle but would defeat a car.

As for John, his hand was still clasped inside his coat but he was not reaching for a weapon. He was desperately trying to staunch blood from the bullet wound in his chest. The men in the car kept on shooting. This time they got him in the leg, toppling him from the cycle. On the ground, he managed to find his weapon and, desperately fighting the rising nausea, shot straight at the car's windscreen, killing one of the Germans. Then he fainted.

The second car, thwarted in the attempt to find Lillilund at the top of Rosenvaengets Allé, sped back, screeching to a halt by the buckled bicycle. One of the Germans got out, scooped up John's pistol and brought its butt crashing down on the saboteur's head. Then John was picked up and thrown over the bonnet of the black saloon.

Within an hour, Lillilund had made contact with a number of Holger Danske members who were able to give him the grim news of John's capture.

He declared: 'Somewhere, there just has to be an informer. What do we do about this Mrs Delbo?'

It was necessary to concoct some plan that would clear or condemn the Norwegian dressmaker. By mid-morning some of the main details had been worked out. Lillilund rang Mrs Delbo and came straight to the point: 'This is

Mr Finsen. I suppose you know that John was taken this morning?'

Her reaction of horror seemed genuine enough. 'What are you going to do now?' she asked, with every sign of anxiety.

Lillilund urged: 'It's absolutely vital I get to Sweden tonight. If I stay here I might as well commit suicide. I must see you before I go.'

'Where are you now?'

He merely said that he would be at her apartment by three o'clock.

The two lovers who strolled down the grubby back street near the Trianglen junction appeared interested in no one but themselves. Occasionally, they stepped into various doorways to embrace passionately. They seemed to show no interest at all in the two black saloons, one at either end of the street, or in the handcart covered with Christmas trees outside No. 4. A man in a black leather trench coat left his vehicle and began talking to the street seller. The two lovers ignored that, too.

But, as agents of Holger Danske, they had both noticed the ugly snout of the sub-machine-gun which peeped through the Christmas trees.

Jens Lillilund did not keep his afternoon appointment with Hedwig Delbo.

At the hastily convened meeting later the same day, one of the saboteurs, suffering from a bad cold, blew his nose noisily and told his companions: 'I've stayed at this woman's apartment. It could have been any of us in John's shoes. I'll do it.'

It was then that they showed the man with the cold the pistols whose barrels were about a quarter of an inch in diameter and around a foot long. He took in the triggers of bent metal tubing and the handgrips which, when unclipped, became magazines for the 7.65 mm bullets. The main virtue of the weapon was that firing it made no more noise than a sharp slap on the wrist. It was British made, had never found its way into any armaments museum, and was created specifically for the assassination of traitors. As far as anyone knew, there were no more than 150 currently in Denmark.

Two afternoons later, a newspaper seller looked out of his shop on the corner of the street where Hedwig Delbo lived. On grey winter afternoons it was usually deserted, but now a group of young men were loitering in doorways. At around four o'clock, another man arrived. He seemed to have a bad cold and was blowing his nose vigorously.

The newspaper seller did not like what he saw. He went to the back of his shop and lifted the telephone.

The man who fingered the silent pistol was about to enter No. 4 when the police streamed into the street. He turned round and sprinted into the apartment building opposite. An old woman answered his tap on the ground floor.

He shoved past her and slammed the door, reaching for his knife to slash the telephone wires. Then he positioned himself in the front room to watch the police round up the Holger Danske men who had presented a sitting target. He was even able to see the outline of Hedwig Delbo in the window of her own apartment. She appeared totally oblivious of the commotion.

After the police had left, the man with the cold apologised profusely to the old woman, tossing her some money to have the telephone repaired. Then he sneaked away, crossed Copenhagen and rejoined his comrades.

He commented bitterly: 'A total blunder. We might as well have told them we were coming. We'll have to try again in a hurry.'

'No guards, this time.'

Even if there was to be a smaller cast for the new attempt, there was an additional risk, which involved stealing a Gestapo car. But Lillilund reckoned that, provided the car could be ditched quickly, it would be worth it; no police would dare stop an SS vehicle without good reason.

As the car sped towards the target's apartment, other members of Holger Danske telephoned the Rosenvaengets Allé police station, where their comrades were being held. Holger Danske had friends there. A few hours later, the officers on duty were remiss enough to leave a back door open. . . .

One of the resistants at the wheel of the stolen car looked anxiously at the would-be killer with the silent pistol. 'Your cold must be killing you. Your eyes are watering terribly. Are you sure that you are up to the job?'

The man made reassuring noises. In his mind's eye he saw Hedwig Delbo placidly sewing dresses, unaware of what was in store for her. It gave him no satisfaction. Sabotage was one thing, liquidation quite another.

There were three men in the car and they parked it a short distance away from where Mrs Delbo lived. All blackout curtains had been drawn for the night and there was a heavy silence. The killer allowed himself to blow his nose one last time. Then he pocketed his handkerchief and pulled out the silent pistol.

The rap at the door was answered instantly by a slightly nonplussed Mrs Delbo. She recovered quickly and invited him in.

Her back was to him now and he waited until she had opened the living room door and turned to face him. She pushed the back of a clenched fist to her mouth in a gesture of horror. What he had not reckoned on was the scream which masked the slap of the bullet. Mrs Delbo crumpled forward and the assassin readied the weapon for another shot. But the gun jammed. His temples were throbbing now and he realised that his heavy cold had turned to 'flu.

The killer staggered away.

But the job was not yet done. Even in death, Mrs Delbo would spell danger. It was necessary to tip off friends at the Rosenvaengets Allé police station. The killer took on the job himself. His reception was explosive. The police informant yelled: 'You *idiot*! That woman you think you

189

killed is in the next room and singing your name to the Gestapo. Get out!'

The whole of Denmark was alerted. Hundreds of photographs of the man with the cold were circulated.

That Mrs Delbo had survived the attempt was in no doubt; now she appeared to have vanished off the face of the earth. Jens Lillilund and the entire Holger Danske sweated with anxiety, a form of purgatory they were forced to endure until the new year. Then Holger Danske received a call from a contact in the Copenhagen office of Thomas Cook.

Hedwig Delbo had surfaced at last. And she was leaving Cook's at six o'clock that evening for a Lufthansa flight to Norway.

There could be no question of any fresh attempt being made in the travel agency; that would blow the contact. A swift bullet from a passing car on the way to the airport seemed more sensible. It was rapidly set at naught when the resistance driver picked for the job had a flat tyre. He eventually reached the travel agency, only to be told: 'She left five minutes ago. It would have been highly dangerous if we had held on to her.'

News of the latest failure was flashed to SOE in London, who made it clear that the matter was now in the hands of the Norwegian resistance. It was a body blow to the pride of Holger Danske; there was a certain wry consolation though for Lillilund on learning that, after another attempt in Bergen, the woman had escaped yet again.

But it turned out that Hedwig Delbo somehow felt safer in Denmark than in her own country. She returned, but there was no trace of her until a telephone call to the bookshop of Mogens Staffeldt.

The informer, a fellow bookseller in Copenhagen who kept busy throughout the occupation with varied tasks, told Staffeldt: 'I think I've seen her. A Norwegian-speaking woman came into my shop for a book from our lending library. When I told her the book was out, I asked if I

190

could send it. She looked nervous and said she would call again.'

Several days later, the woman had been back – calling herself Mrs Dam and giving a telephone number.

Holger Danske could scarcely have survived without friends in the Copenhagen telephone service. There was no listing for a Mrs Dam and finding an address from a mere number was difficult.

'Difficult but not impossible?' pleaded Jens Lillilund. The address, it was eventually revealed, was in the Sankel-marksgade area.

Mogens Staffeldt was instructed: 'Ring Mrs Dam and tell her you have the book.'

The two Danish policemen who spotted the car parked outside Mogens Staffeldt's bookshop were conscientious souls. The car, on inspection, had no petrol-ration stamp on the windscreen. What was it doing there? The driver, catching sight of them in the mirror, became nervous. 'We'd better go,' he muttered to his companion.

The woman who had given her name as Mrs Dam turned up a few minutes after the car had driven off.

There was still no proof that this was in fact the elusive Hedwig Delbo. For any man to attempt a lone killing would be madness; the Gestapo would be nearby. But Mrs Delbo was a genuine dressmaker – a call by a woman just might work.

The girl who had posed as one of the lovers in the earlier bid offered: 'I'll call on her and order a dress.'

By the evening she was back and reporting laconically: 'The dress will be ready by 9 March. By the way, the woman is Hedwig Delbo.'

The men who went with the girl now had little patience with the British-made pistol that had been custom-built for disposing of traitors. It had failed them once, and that was enough.

The killers were carrying old-fashioned automatics which would not jam. In Sankelmarksgade, the men entered the building first and climbed to the landing above the apartment.

At the door, the girl pushed the bell several times, and when the target appeared, announced: 'I'm back for my dress, Mrs Delbo.'

The use of the name was the only warning the traitor got.

The two men leapt down the stairs, shoved the girl aside and opened fire. The girl walked coolly down the stairs, leaving her male colleagues to make sure that this time Hedwig Delbo was indisputably dead.

The news of the execution reached the man in prison whom everyone knew only as John. The Germans had not been disposed to give him much medical treatment for the injuries he had suffered through Mrs Delbo's treachery.

They eventually shot him.

22

The dreaded cold northerly wind which each winter bites viciously across Geneva's Lake Léman can be felt just across the border in France, whistling along the mountains and high valleys of Haute-Savoie.

In the closing months of 1943, the most perilous years for the French resistance, this wind appeared to many to be a grim portent of fresh disasters.

One calamity seemed to eclipse them all.

The local Gestapo who pounced on the tall, tweedy Frenchman making his way across the Swiss border might have been forgiven for thinking that they had secured nothing more sinister than a local farmer ignoring the curfew. In fact, they had come close to slashing the very jugular of resistance in Haute-Savoie. The fortunes of the underground movement were primarily in the hands of Colonel Vallette d'Osia, commander of the 27th Battalion of the Chasseurs Alpins in Annecy, the mountain troops forced into disbandment in 1940.

At that time, Vallette d'Osia had urged his followers: 'The armistice is an illusion and one day we will be called upon to take up the struggle against the occupying forces.'

The chance came with the total occupation of France. But by then army dissidents were committed to underground opposition within the Organisation de Résistance de l'Armée (ORA). In Haute-Savoie, under Vallette d'Osia's leadership, by February 1943 it had become a formidable resistance cadre, receiving guns, explosives and medical supplies through parachute drop from England.

But within seven months, the Gestapo had snatched

Vallette d'Osia; the Germans soon realised that they had landed a sizeable fish.

In the sealed compartment of the train to Paris, d'Osia contemplated his two Gestapo guards and an indisputably grim future. He had already decided that he had no intention of testing his powers of endurance under torture in some Paris cellar. He felt a glimmer of hope soon after midnight, when his two guards fell asleep. They had slipped handcuffs on him, but none the less it was an inexplicable blunder that they should have allowed him to sit alone opposite them. The point seemed academic in a compartment with locked doors; he would have to take his chance with the window.

It was a considerable effort for a man built like a tank to get to his feet nimbly and silently, but somehow he managed it. To prise open the window would have been hard enough even with free hands. It was of the standard design in French trains, with two knobs set wide apart for pulling it down. To tug at both simultaneously while wearing handcuffs was out of the question. He pulled first at one and then the other, and there was an inevitable creak, which he felt sure would disturb the guards. Things were a bit easier then because it was possible to place both hands in the centre of the top end of the glass. It came about halfway down, leaving a gap in the top half just wide enough to pass through.

Vallette d'Osia catapulted through the window, after counting the seconds between telegraph poles. The train was passing along an embankment, which meant that he would have further to fall but possibly on to a softer surface. It seemed an age before he hit the ground, but he forced himself to stand up immediately, foregoing the luxury of even a breather.

It was as well. Behind him, the embankment erupted with gunfire and he heard the cry: 'Stop, a terrorist has escaped.' Even before the train came to a halt, he had melted away.

The news of his arrest had plunged the resistance of

Haute-Savoie into gloom and fear. An entire agonising week stretched out before news was received of a bedraggled, handcuffed figure appearing at a farmhouse near Dijon.

The apparition had told the startled farmer: 'I'm Vallette d'Osia and I've just jumped from a train.'

The reaction was hostile. The farmer was a true patriot and no collaborator, but he was a family man and he had heard plenty about Gestapo and Milice stooges. Colonel Vallette d'Osia of the Chasseurs Alpins was locked up unceremoniously until his identity was confirmed.

There was no question of returning to his position within the resistance or, indeed, remaining anywhere in Haute-Savoie. The hounds of the Gestapo would be baying for blood; the threat to others would be as real as if his capture had been successful. In late October 1943, Colonel Vallette d'Osia was flown to England by SOE.

He was by no means the only serious loss.

Felix Plottier, creator of the maquis in Haute-Savoie, acting initially under the order of Vallette d'Osia, had proved himself a formidable opponent of the Milice, the assiduous lackeys of the Nazis in occupied France.

As the dedicated evaders of forced labour made their way to Bonneville, the local Juge d'Instruction tetchily issued a warrant for the arrest of 'Felix Xavier Arthur Plottier, born 1 November 1908 in Bonneville, son of Maurice François Joseph and Marie Josephine de Freyre.'

Plottier was 'accused of attacking the external security of the State and forming a group of felons. Height: 1 metre 72, wavy chestnut hair brushed back, blue eyes, sturdily built, always bare-headed. Usually dressed in sports clothes, very athletic, loving the mountains. Could be in Annecy or Aix-les-Bains, where he has relatives, or trying to reach the Swiss frontier. This arrest warrant replaces that numbered S 43. If discovered, advise by telephone or telegram the head office of the Security Police situated in Vichy. . . .'

But Plottier, the zestfully unrepentant resistant, had fallen foul of the Vichy police long before. At the pinnacle of his own personal list of resistance heroes was Henri Frenay, architect of Mouvement pour la Libération Française (MLF), eventually to be known as Combat. This was also the name of the movement's newspaper, which proudly displayed a quotation by Clemenceau: 'In war as in peace, the last word belongs to those who never give up.'

Plottier willingly took on the task of distributing the newspaper in his own region. Inevitably, the local Milice were alerted; he became a marked man.

He recalls: 'From then on, it became impossible to sleep on some nights in our house on the hill outside Bonneville. We had an arrangement with my mother that if I was on the way home after work and the Milice was around she would hang out a towel on the tennis court. It was a coded warning. We slept elsewhere.'

Several times he toyed with the idea of escaping to England and aiding the resistance from there, but the risk was too great: so many of the escape lines had already been severed.

The alternative of remaining in France was, however, scarcely more attractive. Under the Vichy warrant for his arrest, on 28th October Plottier was sentenced in his absence by the special section of the appeal court to ten years' forced labour, 'for taking part in a plot and associating with felons'.

The choice of language was remarkably mild in the circumstances. After all, the warrant referred to the actions of a maquis leader with a twelve-hundred-strong resistant force which had its own camps and dropping zones at the plateau of Glières within the Borne Massif mountain range.

Haute-Savoie itself became too dangerous. The Swiss frontier at Geneva beckoned, a mere twelve miles away.

One night, the breath of the Gestapo warm on their necks, Felix and Joan Plottier crossed into Switzerland, hoping that their two young sons would be able to follow in safety later.

Surrounded by vassal states of Hitler's empire, the Swiss faced the ever present threat that they might be the next country to experience the dubious benefits of Nazi 'protection'. The fear was aggravated with the capitulation of Italy in 1943. All frontier posts that had previously been held by Italians were taken over by the Wehrmacht.

Smuggling arms into France from the Swiss side was still vital to the resistance. But the obstacles were formidable.

Plottier explains: 'These included a twelve foot fence which the Swiss had placed all along the frontier, rigidly guarded by Swiss-German troops. My job was to get arms into France, smuggling them to various points close to the Swiss-French border in the upper Rhône valley and elsewhere into France.'

There was only one way in which the supplies of pistol ammunition, reels of detonating fuse, binoculars, food-stuffs and morale-boosting leaflets could be spirited out: in boxes on men's backs, across the mountains north of Chamonix.

Felix Plottier was a brilliant skier with unrivalled knowledge of the mountains; that made the day when the Swiss caught him a considerable blow to the resistance. It was not the first time he had clashed with the authorities. In the May dawn, an armed patrol swooped down on the maquis group which, intent on shipping arms and supplies, was working closely with its Italian counterpart in the Aosta valley, close to the border between Switzerland and France.

The area of Champéry, where Plottier was arrested, had been proclaimed a military zone closed to civilians. His violation of this edict was bad enough; in addition, Plottier had, under an assumed name, rented a chalet for storing arms.

There followed months of interrogation in prison. Plottier recalled: 'There was no torture, no Gestapo methods. But there was no comfort, either. The jail authorities never tired of telling me that I wouldn't hope to get out in under twenty years for arms trafficking, possessing false identity papers and trespass in the military area of Champéry.'

But the Germans were on the run from France; Plottier's case never came to court and he was freed on payment of fifteen hundred Swiss frances – on condition he quit Switzerland.

By then, the knowledge of their inevitable defeat had fuelled a fresh ferocity in the Germans. They and Darnand's Milice flexed their muscles for fierce engagements in the mountains of Haute-Savoie and the Jura, in the central forests of the Corrèze and in the southwestern vineyards of the Dordogne.

It was a corner of Haute-Savoie, however, that was to be the backdrop for one of the greatest resistance tragedies.

23

Within the vast sprawling range of Borne Massif, which extends for more than twelve and a half miles within Haute-Savoie northwest of Annecy, lies the hollow of rolling grassland which is the plateau of the Glières.

Shaped like an elongated diamond, it stretches five miles northeast to southwest and is a mere one and a half miles across at its widest point. Forests girdle the mountains and the sheer rocks act as stern, uninviting sentinels.

It was natural that the resistance would be attracted by the inaccessibility of the Glières, which seemed virtually impregnable against any large-scale surprise attack. In addition, here was also an ideal dropping zone for parachutes and supplies. Captain Henri Romans-Petit, the successor to Colonel Vallette d'Osia, believed that no more than a hundred maquisards would be needed on the Glières. Such a number, it was reasoned, would be enough to guard the approaches, receive the containers of arms and transport them to storage dumps, ready for allocation to other resistance groups.

But Romans-Petit had reckoned without the staunch individualism of twenty-nine-year-old charismatic Lyons aristocrat Theodose Morel, known as Tom, a product of the St-Cyr military academy who had opted for service in the Chasseurs Alpins and been appointed to command the 27th Battalion at Annecy.

To Tom, the Glières represented a sacred stronghold of Free France and not just a dropping zone for Allied supplies. The leaders of the Haute-Savoie maquis expected mass drops of arms and food, which they saw as infinitely more practical considerations than a paragraph

199

or two in the annals of military glory. In fact, Tom marshalled some 450 members of the maquis to the defence of the plateau under the slogan *Vivre Libre ou Mourir* (Live Free or Die).

On the evening of 29 January 1944, the maquis first came to the Glières. It was at the end of a week in which the mountains had been enveloped in heavy mists. The columns of men groped forward slowly in the snow and darkness; the paths which crisscrossed the plateau were a rink of ice. There was a moment of tragedy when a local fourteen-year-old boy, Noel Avettand, who had come to guide the maquisards, plunged to his death. To many who made that journey, the Glières seemed like the end of the world, a place whose sadness was somehow accentuated by the snow cloaking the landscape in a shroud.

It was, above all, a place where men would fight and die, where down in the dark, still valleys there lurked, not just the Germans, but the French collaborators, the Groupes Mobiles de Réserves with their dark blue and mustard-coloured uniforms, black helmets and black boots, their chests banded with the leather straps bearing their equipment.

The expected arms were dropped in mid-February. On the first night, four aircraft dropped fifty-four containers, to be followed by guns and munitions. The whole venture was unopposed; there was fresh confidence in the leadership of Tom Morel.

But the landings had been witnessed both by the Germans and the Milice; now they could pinpoint the position of the forces on the plateau.

Disaster, when it came to the maquis, was from an unexpected cause.

The waves of aircraft had barely departed before the Germans moved up attack troops to the plateau. At around the same time, Michel Fournier, deputy medical officer to the battalion, went down to Grand-Bornand village to pick up some badly needed medical supplies. Some bargaining between the Milice and the resistants had led to a precarious promise that there would be no interference with emissaries sent to collect such supplies.

Fournier did not return; Tom learnt that he had fallen into the hands of the GMR. There was, Morel realised, little point in appealing to the Vichy authorities on behalf of a fellow Frenchman. Some form of confrontation was inevitable; the impulsive leader of the Glières maquis was in the mood for it.

Morel despatched a special unit; it seized thirty of the GMR contingent with little difficulty. As a gesture, this doubtless relieved feelings, but was robbed of any point when it was learnt that Fournier had been hustled away to Annecy hours before. The maquis leader then made an offer: he would exchange the thirty prisoners for the safe return of Michel Fournier.

What seemed like a reasonable bargain was struck with the Milice. Morel released his prisoners; there was still no sign of the medical officer.

Plainly, it was no good conducting negotiations in the spirit of St-Cyr. A new attack was forthwith launched on the GMR command post at Entremont village.

Tom was determined that this would be no puny act of retaliation; the maquisards went in with rifles, grenades, Stens and Thompson sub-machine-guns, supplemented by two Hotchkiss heavy machine-guns and a single mortar. They succeeded in blasting their way into the GMR headquarters at the Hôtel de France in Entremont, seizing prisoners and swiftly disarming them.

The commander of the post, Major Lefebvre, suppressing his rage with difficulty, demanded the traditional right of an officer to keep his pistol to maintain his honour.

Morel asked coldly: 'What is your honour worth, since you refuse to keep your promises?'

The maquis leader then went on to demand the surrender of the entire garrison against the release of Michel Fournier. It brought the rejoinder: 'I have no intention of surrendering but I suggest you do, here and now. I will not negotiate with traitors.'

Now it was Morel's turn to feel mounting rage, and he saw no reason to suppress it. The use of the word 'traitors' by a representative of Vichy led him to lose his temper completely. He hurled insults at Lefebvre, who suddenly appeared bored with the discussion, abruptly turned his back and prepared to re-enter the hotel.

Then it happened. Totally without warning – beyond spitting out 'Salaud' – Lefebvre swung round and, pistol in hand, fired point-blank at Morel. With a look of mingled bewilderment and fear, the Chasseurs Alpins lieutenant, the hero of the Glières, clutched his stomach, gave a single cough and fell dead.

But within minutes Lefebvre was cut down by a single burst from a machine pistol fired by a maquisard who had accompanied Tom Morel with an improvised flag of truce.

What happened next was inexcusable in military terms but at least understandable in men who had lost a beloved leader. The maquis stumbled into the Hôtel de France, tearing to pieces all who stood in their way. Those members of the Milice who were not shot on the spot threw themselves out of upstairs windows in sheer terror. It was either that or be cut to ribbons with knives and bayonets. When the bloodlust had finally been slaked, the Hôtel de France resembled an abattoir.

It was then time for the resistance to count its own cost. Incredibly, in addition to Morel, the defenders of the Glières had lost just one man: Adjutant Georges Descours, a peacetime policeman from Annecy.

The dazed members of the maquis made the sad journey back to the plateau with the bodies of their two comrades and captured arms and supplies. As far as the foot of the mountain, the remains of Morel and Descours were transported by sledge. But after that, everything had to be unloaded and carried for the rest of the way.

With the stretcher parties leading, the difficult ascent up the steep, snow-choked paths began. Five-and-a-half hours later, at 9 a.m., the long and silent line of mourners was back on the Glières.

The bodies of Tom and his adjutant were taken to the community hospital, where, covered with the flags of Free France and on beds draped and canopied with red, white and blue silk taken from RAF parachutes used in arms drops, they lay in state until the funeral. A round-the-clock guard of honour was mustered; the men stood with heads bowed and with rifle or machine-gun at the reverse.

But the outward show of mourning had to be brief. The maquisards, even before the death of their leader, had been aware of just how precarious their position was.

Somehow they all sensed that the Germans would not keep them waiting long.

During the morning of 11 March, the Milice mounted in force up the western front of the plateau, but after an hour of bitter fighting were driven back. Then, flying out of the sun, a Messerschmitt fighter raked the chalets. Incendiary bullets and cannon shells churned up the snow and splintered the wooden walls, but no one was hit and the buildings suffered little damage.

A second German aircraft flew low on a photo reconnaissance mission. Its photographs revealed four fresh piles of logs which had clearly been stacked to light a further Allied parachute drop.

The maquis awaited the signal from London that would tell them when the aircraft were coming. Then, among the personal messages broadcast after the BBC's nine o'clock evening news that same night, they heard it. The newsreader intoned twice: '*Le petit homme aime le Byrrh, le petit homme aime les tessons de bouteille*' ('The little man likes the apéritif, the little man likes the broken bits of the bottle').

Maquisards were alerted by the throbbing roar of four-engined bombers. The drop was truly gigantic: almost ninety tons of arms and munitions, more than sufficient to arm 4,000 men. All at once, the defenders of the Glières ceased to be useful resisters, but became instead frantic foragers, hunting feverishly all over the plateau for arms that had been scattered in 400 places.

More than one maquisard reflected ruefully that the supplies might just as well never have been dropped, for they became trapped into the sticky embrace of the snow or fell into ravines. Day after day, scores of men scoured the fields, the woods and the snowbanks. It was almost a point of honour to retrieve the arms, thus preventing them from falling into German hands.

As for the Germans, they possessed infinite patience. They were content to wait and watch. There was more than enough time for the task they had planned.

General Julius Oberg, commander of a crack Alpine division, conferred with Luftwaffe commanders, Gestapo chiefs and members of the Milice. A force of some 15,000, together with two air squadrons, was at the Germans' disposal.

The order for a general assault was given on 25 March. Hell came to the maquisards on the Glières. Wave after wave of fire sliced into the plateau; trees suddenly became blazing torches and banks of snow melted away. Fifteen thousand Germans against 500 maquisards.

The Glières was now an entrenched camp, where men dug holes into which they vainly tried to snuggle. All too soon, Captain Maurice Anjot, the successor to Tom Morel and also an officer of the 27th Battalion of Chasseurs Alpins, learnt the strength of the opposition. There were training units throughout Haute-Savoie and operational headquarters had been set up at the Hôtel Imperial at Annecy. The mountain troops, white smocks over their grey field uniforms, advanced up the snowy slopes towards the pine trees held by just twenty maquisard to the east of the massif.

By early afternoon only one maquisard remained alive in the sector. He went on firing until his ammunition was spent. Then came the volley which put paid to him too.

The chiefs of the various sectors were cut off. Forced to abandon his command post, Captain Anjot, his officers, doctors and medical orderlies, together with some severely wounded men, huddled in a cave which, poignantly, lay in the shadow of the simple wooden cross that had been erected above the grave of Tom Morel. By twilight, the plateau was being held by this last core of defenders, and with the light fading from the summits of the mountains of Frêles and Auges came nightfall and silence.

With an attempt at cheerfulness, Anjot commented: 'We have at least saved our honour.'

But another maquisard was more prosaic: 'It's the end of the battalion of the Glières.'

And it was. The decision was made to cease fighting, with the injunction that each survivor should seek to join his original maquis. After a fifteen-hour march in the snow, Anjot and a little group reached the village of Naves.

The Germans were waiting.

In the barrage of machine-gun fire, Maurice Anjot was the first to fall.

Leaderless and dispirited, the remaining maquisards, suffering from cold, hunger and lack of sleep, kept up an endless march, dogged by the Germans and the Milice.

Those who were not mown down by execution squads were dragged, battered and beaten, to hotels and villas in Annecy which had been hastily converted into detention centres. Then they were hauled before token tribunals, condemned as 'terrorists' or 'bandits' and immediately shot.

Total repression had come, not just to Haute-Savoie, but to the hamlets and camps of yet another so-called impenetrable fortress: the proud, grim massif of the Vercors in the eastern Alps.

It has been said that no army corps of engineers could have designed and built a better redoubt for hit-and-run guerillas than God had done in this section of the Alps.

With its sheer walls thousands of feet tall, it dominated the plain of the Rhône and Isère rivers like some vast cathedral glimpsed in a distorted dream. On the map it resembles a huge arrowhead thirty miles long by twenty feet wide. Its limestone had proved more pliable than granite could ever be; the bitter weather had combed it into gorges and deep grottoes, locking it from the rest of France within rugged mountain peaks.

Such a position had hitherto discouraged the Germans, providing welcome cover for the camps of the maquisards. True, there had been punitive raids by enemy columns; villages and houses had been burnt following arrests. But the maquis had behaved strictly according to the textbook rules of guerilla warfare: lightning retaliation followed by withdrawal into the welcome protection of the Vercors passes.

Then came June 1944. The Allied armies were on the coast of Normandy, beginning the slow, agonising push to the frontiers of the Reich. No longer was the role of the resistance to be seen as defensive. The BBC, acting at the behest of General de Gaulle and the French National Committee in Algiers, issued the rallying call: the French underground was to rise and do battle.

But after a series of clashes which left neither side beaten, the Germans launched an attack of ruthless brilliance at the very heart of the Vercors.

The massif was alive with hope on 21 July. To the delighted ears of the maquisards came the roar of aircraft, from the south – the direction of Algiers, headquarters of the French government-in-exile. It seemed too good to be true: the long lines of gliders, forty in all, with airborne troops swooping down from the sky, released by the bombers who had towed them in. Liberation was in the skies!

Up went the ecstatic cry: 'It's the Yanks! It's the Yanks!'

But the black crosses on the wings had the immediate effect of turning the reaction to one of sheer panic: 'It's the Boche!'

And it was. In waves they came, troop-filled gliders in tow, supported by the Fokker-Wolfes and the Dorniers which streaked and roared ahead of the transports, unleashing their bombs and peppering everything with machine-gun fire.

206

The maquisards leapt too late to their machine-guns. One German glider was blasted out of the skies, but most of them were on the ground, their crews setting up heavy machine-guns on the airstrip. The SS fanned out, seizing the village of Vassieux and the neighbouring villages of Mure and Château.

The Germans took their time over leaving Vassieux; they had plenty to do there. Those few who survived had appalling stories to tell when it was all over. People were burnt alive in their homes. The SS perfected its own technique of hanging: two victims were suspended by the neck from opposite ends of the same rope, which was thrown over the branch of a tree. Only one of the victims could touch the ground with the tips of his toes. The two seesawed. Death for each was postponed as one man managed to get his toes to the ground. Eventually, the pressure on the neck would become unbearable and both victims too exhausted to survive.

More than 200 people, many of them elderly peasants, were slaughtered indiscriminately. Corpses were found castrated, breasts cut off, tongues removed. For hostages, it was not merely a question of swift death by firing squad: they were tortured first and then butchered. Death, when it came to maimed and broken men, was by machine-gun fire in public squares.

Members of the maquis were, in one sense, luckier than the civilian population. It was not so easy to pin them down. They were forced to keep moving, to seek the protection of countryside they knew well. Nevertheless, the Germans thoroughly and systematically combed out each plateau.

The maquis was forced to break off the fight and run for high ground in the fir forests, where the Germans, in ignorance of the terrain, did not dare follow. There they stayed until they heard the news of the landing of the French Army in the south and its march up the Route Napoléon towards Grenoble.

Only then could the heroic survivors of the Vercors join with their comrades in the campaigns of liberation.

24

Throughout the four years of Nazi occupation, the city of Paris endured its daily humiliation.

From the fall of Paris on 14 June 1940 to the day of its liberation, 3 August 1944, a Nazi band and a battalion of Wehrmacht circled the Arc de Triomphe. At the stroke of noon, the procession made its way down the Champs Élysée to the Place de la Concorde. Like some massive metronome, their footfalls tolled out to Paris and to all France the passage of another day of occupation. It began on the stroke of the drum major's baton, followed with heavy predictability by *Deutschland, Deutschland ueber Alles* and *Preussens Glorie* (Prussian Glory).

The symbols of oppression were everywhere; from the top of the Eiffel Tower flew the black hooked-cross banner of the swastika. Anyone who wanted to be reminded of the national flag of France had to visit the army museum in Les Invalides, where the banned tricolour was locked behind a glass case.

Even the most compliant of Parisians could not escape the black, white and red sentry boxes barring their way in the rue de Rivoli, around the Place de la Concorde in front of the Palais du Luxembourg.

In the Place de l'Opéra were black-lettered signs indicating such destinations as MILITAERBEFEHLHABER IN FRANKREICH, GENERAL DER LUFTWAFFE and HAUPTVERKEHRSDIREKTION PARIS.

It was true that the ration of each Parisian was two eggs, 3.2 ounces of cooking oil and 2 ounces of margarine. It was equally true that wine was in short supply, and at the pavement cafés it was only possible to get ersatz coffee made from acorns and chickpeas. Gas and electricity as public services might be only a memory, but the weather was good that final August of occupation and Edith Piaf was singing at the Moulin Rouge.

Above all, Paris had survived intact. While other cities had been torn apart, some divine providence had spared Notre Dame, Sainte Chapelle, the Louvre and Sacré Coeur.

But for how long?

Hundreds of miles away, deep within the gloomy drooping pine forests of Rastenburg in East Prussia, Adolf Hitler dreamt of death and destruction. From his FHQ (*Fuehrerhauptquartier*), the German dictator proclaimed his determination to reduce Paris to such a shambles that neither Gaullist nor Communist forces would stand to gain from liberation.

Hitler needed an able and ruthless lieutenant to implement his plans: he summoned to Rastenburg Generalmajor Dietrich von Choltitz, an officer from the western front with promising credentials. In the words of an OKW superior, Choltitz had 'never questioned an order, no matter how harsh'. Plainly he was his Fuehrer's man.

His track record boded ill for Paris. In May 1940, he had been one of those who had ordered the bombing of Rotterdam. At the siege of Sevastopol in the Crimea he had won promotion to general at the cost of an arm wound and devastating losses. But he had taken the city and annihilated it. In the retreat from the Russian front he had left behind only scorched earth. He was well aware of his tough reputation, saying: 'It is my lot to defend the rear of the German army. And each time I am ordered to destroy each city as I leave it.'

As might be expected, there were few things capable of shocking this dedicated soldier with the bearing of a provincial burgomaster; Hitler in August 1944 was the exception.

The Fuehrer, badly rattled by the nearly successful 20 July assassination plot in which a bomb had been placed inside his headquarters, launched into a tirade. He raged: 'Since the twentieth of July, Herr General, dozens of generals – yes, dozens – have bounced at the end of a rope because they wanted to prevent me, Adolf Hitler, from continuing my work.'

Hitler was now in a state of feverish excitement, saliva running from his mouth. Choltitz said: 'He was trembling all over and the desk on which he was leaning shook. He was bathed in perspiration and became more agitated.'

After what seemed an age, Hitler calmed down. He said to Choltitz: 'Now you're going to Paris. That city must be utterly destroyed. On the departure of the Wehrmacht, nothing must be left standing, no church, no artistic monument.'

A fresh thought seemed to strike Hitler. With a twisted grin he added: 'Even the water supply must be cut off so that the ruined city may be prey to epidemics.'

Choltitz stared in horror. Here were not the orders of a military commander but all the pent-up resentment of a raving maniac.

Nevertheless, Generalmajor Dietrich von Choltitz went to Paris.

A light wind swept across the Tuileries Gardens, whipping up the skirts of a pretty girl cyclist. The two men on the balcony of the Hôtel Meurice stared appreciatively at the exposed legs and thighs before the girl was lost to view.

The German turned to his mustachioed companion and said with deliberate casualness: 'It would be a pity to kill the pretty girls of Paris; and destroy their city.'

Raoul Nordling had been the Swedish consul-general in Paris for eighteen years; as a representative of a neutral country, he had the supreme advantage of having feet in both German and Allied camps. It was, he was the first to admit, a bizarre posture. But Paris was a bizarre place in these days.

Choltitz's remark gave the Swede a surge of hope. It

seemed to indicate that the German had not finally made up his mind to implement the appalling order of his Fuehrer. But Nordling was also only too well aware that the Commander of *Gross Paris* was being dangerously provoked.

On the grey, damp Saturday morning of 19 August, the Gaullist faction in the Paris Police Committee of Liberation had taken control of the prefecture. Paris was clearly in a mutinous mood; on the day before, there had been a call for a general uprising. And now, with the seizing of the prefecture, it had begun.

Fifty feet below the streets of the city, a vast air raid shelter, sealed off with steel doors and supplied with air from its own conditioning plant, served as the headquarters of the French Forces of the Interior, now the official name of the resistance movement.

Here were ten miles of underground corridors, built to give access to the water mains connecting with various parts of the city. The choice had proved ideal because only those few Germans whose job it was to supervise the water system even knew the place existed. Those who did had left Paris just before the uprising, leaving a young French colonel and his staff in undisputed possession. Throughout the ensuing battle, messengers made their way along the labyrinth of corridors, able to surface as far away as the Bois de Boulogne, where they could slip into cafés, shops and innocuous office blocks – the nerve centres of the various groups.

The ordinary Parisian had remained largely unaware of what was happening until he left home for work and encountered the traffic. It had gone haywire. Paris was one long traffic jam, and the situation got steadily worse during the day. There were no police to control it. German vehicles, many of them fleeing what they sensed was a capital threatened by invasion, were unable to move.

The organisers of the police strike let four days go by. Then three thousand of them, decked out in civilian clothes, returned to the prefecture. They battered on the gates, stormed the building and installed a new prefect. A few minutes later, from the flagstaff of the building fluttered the first tricolour from a public building in the capital for four years.

But as it turned out, the occupation of the prefecture did not go as smoothly as the insurrectionists had expected. Amid the mêlée, a German truck exploded when hit by an incendiary. German soldiers running for cover were struck by police marksmen. But there was no victory here; an explosive shell from a tank hit the iron gates of the prefecture and blew them open. A young law student, Edgar Pisani, who had been trying to work the switchboard, was lifted out of his chair and flung into the opposite corner of the room.

A German Tiger tank lumbered into the prefecture courtyard. The police defenders, crouching behind sandbags, were no match for such armour – and they knew it.

There was mass panic, with the defenders dashing in terror for the entrance to the metro station inside the prefecture.

One man now seized the initiative. Police Sergeant Armand Fournet, appalled at the sudden rush to escape, ran to the station entrance and blocked it. He waved a pistol and shouted: 'I'll shoot any man who tries to pass me. We must stand together, fight together. It is our only hope of survival.'

Incredibly, the panic-stricken mob halted. Fournet later recorded that he saw a collective look of shame; the men turned back to the courtyard and their posts.

Still the Germans kept up their fierce tank barrage. Policemen on the roof tossed Molotov cocktails towards the tanks – these comprised bottles containing sulphuric acid and several flasks of potassium chlorate.

Choltitz, on his hotel balcony, heard the bursts of gunfire. In a sudden fury, he vowed: 'I'll get them out of their prefecture. I'll bomb them out of it.'

Nordling, still at the commander's side, asked quietly:

'Do you realise what that means? Your near misses will fall on Notre Dame and Sainte Chapelle!'

Choltitz shrugged: 'What alternative do I have?'

The Swede realized that the present insurrection, if it continued, could sound the death knell of Paris, the city where he had spent most of his adult life and which he deeply loved. Already he had done his bit for the Allied cause, against all the rules of Swedish neutrality. He had successfully negotiated with Choltitz for the release of more than four thousand political prisoners.

Now he felt that he must do more: he would plead for the very life of Paris itself. He forthwith suggested a temporary ceasefire for the removal of the dead and wounded.

At first, the German greeted the idea with incredulity. The very suggestion of a ceasefire was a novelty; no such thing had been suggested to him before. This was not the way that the vanquished should talk to a victor; in Choltitz's book there should be total surrender.

A moment's reflection, however, showed him that a truce would release a number of troops tied down in a single action. Furthermore, once an attack was carried out on the prefecture, there could be no turning back.

Nordling waited anxiously for Choltitz to decide; he knew that the defenders of the prefecture could not hold out much longer. His hope was that a temporary ceasefire might ultimately be extended. He was playing desperately for time.

At last, the fat little general, his eyes slits of tiredness, turned to Nordling and said: 'Very well. If it can be shown for just one hour that the FFI officers can control their men, I will accept a temporary truce.'

A mere two hours after giving his undertaking to Nordling, the commander of *Gross Paris* received a terse order from Hitler: 'Prepare the Seine bridges for destruction. Paris must not fall in the hands of the enemy except as a field of ruins.'

It was an insane, purposeless order. Nothing could stop

the advance of the American and French forces. Besides, Choltitz needed the bridges for troop movements within the city. He decided to ignore the order.

But the calling of a ceasefire had taken no account of internal political ambitions. The Communists, thirsting for insurrection and determination to have Paris as their prize, refused to observe any truce.

For Breton seaman's son Henri Tanguy – cover name 'Colonel Rol' – it seemed the fulfilment of a dream. For sixteen years he had been a dedicated Communist, a thorn in the flesh of prewar French governments, and had been ejected frequently from factories for trade union and industrial agitation. He had fought in Spain; his cover name was that of a comrade fighting the forces of General Franco. Now Rol-Tanguy was longing to challenge the Gaullist faction head on.

At first, there were mere fissures in the seemingly solid rockface of the ceasefire. Then the fissures became cracks and the whole structure burst open.

Violence broke out all over Paris.

When it was spent, those involved recalled isolated incidents of horror amid the general carnage. Four truckloads of German troops were ambushed and then set alight with Molotov cocktails. The men staggered screaming through the streets, which soon reeked with the sourness of burnt flesh. Communist resistant André Tollet, who was among those who commandeered the Hôtel de Ville, recorded:

Four German tanks rumbled into the square and started shelling the building.

I saw a young woman, a bottle in her hand, run fearlessly up to the tanks and smash against the side. She ran away as the flames shot up but a German bullet sliced into her and she fell. But she had caused the other tanks to turn tail. She had saved the Hôtel de Ville.

General Jacques-Philippe de Hautecloque was a dour, lean individual whom General de Gaulle had named as trainer and commander of an armoured division for the liberation of Paris. The man who called himself General Leclerc – the pseudonym was adopted to protect the family he had left behind at the time of France's surrender – was in charge of 16,000 men with 2,000 vehicles. All he needed was the signal to advance on the capital.

The Allies were split on the wisdom of sending large forces to liberate Paris at all. General Dwight D. Eisenhower, as Supreme Commander, told de Gaulle: 'I plan to pinch off Paris and let her hang there for future plucking.' Even blunter was Lieutenant-General George S. Patton, who declared: 'They started their goddamned insurrection. Now let them finish it.' Various representations from Paris reached the ears of the Allies: all the signs were that the Germans would not delay indefinitely their wholesale retaliation against the French capital. Eventually, Eisenhower relented: the French would go in.

Around dusk on Wednesday 23 August, Leclerc leaped from an aircraft on a field at Argentan, crying: *'Mouvement immédiat sur Paris!'* And at dawn the triumphant progress of the French 2nd Armoured Division began, as it roared out of its bivouac near Ecouché south of Argentan. A violent rainstorm lashed at the wild, winding country roads; the men, volunteers from every corner of the French Empire, had only one thought. They wanted to be in the French capital, which most of them – drawn from Indochina, Senegal, Tunisia, Morocco, French Equatorial and Central Africa – had never seen. Ahead of them was a bloody slog, in which the American-made Sherman tanks of 2nd Armoured were harried by Tiger tanks.

Paris prepared to celebrate. Its bells had been silent for the four long years of occupation. But now they rang out with the sheer joy of anticipated freedom. The first to peal was the south tower of Notre Dame, followed by Sacré Coeur in Montmartre. And then it seemed as if the whole of Paris was one vast chime.

In the Hôtel Meurice, at a candlelit dinner table,

Generalmajor Choltitz paused for a moment, shrugged, and went on with his meal.

One man in Paris, however, was deaf to church bells and celebration. The news that General Leclerc was on the way acted as a spur to Rol-Tanguy. He knew that time was running desperately short; if his Communist FFI was to be granted any role at all in the liberation, then he would have to move fast. General de Gaulle was also bound to make a grand entrance from his billet at the magnificent Château de Rambouillet. Rol-Tanguy installed himself in the Hôtel de Ville, symbol of Paris's political sovereignty. He reasoned that this was where de Gaulle would surely come. Rol-Tanguy was prepared to greet him as an heroic 'guest' but there would be no deference to him as leader or liberator.

Political manoeuvring aside, France was still at war and there was fighting ahead. The Germans were holding out at the Buttes-Chaumont tunnel, where a number of trains were parked, and the Prince-Eugene barracks of the Wehrmacht on the Place de la République. FFI units threw in everything they had, watching the dwindling of their meagre supplies of ammunition. The German guards at the Buttes-Chaumont were rapidly overcome; more than 125 prisoners were seized, along with arms and munitions.

Leclerc sent one column of men to Versailles, with orders to strike for the northwestern gate, the Porte de Sèvres. This column, in fact, was the smallest, but Leclerc was determined it would make the greatest noise and fool the Germans into assuming that Versailles constituted the main thrust.

The second column was then despatched some five miles to the southeast through the valley of the Chevreuse, entering Paris by Porte de Vanves. As for the main thrust, which he himself would use for his main entry into Paris, that would be entrusted to Colonel Pierre Billote, who would slip south, through Longjumeau and Fresnes, and break into Paris through the southern gateway of the Porte d'Orleans.

Late on the night of the twenty-fourth, the Communists of the FFI fought on desperately in their own bid to liberate the capital. But it was too late. Tough, red-headed tank commander Raymond Dronne swept across the city limits and made history as the first French soldier to come home to Paris.

It was a Paris, moreover, which had gone delirious with joy. A vast tide of humanity engulfed armoured vehicles inscribed with the Cross of Lorraine. Dronne was a handsome man, and he was looking forward to seeing his first Paris girls. As it turned out, there were so many seeking to embrace him, crush him and stroke his uniform that at the end of the day he could remember only one clearly: a heavy girl wearing the red skirt and black bodice of Alsace who had jumped on his jeep and smashed the glass of his lowered windscreen.

Generalmajor Choltitz was well aware that he was going down to defeat. But, he reasoned, any capitulation might as well be carried out in style. He made sure that his uniform was freshly pressed and his boots highly polished. He decided to have a last dinner in the Hôtel Meurice. By tomorrow, he might be dead; if life entailed surrendering to the FFI, to terrorists, then it was probably better so.

As for General de Gaulle, his political antenna was twitching vigorously. He was far too tried a hand to fall in with Rol-Tanguy's ploy and go to the Hôtel de Ville, where he was only too well aware that he would be received as a 'guest'.

He was no one's guest. He was the President of the Provisional Government of the Republic. Moreover, it was his tanks which had liberated Paris.

At the Gare Montparnasse, de Gaulle received the surrender document which Leclerc had previously signed with Choltitz. De Gaulle blazed with anger when he saw Rol-Tanguy's signature; the Communist had insisted on adding his name. From Gare Montparnasse, de Gaulle then drove to his old office at the Ministry of War, which he had left in 1940.

But neither de Gaulle nor the forces of Leclerc had finished with the Germans. By the time it was all over, a further 127 French – soldiers and civilians – were to die. The casualties for the Liberation of Paris amounted to 901 FFI and 582 civilians. A total of 2,788 Germans died.

It was the civilians who suffered most as a suicide squad of Germans clashed with liberators storming the Foreign Office. A volley of gunfire drove back the French. Then heavy fighting erupted around the back entrance to the building. The tanks were in the front line now, shelling the German positions and setting fire to the ministry. Flames from one of Leclerc's tanks licked into the crowd. Many bystanders were killed before the Germans were wiped out.

The victorious troops broke into Gestapo headquarters at the Hotel Majestic in the Étoile. After that, they were watched by a delirious crowd, who at long last saw the hated swastika torn from the Arc de Triomphe and replaced by the flag of France. Shortly after noon, the tricolour flew from the Eiffel Tower.

It was not a tricolour to satisfy the stickler for accuracy. It was fashioned from three ancient bed sheets stuck together. One was dyed pink, one a decidedly pallid blue, and the third was a washy grey.

But it was a tricolour, nonetheless. And at noon on 25 August 1944, that was all that mattered.

Earlier, Generalmajor Choltitz, at his desk at the Meurice, had long given up marking the large map of Paris with red crosses to show the penetration of Leclerc's forces. Soon, he reflected ruefully, he would be running out of pencil. It would be more pleasant to have one last glass of wine with his officers.

That done, he retired to a small room in the hotel and waited.

A few hours later, the Commander of *Gross Paris* faced Lieutenant Henri Karcher of the army of General de Gaulle. For such an historic event, the encounter was curiously banal. Karcher merely took Choltitz's gun as the symbol of his surrender, saying: 'Follow me!'

When Choltitz arrived at the prefecture as a prisoner, the close-shaven, well-scrubbed and perfectly uniformed German general stood to attention before a scruffy, unshaven Frenchman with mud-caked American GI boots and a travel-stained uniform. For a moment, it looked as if General Leclerc was the vanquished and Choltitz the victor.

The two men got down to discussing the surrender document, but their deliberations were interrupted by an angry Rol-Tanguy demanding admittance to watch the signing of the surrender of the city he had defended for six days. An embarrassed Leclerc agreed.

General Charles de Gaulle, who had left Paris in June 1940 as an obscure brigadier general, returned a hero on the afternoon of 25 August. He insisted on riding through the city, contemptuously defying snipers and stray bullets in an open French-made Hotchkiss car. Nothing would have induced him to have paraded in an American jeep.

The square on the Boulevard Montparnasse was alive with Parisians. To the chorus of 'De Gaulle! De Gaulle!' he stretched out his arms high and wide in a huge V-sign.

Behind the scenes, however, things were less happy. Although they understood the reasons for it, a number of de Gaulle's followers were uneasy over his refusal to go to the Hôtel de Ville. His hatred of Rol-Tanguy, it was felt, could be construed as a direct boycott of the resistance and all it stood for. Such a slap in the face would make the future governing of France much harder. In the end, de Gaulle allowed himself to be persuaded.

Most Parisians remained unaware of all this. In any case, even if they had known, it is doubtful they would have cared. On the streets and boulevards, they were too busy prancing about in German helmets. Members of General Leclerc's forces had their faces stained scarlet with lipstick.

At the Hôtel de Ville, de Gaulle was asked if he would go out on the balcony and proclaim the Republic. His response was in itself guaranteed to render his legend immortal.

There was an icy silence. Then in tones shot full with contempt, de Gaulle snapped: 'The Republic has never ceased to exist!'

Thousands were singing and embracing, sharing the joy of liberation with those who had made it possible. These experiences made up the memories that Parisians were to cherish down the years. The most sublime moment of all was when, dark and miserable for four long years of cruel repression, Paris suddenly lit up.

Arc lights threw the Eiffel Tower into sharp relief. The Palais de Chaillot, Les Invalides, Notre Dame, all suddenly leapt miraculously out of the night. The Sacré Coeur, above Montmartre, became a giant, shining translucent wedding cake. Those inside Notre Dame would for years recall the voice of de Gaulle intoning every verse of the Magnificat.

But Paris was also cruel and bitter and brimming with revenge. There was the woman, her face suffused with hatred, who spat full in the face of Generalmajor Choltitz with the scream of *Bâtard!* On the Place de Chatelet, French captors, forced their prisoners to witness the sight of young girls, their head shaved and their breasts bare, sporting signs reading: 'I WHORED FOR THE GERMANS'.

In the St-Antoine hospital, a wounded and unconscious German was slowly strangled, his Knight's Cross ripped from his neck. The few remaining snipers in the city who were caught never reached the POW cages: the crowd beat them to death. A special hatred was reserved for members of Choltitz's staff on their way to captivity. All along their path they faced a jeering, raging mob who tore the uniforms off their backs, clubbing and kicking them.

Old habits die hard. In the restaurants and hotels, suddenly doing roaring business, harassed waiters could perhaps be forgiven for still adding the mandatory Vichy sales tax to their bills. Indignantly, diners deducted the amount.

One man remained largely unmoved by the mood of celebration in Paris. General Charles de Gaulle muttered to a colleague: 'The struggle for the rest of France is just beginning.'

And not just for France. Far to the north in the Netherlands, resistance steadily became even more bitter.

Here tragedy was just beginning.

25

Throughout the years of Nazi oppression in the Netherlands, Hanns Albin Rauter exercised his awesome powers from the barrel of a gun.

It was not just that he was Generalkommissar; after all, there were four of those in the country. He was something infinitely more imposing: Generalkommissar fuer des Sicherheitswesen (Commissioner General for Public Safety).

Even this was not the end of the parade of titles; there was, of course, the even more powerful Hoehere SS und Polizeifuehrer Nordwest (Higher SS and Police Leader).

As such, Rauter spelt terror throughout the Netherlands. His rule, as cruel and merciless as his chief, Heinrich Himmler, could have wished, reached the very pinnacle of power in 1944 as the spectre of defeat for Nazi Germany rose menacingly after D-Day.

Rauter was by then no longer simply a policeman but chief executioner of the Netherlands, with squads of killers on permanent standby. Captured resistance workers were immediately put up against the wall. There were no fancy irrelevancies such as trials; dissidents were termed *Todeskandidaten* (death candidates), and there was no limit to the numbers that could be despatched summarily.

Furthermore, their executions took place in public; bodies were left rotting by the roadside. By late summer 1944, Rauter had fully earned the nickname 'Hangman of the Netherlands'.

He doubtless relished the title, but by that stage of the war he also had his worries. The allied armies were racing towards the Dutch border. The Netherlands would become once again a major theatre of war; it needed troops to defend it, not policemen.

His parade of ranks and titles came to the rescue. By June 1944, Rauter had already been appointed to the military rank of General der Waffen-SS, enabling him to report to Generalfeldmarschall Walther Model, commander of Army Group B, at his Headquarters at Oosterbeek. Rauter still controlled a number of Waffen-SS units and was determined to put them to good use.

The need was pressing; the Allies had landed at Arnhem. Rauter speedily left the Hague, and drove to a new headquarters at Apeldoorn, lying to the northeast. There was no question where the bulk of his forces should go; they were forthwith ordered to Arnhem, which lay to the south east of Apeldoorn. The Germans sustained heavy losses against British airborne troops, but after ten days of savage fighting the Allies withdrew. In the overall scheme of the war, it was a mere setback; but Rauter greeted it ecstatically as a key victory.

In terms of career prestige, the performance of his forces at Arnhem had done him nothing but good. Indeed, Kampfgruppe Rauter was raised to the status of a provisional corps and assigned a sector of the front along the Rhine and Waal rivers from Emmerich, just inside Germany, to Tiel, in the Netherlands, west of Arnhem.

In terms of numbers, Rauter possessed formidable military muscle. He tended it with consummate devotion, driving out daily to visit forward posts and inspect defences. His new responsibilities made him disenchanted with his old police work. However, Arthur Seyss-Inquart was still a figure with whom to reckon, and past responsibilities could not be disregarded. The Reichskommissar had moved to his own headquarters closer to the Fatherland and was now at Apeldoorn; he expected Rauter to drive there for a conference every Wednesday morning. The journey was made by Rauter from Corps Headquarters at Didam, a village ten miles east of Arnhem.

It was a routine that the Higher SS and Police Leader

followed faithfully. Then on Tuesday 4 March 1945, he changed his timetable.

That week, he was faced with two conferences at Apeldoorn. He was required at 25th Army headquarters as well as calling on Seyss-Inquart. He decided to allow himself rather more time and start out on Tuesday evening, breaking the journey at his usual hotel.

Orders were given to his driver to have the car ready for 10 p.m. It seemed an unimportant change of schedule. But for Hanns Rauter the consequences were to be dramatic.

The Netherlands had evolved its own form of maquis warfare; by September 1944 this meant the activities of the unified Dutch resistance under the banner of *Binnenlandse Strijdkrachten* (Dutch Interior Forces) under the overall command of Prince Bernhard. One of the areas in which it operated was District 6, comprising the Veluwe, an undulating forest region with extensive heathlands and large wooded tracks.

And at the core of the district, in the town of Apeldoorn, was a cell which, for resistance resources, was not at all badly served. The GC-Groep, favoured for the more risky operations, could boast a healthy supply of Sten guns, pistols and grenades.

GC-Groep had something else fiercely envied by other resistants – some genuine SS uniforms. It was generally agreed by jealous rivals that, when it came to the element of surprise, the GC-Groep had an unfair advantage.

Every group had its hero and District 6 proved no exception. Geert Gosens was a high-spirited young mechanic with, by common consent, rather more than his fair share of luck. There was the time when a posse of SD swooped on his house, where he had been hiding transport used by the resistance.

Gosens, who at the time of the raid had been asleep on the first floor, clambered to safety over the roof, clad only in underpants. The experience increased his adrenalin: the next day he came back with his Sten and opened fire on the Germans who were in the act of removing vehicles from the garage. He had the satisfaction of flattening the tyres and making good his escape yet again. Unfortunately, the vehicles were not recaptured.

The transport problem was acute for the resistance. On Tuesday 6 March, news reached BS that a single Wehrmacht truck was due to collect a sizeable quantity of pork for distribution to the Wehrmacht. It was to be picked up from a butcher in the nearby village of Epe the following morning.

The Apeldoorn BS Sabotage Commander forthwith instructed Gosens and his team to seize the meat.

For Gosens, the challenge was irresistible; the method he favoured conformed with everyone's popular idea of the model resistant.

Gosens reasoned that, since the group already possessed German uniforms, the problem was halfway solved. All that remained was to dress up the team and drive up in a truck before the genuine Germans were due and seize the meat.

That, of course, left the question: where was the right sort of truck to be found? To all questioners, Gosens shrugged with a grin: 'Steal it, of course.'

He set about picking a small team with the necessary loyalty and experience. The most important matter to be decided was where the ambush should happen. On the advice of one of the resistants, Wim Kok, in normal life a member of the Dutch Mounted Police, Gosens opted for the road to Arnhem.

It had the big attraction of being quiet and sparsely populated; it ran through woods offering ample cover. In addition, the team had a nearby campsite bolt hole. Their courage was fuelled by the fact that their resistance had previously ambushed and fired a German car, there-after taking the occupants prisoner. Success of that kind was apt to be infectious; there was general agreement that it was well worth trying again.

Shortly before 10 a.m. on the chosen day, the team set off on bicycles for the Arnhem road. Except for Kok, who elected to wear his everyday police uniform, the men were dressed as Germans. Sep Koettinger, an Austrian member of the Waffen-SS who had deserted to the Dutch, masqueraded as an SS-Oberscharfuehrer (Quartermaster Sergeant), while Gosens and his fellow Dutchman Henk de Weert were both dressed in the uniform of Rottenfuehrers (corporals). The other two, Dutchman Karel Pruis and another turncoat Austrian, Herman Kempfer, appeared to be SS private soldiers. All bristled with Stens except Gosens, who was content with his Walther pistol.

Concealed by a grass verge just beyond an inn called De Woeste Hoeve, the men lay in wait. Then out of the darkness came the sound of a heavy vehicle coming from the direction of Arnhem. The party climbed out of its ditch. Each man had his allotted task. Koettinger switched on his torch.

Seated next to the driver of the grey six-cylinder BMW convertible, Hanns Rauter tensed as he peered ahead, catching the flash of a white light and, in the glare of his own black-out shielded headlamps, two uniformed men signalled the car to halt.

Rauter's long stint as police chief had instilled in him a strong sense of suspicion and self-preservation. What was this? Only a short while ago he had decreed that nowhere in the Netherlands, at any time of day or night, were patrols to halt traffic in open country. Such patrols were instructed to operate only in built-up areas or on the outskirts of towns and villages.

Whatever was ahead, Rauter did not care for it. As he reached for his machine-gun, he yelled: '*Achtung*! . . . be ready . . . probably terrorists!'

Rauter's driver was ordered to plough on. To his orderly, Oberleutnant Exner, who toted a sub-machine-gun, Rauter barked:

227

'Defend the rear!'

It was then that the driver, through inexperience, committed a major blunder: he applied his brakes. As the car slowed, Rauter found himself looking directly into the eyes of one of the resistants and shouting: 'What's wrong, man? Don't you know who we are?'

Gosens realised the truth: not only had they all failed in their original plan to stop a lorry but had exposed themselves to some top Nazi brass.

Gosens pulled the trigger: Rauter slumped with the impact of the first blast. As if on some prearranged cue, De Weert and Pruis let loose with their Stens. For the next few seconds, the bullets raked the BMW in merciless fire. Oberleutnant Exner, facing rearwards with his weapon, died instantly. A bullet sliced into the driver's right ear and he slumped forward, dead. Rauter, himself bleeding profusely, took the weight of the dead driver, whose hand still clasped the hand-brake.

Through extraordinary good luck, Hanns Rauter was not dead. The first bullets, which had torn the car's windscreen apart, had smashed through the fingers of his right hand and sliced through the jawbone and through one of his lungs. In addition, a bullet from the rear had penetrated through the neck vertebrae; his body had slumped forward into the windscreen.

Rauter, struggling through the haze of unspeakable pain, managed to shove his dead driver aside and pull himself up by the windscreen frame. His only reward was an additional bullet through his left armpit and another which grazed his left arm.

A heavy curtain of silence descended on the stretch of road, fractured by the macabre horror of a death rattle from one of the dying. Then there was another sound: some sort of vehicle was approaching from the direction of Arnhem. The threat to the BS men was appalling: the magazines of their Stens were empty and there could be no question of pushing the BMW out of sight. The only course was to grab the bicycles and hide in the ditch on the west side of the road.

The Wehrmacht truck pulled up next to the bullet-ridden car. For a few agonising seconds, the hidden men heard its engine running. Then a door was slammed and the vehicle rumbled off at speed towards Apeldoorn.

The resistance group waited a few minutes before gingerly venturing out and approaching the BMW. The batteries of their torches were getting weak and they could see little. When they heard the sound of another car approaching, it seemed good sense to withdraw to that secret campsite a few miles to the east.

As for Rauter, he lay helpless with his injuries until around 6 a.m. Then he was discovered by troops with horse-drawn transport on the way to some training grounds. They wasted no time, storming into De Woeste Hoeve and commandeering the telephone in a desperate bid to reach the German authorities at Apeldoorn. Before long, an ambulance was streaking towards De Woeste Hoeve. Even though he had lost an enormous amount of blood and was desperately frozen with cold, Rauter, who still had some secret documentation with him, managed to hand it over before he was rushed to hospital for a life-saving blood transfusion.

The eighteen miles between Apeldoorn and Arnhem forthwith became the exclusive territory of the Sicherheitsdienst.

The sinister umbrella of the Nazi party, enveloping the all-powerful Gestapo, speedily despatched a two-man team to the area of the shooting, where the BMW remained with its two corpses.

The SD men were characteristically thorough; they made plaster moulds of all tyre tracks, mustered Dutch police representatives and ordered one of their photographers to record the aftermath of the incident as exhaustively as he could. The SD team was no less industrious when it came to investigating the possible role of the adjacent De Woeste Hoeve.

An incident room was established at the inn; inhabitants and neighbours were grilled mercilessly. All, predictably, professed total ignorance of events. Fortunately for them, they were allowed to go free. The SD apparatus, doubtless feeling the hot breath of Heinrich Himmler on its neck, had no time at that stage for idle acts of revenge: the actual would-be assassins of Generalkommissar Hanns Albin Rauter were considered the biggest game.

Despite the luck of those at the inn, what followed constituted the toughest reprisals of the entire occupation of the Netherlands – and some of the worst war crimes committed during the Nazi occupation of the west.

With Rauter out of action, it was inevitable that another leading member of the SD would take centre stage. The role fell on one of Himmler's keenest and most conscientious lieutenants. SS-Brigadefuehrer Dr Eberhardt Schoengarth, Rauter's deputy, set about his mission of revenge with relish.

Schoengarth had a meeting with Seyss-Inquart and came straight to the point: an attack on the highest official of the Netherlands called for 'the severest punishment'. Schoengarth was the man of the hour and he was determined to make the most of it. Himmler, he declared, had instructed him to shoot 500 prominent citizens taken as hostages.

Seyss-Inquart applauded the thinking of the SS man; in practice, he was in no position to protest. Schoengarth was now free to go shopping for hostages.

The various SD chiefs in the Netherlands were instructed to produce fodder for the firing squads. Some thirty *Todeskandidaten* in The Hague formed the nucleus of victims: it was far from being enough for Schoengarth, who declared: 'It doesn't matter if they are *Todeskandidaten* or not. Looters or curfew-breakers will do.'

De Woeste Hoeve was chosen as the site for many of the executions. A 150-strong team of Ordnungspolizei lined up prisoners in five groups of 20 and one of 16. Within half an hour, a long line of men lay by the side of the road. Next to the bodies a notice was set up: 'This is what we do with terrorists and saboteurs.'

Gosens and the other saboteurs who hid out and survived the purges learnt of these and other executions with horror; none had envisaged retaliation on so savage a scale. All they could do was hold up in their campsite fastness and wait for the wave of killings to cease. A total of 263 people were shot in reprisal for what the Germans still thought of as a planned assassination bid.

But any satisfaction the Germans may have felt for their acts of revenge was short-lived. For the end of the Nazi rule in the Netherlands was fast approaching.

On an evening in the summer, the Nationaal-Socialistische Beweging leader Anton Mussert had chaired a meeting of his chief functionaries at NSB headquarters in Utrecht. A bare two months earlier, after D-Day, Mussert had sworn that he would never be displaced: moreover, he had refused to prepare a contingency evacuation scheme for the wives and children of his members.

There had, however, been rapid progress by the Allies, since the British 21st Army Group had taken no time off to celebrate the liberation of Paris, but had steamrollered on to liberate northwestern France and by 4 September had taken Antwerp. Now Mussert, shorn of much of his arrogance, was at last prepared to discuss the very real possibility of evacuating women and children to Germany.

It was a reasonably calm gathering of Mussert supporters. The calm did not last long. False rumours had reached the Netherlands that the Allies were at Breda: well north of the Belgium border and on a direct line to Rotterdam. It was enough to throw thousands of NSB members into panic. On 5 September, which the Dutch were later to dub 'Mad Tuesday', Mussert supporters fled their homes, leaving everything behind. Their leaders, with the exception of Mussert, were the first to go; NSB mayors left their posts and Nazi officials fled from their uncleared desks. Yesterday's fanatical idealists, who had promised to fight to the last man, melted away. And so, incidentally, did scores of Germans. The wife of the Reichskommissar, Gertrud Seyss-Inquart, left the Hague for Salzburg in Austria with five suitcases.

In fact, it was not until 4 May 1945 that the Netherlands and Denmark were surrendered unconditionally to Field Marshal Sir Bernard Montgomery, five days before the final ratification in Berlin of Germany's unconditional surrender. In Hilversum, the radio repeated an endless warning: 'The Germans are still around', but it was largely ignored as total strangers talked, laughed and shook hands on the streets. Throughout the occupation the Germans had allowed only six stanzas of the Dutch national anthem, the 'Wilhelmus,' to be sung. Now the crowds chorused the anthem in full, with the forbidden first verse: 'Wilhelmus of Orange, I am of Dutch blood, true to the Fatherland until death.'

Southeast of Utrecht, General Johannes Blaskowitz, commanding German Army Group H in the west, surrendered his 120,000 men to the Canadian army. In Utrecht itself, the jubilant Dutch sprang aboard Allied armoured vehicles, while the resistance still grappled with snipers. The Prime Minister of the Netherlands, Professor Peter Gerbrandy, who was still in London, confirmed the signing of the capitulation, telling the Dutch people: 'The German Reich with its criminal elements . . . is beaten. Drink the cup of joy, but do not forget the suffering that is mixed in it.'

It was a needless plea; the memories of the suffering were only too great, and to this day the Dutch do not allow themselves to forget. Immediately after the liberation, a simple memorial was erected at De Woeste Hoeve to commemorate the victims of the reprisals of 8 March 1945. Those who had been executed were buried in a mass grave at the Heidehof General Cemetery at Ugchelen, southwest of Apeldoorn. Six weeks later, after the liberation, the bodies were exhumed for the gruesome task of identifying them from clothing and personal effects. A large number were interred at the National Cemetery of

Honour at Loenen, built by the Dutch War Graves Commission and inaugurated in 1949.

Perhaps the most telling reminder of all is a grim, stark statue of a man which stands on a plinth in a clearing at the end of a country road. Called 'Man before the firing squad', it is a reminder of the death of forty-nine inmates of Amersfoort concentration camp who had been included in the reprisals.

For the nation that grieved, the only balm was the machinery of justice which was now turned on the oppressors. Hanns Albin Rauter, still suffering from the effects of his injuries, came into the hands of the Dutch authorities to be tried for his four-and-a-half-year reign of terror. He protested to the court that he implored both Arthur Seyss-Inquart and Brigadefuehrer Schoengarth to refrain from reprisals following the assassination attempt. To the court it sounded either like a direct lie or a cowardly deathbed repentance. It made no difference. On 25 March 1949, he was executed.

Schoengarth, too, went to his death, as did Anton Mussert, arrested without a struggle by the resistance in Utrecht. After a trial, Mussert was shot by firing squad at Scheveningen, where so many resistance fighters had met their deaths.

But the German tenure in Holland had left a legacy; the purges of collaborators began.

Some countries salved their consciences by herding even their most minor traitors before firing squads; others escaped the net altogether.

In Belgium, it was generally agreed that Leon Degrelle possessed nothing less than the luck of the devil.

26

Faced with the collapse of all his dreams, Leon Degrelle had, nevertheless, remained intent on holding on to the last vestiges of power, not only within his own Rexist movement but as one of Heinrich Himmler's chosen within the elite field grey legions of the Waffen-SS.

In 1941, Degrelle joined a legion of Walloon volunteers to fight on the eastern front. Recruitment for the legion was brisk; there were some twelve hundred volunteers; Degrelle was one of the earliest. This, however, was not his first attempt to don a German uniform. In the months before Hitler's attack on Russia he had applied unsuccessfully to join the Wehrmacht. But his Nazi masters had felt he would be of greater value as a politician. As the conflict wore on and it became apparent that the Germans needed every fighting many they could get, his offer was eventually accepted.

The Walloon legion was flung into the cauldron of the Russian front. Although he had no military experience, it was generally agreed that Degrelle was a good soldier and his rise through the ranks was spectacular. Between December 1943 and February 1944, five Wehrmacht divisions and the Waffen-SS Viking Division, which included the Walloons, were encircled at Cherkassy in the Ukraine. Of the 56,000 beleaguered troops, 35,000 had punched their way out, covered by the tenacious men of Viking.

Of the 2,000 Walloons involved, just 632 survived. Lucien Lippert, the Brigade Commander, was killed; his place was taken by the newly promoted SS-Sturmbannfuehrer Leon Degrelle.

On his return to Belgium, Degrelle was determined to

make the most of what was hailed as the triumphant resistance at Cherkassy. A spectacular parade on 27 February 1944 was staged at the Sports Palace in Brussels and a portrait of Lippert was displayed prominently on the rostrum.

A few days later, a similar gathering was held in Charleroi. The German radio in Belgium, broadcasting in French, had a suitable enthusiastic report. It proclaimed:

Leon Degrelle, standing on a tank, passed through . . . at Charleroi, saluting the crowd with raised arm. The sight of the columns of the Legionnaires with the tricolour decorated with the Cherkassy badge, moved the huge crowd deeply. On the Place de l'Hôtel de Ville, decorations were awarded to 150 men who distinguished themselves on the eastern front. The band of the SS Leibstandarte Adolf Hitler played a slow march.

As a tribute to his own troops, Degrelle allowed himself a defiant peroration: 'We were a battalion and became a brigade. Tomorrow we will be a division.'

But any talk of tomorrow was pure illusion. In far better shape than the Waffen-SS, fuelled with Nazi ideology and precious little else, was the British guards armoured division, which stormed to victory from the beaches of Normandy to Cuxhaven on the Elbe estuary. When the Germans began their retreat to the Rhine, the guards division was the right flank formation of the British 2nd Army.

The division advanced from Douai, crossing the Belgium frontier on 3 September; by nightfall it had swept into the capital from the north and east.

Alexander Clifford of the *Daily Mail* wrote:

By the time we reached the suburbs of Brussels our hands were limp, our faces covered with lipstick, our car loaded with fruit and flowers, and our ears deafened with cheering. . . . It was an hour before we could move our vehicles. It was astounding that they did not crumple up beneath the weight of the Belgians, who used them as grandstands. Many of these people were in tears.

It was a rare and moving sight. If you got out of your car, in half a second you were overwhelmed and wildly kissed again and decorated with flowers and made to drink wine.

It was as if suddenly the Belgians lost all instincts of fear; from hastily abandoned German slit trenches they watched the British troops advance past the red glare of the Palais de Justice, which the Germans had put to the torch. The few pockets of resistance that remained were swiftly mopped up. Even the quick stutter of German machine-guns and the deep slam of the British tank weapons caused no panic or a sudden scuttle into homes and shelters.

In the Grand Place, on the steps of the Hôtel de Ville, the crowd burnt Hitler in effigy. All the relics of transport vehicles that could be found were dragged to numerous bonfires. At the former Gestapo headquarters, documents and files were also burnt by a delirious mob.

But there were those whose motives had little to do with the joy of liberation. Collaborators were covering their tracks.

Among them was Leon Degrelle. The sweepings of the Walloon, Flemish and French SS divisions had been hastily assembled as the pretentiously termed 'SS Army Corps West' to fight in the path of the Soviet advance into Pomerania.

It all proved useless. The Russians were unstoppable; most of the Flemish SS fell into Soviet hands, the French SS was a disintegrated flotsam on a sea of fleeing military and civilians. The Walloons fared rather better. Some remnants were evacuated by sea to Copenhagen, while others, Degrelle among them, made their way overland Schleswig-Holstein.

Imminent defeat, the annihilation of past hopes and dreams, the total collapse of the Third Reich – these things were now brutally obvious to most of those Rexists whose loyalty was strained to the uttermost.

But Degrelle insisted that all was by no means lost.

There was time for one last bold gamble. It rested on the say-so of just one man.

In the north of Germany, Heinrich Himmler roamed aimlessly round his headquarters, which were now at Ploen, on the borders of Denmark. Adolf Hitler had opted for a suicide pact with his wife Eva Braun. The Fuehrer's designated successor was Grossadmiral Karl Doenitz, who had no intention of employing Himmler in any capacity whatever.

Degrelle proposed a meeting at Malente, near Kiel. It turned out to be a grotesque pantomime; Degrelle was driving a Volkswagen powered by potato schnapps, and Himmler, looking faintly ludicrous in a crash helmet, was at the wheel of his own vehicle.

Degrelle came straight to the point, asking: 'What do you want of my Belgian SS? I am proposing that we either establish a northern redoubt in Norway or else disperse into some sort of Werewolf group.'

The Rexist leader had got wind of the underground civilian army which had been recruited and trained by the SS against the Allies, who were overrunning Germany. Surely such a group could be reinforced.

To Degrelle's consternation, Himmler appeared listless and uninterested. In an attempt to master his exasperation, Degrelle demanded of the Reichsfuehrer-SS: 'What *are* your plans?'

At that moment, the charade was interrupted by Allied aircraft sweeping down on Himmler's retinue. The party dived for the nearest ditches. Himmler was shocked, rebuking his staff by protesting: 'Discipline, gentlemen, discipline!' After the party had scrambled from the ditches, the two men bade each other farewell, Degrelle's question unanswered. Himmler was intent only on making his way through Allied fire to some imagined haven in Flensburg.

Still Degrelle refused to give up. How about sympathetic forces in Denmark? There were none willing to do business with him. All hope was now pinned on Vidkun Quisling, the bombastic Norwegian traitor, who was already shivering in the shadow of the firing squad. All Quisling was anxious to do now was present an image as his country's saviour.

Degrelle, the last hope gone, saw no reason to offer himself for slaughter. A private aircraft belonging to Hitler's Minister for War Production, Albert Speer, had been supplied to Quisling in case he should wish to escape to Spain. He showed no inclination to accept the offer; Leon Degrelle took his place.

Liberation was not simply a matter of wine-induced euphoria on the streets of Brussels: the newsreel and newspaper photographers followed sorrowing wives and mothers who laid their wreaths beneath the low drop gallows of Breendonck fort, situated between Brussels and Antwerp. Here many of their men had been slowly throttled to death. There were the rooms in which victims had been subjected to alternate blasts of fiery-hot and ice-cold air, and there were pulleys from which prisoners were slung.

The cameras recorded one particularly poignant moment: a black-garbed widow in the castle courtyard removing a sliver of wood from the stake against which her husband had stood before a firing squad.

And now special courts in Belgium were set up, manned by two civilian and three military judges. According to one set of records, some 100,000 persons were arrested, but only 87,000 were subsequently brought to trial; of these, around 10,000 were acquitted. Sentences of death were passed on 4,170 people, of which 230 were actually carried out.

As for Degrelle, he was eventually sentenced to death by a Belgian court in his absence. In 1946, he found his way to Argentina, later returning to Spain, where he managed to withstand all bids to extradite him to Belgium.

In the mid-1980s, the French-speaking channel of the Belgian television service ran him to earth in his luxurious

238

Madrid home. The decision to run three lengthy programmes on Degrelle and his wartime collaboration led to bitter protests from organisations of resistance fighters and survivors, particularly when it was learnt that the interviews had been filmed some years earlier but that the authorities had then judged it impossible to show them.

In more than an hour of detailed exchanges with Maurice de Wilde, a specialist on the record of wartime collaboration, Degrelle angrily refuted documentary evidence from SS headquarters in Berlin that he was willing, not only to raise volunteers to fight 'the Godless Communists in the east', but effectively hand over both the Walloon and Flemish regions in Belgium as a virtual German protectorate. Such an allegation, Degrelle insisted, was 'absolute rubbish'. He claimed that reference to the 'Reich' in those documents referred, not to a German Reich, but to 'a union of Western European peoples, each guarding its own proper identity – an idea which I always defended'.

Confronted by transcripts of his own speeches in which he referred to the French-speaking Walloons as 'part of the great Germanic community', Degrelle stated that until the early Middle Ages Wallonia was part of the German empire founded by Charlemagne. He also claimed that these historical references helped to win concessions for Wallonia from Hitler and Himmler. Indeed, Himmler had let Degrelle's 4,000 Walloon-SS volunteers have their own national flag and use the French language in military orders.

Over the years, Degrelle delighted in holding court to anyone who would listen, and readily granted interviews in his study crammed with books, video cassettes and memorabilia. When pressed, he was even ready to strut in his old SS uniform.

27

The twelve-year-old Third Reich of Adolf Hitler, envisaged to last for a thousand years, crumbled to death in the last days of April and the start of May 1945.

On 30 April, the brain which conceived it rotted among the ruins of the Berlin Chancellery. Hitler had presided over the last of his noon situation conferences in his underground bunker fortress. The Fuehrer had listened without emotion to news of heavy fighting in the Tiergarten and the Potsdamer Platz, only a few blocks away from the Chancellery. At about 3.20 p.m., he and Eva Braun withdrew to the Fuehrer's suite. Outside the door, the inhabitants of the bunker waited. Hitler shot himself with his Walther 7.65 calibre pistol, probably biting into a poison capsule at the same time. Eva Braun took poison.

On 4 May, the German High Command surrendered all German forces in northwest Germany, Denmark and the Netherlands to Britain's Field Marshal Montgomery. The BBC Danish radio delivered the news to Denmark at 8.35 the same evening.

Danish families greeted the news by placing lighted candles on window sills. Danish intelligence agents, however, were more energetic. They were posted on the Jutland-Danish border to pluck hundreds of suspected traitors, Gestapo agents and SS officials from the columns of retreating Germans and wandering refugees.

Within six weeks of the liberation, more than eleven hundred arrests had been made at the border. The number of those seized within Denmark totalled 20,000, among them hundreds of 'field mattresses' – young women who had slept with German soldiers. It was a sign of the prevailing bitterness that the death penalty, whose introduction had been successfully resisted during the occupation, was restored for the worst cases of collaboration. Not only did Denmark reauthorise the death penalty, but it was made retroactive to the years of Nazi rule.

One of the most fortunate of the leading figures of the occupation was the German plenipotentiary, Dr Werner Best, whose death sentence was commuted to five years. Best was able to argue successfully that German officials in Berlin had initiated the action against the Jews and that, therefore, he could not in justice be held responsible for their fate.

The authorities made sure that those arrested, whatever their ultimate fate, suffered maximum humiliation. In the major Dutch cities, groups of suspected collaborators were driven through streets in open trucks, their hands raised high in abject surrender.

Some of the reprisals were so savage that the Danish branch of the War Resisters International Council, a pacifist organisation, urged the new Danish government to disband all resistance movements, so that alleged collaborators could be arraigned before properly constituted courts.

As for Norway, pious warnings were issued by the authorities against private settling of scores, but it was hard to slake the thirst for individual vengeance. As if fully aware of their likely fate, Reichskommissar Josef Terboven and Obergruppenfuehrer Rediess of the SS blew themselves up in a bunker located in the residence of the Crown Prince.

There remained Vidkun Quisling.

As the situation became progressively worse for the Germans, he steadily retreated from reality, nurturing futile dreams of eventually ruling an independent country which, with the help of a reconstituted Reich, would turn on Russia in a sort of 'Nordic defence'.

With the announcement of the German surrender in Denmark, he had contacted Terboven to see if further catastrophe could be avoided. Terboven had been blunt: 'The best thing for you is to get out of the country.' Then had come the offer of an aircraft to fly him to Spain, and there had been talk of a long-range U-boat making for South America.

It was a measure of just how deluded Quisling had become that he stoutly rejected both offers, optimistic that he could easily justify his wartime actions.

Quisling returned to his luxurious villa, clinging fatuously to the title of Minister President and entrusting his safety to his few remaining Hird bodyguards. He could scarcely credit the message he soon received from police headquarters: he must turn himself in on 9 May at 7 a.m. or be formally arrested.

He expostulated: 'I am being treated like an ordinary criminal.' The retreat into fantasy went even further. He attempted to plead on the telephone with Crown Prince Olav in London. The operator refused to connect the call.

Shortly after 6.15 a.m. on the day that the police had designated, Quisling, in greatcoat and soft felt hat, stepped out of the Mercedes Benz limousine which had been a gift from Hitler. It was the last comfort he was ever to know. Preliminary questioning over, he was locked into a bleak cell with a toilet bucket and a few sticks of furniture. Three months later, the trial began in the large assembly hall of Oslo's Freemasons' Lodge, which was doing duty as a courtroom.

If he had any remaining illusions of power or prestige, they were swiftly shattered. From the outset the mood of the court was hostile. Quisling complained to the judge that he had lost thirty-five pounds in weight, only to be told coldly: 'That is nothing to what some of our people lost when you put them in concentration camps.'

The charges were all-embracing: the prosecution was determined that Quisling should escape nothing. Allegations ranged from conspiracy to murder and complicity in the deportation of Jews, to theft of possessions from the royal palace and drunkenness and debauchery. His guilt on the main charge of treason was incontestable, but there were those who felt considerable uneasiness at the hostility displayed towards him.

There was a widespread feeling that a fair hearing in such an atmosphere was impossible. There were even allegations that the prisoner had been subjected to a vigorous physical and psychological examination, including electrical probing of the brain. Quisling was pronounced sane and the trial continued. But the doubts persisted.

Quisling's eight-hour speech in his own defence was a rambling self-justification. He proclaimed: 'To me, politics is not a matter of party interests, professional job-seeking, or personal ambition and lust for power. It is a matter of self-sacrifice and practical action in the service of the historical development for the benefit of one's own country and to promote the realisation of God's kingdom on earth which Christ came to establish. If my activities have become treasonable, as they have been said to be, then I would pray to God that for the sake of Norway a large number of Norway's sons will become such traitors as I, but that they will not be thrown into jail.'

There were no signs of repentance. Indeed, he assured the court that, given the chance again, he would have taken the same course. Only the minor charges seemed to sting him into indignation.

He was acquitted of these, but sentenced to death for murder and treason. At 2 a.m. on 24 October, Quisling was rushed in a police car to Akershus Castle, shoved unceremoniously against a wall and despatched by a ten-man firing squad.

The death of the more prominent Nazis who had extended their influence over all the occupied countries of the west inevitably overshadowed the fate of lesser fry. Heinrich Himmler, for example, held his last staff conference at Flensburg on 5 May. At 2 p.m. on 23 May, he blundered into a British checkpoint at Bremervoerde. Six hours later he was identified, stripped and searched. As an army doctor's fingers groped in his mouth, he bit on the concealed poisoned capsule. Fifteen minutes later he was dead. A blanket was thrown over his corpse and two days later he was buried in an unmarked grave.

At the Nuremberg trial, Alfred Rosenberg, the 'party philosopher' who had headed the Nazi party's office of foreign affairs, was convicted of four charges; the judgement linked him closely to Hitler's invasion of Norway. It stated: '. . . Rosenberg arranged for Quisling to collaborate closely with the National Socialists and to receive political assistance from the Nazis.'

He was sentenced to death and hanged for war crimes at Nuremberg on 16 October 1946, along with Keitel, Ribbentrop and Seyss-Inquart, all of whom had had major roles in the Nazi invasion of the west.

Himmler, seemingly, was not the only Nazi war criminal to be consigned to the oblivion of an unmarked grave. Mystery surrounded the last day of Gustav Simon, Gauleiter of Hitler's 'Moselleland', who, early in 1945, left a shattered Luxembourg in a vain bid to reach Berlin for fresh instructions. Trapped in Westphalia, Simon hid under an assumed name in the British zone of occupation; by December a certificate issued in Paderborn recorded his death, but no accompanying details were released. There were unsubstantiated rumours that the certificate was a fake and that Simon had been smuggled back to Luxembourg and murdered by members of the Red Lion of Luxembourg resistance group.

As an act of revenge, it would have had a certain logic. During the occupation, members of the Red Lion had perished in front of firing squads in the concentration camp at Hinzert, after digging their own graves.

The tiny duchy had experienced the fallout from Hitler's last major initiative in the west: a bold counterattack in December 1944 through the forests of the Ardennes, in the so-called Battle of the Bulge. Part of the territory involved comprised the northern half of Luxembourg.

Hitler's object was to recapture Antwerp; for the fruitless gamble, he snatched valuable units and tanks from the Russian front, together with the last remnants of the Luftwaffe and some 250,000 troops.

Under the full force of the onslaught, isolated villages in the Ardennes mountains were taken by surprise. There had been no time for evacuation; the Germans carried off men between fifteen and seventy for forced labour in the already shattered Reich. On a stretch of sixty miles along the German frontier to a depth of five miles there was wholesale eviction to create a no-man's-land for military operations.

The German initiative in the Ardennes was soon lost; Hitler's last dramatic gesture postponed the balm of full liberation for Luxembourg under the final year of the war.

28

In France, the search for collaborators took on all the ardour of a mission. The purge – known as *l'épuration* (purification) – lasted from September 1944 to the end of 1949.

Just over 2,000 death sentences were handed down, but women and minors were automatically exempted by General de Gaulle. These figures took no account of private vengeance or of collaborators summarily executed in the period immediately after liberation.

Many of these executions, of dubious or nonexistent legality, were carried out with a swift barbarity that would, in many cases, have done credit to the Milice and even the Gestapo.

It was to be years before the deep, festering wounds of *l'épuration* were to heal. And, even then, scars remained.

International attention focused on the two most famous collaborators of them all.

Maréchal Pétain was whisked away from Vichy by the Germans; while at the Hotel Matignon in Paris Pierre Laval, his luggage packed, luxuriated in a marble bath. It was his last indulgence and also his last day in France before he too was taken to Germany.

On 23 July 1945, Maréchal Pétain was arraigned on a charge of treason. Alone of the Vichy survivors, he requested to be allowed to return to France to stand trial: 'At my age, there is only one thing one still fears. That is not to have done all one's duty, and I wish to do mine.'

In court, he wore the simplest uniform of a Maréchal of France and the Medaille Militaire, the only decoration shared by simple soldiers and great commanders. His lawyer begged him to take his Maréchal's baton into court, only to receive the scornful reply: 'That would be theatrical.'

In his last words to the court before sentence, Pétain said: 'My thought, my only thought was to remain with the French on the soil of France, according to my promise, so as to protect them and to lessen their sufferings.'

Whether this was the simple truth or a desperate bid for sympathy, no one could tell. But it made no difference; the court remained unmoved. On 15 August, the ninety-year-old Maréchal was sentenced to death. President de Gaulle commuted the sentence to life imprisonment and the old man was confined on the Ile de Yeu off the Vendée coast. By June 1951, he had become almost totally senile and was released. Within a month he was dead, passing away within two days of the ex-Crown Prince Rupprecht of Bavaria, his old adversary at Verdun in the World War One.

Two months after the trial of Pétain, it was the turn of Pierre Laval, for whom the French reserved a special hatred. The proceedings in court could only be described as an undignified shambles; imprecations were hurled constantly from the public gallery. On 14 October, four days after being sentenced to death, Laval took poison. But France was determined to have its revenge and the stomach pumps went to work; the doctors kept him alive long enough to face the firing squad.

The men of the Glières who had perished in the German cleaning-up operations of February and March 1944 were avenged spectacularly the following August. The liberation of the Department of Haute-Savoie was to be down to the glory of the resistance alone.

German retreat did not mean that the enemy had done with Haute-Savoie. All those Germans stationed in the southeast were ordered to assemble in the area of the Rhône Valley, to stem the thrust that the Allies were bound to make to the north. In particular, the Germans were told to make their way quickly to the city of Lyons, which was to be fashioned as a strongpoint to delay the junction of both southern and northern Allied armies.

The key objective for the liberators was the town of Annecy, where most of the Wehrmacht and Gestapo had been stationed.

At the same time, the order went out to the maquis: attack all the enemy posts on the line of retreat.

Arms were distributed to the different camps. But it was not just the maquis who had caught the scene of battle. There was now a new people's army. An eyewitness, recalling the events a year later, wrote:

... This new people's army, though poor in weapons, held itself with pride. There were no uniforms, but there was faith. ... Everyone joined in keenly; the butcher, the baker's apprentice, the postal employee, the schoolmaster, the factory worker and· the peasant – everyone still in his working clothes, with a weapon different from his neighbours; all supporting the action of the maquisards, themselves so variously attired that the people's army made a very odd appearance. One would be wearing an old tin hat dating from the war of 1914–18; another had treasured his old French sailor's cap with a red pompom; a third had on a fireman's helmet. Many were in shorts, hair in the wind and chests bare. ...

As the columns of maquis made their way down the mountain paths, they were held up at the farms by peasants who, leaving their field work, rolled out barrels of cider into the open to refresh the fighters.

The focal point for the twin assault of the maquis and the citizen army against the regrouping Germans was a sector between Marignier and Cluses, in a part of the valley of the Arve, to the east of Bonneville.

It was soon clear to the maquis that Cluses required its urgent attention. On the morning of 18 August, Bonneville signalled that a column of German lorries, reinforcements from Annecy, was moving up the main highway to Cluses, where the Germans already had a significant advantage of arms, including antitank weapons and captured French 75 mm guns.

The maquis, hidden in the fir forests, thickets and bushes which lined a road, opened up on the lorries loaded with men and guns. The Germans were forced to a halt in the vain effort to clean up an opposition which was virtually invisible. Their progress was inevitably slow; they were approaching two critical points, the Bridge at Vougy and the crossing at Scionzier, where the road snaked through a narrow street of houses bunched closely together.

The tactics of the maquis were to let the German column pass Vougy Bridge, so as to trap it between two bottlenecks at Cluses and Vougy. Of the 150 lorries that had left Annecy in convoy, only thirty managed to penetrate beyond Vougy Bridge. Along a thirty-mile stretch of road, the Germans were harassed by the maquis.

Bright flares and the path of tracer bullets from the dark heart of the mountains cut through the still of night at Cluses. The engagement went on until 2 a.m. In a sudden lull, the Germans attempted a bold move.

The inhabitants of Cluses remained huddled behind closed doors and windows. In silence, the Germans pushed their lorries to the point of exit from Cluses towards the national highway. No one risked switching on the engines of the vehicles, but, if the inhabitants of Cluses had snatched a few hours of sleep, the maquis had allowed themselves no such luxury.

They returned to the attack, firing into the convoy with the weapons supplied to them on previous Allied air drops. The progress of the German lorries, now making in the opposite direction towards Annecy, was even closer than the day before. Not a single vehicle or its occupants made the road crossing at Vougy. A well-placed machine-gun hidden in a roadside ditch sliced into one car that had tried to make a passage. Its five occupants, senior officers of the Gestapo at Cluses, were killed.

Other Germans made a bid to reach the Swiss frontier by crossing the Arve, but the foaming icy torrent proved too much. Many were drowned; those who managed the crossing had lost all will to fight and surrendered meekly enough.

By early evening, lorryloads of German prisoners, the vehicles churning up the hot dust of high summer, made their way to Marignier.

German casualties were put at around 500. Losses for the maquis were around thirty dead and a few wounded.

The final act in the liberation of Haute-Savoie took place the following day, 19 August, in front of Annecy, where all the maquis had assembled. Enemy strongholds were seized; the rump of the German garrison and members of the Vichy were arrested.

Partisans sported berets, military caps and open shirts, rounds of ammunition dangling from their belts. The atmosphere was festive. But it told only half the story. While one section of the resistance permitted itself to relax, another was on the move. Female collaborators were punched and kicked out of their houses, and stripped to the waist while their heads were shaved.

German prisoners fared comparatively well. It was the Milice that the partisans were seeking. There was not much discrimination about arrests; most people remembered only the brutality which the forces of Vichy had committed in Haute-Savoie, under the orders of the local Prefect, Charles Marion.

Now raw young recruits to the Milice were bracketed with hardened criminals. Many of them had not taken part in combat; nonetheless, they were arraigned in a series of field courts martial. Later, passions were to cool a little, but there were many cases where it was hard to tell vengeance and justice apart.

The more level-headed of the maquis, keen to preserve at least some trappings of legality, held villagers at gunpoint to prevent any bloodbath. Some 200 Milice in Annecy were hastily piled into trucks and taken up the mountain to the village of Grand-Bornand, where they were placed in the local dance hall.

Jean Comet, a regional prosecutor who had originally gone into hiding when the Germans rounded up court officials known to be hostile to collaboration, speedily offered his services as prosecutor at the forthcoming courts martial at Grand-Bornand.

The night before the trial, he drew up a list of responsibilities. The charges were fashioned in such a way as to avoid any future accusation of crude vengeance. Mere membership of the Milice was proclaimed to be the least heinous offence, followed by slightly more serious charges against those who had served but not taken part in actual combat against their fellow Frenchmen. But it was made clear to the resistance judges that the only possible verdicts on treason charges were Guilty or Not Guilty; the penalty was to be death.

It was calculated that at least three-quarters of the Milice would be found guilty of serious crimes; seventy-five coffins were ordered from a carpenter; local people were put to work digging a pit outside the village.

At 10 a.m. on 23 August, the Milice prisoners were mustered into the dock in groups of twenty, protected by armed partisans.

The trial went on all day and most of the night. Throughout, the judges were careful to give the defence fair play; lawyers for the accused made much of the fact that their clients were young and had been seduced by Vichy propaganda. Twenty-one of the defendants were acquitted, but that did not mean instant release: few of them would have left the court building alive. Besides, there were lesser charges to be answered. Seventy-six Milice were found guilty of crimes carrying the death penalty, and the judgment noted that 'present military circumstances require that these sentences be sanctioned with great energy'.

There was quick absolution from the village priest. Death certificates had been completed and coffins num-

251

bered. The convicted men had an opportunity to write a last letter and bequeath their possessions. Five stakes were set up at the execution site. The prisoners, led out in alphabetical order, were given the option of blindfolds. At the moment of execution they shouted: 'Long live the Maréchal!' or 'Long live France!'

The shootings, which began just after dawn, continued throughout the day.

29

The continent of Europe had been prostrated by war. In the centre of misery and destruction lay Germany. Bombing had gouged the heart out of her towns, cities and industries. For every ton of bombs dropped on Britain, 315 had descended on Hitler's Reich.

In 1945, the vast majority of Berliners were struggling to survive on about 800 calories a day.

Burst water mains and ruptured sewers spread typhoid. Mosquitoes fed on corpses rotting in the rubble and then spread dysentery. In July, six out of every ten babies born in Berlin perished.

In the rest of Europe, a feeling of anticlimax followed the euphoria of liberation. There was, of course, the very considerable consolation that a brutal occupation force had been driven out. These feelings were shared by the one section of the United Kingdom to be forced under the Nazi heel. As late as 7 May 1945, the Germans in Jersey, the largest of the Channel Islands, had made preparations to reinforce the fortifications. Six days later, after the surrender, a convoy of fifty ships arrived off the Channel Islands bringing with them luxuries only dimly remembered since 1940 – flour, meat, biscuits, tea, chocolate, tobacco, soap, coal and gas. Even the German workers cheered lustily as the first landing craft nosed its way into Jersey's port of St Helier.

For some members of the French maquis, there were still matters of uncompleted business.

Felix Plottier, the unrepentant resistant clapped in jail by the Swiss under his alias of Felix Fournier, was uneasy.

It was true that he had been released from prison, but the terms of the deportation order made it clear that he would be banned from Switzerland for life. Since he lived a mere twelve miles from the frontier, had many Swiss friends and needed to travel there for his business, the ban was more than mildly vexatious. Immediately on leaving jail, he sought out a senior Swiss official.

The man's demeanour was arctic; the ban must be allowed to stand. He intoned with heavy gravity: 'We cannot rescind the order prohibiting the entry of Monsieur Felix Fournier into Switzerland. If Monsieur Fournier attempts to enter our country again he will be arrested.'

There was a pause; the man's aura of disapproval filled the room. Without relaxing a muscle, he added: 'However, we have no record of a Felix Plottier and there is therefore no prohibition against such an individual entering Switzerland.'

Plottier played the game to the last; he gravely shook hands with the official and took his leave.

Felix and Joan Plottier, back in Bonneville, prepared to pick up the threads of their lives. But first they would give themselves a treat. In a barn near their home, buried beneath faggots of wood, lay their magnificent red and black Simca coupé.

They soon discovered that all it needed to be roadworthy was a new set of tyres.

PEN & SWORD MILITARY CLASSICS

We hope you have enjoyed your Pen and Sword Military Classic. The series is designed to give readers quality military history at affordable prices. Pen and Sword Classics are available from all good bookshops. If you would like to keep in touch with further developments in the series, including information on the **Classics Club**, then please contact Pen and Sword at the address below.

Published Classics Titles

PEN AND SWORD BOOKS LTD

47 Church Street • Barnsley • South Yorkshire • S70 2AS

Tel: 01226 734555 • 734222

E-mail: enquiries@pen-and-sword.co.uk • **Website:** www.pen-and-sword.co.uk

LEGIONS
OF DEATH

&

CROSS
OF IRON